The Pistol Book

JOHN WALTER

arco

ARCO PUBLISHING, INC
NEW YORK

Published in 1984 by
Arco Publishing, Inc.
215 Park Avenue South
New York, NY 10003

For Sue . . . again

ISBN 0-668-05995-8
Library of Congress Catalog Card Number: 83-72220

Printed and bound in Great Britain by
Robert Hartnoll Limited, Bodmin, Cornwall

Preface and acknowledgements

The Pistol Book has proved interesting to compile—but by no means easy and frequently exasperating. Unfortunately, there has not been enough space to provide a history of the handgun, however brief, and other parts of the project—a regionalised gunsmiths' register and other long-term objectives—have been deferred. So many details were supplied, and so many differing models discovered during research that the project has crystallised as a company-by-company directory supported by a brief introduction, benefitting greatly from skilful editing and revising, each stage condensing material a little more elegantly. Compared with the preceding book in the series, *The Airgun Book*, the pistol book presents a totally different aspect; this should not come as much surprise. The airgun book was distributed in a market where little attention had been given to theory; as far as pistols are concerned, however, interior and exterior ballistics have been subjected to such copiously detailed studies as Mann's classic, *The Bullet's Flight, Hatcher's Notebook*, ballistic and reloading manuals and countless other sources. I could not hope to add much to such monumental achievements, other than by contributing the assessment system discussed in Appendix 1. I see my role simply to collect in a central, accessible one-volume source details of as many handguns as possible, whether firing ball cartridges, black powder, blanks or even signal flares.

Our directory is nothing if not diverse: not only are more than six hundred guns listed, but also a hundred or more manufacturers, not even counting makers of parts and accessories, wholesalers and distributors.

Some companies are small; others, multi-national conglomerates. Some have been helpful, often through well organised public relations machinery; others declined to assist our research, which I find hard to understand in a highly competitive business. Consequently, inconsistencies will be found in the style and content of a few individual entries. The implications are twofold; there are occasions on which incomplete data have been used in the absence of anything better, and merely by devoting space to uncooperative manufacturers (obligatory, for the sake of completeness) we have denied space to those which responded quickly and willingly. I must apologise to the many companies which gave me much *more* assistance than I needed, particularly Smith & Wesson, details of whose complicated history and extensive product range I reluctantly compressed into a small pre-determined space. The occasional sparseness of illustrative material reflects the fact that some companies supplied more data than pictures.

The Pistol Book has been written to satisfy an international rather than parochial market, with all the attendant problems; for example, the products of Amadeo Rossi, important in the Americas, are uncommon in the United Kingdom. The initial draft of the Rossi section contained details only of the handful of revolvers seen in the United States of America; Rossi then supplied details of its enormous product range, and the size of our 'Rossi' section illustrates the difficulties of relying too greatly on the affairs of one *national* market.

This 'internationalisation' has forced the inclusion of companies about whom virtually nothing is known—and whose entries consist, in some instances, of little more than a name and address. Data came from a variety of sources, not all of unimpeachable accuracy, as it is impossible to fire every gun personally.

The Pistol Book, like its airgun predecessor, may well appear in translation and further editions; manufacturers, distributors and readers wishing to supply pertinent details, fill gaps or correct errors are encouraged to contact me by way of the publisher whose imprint may be found at the beginning of the book. Despite all the help I have received, however, responsibility for the opinions expressed and as yet unnoticed mistakes remains entirely mine.

It is always difficult to acknowledge satisfactorily the help offered by many individuals, companies and government bodies during the preparatory work, or give due credit to the many printed sources that have been consulted. A few of the latter have been noted throughout the text, where appropriate, but I am afraid that I must take recourse to that perennial authors' stand-by—and list my thanks alphabetically. I sincerely hope that the people whose assistance I value most greatly will take no offence . . .

Ms Tamara Angerman, Oy Sako Ab; Astra-Unceta y Cia; Sr Enrico Attia, Italo-Trade SpA; Herr Martin Barthelmes, Fritz Barthelmes Sportwaffenfabrik; Bauer Firearms Corporation; Pietro Beretta SpA; Ing. Francesco Bernardelli, Vincenzo Bernardelli SpA; Herr J. Bischof, Em-Ge Sportgeräte GmbH & Co. KG; Mr Patt Bogush, Colt's Inc.; Sr Luis Antônio Borba dos Santos, Sales Manager, Amadeo Rossi SA; Mr Geoffrey Boxall, Oliver J. Gower Ltd; Embaixada do Brasil, London; Mr Geoffrey H. Brown, Viking Arms Ltd; Sr Miguel Ruíz Cruz, Sales Director, AFAMSA; Mr Ian Edgar, Edgar Brothers; Erma-Werke GmbH; Mr Edward C. Ezell; Mr Val J. Forgett, President, Navy Arms Company; Freedom Arms; Sr Rino Galesi, Rigarmi; Dr Rolf Gminder; Mr Hank Goodman, President, Hopkins & Allen Arms; Herr Joachim Görtz; Mr Colin Greenwood, Editor, *Guns Review*; Mr Roger C. Hale, Sales Director, Parker-Hale Ltd; Mr Donald E. Hard, Executive Vice-President, Wildey Firearms Company; Mr Earle G. Harrington, Advertising Manager, Harrington & Richardson, Inc; Herr P.F. Hediger, Hämmerli Jagd- und Sportwaffenfabrik AG; Mr Brian T. Herrick, Vice President Marketing/Sales, High Standard, Inc.; Herr Peter Hoffmann, Carl Walther Sportwaffenfabrik GmbH: Mr Ian Hogg; Mr Roy C. Jinks; Mr P.A. Keegan,

Director of Advertising, Charter Arms Corporation; Mr Geoffrey Kenshole, Peregrine Arms; Mr John C. Leak, Vice-President, Sterling Arms Company, Inc; Llama–Gabilondo y Cia; Lyman Products Corporation; Mr Arthur Matthews, Arthur E.S. Matthews Ltd; Mauser-Jagdwaffen GmbH; Mr Tim Pancurak, Thompson/Center Arms; Mr Brett Parsons, Sales Manager, Sterling Armament Company; Sr Giuseppe Pietta, Pietta F.lli; M A. Renard, Defence Products Co-ordinator, Fabrique Nationale Herstal; Röhm GmbH: Herr Karl Schäfer; Mr Joseph J. Schroeder Jr; Herr Alex Seidel, Heckler & Koch GmbH; Smith & Wesson; Mr Jan Stevenson, Editor, *Handgunner*; Umarex Sportwaffen GmbH & Co. KG; Mr Stephen K. Vogel, President, Sturm Ruger Export Company, Inc.; Herr Hans-Hermann Weihrauch, Hermann Weihrauch KG; Mr Robert E. Weise, Stoeger Publishing Company; and the many authors and reviewers whose works I consulted.

The progress of a book is rarely smooth and production hitches inevitably occur. I would like to thank my editor, Michael Boxall, though (to ensure his reputation remains unsullied) I admit that the last-minute entries escaped his deft touch. The production team at Arms & Armour Press turned a Nelsonian eye to my over-optimistic scheduling, for which indulgence I and my sanity are grateful, and my colleagues at Pacific Press worked enthusiastically to ensure that work was completed on time. I am particularly grateful for the encouragement of Ron and Jackie Shenton, who bullied me when I needed it; Dennis Banbury, Gerry Petrosino, Ken Dudgeon and Jędrek 'Andrew' Jaworski of Z. Jaworski & Son also deserve my thanks many times over for their patience, enthusiasm and ability to do the impossible when all seemed lost. Lastly, but by no means least, I owe a special debt to my wife Sue—part-time proofreader, paste-up artist and purveyor of endless black coffee—and to our families, who believe we have emigrated.

John Walter, Harrow, 1983

How to use the directory . . .

Each major entry is accompanied by a series of symbols, the significance of which is explained below. These show the company's product range at a glance.

A major entry, indicated by the **large, bold serifed** face headline. These are accompanied by the company address and details of the principal distrtibutors in Britain and the United States of America (where known). There is also a brief description of the company

Each gun entry has a **bold sans-serif headline,** followed by a description and *data* in medium type.

Smaller companies of whom little is known, or who failed to reply during our research, are given entries in smaller **bold, serif type** followed by a few lines in serifed medium.

---

bird's head butt usually exhibits a sharper radius than the Kentucky guns, the stock is half rather than full length, and once again - the furniture is brass.
Cal. 0.50in. 12.7mm. All other data as Kentucky Pistol.

Agner

Agner–Saxhøj Products, Denmark

British agency: Parker-Hale Ltd, Golden Hillock Road, Birmingham B11 2PZ, England. US agency: standard warranty: unknown.

The Agner target pistol has only recently made its début in Britain, little being known about its manufacturer at the time of writing.

Agner M80

Target pistol. This interesting, unusual Danish-made gun appeared in Britain at the beginning of 1983—the first product of a small and hitherto unknown Danish manufacturer. Made largely of stainless steel, the Agner is intended for standard and rapid fire competitions. It undoubtedly possesses some very unusual features—such as a combination safety catch and locking key on the left side of the frame behind the trigger, an integral dry-firing device and an unconventional fully adjustable trigger. It also features, according to its accompanying promotional literature, 'a new concept in weight displacement which allows for accurate rapid fire even with high velocity ammunition'. The grips are well finished anatomical-pattern walnut, and the whole gun shows evidence of careful thought in its design and construction. It is too early to assess its potential, but early reports agree that the Agner will soon be jockeying for a place among the leading guns in its class—even though it is by no means the cheapest.
Cal. 0.22in LR rf. Mag: detachable box, catch above grip on left side of frame. Mag cap, rds: 5 Trg: SA, internal striker (?). Wt, Loa, Brl: NA, but within ISU competition rules. Sft: rotary 'key' on left side of frame behind trigger, down to safe, horizontal to fire, upwards to lock.

American Arms & Ammunition Company

1015 NW 72nd Street, Miami, Florida 33150, USA. This company handles the Budichowsky TP-70 personal defence pistol in the United States (associated with Korriphila in Germany—qv), together with a large-calibre military pistol from the same source.

Arcadia Machine & Tool Company (AMT)

Formerly 11666 McBean Drive, El Monte, California 91732, USA, but now apparently in Covina, California. No details were received from AMT in time for inclusion.

AMT Hardballer

General purpose pistol. This is a derivative of the Colt Government Model, though built of largely new parts. The external differences are considerable, as the Hardballer has a modified squared slide with its adjustable sights mounted on a top-rib. Several slide lengths are available. The basic operating system, however, parallels that of the Colt Government Model (qv).

Back-Up

Personal defence pistol. This, as its name suggests, is a small pocket automatic chambering 0.22in LR Hyper Velocity rimfire ammunition. Made largely of stainless steel, the Back-Up is 5in (13cm) long and weighs about 18oz. or 510gm, with an empty eight-round magazine. The manual safety lies on the left side of the frame, but there is also a grip safety unit.

Armigas-Comega

Costruzioni Meccaniche Gardonesi Attilio Zanoletti, Via Valle Inzino 34, I-25063 Gardone Val Trompia (Brescia), Italy.

British agency: currently none. US agency: currently none. Standard warranty: unknown.

Armigas was founded in 1961 to make rifles and pistols powered by carbon dioxide, for which it is better known than as a bona fide gunmaker. During the 1960s, however, small quantities of a blowback personal defence pistol, the Titan (wrongly attributed elsewhere to Tanfoglio), were made alongside the gas guns.

Armi-Jäger

Armi-Jäger di Armando Piscetta SRL, Via Campazzino 55/b, Milan, Italy.

British agency: Scalemead Arms Co., Unit 3, Diplocks Way, Hailsham, East Sussex BN27 3JF, England. US agency: no sole distributor. Standard warranty: 12 months

Armi-Jäger is better known for its rimfire autoloaders—including near-replicas of the AK 47 and the US M16A1 Armalite—though a series of cartridge revolvers and deringers is also made.

Baby Frontier

General purpose revolver. This rimfire derivation of the Frontier has an exchangeable cylinder and a firing pin suited to rimfire ammunition—but is an otherwise conventional Colt Peacemaker 'Western' copy, albeit to two thirds scale. The guns are blued with plain wooden grips. A long-barrel (20in. 52cm) 'Buntline' version has also been made in small numbers.
Cal. 0.22in LR or 0.22in Magnum rf. Otherwise generally as Frontier, except Brl, in mm: 3.9, 4.7 or 5.9:100. 120 or 150

Frontier

General purpose revolver. This is another near-fascimile of the Colt Peacemaker, made in a variety of styles and calibres—neither the best of copies nor the worst, and representing quite good value. The Armi-Jäger revolver can be obtained in blue or plated finished, the former often featuring a case-hardened frame and the latter, extensive engraving. Grips are wood or chequered rubber. The rimfire version has interchangeable cylinders chambering standard or magnum cartridges.
Cal. 0.22in LR rf or 0.22in Magnum rf, 0.357in Magnum, 0.38in Special, 0.45in Long Colt. Mag: cylinder. Mag cap, rds: 6. Trg: SA, exposed hammer. Wt. Loa: see Colt version. Brl, in mm: 4.7, 5.9 or 7.1:120, 150 or 180. Rf: 7L? Sft: half-cock notch.

Super Frontier

Target and general purpose revolver. This variant of the Jäger Frontier has a long barrel, adjustable sights, a square-backed trigger guard and a long army-style walnut grip.
Cal. 0.22in LR rf, 0.35in Magnum. 0.44in Magnum. Otherwise generally as Frontier, except Brl, in mm: 5.9/150 (0.22. 0.357in) or 7.1:180 (0.44in).

Teodoro Arrizabalaga Guisasola

Avenida del Generalismo 2, Eibar, Guipúzcoa, Spain. Spanish export directories record this company as a manufacturer and exporter of shotguns, sporting guns and muzzle-loading handguns. No information about these has yet been elicited from Spain.

AFAMSA, AGNER, ARCADIA MACHINE & TOOL, ARMIGAS, ARMI-JÄGER, ARRIZABALAGA **25**

Contents

Entries in **bold type** refer to manufacturers sufficiently important to be given extended coverage. Lesser makers, wholesalers, etc, are shown in medium.

Alphabetical order has been followed wherever possible, but the late arrival of some information has resulted in a few unavoidable anomalies.

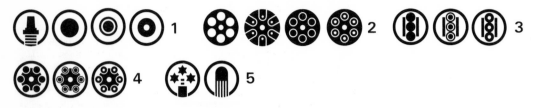

Above: the classification symbols used in this book. from left to right, in groups. **1** percussion and flintlock pistols; single-shot pistols (general); single shot, rimfire; single shot, centrefire. **2** revolvers (general); percussion revolvers; rimfire revolvers; centrefire revolvers. **3** automatic pistols (general); rimfire automatics; centrefire automatics. **4** mechanical and other repeaters (general); rimfire repeaters; centrefire repeaters. **5** signal, pyrotechnic and starting pistols; air and gas-powered pistols.

The classification system

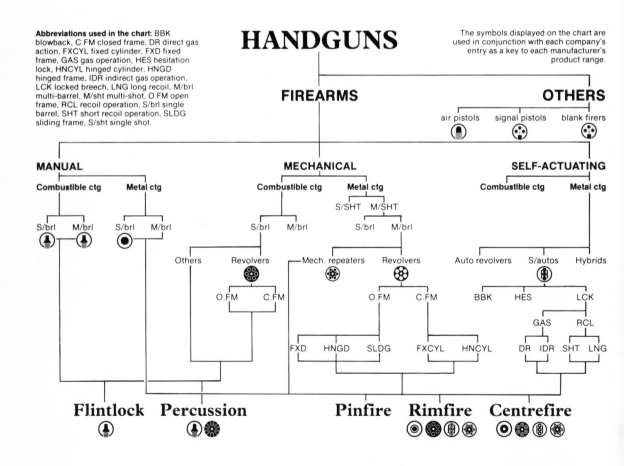

MILITARY PISTOLS

Though many operating systems and locking devices have been applied to automatic pistols, the Browning link system has become by far the most popular means of locking a large-bore automatic—and deservedly so, as it is strong, simple, reliable and very durable indeed even though the guns in which it is incorporated are rarely as elegant as—for example—the Parabellum.

At the end of the First World War, in which many thousands of Browning system M1911 service pistols had been made by Colt, Remington and other contractors for the US Army, Browning began to spend more time at the Herstal (Liège) factory of Fabrique Nationale d'Armes de Guerre, a company which had been making his blowback designs since 1897. Here, in collaboration with the company Bureau d'Études, he perfected what was to become the 'High Power' or GP Mle 35. Most of the design work had been completed, and the patents sought, when Browning died suddenly in 1926; the perfection of the gun, therefore, must be credited to Dieudonné Saive and the FN technical staff. The pistol was marketed from 1935 onwards, appearing more or less concurrently with 'Brownings' modified by Tokarev in Russia, Wilniewczyc and Skryzpinski in Poland, and Petter in France (Switzerland?). The principal difference between the US Army M1911 and the GP, apart from the fact that the latter chambered the 9mm Parabellum round and had a 13-round magazine, lay in the design of the barrel-depressor unit: the M1911 has a swinging link, which was replaced on the GP by a cam-finger system that promised greater reliability. By 1939, small quantities of the GP had been delivered to the Belgian, Latvian and Estonian armies, and large numbers were subsequently made for the Wehrmacht during the German occupation of Belgium during the Second World War; others were made for the Canadian Army during the same period, and thus the GP had the rare distinction of manufacture and use by *both* sides at the same time. After the end of the war, with what could have been its principal rival (the Walther P 38) effectively prevented by the Allies from competing on the world markets, the GP proved to be a worldbeater. Currently, it serves the armed forces and police of sixty-five countries and thus—by any yardstick—must be considered the most successful handgun in history.

(Illustrations by courtesy of Fabrique Nationale.)

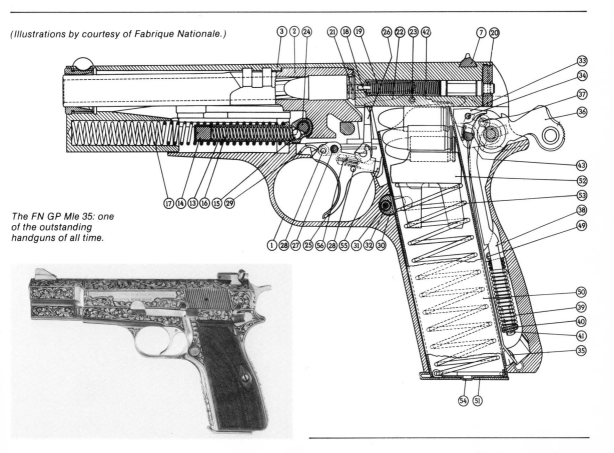

The FN GP Mle 35: one
of the outstanding
handguns of all time.

The only challenger to the GP in the immediate postwar years was the US M1911/M1911A1 series, many guns being available from surplus stocks. The Walther P 38 would probably have been another, because the heyday of the Parabellum (Luger) was well past even though mass production of the German army P 08 had continued until 1943. The P 38 is a more complicated design than the GP and its magazine held only eight rounds, but it did have the double-action trigger system which its rival lacked. Designed in the mid 1930s, the P 38 had been adopted by the German forces in April 1940. Such large quantities had been made by 1945—and on into 1946 in the Mauser-Werke Oberndorf factory, under French supervision—that the P 38 equipped many French units in Indo-China into the 1950s and the East German Volksarmee and Volkspolizei pending the substitution of Russian designs. The Allied occupation of Germany, however, prevented work on the postwar version of the P 38 until 1954 and it was 1957 before the pistol was re-adopted by the Bundeswehr. The intervening years had enabled FN to consolidate the pistol market with the GP, and, as a result, the P 38 (renamed P 1 in 1963) only sold to Austria and Portugal. The once-assured position of the P 1 in Germany is now being challenged by guns such as the P 6 (the SIG-Sauer P 225) and P 7 (Heckler & Koch PSP), though Walther has attempted to bring the design a little more up to date with the P 5.

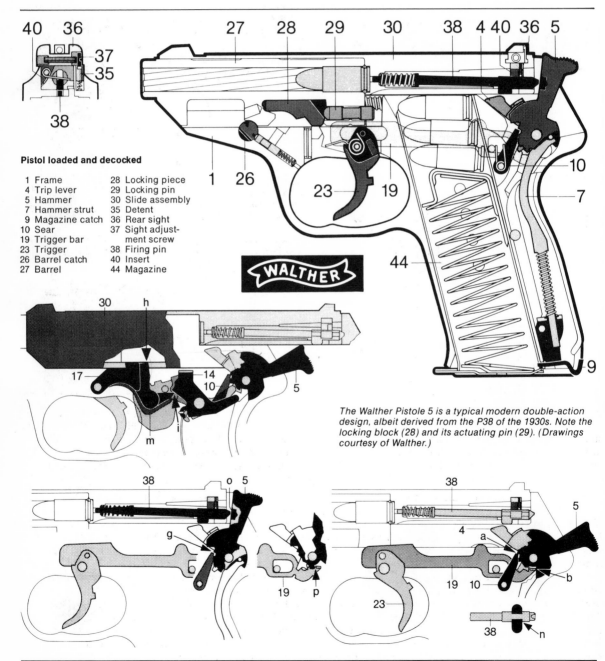

Pistol loaded and decocked

1 Frame	28 Locking piece
4 Trip lever	29 Locking pin
5 Hammer	30 Slide assembly
7 Hammer strut	35 Detent
9 Magazine catch	36 Rear sight
10 Sear	37 Sight adjust-
19 Trigger bar	ment screw
23 Trigger	38 Firing pin
26 Barrel catch	40 Insert
27 Barrel	44 Magazine

WALTHER

The Walther Pistole 5 is a typical modern double-action design, albeit derived from the P38 of the 1930s. Note the locking block (28) and its actuating pin (29). (Drawings courtesy of Walther.)

Several companies have emerged since the end of the Second World War as important suppliers of automatic pistols, apart from those such as Fabrique Nationale and Walther (both of which also had a long prewar history).

Schweizerische Industrie-Gesellschaft of Neuhausen-am-Rheinfalls, better known by its acronym SIG, benefitted from a decision taken by the Swiss armed forces to replace the ageing Borchardt-Lugers with the SIG-Petter SP 47/8 (or Ordonnanzpistole 49), a variation of the Browning link system developed for the French in the mid 1930s and perfected during the war. This gun is undeniably well made, with its slide bearing surfaces running, uniquely, inside the frame; as a result, it has a reputation for exemplary accuracy and near-perfect functioning, but is also very expensive. SIG, therefore, has co-operated in recent years with J.P. Sauer & Sohn of Eckernförde in Germany and has developed the simplified P 220 and 225. These certainly lack the manufacturing quality of the original SIG-Petters but are appreciably cheaper and (by all accounts) work just as well. The 220 has been adopted by the Swiss army as the Ordonnanzpistole 75 while the P 225 has done well enough in the West German police pistol trials to have been adopted by several state police forces as the P 6.

Left: the ultra-modern SIG-Sauer P220 dismantled into its main components. **Above and below:** the line drawings feature the Walther P5. 28 is the locking block; 29, the actuating pin.

Pietro Beretta of Gardone Val Trompia (Italy) is a long-established pistol maker currently enjoying a renaissance. Beretta supplied the Italian forces with many thousands of pistols—simple blowbacks—between 1915 and 1945 and has since continued to prosper. In addition to the simple designs, the company has developed a series of variations on the locked-breech Mo. 951 or 'Brigadier'—adapting some ideas from the Walther P 38—and the latest guns are good enough to have won the recent US Army pistol trials. The pistols, though lacking some of the constructional strength of the prewar P 38, serve with the armies of Italy, Israel and Egypt.

A comparatively new name is that of Heckler & Koch of Oberndorf, maker of a series of delayed-blowback pistols designed by Herbert Meidel. These—the P 9, 9 S and 9 Sport—are the archetype German semi-automatic: well made, double-action and elegantly engineered, but extremely complicated and thus expensive. The design appears to have been based on the German MG 42 and, perhaps, the Czechoslovakian vz.52 pistol. Recently, however, H&K has sought something different. This has led to that most curious of pistols, the VP 70—largely made of synthetics and, in some of its guises, fitted with a three-shot burst facility. This lets it operate as a kind of submachine-gun, but without the normal penalties of climb and waste of ammunition. The VP 70 is possibly a little out of step with current trends elsewhere, but may yet prove to be a pointer to the future. Apart from a personal-defence pistol, the HK 4, distinguished by no fewer than four exchangeable barrels, H&K also offers the new Polizei-Selbstladepistole or PSP. This is an extremely interesting design using a form of delayed blowback in which gas, bled from the barrel, opposes the rearward movement of the breech until the chamber pressure has dropped to a safe level. Other unusual features include a grip safety which, though by no means a new idea, is rare on a contemporary handgun. The PSP also performed well in the German pistol trials and has been adopted by many Federal agencies as the Pistole 7.

In the United States. Smith & Wesson has made a concerted effort to loosen the hold Colt has maintained on service pistol contracts—the M1911A1 and an assortment of general officer and other derivatives having remained issue throughout several reassessments of the role of the pistol in the modern army. So far, none of these has provided a suitable replacement for the handgun; indeed, I believe that, so long as they recommend hybrids of the pistol and the submachine-gun, none will ever succeed. Smith & Wesson pistols are also based on the well-tried Browning link system, but have usually been double action and often have large-capacity magazines: additionally, they chamber the 9mm Parabellum cartridge rather than the 0.45in ACP. The best known are the S&W Models 39 and 52, now supplemented by newer derivatives (see directory section). Limited service has been seen with the US Navy and special forces, but the Colt is still the standard army handgun.

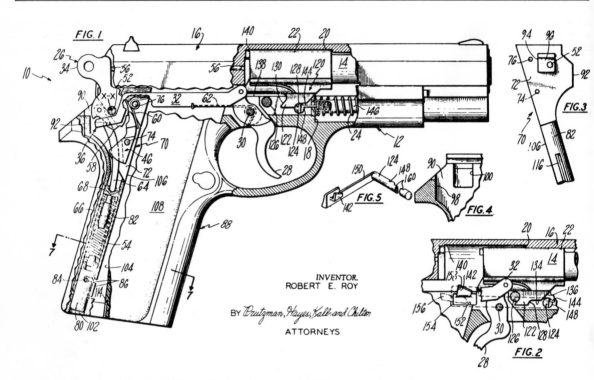

INVENTOR.
ROBERT E. ROY

BY *Prutzman, Hayes, Kalb and Chilton*

ATTORNEYS

The Colt Stainless Steel Pistol, or SSP, was developed in the early 1970s as a possible replacement for the Government Model. It awaits a change in its manufacturer's policy before production can be undertaken. The illustration comes from its US patent specification, by courtesy of the US Patent Office.

Though military guns made behind the Iron Curtain are rarely seen outside their country of origin—Eastern bloc target pistols, however, are quite common—guns made in Czechoslovakia are the exception. The most common of the Czech handguns has been the vz.52, a roller-locked design which may, perhaps, have influenced the design of the Heckler & Koch P 9 series. Recently, however, the CZ factory has produced another gun, apparently intended largely for export and based on the well-tried Browning link system as improved by the FN GP Mle 35. This is known as the vz.75 and has a 15-round staggered-column magazine. Some reviewers have placed this gun—wrongly, in my view— well down the list of desirable combat pistols, yet it has several very good features. The finish on some early specimens was not in the class of most Western products, but this—as the pre-1945 Russian submachine-guns testify—is not necessarily an indication of unreliability or mechanical inefficiency.

The Russian service pistol, an unlocked-breech type known as the PM or Makarov, is rarely seen outside the Soviet bloc and does not represent any advance in combat pistol technology. The Hungarians offered the rather anonymous 'Tokagypt 58' to the UAR in the late 1950s, but the armed forces preferred the Beretta Mo. 951 and the Tokagypt was speedily relegated to the reserve and then to the police. Though many Hungarian-made personal-defence guns will be encountered—based, for the most part, on the Walther PP—there is also a new military pistol known in Britain as the FÉG after the manufacturer's trademark. Amazingly, this is almost a direct copy of the GP Mle 35; so close, indeed, that some of the parts are said to be interchangeable. The Hungarian derivative has a slightly different external shape and rather poorer quality, but it undoubtedly inherits the ruggedness of its prototype.

Most of the lesser manufacturers of automatic pistols, though they often make guns in great quantity, are content to let others create the designs; the larger Spanish Llamas and Stars, for example, are based closely on the US Colt M 1911A1 (the smaller guns are usually blowbacks). Recently, however, the maker of the Llama—Gabilondo y Compañía of Eibar—has introduced an interesting, American-designed pistol called the Omni, available either in 9mm Parabellum or 0.45 ACP. Fantastic claims as to efficiency of this gun have been made and it may be that, after it has seen widespread service, some of the 'new' features will prove less desirable than was initially thought; equally, the locking mechanism is *still* a derivative of the Browning link. However, as Spanish manufacturers in general have achieved very little in automatic pistol design since 1945, Gabilondo is to be congratulated for introducing what is, in many ways, a remarkable design. Further details of the Omni will be found in the relevant directory section.

The Spanish, in common with the Italians, are apparently clinging to traditional gunsmithing techniques. Most of their products, therefore, exhibit machined gunmetal components, rather than widespread use of synthetics. The trend in other European countries—notably in West Germany as exemplified by Heckler & Koch—is towards simplified production systems such as investment casting and increasing use of synthetics for unimportant parts.

At the time of writing, the pistol retains at least a small importance in military circles; few armies, for example, have yet abandoned it altogether. Inroads on its popularity have been made by the Czechoslovakian Scorpion machine pistol, and more particularly by the American Ingram. Even these cannot be classed as satisfactory one-hand guns, however, and the archetype military pistol remains a large locked-breech design, often double action, chambering the 9mm Parabellum (or, to a lesser extent, the 0.45in ACP) and holding up to eighteen rounds in its magazine. Safety features are usually excellent and reliability unimpeachable. What progress will be made in the next decade is, understandably, difficult to predict after the apparent failure of attempts such as the American Personal Defense Weapons Program, together with the Colt 'arm gun' and SCAMP projects, to evolve a replacement for the pistol that can be used with one hand. Apart from obvious trends such as simplified manufacturing techniques—stamping, pressing, investment casting, synthetic parts—it is quite likely that some steps will be taken towards perfecting the caseless or self-contained projectile. Several attempts have already been made (like simplified production methods, the caseless round dates back to the Second World War), but only the MBA Gyrojet has seen any measurable success. This 'pistol' fired a small rocket, but was cursed with inaccuracy . . . the traditional failing of cartridges that consume integral propellant. The Gyrojet enjoyed a brief heyday in the 1960s, but has since disappeared. I have no doubt that it will re-emerge in a differing guise, as its great merit—simplicity—has much to commend it to a pistol manufacturer. It is interesting that Heckler & Koch, well known for its rather radical pistol designs, has already developed an automatic rifle firing a caseless cartridge.

Below: the Ingram submachine-gun is a popular 'handgun substitute'. (Photograph by courtesy of Ian Hogg.)

Commercial guns can be categorised in several ways, by calibre, manufacturer or even model. This book, however, will settle for a 'categorisation by class':
(a) Sporting guns. (b) Target guns. (c) Personal defence and general purpose guns.

SPORTING GUNS

The 'automatic' and the revolver occupy equal prominence in this class. Though many would doubt the utility of a handgun as a sporting gun—and equally many would press its merits—the last few decades have seen the development of some extremely powerful cartridges and the guns in which to use them: 0.357 Magnum, 0.41 Magnum, 0.44 Magnum etc. Most of these are revolver cartridges, the best of the guns being made by the leading US companies, S&W, Colt, Ruger and Dan Wesson, though there are some lesser known participants. The most powerful gun of all is claimed to be the 44 Auto Mag, a recoil operated rotating-bolt-locked pistol (made by a confusing array of contractors and subcontractors) that has finally overtaken the legendary Gabbett-Fairfax 'Mars' in the all-time power stakes . . . after eight decades of effort. There is also the gas-operated Wildey, externally resembling the Government Model Colt but internally quite different, which claims an similarly astounding power level.

On a much less exciting plane, there are many guns—generally revolvers in the USA but a much headier combination of revolver and auto in Europe—used for what is normally termed 'plinking', *i.e.* use on non-regulation paper, animate or other targets, or simply shooting at tin cans.

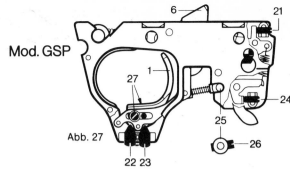

Mod. GSP

Abb. 27

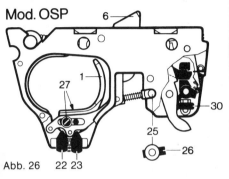

Mod. OSP

Abb. 26

Hämmerli 232

These three guns testify to the diversity of the present-day target pistol.

Top: the Sauer Western Target revolver, now made in Italy.
Middle: the extraordinary-looking Hämmerli 232 rapid fire pistol with its hand-enveloping Morini grip.
Bottom: the FN Practice 150 is a trainer for the FN International II.

The drawings depict the detachable trigger unit of the Walther OSP, giving a clear indication of the complexity to be expected in a target pistol.

Photographs and drawings appear by courtesy of the manufacturers concerned.

TARGET PISTOLS

This category contains the most interesting group of guns and—without doubt—the most sophisticated. There is also a bewildering permutation of classifiable subvarieties.

'Practical Pistol'
This is a comparatively new class, intended to combine the best of target shooting with the excitement and interest-value of a staged 'realistic' environment in which the shooter is expected to complete an obstacle course, reload, and fire with either hand on penalty of time and scores. The guns used for practical pistol shooting are inevitably large-calibre automatics or much more rarely revolvers; the GP35 & Colt 1911A1 are among the most favoured, but most competitors 'customise' their weapons and a considerable amount of minor modification is permitted. This in turn has led to many variations on grips, sights, trigger guard shapes, frames and magazine designs, and the rise of a minor industry to satisfy the demand.

'Long Range Shooting'
As far as handguns are concerned, this is also a comparatively recent innovation; though historical precedents may suggest the contrary, the prototype of the modern long-range gun is most plausibly the modernistic plastic-gripped 0.221 Remington XP100 Fireball introduced in 1962 to fire a bottle-necked cartridge allying a very high muzzle

velocity with—in pistol forms—an extremely flat trajectory. This facilitates shooting out to several hundred yards with commendable accuracy, assisted, of course, by optical sights. The XP100 and the block-action Thompson/Center Contender, descendants of a long line of Continental block-action guns, can be said to have inspired the current fascination with long range shooting. Many of the guns to be seen are privately made, though others are the products of small but highly specialised gunmakers.

Standard Pistol

This is, perhaps, the branch of the sport with the greatest number of participants. Guns designed for deliberately-aimed fire inevitably incorporate considerable mechanical refinement—exceeded only by the 'Free Pistols' and possibly the rapid fire guns—and have the considerable weight necessary to minimise disturbance on pulling the trigger. Features such as the sight radius and the minimum pull weights are regulated (and the rules written and re-written) by the sport's governing bodies, while manufacturers constantly strive to gain a march on their rivals.

Standard pistols are intended for a combination discipline, in which some of the advantages of the Free Pistols must be combined with some from the specialised rapid-fire guns. Consequently, far greater variety of shape and refinement may be found among the Standard Pistols than in any other single class.

Rapid-fire

Rapid-fire guns are among the most interesting of target pistols, destined for precise, closely defined competition shooting. The majority of targets consists of frames bearing silhouettes—usually stylised human figures—which present themselves for a brief, pre-determined instant and then rotate to present a non-scoring edge; the process then continues for several shots. The rapid-fire guns are universally characterised by one feature: ultra-low power to reduce the recoil impulse to its minimum practicable level while maintaining flawless functioning. Low recoil has the twin advantages of minimising disturbance on firing and reducing the time taken to get back to the point of aim. Considerable weight helps, as does light trigger pull and, if possible, a low bore axis: the lower the turning couple set upon firing the less the displacement (the 'straight line' theory). The search for perfection has led to some bizarre solutions; for example, the Russian MTsZ-1 appeared at the 1956 Olympic Games with its barrel *below* the line of the trigger guard and sights carried at normal height on a special rib. The gun was really a conventional upside-down automatic . . . and was subsequently banned from competition because of its excessive length.

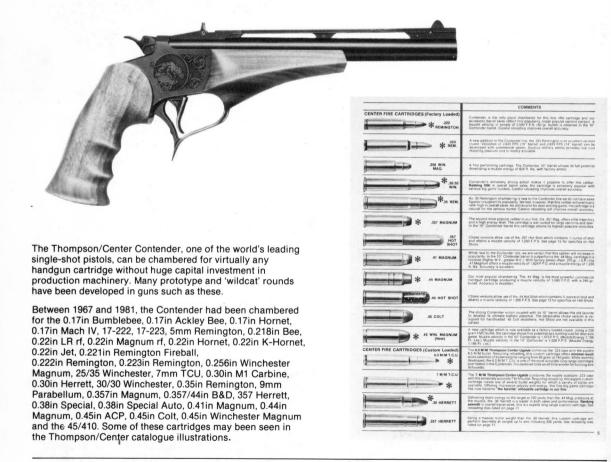

The Thompson/Center Contender, one of the world's leading single-shot pistols, can be chambered for virtually any handgun cartridge without huge capital investment in production machinery. Many prototype and 'wildcat' rounds have been developed in guns such as these.

Between 1967 and 1981, the Contender had been chambered for the 0.17in Bumblebee, 0.17in Ackley Bee, 0.17in Hornet, 0.17in Mach IV, 17-222, 17-223, 5mm Remington, 0.218in Bee, 0.22in LR rf, 0.22in Magnum rf, 0.22in Hornet, 0.22in K-Hornet, 0.22in Jet, 0.221in Remington Fireball, 0.222in Remington, 0.223in Remington, 0.256in Winchester Magnum, 25/35 Winchester, 7mm TCU, 0.30in M1 Carbine, 0.30in Herrett, 30/30 Winchester, 0.35in Remington, 9mm Parabellum, 0.357in Magnum, 0.357/44in B&D, 357 Herrett, 0.38in Special, 0.38in Special Auto, 0.41in Magnum, 0.44in Magnum, 0.45in ACP, 0.45in Colt, 0.45in Winchester Magnum and the 45/410. Some of these cartridges may be seen in the Thompson/Center catalogue illustrations.

*Three generations of the Hämmerli falling-block action match pistols are shown here. **Top to bottom:** the Modell 104, the MP33 and the Modell 152 electronic, dating from 1962, 1933 and 1978. (Courtesy of Hämmerli.)*

Hämmerli

A great number of 'innovations' designed to improve rapid-fire guns have appeared in the last few years. One undeniable improvement has been the removal of the backsight to a fixed mounting independent of the slide, usually a 'saddle' or hollow bridge through which the slide recoils. There are several 'proprietary' magazines and also several attempts to reduce muzzle climb or jump—even the exceptionally low-powered 0.22 short has to exert considerable force to operate the action—and most have taken the form of ports drilled into the barrel from above, forming a type of muzzle brake or compensator. There is, however, another advantage: all or any of the ports may be closed—usually by inserting small blind screws—to adjust the compensating effect to different brands and powers of ammunition. Some guns have been made with interchangeable barrel, trigger or slide assemblies to enable an owner to perform (or practise) differing disciplines. Typical are the West German Walther, GSP and the Finnish Sako guns.

Various kinds of ignition systems have been attempted, the goal being the shortest possible lock-time (*i.e.* the period elapsing between the release of the striker/hammer and ignition of the chambered round, measured in milliseconds), and the smallest interaction between mechanical parts. Experiments have been made with a number of mechanical systems—as is to be expected—and even a few electronic systems. However, most of the latter are to be found on the FREE PISTOLS.

In addition to the trigger systems, there has been a huge variety of grip designs, the majority featuring at least a thumb-rest and a large proportion with adjustable palm shelves or 'wraparound' extensions enabling the owner to achieve optimal grip for his individual requirements.

Free pistols
The modern free pistol—the best developed handgun currently available—is in my opinion, a worthy successor to the duelling pistol, in which case its history may be said to have been a Central European development. Although sophisticated percussion target pistols had been produced in France by gunmakers such as Le Page, and the primer-propelled Flobert 'parlour' guns had originated there too, it was in the area bounded by Southern Germany, Switzerland, America and Bohemia that the free pistols was properly developed.

Target shooting in Central Europe was a very highly codified, organised and controlled sport—even in the mid nineteenth century—and by the end of the 1890s, several advanced pistols had been developed. Some had been offered by Dreyse (a company which ceased to exist in 1901), but the best known and most successful of the pre-1914 guns was the Tell (sometimes called the William Tell) pistol, patented in 1909 and made by Ernst Friedrich Büchel of what was then Zella St Blasii. A Tell won the 1911 world championship competition in Rome and continued its dominance in Rome again in 1926. Büchel then produced an improved gun known as the Luna and, until his company was bought out by Udo Anschütz, continued to make Luna pistols alongside the Tell. Anschütz then made the Luna together with its own 'Rekord', which gained the gold medal at the 1936 Olympic Games. Unfortunately, production of these outstanding examples of the gunmakers' art ceased with the Second World War and never resumed.

Like the Luna, Tell and Rekord—and countless other German and Swiss guns—the Hämmerli was a dropping block action free pistol with a highly sophisticated set (or 'hair') trigger system. Unlike 'rapid fire' pistols, in which speed was of the essence and an auto-loader virtually obligatory, the free pistols were inevitably single shot; this rule still holds. The first Hämmerli gun was the modified Martini-actioned MP Modell 33, produced from 1933 until it was supplanted after 1949-50 by the improved Modell 100. This was replaced, in turn, by a series of revised guns culminating in the Modelle 106 and 107, production of which finally ceased in 1971-2 when serial numbers had reached 33788. Their replacements were the Modell 150, which has a mechanical trigger system, and the electronically-triggered Modell 152.

The modern free pistol is an extraordinarily complex tool: often very curious-looking, like the Italian Pardini with its ultra low barrel line, and generally lacking the elegance of its previous predecessors. Electronic ignition, though not new (High Standard attempted it in the early 1960s), has yet to replace the mechanical systems and several guns can still be obtained in the classic mould—even though the Hämmerli-Martini is no longer in production. Typical of these is the Zentrum, made in the GDR.

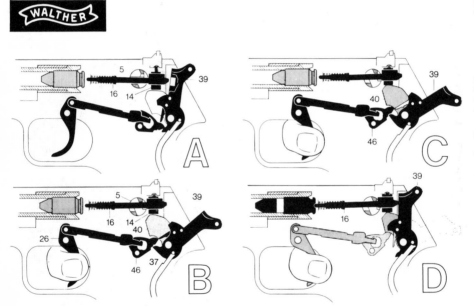

(Diagrams by courtesy of Walther.)

These drawings depict part of the trigger cycle of the Walther PP Super. *A* shows the system at rest, when the head of the firing pin (16) enters a recess in the hammer face (39) and cannot be driven forwards. *B* shows how a pull on the trigger rotates the hammer by means of the lifting arm (37), while at the same time raising the firing pin (16) by way of the blade (40). At *C*, the hammer slips from the lifting arm and flies forward to strike the firing pin (*D*). The cycle can now begin again.

GENERAL PURPOSE AND PERSONAL DEFENCE GUNS

This class contains a considerable variety of guns, revolvers and semi-automatics alike, and may be conveniently split in half.

General Purpose Guns

These are the weapons of the police and similar organisations. In the USA they are mainly revolvers—the recent trend has been towards large-calibre magnums—while Europeans have always favoured semi-automatics, typified by the Walther PP. There have been exceptions, of course: some German units, and Swiss cantonal forces, have favoured the full size Walther P1 and the SIG SP210. And, until recent years, the British favoured Webley revolvers. As far as the revolvers are concerned, the principal US suppliers are Colt and Smith & Wesson (both long established), a supremacy recently challenged by Charter Arms, Sturm, Ruger & Co. and Dan Wesson. No products of lesser manufacturers are currently as widely distributed. Few worthwhile advances in revolver technology have been made since the early twentieth century, as the patents sought by Colt and Smith & Wesson testify, though the US Gun Control Act of 1968 inspired frantic development of 'transfer bar' safety systems for revolver lockwork. This has finally removed the problem of the firing pin accidentally igniting a chambered round: a well known failing of the Colt Peacemaker, which caused the Wild West pistoleer to ride with the hammer down on an empty chamber.

Other recent trends have included the development of an intermediate cartridge—more powerful than the long established but under-powered 7.65 and 9mm ACP, but less powerful than the equally long established 9mm Parabellum. This has led to pistols developing more power than traditional blowback general purpose pistols while remaining sufficiently low powered to make a breech lock superfluous. However, too few such guns have been accepted to loosen the grip of the two power bases:

a) guns such as the SIG Sauer P225, Walther P5 and similar locked breech guns

b) the sophisticated double action blowbacks such as the Walther PP and PPK—still in production after fifty years—the FN-Browning Model 40, Beretta 81/84 series, and the latest Astra and Stars.

Personal defence

This is another confused category, containing a variety of small revolvers, semi-automatics and even modern versions of the deringer. The guns in this group are kept by police and undercover agents, in desk bureaux, in handbags, glove compartments, attaché cases and other places where small size is advantageous. Their principal drawback is low power, since the most popular cartridges are the 0.22in LR, 0.25in ACP/6.35mm Auto, 0.32in ACP/7.65mm Auto and 0.380in ACP/9mm Short, none of which is an especially effective man-stopper. In some cases, though, this lack of power can be a definite advantage, as it permits low weight, low recoil impulse and enhanced controllability.

The desirability of widespread private ownership of personal defence handguns has often been questioned; in Britain, for example, a succession of punitive legislation has kept such ownership to a minimum—which is not to say that there are no guns of this type in circulation. In the USA, state laws differ greatly; some states do almost nothing, while others, such as California, have quite strict controls on handguns (though not necessarily on longarms). Additional

Below: an exploded drawing of a typical Smith & Wesson revolver. **A** is the Model 10 Military & Police, in 0.38in Special calibre with a 4in barrel. **B**, the same gun with the optional heavy barrel. **C**, the Model 15 Combat Masterpiece, and **D**, the Model 18 Combat Masterpiece.

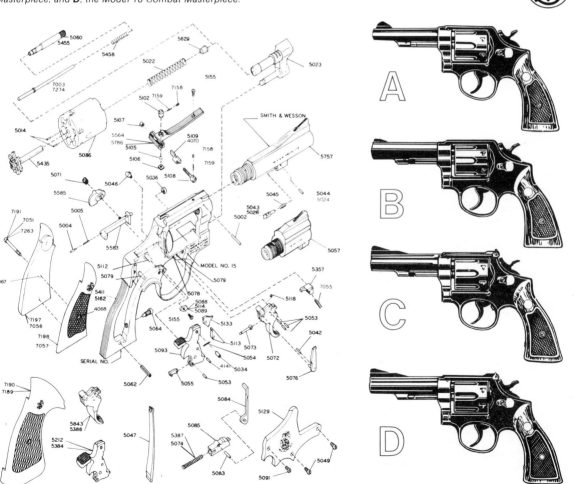

Federal laws have also prohibited the sale of guns measuring less than 4 inches high . . . and forced the removal of the Walther PPK from the US market. Precedents for restrictions of this type included the notorious Austro-Hungarian '20cm' law of the early twentieth century, which led to the appearance of unlikely long-barrelled pocket pistols.

The story of the small guns can again be traced back through the centuries, to the small flintlocks of the eighteenth century. It runs through the line of pepperboxes, small percussion and pinfire revolvers, a collection of cartridge-firing deringers, palm-squeezer and similar designs, to the small pocket automatics. Among the first and most successful of these was the Browning of 1906. The pocket automatic was a popular design; cheap to produce and easy to conceal on account of its flatness, many millions were manufactured. In addition to the guns made by properly established firms such as Fabrique Nationale and Colt, fantastic quantities were made in Eibar (Spain) and Liège (Belgium) more with an eye to quantity than quality. Their names ran the gamut from A to Z, and many were to prove as dangerous to the firer as to the target. Mercifully, the restriction of the modern gun markets, more stringent proof laws, better educated and more discerning clientele, and a general rise in material quality have now removed most of the inferior products from the market. The two main trends in the construction of present-day pocket and personal defence pistols have been towards the reduction of size and weight while improving safety. The development of strong, lightweight alloys has been invaluable, and one notable landmark in this class was the introduction in the early 1930s of the Walther Polizei-Pistole, patented in Germany in 1929; this gun had one of the first commercially acceptable double-action trigger systems and was such a success that many of today's double-action personal defence pistols are little more than copies of the Walther. The original is, in fact, still in production in Walther's Ulm/Donau factory and shows no signs of approaching obsolescence. It can even be argued with some justification that *every* gun of this class, whether a direct copy of the PP or using different lockwork, was inspired by the exploits of the prewar Walther organisation.

The typical modern pocket automatic or revolver is, as a result, far better made than its early twentieth-century counterpart.

Blackpowder shooting

This has seen a tremendous upsurge in recent years. Naturally, such shooting is messy, inconvenient and ineffectual compared to modern weaponry, but to cling to this view alone is to miss the point entirely; an element of nostalgia lies in 'powder burning'—the re-enactment of US Civil War skirmishes being one extreme—and this kind of shooting often breeds a cameraderie unique among shooting fraternities. Though competition shooting is, undeniably, as seriously contested with these old timers as in any other branches of the sport, anyone who has partaken in blackpowder competitions (especially internationally) will be well aware of their unique flavour; where else in shooting could national teams be found bedecked as Japanese Samurai, Confederate sharpshooters, English Gentlemen or soldiers of the French Revolutionary Wars?

Their handguns come in many types, the most numerous being percussion revolvers . . . perhaps as popular now as in their mid nineteenth century heyday. Most of the modern guns, made by reputable manufacturers, are undoubtedly stronger and better made than all but the best of their antecedents. The rise of shooting the replica revolvers—re-creations would, perhaps, be a better term—has contributed greatly to the prosperity of the Italian gunsmithing industry, particularly in the Gardone valley where almost every gunmaker (and there are many) produces flintlock and percussion pistols or copies of the ubiquitous Colt and Remington revolvers. This success has been credited in particular to Val Forgett of Navy Arms (qv), whose launch of 'Reb' and 'Yank' percussion revolvers in the United States opened the floodgates. Thus, comparatively youthful companies such as Uberti have quickly established themselves as purveyors of good quality blackpowder guns. Even Colt now proffers recreations of some of the most famous revolvers in firearms history. And while almost every modern percussion revolver still derives from a Colt or Remington prototype, attempts have been made to improve on the nineteenth century. The most impressive has been the production by Sturm, Ruger & Co. (qv) of the Old Army revolver, perhaps the finest percussion revolver yet developed. Clearly, then, much life remains in this sport.

Right: the Colt Navy revolver of 1851, shown here in exploded form, is among the best known of all percussion revolvers. It is currently being re-created by Daffini, Pietta, Rigarmi, Uberti and many other Italian gunmakers, in addition to Colt itself. The quality of many reproductions is high–the Colt and Uberti patterns are generally regarded as the best, with Pietta's only a short distance behind–but those made by less well established companies are often little better than mediocre. However, owing to compulsory proof in Italy and Spain, they are rarely so poor as to be dangerous.

Operating systems

Describing the operating systems of handguns presents a series of unique problems. It has been attempted by many people at many times, usually with only a modicum of success. This book's attempt takes the form shown in the chart on page 5, which is intended to facilitate tracing a path through the complexities of handgun operation . . . which could be enlarged to fill an entire book. R.K. Wilson's *Textbook of Automatic Pistols* is one such example, dealing exclusively with all but one part of the subject area. Wilson's elegant descriptions of the mechanisms and their intricacies are among the best ever written; but, without the benefit of diagrams, few of us could reconstruct the action after reading its description. *The Pistol Book* obviously cannot devote space to detailed discussion of the operating principles, yet a few brief details are obligatory.

The three basic classes

1 Those handguns firing self-contained ammunition and relying entirely on manual operations to load and extract and/or eject the spent case. This category contains single shots (a class now making a comeback) and such things as pepperboxes or double deringers with manually rotated barrel clusters.
2 Those in which the majority of the loading, indexing and extraction and/or ejection operations are achieved by means other than *direct* manual control. This includes guns in which these 'automatic' operations are achieved mechanically, even though some part of the process may be achieved as a result of manual operation. The best known example of this class is the revolver, in which turning the cylinder and operating the trigger system is achieved by the firer's hand, despite the linkages involved, though the short-lived mechanical repeater of the late nineteenth century is another.
3 Those in which operations such as loading, extraction and ejection are accomplished by the mechanism itself, the only part played in the cycle by the firer being to prepare the system for the first shot—pulling the slide back in an automatic—or tripping the sear before each shot.

CLASS 1: MANUAL OPERATION

These guns are now mainly single-shot, a class finding increasing acceptance and distribution, particularly as it can be chambered for almost any cartridge. The most efficient of these is the comparatively modern Thompson/Center Contender, designed by Warren Center in the early 1960s, which has been chambered for more than twenty cartridges between 0.17in (a passing craze) and 0.45in. This gun has perhaps the simplest possible exchangeable barrel. The barrel units are retained by a transverse pin, itself retained by the fore-end; to remove the barrel, the fore-end is detached, the axis pin removed, the old barrel replaced and the axis pin and fore-end refitted. Most modern single-shot guns have dropping-block actions—the Hämmerli free pistols, Models 100 to 107, were Martinis—and some of the latest have sophisticated electronic trigger units.

CLASS 2: MECHANICAL OPERATION

These guns may also be subdivided into simple and multi-barrel types. The latter is now a rare bird, but there are still several two-shot fixed-barrel cluster deringers based on the nineteenth century Remington pattern. There are, however, many modern representatives of the single-barrel mechanically-operated gun even though the mechanical repeater is moribund. Here, of course, we encounter the revolvers.

Revolvers have had a long and equally complicated history of mechanical development. Virtually every type of frame construction, trigger system and extraction/ejection mechanism has been introduced at one time or another; some worked and stood the test of time—others worked yet did not—and more than a few were complete disasters. The chart indicates the subdivisions, the principal of which are 'open' and 'closed' frame. For the purposes of this work, the distinction between the two is precisely drawn: open frames are any that are made in two or more pieces regardless of how they may interlock, while closed frames are solid one-piece forgings. By this definition, guns such as the Colts and Smith & Wessons, even though their cylinders are carried on laterally-hingeing cranes—not a new idea: see Albini's patent of 1869—are defined as 'closed' frame patterns. This feature apart, however, there is little variety among the closed or solid-frame designs; many have loading gates and/or ejector rods, but these are variations of *detail* rather than principle.

Open-frame revolvers come in a much more interesting variety. They may be conveniently segregated into (i) hinged frame, and (ii) sliding frame.

Hinged frame
This has been surprisingly popular, as it offers the chance of simple and efficient auto-ejection, albeit balanced against theoretically weaker construction. And, just as the solid-frame gun has a long-established pedigree—back to the Remington of 1858 and beyond—the hinged frame has also enjoyed a long life. There was, for example, the big bore

Long recoil operation

a barrel spring
b bolt lock
c bolt
d unlocking device
e bolt spring
f bolt latch
g lock open
h spent case extraction
i bolt latched
j lugs engaged
k bolt unlatched

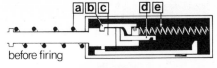

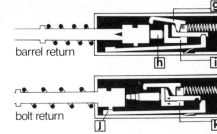

before firing

barrel return

end of recoil

bolt return

Short recoil operation

a barrel spring
b counter-recoil buffer
c recoil buffer
d bolt lock
e accelerator
f unlocking cam
g bolt spring
h backplate buffer

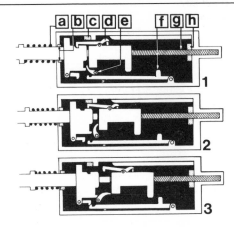

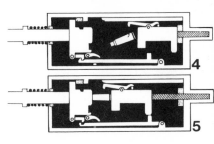

Diagrams from *Military Smallarms of the Twentieth Century,* by Ian Hogg and John Weeks (Arms & Armour Press, London, 1973 to date).

Below: *the Steyr-Daimler-Puch Model GB, a modern gas-operated design. (Courtesy of Ian Hogg.)*

Smith & Wessons beginning with the American Model of 1869 made to W.C. Dodge's patents. The majority of the British Webley series (and all of the government models) showed this type of operation, in which the barrel/cylinder group is hinged at the front end of the frame and tips downwards to eject the cylinder contents. Many modern Harrington & Richardson revolvers feature this system, but there are few other representatives.

There have been a few bizarre guns in which the barrels hinge upwards, usually around a lateral pivot above the frame behind the cylinder, and even a couple in which the barrel/cylinder combination pivots laterally around a vertical pivot at the lower front end of the frame. Most of these ill-starred aberrations rapidly disappeared—they were neither as convenient nor as efficient as the downward-hingeing barrel pattern, which lent itself better to auto-ejection systems.

Sliding frame

Revolvers with sliding frames—perhaps more accurately described as 'sliding barrel'—are relatively unusual. There were a few early attempts to develop guns in which the cylinder could be *replaced* with another, but these were rapidly superseded by more conventional designs in which the the cylinder remained part of the whole. The sliding frame group contains the Galand & Somerville, which was patented in Britain in 1870 and for a brief spell the service revolver of the Russian Navy, and the American 'Merwin & Hulbert', which was made by Hopkins & Allen. Both were auto-extractors.

There was also a hybrid system featuring a downward hingeing barrel which pulled the cylinder forward along the frame in such a way that the cylinder axis pin remained parallel to the frame during the entire operation. The most noteworthy example of this is the British 'Enfield' revolver of 1879, rapidly superseded by the more efficient Webley.

All modern revolvers are either of the solid-frame pattern—'western' copies with cylinders carried on laterally movable yokes—or alternatively of the tip-down hinged-frame pattern.

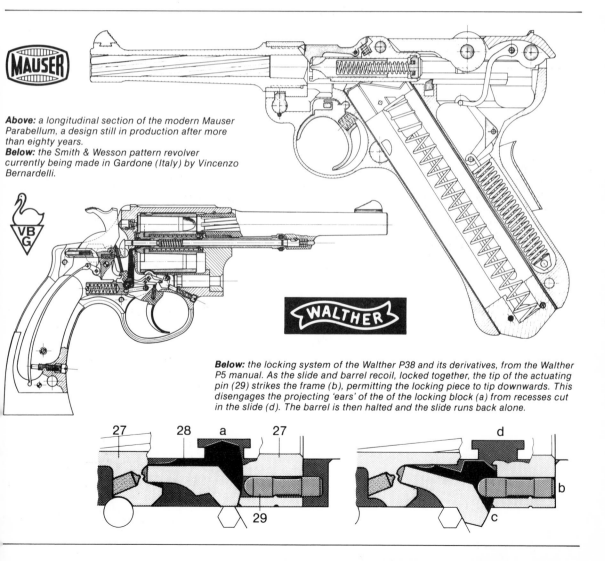

Above: *a longitudinal section of the modern Mauser Parabellum, a design still in production after more than eighty years.*
Below: *the Smith & Wesson pattern revolver currently being made in Gardone (Italy) by Vincenzo Bernardelli.*

Below: *the locking system of the Walther P38 and its derivatives, from the Walther P5 manual. As the slide and barrel recoil, locked together, the tip of the actuating pin (29) strikes the frame (b), permitting the locking piece to tip downwards. This disengages the projecting 'ears' of the of the locking block (a) from recesses cut in the slide (d). The barrel is then halted and the slide runs back alone.*

CLASS 3: SELF-ACTIVATING SYSTEMS

This category embraces 'self-loaders' and 'automatics', in which the manual actions of the firer are reduced to a minimum. It, too, is easily subdivisible, the criterion being the strength (or otherwise) of the breech-lock—(i) unlocked breech, (ii) hesitation or partially locked breech and (iii) locked breech.

Unlocked breech.

Otherwise known as 'blowback' or 'case projection', this system consists of a heavy breechblock and a stiff spring. Consequently, all that opposes the movement of the bullet forwards, and the resultant backward movement of the cartridge case, is the radial pressure which tends to stick the casewalls to the chamber, the inertia of the breechblock, a modicum of friction to be overcome as the parts move, and the resistance of the recoil spring(s). The breechblock needs to be heavy and the recoil spring(s) sufficiently powerful to prevent the breech opening too quickly or casehead separations and similar ammunition problems ensue. An unlocked breech, however, generally brings the advantages of simplicity and, provided that the gun has a solidly attached slide incapable of being blown off backwards, there is no doubt that the 'blowback' system is quite acceptable. It is popularly believed that unlocked-breech guns should not be chambered for cartridges more powerful than (for instance) the 9mm short, alias 0.380in ACP. Though there is some merit in this rule, the Spanish Campo Giro and its better known derivative, the Astra, handle cartridges as powerful as the 9mm Parabellum and 9mm Largo in perfect safety. There has also been a handful of blow *forward* designs in which the movable barrel is projected forwards from the standing (or fixed) breech. The best known representatives have been a Mannlicher (1894) and the Schwarzlose of 1908, though the system has recently reappeared. Its principal merits are simplicity, safety and rugged construction; drawbacks include an understandably odd recoil pattern and inferior accuracy compared to conventional blowbacks.

Hesitation lock

These guns are, it is claimed, a means of combining the simplicity of the unlocked-breech types with the safety (at least partly) of a bona fide breech lock. The results have been inconsistent: some guns have worked well, others have been complete disasters. The earliest exponent was the Schönberger of 1892, but the most completely successful have been the Savage (Searle's patent, 1905), which has a rotary 'lock' turning through only about 5°, the Czech vz/52 and the modern Heckler & Koch P9 system credited to Herbert Meidel, both of which use a minor variation of the roller-lock pioneered by the MG42. At the 'disaster' end of the market has been the Kimball, perhaps 250 of which were made in Detroit during the 1950s. This chambered the powerful US 0.30in M1 Carbine cartridge and relied on a combination of a small free barrel movement and a grooved chamber to delay opening of the breech. Unfortunately for its champions, however, propellant fouling often transformed the Kimball into an ordinary blowback with potentially disastrous consequences—particularly as the slide was halted only by two small lugs at the rear of the frame which could (and did) fail under severe battering. The slide could even be blasted off the frame towards the firer, which aptly illustrates the advantages of a closed or captive frame/slide design in blowback or locked breech types. Consideration of hesitation locks cannot be left without acknowledgement of the 'Blish Principle' (that friction between two differing metal surfaces increases under pressure) embodied in the Thompson submachine gun. The efficacy of the lock—which originally consisted of a bronze H-piece sliding diagonally to release the gunmetal breechblock from the gunmetal receiver—has been widely questioned, and the last 'Tommy Guns' functioned quite happily as blowbacks. Yet the Blish lock is probably a satisfactory delay mechanism in its own right. Towards the end of the 1920s, Thompson produced an automatic rifle, one of the all-time best hesitation lock catastrophes, to compete in the US Army trials against the toggle-locked Pedersen—nearly the greatest hesitation-lock success—and the Garand. The Thompson gets a mention here because it is an effective illustration of the dangers of too short a delay period; it ejected fired cases with such impressive violence that their mouths would stick into oak boards. Modern representatives include the MAB Model N, which uses another of the rotary delay systems; the Heckler & Koch PSP (P7), with an efficient delay system in which a gas bleed is used to oppose the opening of the breech until the gas pressure has dropped to a safe level; and the Italian Benelli M76.

Positive lock

The locked breech 'automatic' pistol has attracted infinitely more attention from inventors, engineers and manufacturers alike than the revolver—and the problems associated with the development of an efficient self-loading mechanism (however much revolver makers care to deny it) have been infinitely more difficult to solve. Virtually every conceivable locking system has been attempted, with every conceivable amount of success. The history of the automatic pistol, notwithstanding the huge contribution of the American John M. Browning, is also very much a European one. The principal categorisation of locked-breech guns is derived not from the mechanics of the lock itself—there are too many variations—but rather from the source of power.

GAS OPERATION is the less popular, though well pedigreed method. The power necessary to unlock the slide and force it backward is derived from the propellant, there being two major subclasses: *direct* operation where the gas impinges directly on the piston or breechblock, *indirect* when it is used to load intermediate levers or springs. Gas operation has several merits—it can lead to a simpler mechanism—but one principal drawback: fouling can often render the gun inoperative, though the influence of fouling has gradually decreased in direct proportion to advances in propellant technology. The American Wildey of 1974-5, based on a Husqvarna design of 1970, is gas operated, as is the Steyr GB and the hesitation locked Heckler & Koch PSP, but it remains to be seen whether gas systems will triumph.

RECOIL OPERATION derives its power from the reaction set up in the the gun on firing, when the moving bullet is counterbalanced by an equal force moving backwards. In a 'fixed' gun, such as a revolver, the rearward velocity is muted by the weight of the entire gun and the energy subsequently dissipates into the firer's arm, shoulder and back muscles. In a recoil-operated auto-loader—though some of the recoil forces ultimately disappear in the same manner—part of the power available is adapted to open the breech-lock and push the slide back past the cocking position. As in gas-operated pistols, return of the parts and re-locking of the breech are accomplished by springs compressed during the initial backward movement.

Recoil operation is subdivisible into two groups: *short recoil* and *long recoil*. Various definitions of these have been attempted, but those involving arbitrary dimensions ('more than an inch') make no allowance for the great differences encountered not only among calibres, but also between cartridge case lengths. The best definition, therefore, is *long recoil:* locked travel greater than the length of the cartridge case; *short recoil:* locked movement less than the length of the cartridge case. This has little or nothing to do with the power of the cartridge: in the instance of the 9mm Parabellum, the 'cut off' dimension would be 19mm, whereas for the 6.35mm Auto (0.25in ACP) it would be less—and for the 0.22in Magnum rimfire, appreciably greater. Long-recoil pistols have included the Frommers, the Roth-Sauer and Roth-Steyr, and an 1895-vintage Schwarzlose; most of the remainder, however, have featured short recoil.

Recoil operation is illustrated on page 20.

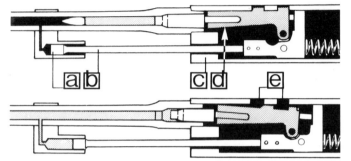

a b   c d   e

Recoil operation is illustrated on page 20.

Gas operation—direct

a   gas piston
b   operating rod
c   receiver
d   breechblock
e   locking lugs

A   locked position; the bullet is travelling down the barrel, but no gas has yet been bled off into the piston chamber
B   unlocking taking place; part of the propellant gas has been bled off into the piston chamber and has forced the piston back against the breechblock carrier

Recoil operation is widely favoured for pistols because of its reliability, which counteracts a tendency towards complexity—though many recoil-operated handguns, such as the Parabellum (Luger) remain masterpieces of the toolmakers' art. Finally, however, simpler and more durable designs have been evolved, exemplified by the Browning-designed US M1911 (Colt) pistol. And though the Germans in particular have clung to complexity—the Walther P 38 and the Heckler & Koch P 9 series are recent examples—the trends are now towards the strong, simple and cheap construction embodied in the SIG-Sauers, using stampings, precision castings and synthetic parts wherever practicable. Recoil operation is less favoured than gas for machine-guns, in which limitations of space and volume are of less consequence than in handguns and where, therefore, the problems of gas fouling can be minimised.

Locking systems

These have come in tremendous variety: tipping blocks, oscillating blocks, dropping barrels, rotary breechblocks, toggle-joints, links, bolts, rollers and almost every plausible solution (not to mention many implausible ones!) having been tried in the last hundred years. The most popular and durable has proved to be the Browning dropping link, designed in its original form in the 1890s, patented in 1897 and subsequently refined several times before being 'perfected' in 1909 and latterly in 1925-6. In its final form, it consists of a tipping barrel controlled by a pivoting link (or cam finger in the GP and other recent designs) under the breech. Recoil causes this unit to pull lug(s) atop the barrel from locking recesses in the underside of the slide, after which the slide is freed to run backwards. The Browning system is currently featured by the Colt M1911/M1911A1 and its derivatives—still in production after seven decades—and the FN Browning GP Mle 35; in addition, the SIG-Sauer P 220 and 225, the bigger Spanish Stars and Llamas, the SIG P 210 series, the Smith & Wesson M 39 and M 52, the Russian Tokarevs and their variations, the latest FÉG pistol and the Czech CZ vz.75 all feature much the same system . . . and there have been many others, such as the Polish wz/35 Radom and the French Petters, which are no longer in production.

No other system has approached the Browning link/cam systems for popularity. The survival of the toggle-lock incorporated in the Parabellum (Luger), still in production after more than eighty years despite a gap between 1943 and the late 1960s, owes more to sentiment than to mechanical efficiency. The design, elegant though it be, is fantastically complicated, difficult to manufacture and more than a little temperamental. The mechanism of the Walther P 38, the replacement for the Parabellum in German service and now known to the Bundeswehr as the P1, is another survivor from prewar days. Incorporating a separate locking block under the barrel and operated by short recoil, it can be said to have influenced the Beretta 951 and its newer derivatives. But even these, however, have failed to displace the Browning Link from its pre-eminent position.

AFAMSA

Avenida Francisco Cambó 14-5° E, Barcelona-3, Spain

British agency: none. US agency: none. Standard warranty: unknown.

A small specialist manufacturer of muzzle-loading pistols, with an estimated annual output of five thousand guns in 1982, AFAMSA was founded in October 1962. Its name is an acronym of Asociación de Fabricantes de Articulos Manufacturados SA, which suggests that it was, at least initially, a collective of even smaller workshops. It was certainly listed as an export agency rather than gunmaker.

Modelo 1800 or English Model 1800

Target pistol This elegant blackpowder gun is loosely based on the English pistols of the late eighteenth and early nineteenth centuries, though it is by no means a true replica and some of its features recall French influence. It has a browned German-made target barrel, an adjustable trigger and an engraved 'in the white ' lock inscribed LONDON. This is usually a flintlock—more in keeping with the overall style of the gun—but a percussion alternative may be obtained as well. The European walnut half-stock has a chequered round butt and German silver mounts.
Cal: 0.45in, 11.4mm. Mag: none. Trg: SA, external hammer. Wt, oz/gm: 44.0/1245. Loa, in/mm: NA. Brl, in/mm: NA. Rf: yes–style uncertain. Sft: none except half-cock position on hammer.

Below: *the Agner M80. (Courtesy Parker-Hale Ltd.)*

Modelo 1810 or English Model 1810

Target pistol. An undeniably elegant, but untypically English design, the Modelo 1810 features a German-made precision match barrel and double set-triggers. The barrel is browned, the plain lock 'in the white' and signed LONDON, and the European walnut half-stock has a rounded chequered butt. The mounts and inlays are of German silver.
Data: generally similar to the Modelo 1800 (qv).

Model 10 Kentucky Pistol

General purpose pistol. This is an interesting blackpowder gun featuring a conventional leaf-spring front-action lock. The octagonal barrel and lock are usually browned, while the furniture on the full-length beech stock—ramrod, pipes, barrel key escutcheon, sideplate, nose cap—are brass castings. The sights are adjustable by driving them across their dovetails, the elegant trigger has a back-curled tip and the butt is a bird's head type. The AFAMSA pistol is also available as a flintlock (Modelo 10FL) or even in build-it-yourself kits (Modelo 10K with a percussion lock, Mod. 10FL with a flintlock). One feature of the design is the relative ease with which the two ignition systems can be interchanged.
Cal: 0.45in, 11.4mm. Mag: none. Trg: SA, external hammer. Wt, oz/gm: 48.0/1360. Loa, in/mm: 15.5/394. Brl, in/mm: 10.0/254. Rf: 12 R?. Sft: none except for half-cock position on the hammer.

Mountain Pistol

General purpose pistol. The Mountain Pistol is a derivative of the Modelo 10 Kentucky (qv), but only in its percussion-ignition form. Its features include a case-hardened lock, with its associated colours, and a chequered beech stock. The

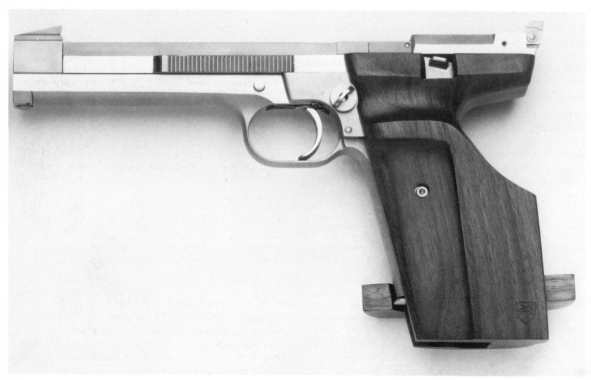

bird's head butt usually exhibits a sharper radius than the Kentucky guns, the stock is half rather than full length, and—once again—the furniture is brass.
Cal: 0.50in, 12.7mm. All other data as Kentucky Pistol

Agner

Agner–Saxhøj Products, Denmark

British agency: Parker-Hale Ltd, Golden Hillock Road, Birmingham B11 2PZ, England. US agency, standard warranty: unknown.

The Agner target pistol has only recently made its début in Britain, little being known about its manufacturer at the time of writing.

Agner M80

Target pistol. This interesting, unusual Danish-made gun appeared in Britain at the beginning of 1983—the first product of a small and hitherto unknown Danish manufacturer. Made largely of stainless steel, the Agner is intended for standard and rapid fire competitions. It undoubtedly possesses some very unusual features—such as a combination safety catch and locking key on the left side of the frame behind the trigger, an integral dry-firing device and an unconventional fully adjustable trigger. It also features, according to its accompanying promotional literature, 'a new concept in weight displacement which allows for accurate rapid fire even with high velocity ammunition'. The grips are well finished anatomical-pattern walnut, and the whole gun shows evidence of careful thought in its design and construction. It is too early to assess its potential, but early reports agree that the Agner will soon be jockeying for a place among the leading guns in its class—even though it is by no means the cheapest.
Cal: 0.22in LR rf. Mag: detachable box, catch above grip on left side of frame. Mag cap, rds: 5 Trg: SA, internal striker (?). Wt, Loa, Brl: NA, but within ISU competition rules. Sft: rotary 'key' on left side of frame behind trigger, down to safe, horizontal to fire, upwards to lock.

American Arms & Ammunition Company

1015 NW 72nd Street, Miami, Florida 33150, USA. This company handles the Budichowsky TP-70 personal defence pistol in the United States (associated with Korriphila in Germany—qv), together with a large-calibre military pistol from the same source.

Arcadia Machine & Tool Company (AMT)

Formerly 11666 McBean Drive, El Monte, California 91732, USA, but now apparently in Covina, California. No details were received from AMT in time for inclusion.

AMT Hardballer

General purpose pistol. This is a derivative of the Colt Government Model, though built of largely new parts. The external differences are considerable, as the Hardballer has a modified squared slide with its adjustable sights mounted on a top-rib. Several slide lengths are available. The basic operating system, however, parallels that of the Colt Government Model (qv).

Back-Up

Personal defence pistol. This, as its name suggests, is a small pocket automatic chambering 0.22in LR Hyper Velocity rimfire ammunition. Made largely of stainless steel, the Back-Up is 5in (13cm) long and weighs about 18oz, or 510gm, with an empty eight-round magazine. The manual safety lies on the left side of the frame, but there is also a grip safety unit.

Armigas-Comega

Costruzioni Meccaniche Gardonesi Attilio Zanoletti, Via Valle Inzino 34, I-25063 Gardone Val Trompia (Brescia), Italy.

British agency: currently none. US agency: currently none. Standard warranty: unknown.

Armigas was founded in 1961 to make rifles and pistols powered by carbon dioxide, for which it is better known than as a bona fide gunmaker. During the 1960s, however, small quantities of a blowback personal defence pistol, the Titan (wrongly attributed elsewhere to Tanfoglio), were made alongside the gas guns.

Armi-Jäger

Armi-Jäger di Armando Piscetta SRL, Via Campazzino 55/b, Milan, Italy.

British agency: Scalemead Arms Co., Unit 3, Diplocks Way, Hailsham, East Sussex BN27 3JF, England. US agency: no sole distributor. Standard warranty: 12 months

Armi-Jäger is better known for its rimfire autoloaders—including near-replicas of the AK 47 and the US M16A1 Armalite—though a series of cartridge revolvers and deringers is also made.

Baby Frontier

General purpose revolver. This rimfire derivation of the Frontier has an exchangeable cylinder and a firing pin suited to rimfire ammunition—but is an otherwise conventional Colt Peacemaker 'Western' copy, albeit to two thirds scale. The guns are blued with plain wooden grips. A long-barrel (20in, 52cm) 'Buntline' version has also been made in small numbers.
Cal: 0.22in LR or 0.22in Magnum rf. Otherwise generally as Frontier, except Brl, in/mm: 3.9, 4.7 or 5.9/100, 120 or 150.

Frontier

General purpose revolver. This is another near-facsimile of the Colt Peacemaker, made in a variety of styles and calibres—neither the best of copies nor the worst, and representing quite good value. The Armi-Jäger revolver can be obtained in blue or plated finished, the former often featuring a case-hardened frame and the latter, extensive engraving. Grips are wood or chequered rubber. The rimfire version has interchangeable cylinders chambering standard or magnum cartridges.
Cal: 0.22in LR rf or 0.22in Magnum rf, 0.357in Magnum, 0.38in Special, 0.45in Long Colt. Mag: cylinder. Mag cap, rds: 6. Trg: SA, exposed hammer. Wt, Loa: see Colt version. Brl, in/mm: 4.7, 5.9 or 7.1/120, 150 or 180. Rf: 7L? Sft: half-cock notch.

Super Frontier

Target and general purpose revolver. This variant of the Jäger Frontier has a long barrel, adjustable sights, a square-backed trigger guard and a long army-style walnut grip.
Cal: 0.22in LR rf, 0.35in Magnum, 0.44in Magnum. Otherwise generally as Frontier, except Brl, in/mm: 5.9/150 (0.22, 0.357in) or 7.1/180 (0.44in).

Teodoro Arrizabalaga Guisasola

Avenida del Generalisimo 2, Eibar, Guipúzcoa, Spain. Spanish export directories record this company as a manufacturer and exporter of shotguns, sporting guns and muzzle-loading handguns. No information about these has yet been elicited from Spain.

Astra–Unceta y Compañía SA

La Vega s/n, Apartado 3, Guernica (Vizcaya), Spain

British agency: Viking Arms Ltd, Summerbridge, Harrogate HG3 4BW, North Yorkshire, England. US agency: Interarms, 10 Prince Street, Alexandria, Virginia 22313, USA. Standard warranty: 12 months?

Founded in Eibar in 1907 by Juan Esperanza and Pedro Unceta, this company made many thousands of cheap blowback and personal defence pistols prior to the move to Guernica in 1913. Military-style pistols were made from 1916, when the Spanish army adopted the Campo-Giro. In 1921 the company adopted the name Esperanza y Unceta though the Astra tradename had been used since 1914. It benefitted greatly when the Spanish adopted the Astra-modified Campo-Giro pistol, the Modelo 1921, an outstandingly successful design which has remained in production until the present day (see Modelo 4000 Falcón). The name changed to Unceta y Compañía in 1925 and then to Unceta y Compañía SA in 1942. The product range was expanded in the late 1940s to include pneumatic drills and textile machinery, and the manufacture of shotguns commenced in 1954. Finally, in 1955, the Astra acronym was added to the official trading name. Astra–Unceta y Cia SA is now the leading Spanish gunmaker, marketing a large range of solid and dependable pistols and revolvers.

Cadix

General purpose revolver. Introduced in 1958 (1969 in 0.22in Magnum rf), the well-made double-action Cadix is based on Smith & Wesson practices, with its cylinder mounted in a yoke and swinging out of the left side of the frame. The thumb-latch lies on the left side of the frame below the hammer. There is an inertia-type firing pin and typically S&W lockwork, while the adjustable backsight consists of a laterally movable sight-blade insert and a vertically movable spring-steel rib dovetailed into the top of the frame. The ejector rod housing has a very distinctive shape, while the rear of the trigger guard has a prominent flattened section; the result is a rakish appearance rarely confused with other guns. The grips are usually chequered wood or simulated mother-of-pearl grips, and the Cadix can also be obtained in 'de luxe' chromed, engraved, silver-plated or gold damascened finishes.

Cal: 0.22in LR rf, 0.22in Magnum rf, 0.32in S&W Long or 0.38in Special. Mag: cylinder. Mag cap, rds: 5 (0.38in), 6 (0.32in) or 9 (0.22in). Trg: DA, external hammer. Wt, oz/gm: 25.2-28.8/715-815. Loa, in/mm: 8.9 or 10.8/225 or 275 (9.0-11.0/229 or 279 in 0.38in Special only). Brl, in/mm: 4.0 or 6.0/102 or 152. Rf: 6 R?. Sft: inertia-type firing pin

Modelo Camper

General purpose pistol. This long-barrelled version of the Cub (qv) was made for a decade from 1956. Its longer barrel did little to improve its performance and the original Cub was undeniably more readily concealed; consequently, it met an early demise.
Cal: 0.22in Short or 0.25in ACP (6.35mm). All other data, apart from barrel length, identical with the Cub.

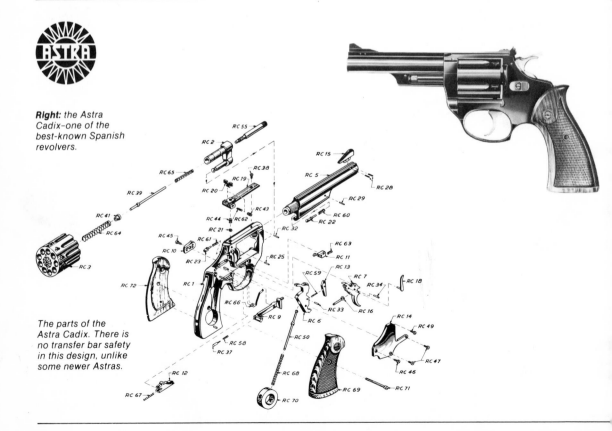

Right: *the Astra Cadix–one of the best-known Spanish revolvers.*

The parts of the Astra Cadix. There is no transfer bar safety in this design, unlike some newer Astras.

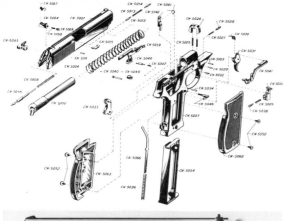

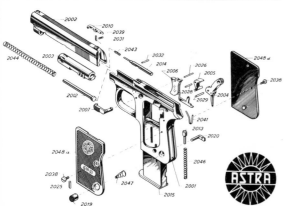

Modelo Constable (or Modelo 5000)

General purpose pistol. The Constable, dating from 1965, is Unceta y Cia's contribution to the genre of guns typified by the Walther PP—which superficially at least, the Constable greatly resembles. There is a double-action trigger system with a firing pin interlock preventing accidental discharge, and a barrel-type manual safety which allows the hammer to be dropped safely (if a little disconcertingly) onto a loaded chamber. The Astra design is a little more rakish than the Walther—it is, after all, a much newer design—and has a 'yoke' type dismantling catch ahead of and above the trigger aperture. De luxe chromed, engraved and damascened versions may also be obtained.
Cal: 0.22in LR rf, 0.32in ACP (7.65mm) or 0.380in ACP (9mm Short). Mag: detachable box in butt, crossbolt catch behind trigger. Mag cap, rds: 7 (9mm), 8 (7.65mm) or 10 (0.22in). Trg: DA, external hammer. Wt, oz/gm: 22.8-24.0/646-680. Loa, in/mm: 6.6/168. Brl, in/mm: 3.5/89. Rf: 6 R?. Sft: radial lever on left side of the slide, moves up to 'fire'; firing pin block; inertia-type firing pin.

Constable Sport

General purpose pistol. This was a sporting version of the standard Constable, or Modelo 5000, with a longer barrel, optional extra barrel weights, and more sophisticated sights. It was superseded in 1979 by the TS 22 (qv).
Cal: 0.22in LR rf. Data otherwise as Constable except for dimensions.

Modelo Cub (or Modelo 2000)

Small personal defence pistol. This small gun is an uncomplicated blowback, making its first appearance in 1955. It is a straightforward derivative of the 1906 model Browning, but with an external hammer. Its barrel is retained in the frame by three partly circumferential ribs. The Cub is very easily concealed, but it is very low powered and a poor man-stopper. Its sights are rudimentary—a small raised front sight and a short groove-type backsight formed as part of the slide. In addition to the standard plain gun, chromed, engraved and gold damascened de luxe versions (*modelos de lujo*) may be obtained to special order. Grips may be wooden or synthetic. This gun also masqueraded as the 'Colt Junior', with slides marked MADE IN SPAIN FOR COLT. Astra reports that 73,075 guns were made until the Gun Control Act of 1968 prevented Colt importing them.
Cal: 0.22in Short rf, 0.25in ACP (6.35mm). Mag: detachable box in butt, catch on lower left side of butt. Mag cap, rds: 6 (0.22in) or 7 (0.25in). Trg: SA, exposed hammer. Wt, oz/gm: 12.4 or 12.7/350 or 360. Loa, in/mm: 4.4/112. Brl, in/mm: 2.3/57. Rf: 6 R?. Sft: radial lever on left side of frame behind trigger (moves down to fire); hammer safety prevents slip during cocking.

Modelo Falcón (or Modelo 4000)

General purpose pistol. The Modelo 4000 appeared in 1956 to replace the 3000, which dated from the end of the Second World War. The basic design is much older: the original Astra automatic was the Campo-Giro, adopted by the Spanish armed forces in 1913. This subsequently became the Astra Modelo 400 (militarily: Modelo 921), the first of a series of similar blowbacks characterised by an unusual tubular slide concentric wih the barrel and mainspring. The slide remains open when the last round has been fired and ejected, after which the magazine can be withdrawn. The Astra is an old but efficient design. Its principal demerit, other than the unlocked breech, is simply that it *looks* an old design.
Cal: 0.32in (7.65mm Short), 0.380in (9mm Short). Mag: detachable box in butt, catch on bottom left side of butt. Mag cap, rds: 7 (9mm) or 8 (7.65mm). Trg: SA, exposed hammer. Wt, oz/gm: 22.8 or 23.6/646 or 668. Loa, in/mm: 6.5/164. Brl, in/mm: 4.4/112. Rf: 6 R?. Sft: radial lever on left side of frame behind trigger (moves down to fire); magazine safety; hammer safety prevents hammer-slip during cocking.

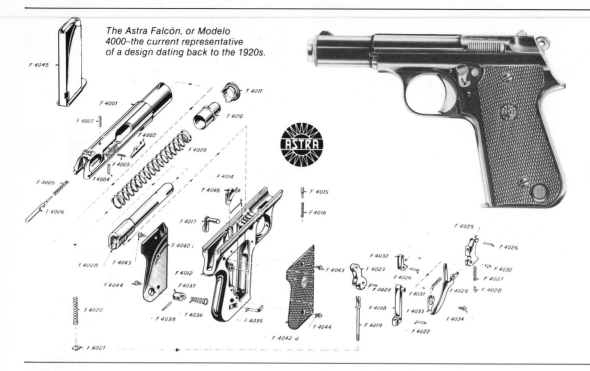

The Astra Falcón, or Modelo 4000–the current representative of a design dating back to the 1920s.

Astra Match

Target revolver. Dating from 1976, this good quality gun is intended for shooting under UIT rules, and derives from S&W principles by way of the Astra Cadix. Its single-action lockwork permits a lighter trigger pull and faster hammer fall, even though the hammer must be manually cocked before each shot. The trigger pull may be altered by inserting a key in a slotted-head adjuster on the backstrap and the tension in the mainspring can also be regulated. The backsight is fully click-adjustable laterally and vertically, while the broad square front-sight blade is specifically intended for target shooting. There is also a broad, serrated trigger shoe and chequered oversize target-style wooden grips.
Cal: 0.38in Special. Mag: cylinder. Mag cap, rds: 6. Trg: SA, external hammer. Wt, oz/gm: 43.2/1230. Loa, in/mm: 11.3/286. Brl, in/mm: 6.0/152. Rf: 6 R?. Sft: 'transfer bar' hammer block; inertia-type firing pin.

Modelo NC-6 (or New Cadix)

General-purpose revolver. This is simply a modified, modernised version of the basic Cadix (qv), with improved safety features. However, the NC-6 is otherwise practically identical with its predecessor—an S&W derivative of adequate quality and performance.
Cal: 0.22in LR rf, 0.22in Magnum rf, 0.32in S&W Long or 0.38in Special. Mag: cylinder. Mag cap, rds: 6 (0.32, 0.38in), 8 (0.22in). Trg: DA, external hammer. Wt, oz/gm: 25.8-28.8/730-815. Loa, in/mm: 9.1 or 10.9 (11.1 in 0.38in Special)/232 or 278 (282 in 0.38in Special). Brl, in/mm: 4.2 or 6.0/106 or 152. Rf: 6 R?. Sft: 'transfer bar' hammer block; inertia-type firing pin.

Modelo TS-22

Target pistol

The TS-22 appeared in 1979, a variation of the A-50 (qv) with which it is mechanically identical. The most obvious alterations are the extended slide, the extension being dovetailed vertically onto the standard slide immediately ahead of the retraction grooves—which now lie at the front rather than the rear. The fully adjustable sights lie on a raised ramp forming part of the combined slide extension and muzzle weight, while there are also lengthened thumbrest-style wooden grips. An extended floorplate is fitted to the TS-

22 magazine. Apart from these features, it is an A-50, but it is competitively priced and the equal of many a more expensive design. The Astra, interestingly, bears a considerable resemblance to the earlier Italian Bernadelli Modello 69 (qv), though the 69's slide extension does not reciprocate.
Cal: 0.22in LR rf. Mag: detachable box in butt, crossbolt catch on left side of frame behind trigger. Mag cap, rds: 10. Trg: SA external hammer. Wt, oz/gm: 35.3/1000. Loa, in/mm: 9.3/235 Brl, in/mm: 6.0/152. Rf: 6 R?. Sft: as A-50.

Modelo 41

General purpose revolver. Also known under the general designation 'Modelo 44', this enlargement of the Modelo 357 (qv) chambers a larger and more powerful cartridge. It is a derivation of S&W principles—once again—with a laterally-opening cylinder mounted on a yoke in the frame. It incorporates a perfected transfer-bar safety system and, like most modern Astra revolvers, features a fully adjustable back sight. Additionally, it offers acceptable quality at a modest price.
Cal: 0.41in Magnum. Remainder of data: see Mod. 44.

Modelo 44

General purpose revolver. A variation of the 41, described previously, this gun chambers perhaps the most effective 'man stopper' amongst revolver cartridges, though one that produces excessive recoil and, therefore, takes some handling. This was the first of the series of Astra Magnum revolvers, Models 41, 44 and 45.
Cal: 0.44in Magnum. Mag: cylinder. Mag cap, rds: 6. Trg: SA, external hammer. Wt, oz/gm: 45.2 or 46.0/1280 or 1310. Loa, in/mm: 11.5 or 13.8/293 or 350. Brl, in/mm: 6.0 or 8.5/152 or 216. Rf: 6 R?. Sft: 'transfer bar' hammer block; inertia-type firing pin.

Modelo 45

General purpose revolver. This is another variation of the Modelo 44 (qv), chambering an older—and, in its normal forms less effective—cartridge, the 0.45in Colt. The revolver will appeal to the shooter who already has a gun in this calibre and to those who hand load, as it is strong and quite reliable.
Cal: 0.45in Colt. Data otherwise as Modelo 44.

Modelo A-50

General purpose pistol. This is a derivative of the Modelo 5000 or 'Constable', with which it shares its basic design. However, the A-50 is simplified in the sense that the slide-release catch (formerly above the left grip behind the trigger) has been eliminated and the slide-mounted safety moved down to the frame behind the left grip. These revisions allow a certain amount of simplification, but greatly reduce the safety inherent in the gun—though not to a dangerous degree.
Cal: 0.32in (7.65mm Short) or 0.380in ACP (9mm Short). Mag: detachable box in butt, crossbolt catch on left of frame behind trigger. Mag cap, rds: 7 (9mm) or 8 (7.65mm). Trg: DA, concealed hammer (?). Wt, oz/gm: 22.9 or 23.4/650 or 660. Loa, in/mm: 6.6/168. Brl, in/mm: 3.5/89. Rf: 6 R?. Sft: radial lever on left rear frame, moving down to 'fire'; hammer block safety; inertia-type firing pin.

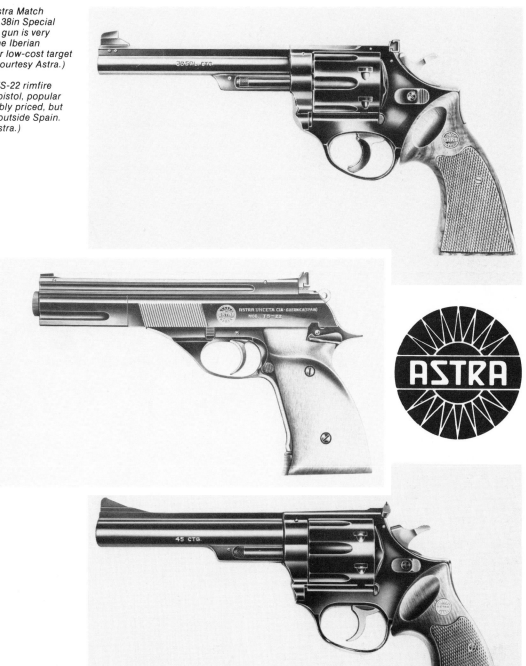

Right: the Astra Match revolver in 0.38in Special calibre. This gun is very popular in the Iberian Peninsula for low-cost target shooting. (Courtesy Astra.)

Below: the TS-22 rimfire semi-target pistol, popular and reasonably priced, but uncommon outside Spain. (Courtesy Astra.)

Right: the Modelo 45 revolver, a centrefire Smith & Wesson inspired design greatly resembling the models 41 and 44. (Courtesy Astra.)

Model A-80

Military and police pistol. The A-80 is Unceta y Cia's answer
to the problems of providing this class of pistol in the 1980s
and represents a complete departure from the previous
military/paramilitary guns based on the Campo-Giro
blowback system; instead, the designers have combined the
Browning/FN cam-finger dropping-barrel lock and a double-
action trigger system inspired, perhaps, by the Walther P 38.
To this has been added a de-cocking system adapted from the
prewar Sauer 38H (and now exemplified by the SIG-Sauer P
220 and 225), and the result is an efficient but unoriginal
design—yet one which will hold its own against all but the
very best of its rivals. The compact, well made and acceptably
finished A-80 is more traditionally-made than some of its
competitors (which is not implied criticism) and may yet prove
to be more acceptable to a market still suspicious of synthetic
parts; there may be a slight weakness on the left side of the
Astra frame, where metal is cut away from the magazine well,
but the A-80 should make a strong challenge for a share of the
market during the 1980s. One interesting feature is the de-
cocking lever, which can be supplied for right- or left-handed
users.
*Cal: 7.65mm Parabellum, 9mm Parabellum, 0.38in Super Auto,
0.45in ACP. Mag: detachable staggered-column box, catch on
butt heel. Mag cap, rds: 9 (0.45in), 15 (others). Trg: DA,
external hammer. Wt, oz/gm: 33.7-34.7/955-985. Loa, in/mm:
7.1/180. Brl, in/mm 5.6/142. Rf: 6 R?. Sft: de-cocking lever and
firing-pin lock; inertia-type firing pin.*

Above: *the Astra A-80 military and police pistol is a typical
modern double-action design with a large capacity magazine.
Chambering the most popular of the service pistol rounds,
including the 9mm Parabellum and the 0.45in ACP, it uses yet
another variation of the Colt-Browning system as modified by
Fabrique Nationale, Petter, SIG and others. (Photograph by
courtesy of Astra.)*

Below: *an exploded drawing of the Astra A-80. Note the single
locking rib on top of the barrel and the cam-finger actuator
(103) beneath the breech.*

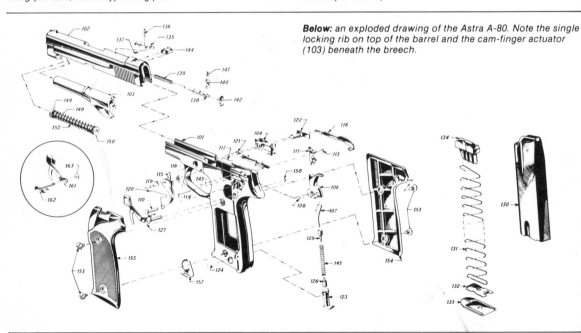

Modelo 250 and 250 Inox

Small personal defence revolver. This gun is a smaller,
lightened derivative of the 960 (qv), sharing the same transfer
bar safety system. However, the barrel is appreciably shorter
and the back sight is little more than a groove cut
longitudinally in the top of the frame. The gun is made in four
different chamberings, in the smallest of which (0.22in LR and
Magnum rf) it is neither powerful nor especially accurate. The
0.38in Special is an appreciably better man-stopper. Its usual
finish is blued, with chequered wooden grips, but the Modelo
250 Inox is made of stainless steel.
*Cal: 0.22in LR rf, 0.22in Magnum rf, 0.32in S&W Long or 0.38in
Special. Mag: cylinder. Mag cap, rds: 5 (0.38in), 6 (0.32in) or 9
(0.22in). Trg: DA, external hammer. Wt, oz/gm: 22.4-23.3/635-
650. Loa, in/mm: 6.6/166. Brl, in/mm: 2.2/55, but 2.0/51 in
0.38in Special. Rf: 6 R?. Sft: 'transfer bar' hammer block;
inertia-type firing pin.*

Modelo 357 and 357 Inox

General purpose revolver. The Modelo 357, which first
appeared in 1972 and derived directly from the Cadix, was the
first Astra revolver to feature the transfer bar safety system; it
was also the first to chamber the powerful magnum cartridge
necessary to compete with guns being made by Colt, Smith &
Wesson and others in the USA. The Astra has an adjustable
back sight whose spring-steel base is dovetailed longitudinally
into the top of the frame, lateral adjustments being effected by
moving the front sight blade laterally. The revolver is generally
supplied in blued finish, with chequered wooden grips, but de
luxe versions—*modelos de lujo*—are also to be had. The 357
Inox offers stainless steel construction. There are barrel
lengths from 3in (76mm), best for personal defence, by way of
4in (102mm) and 6in (152mm), best for general purposes, to
8.5in (216mm)—the most accurate of the series but perhaps a
little unwieldy.

Cal: 0.357in Magnum. Mag: cylinder. Mag cap, rds: 6. Trg: DA, external hammer. Wt, oz/gm: 37.8-46.0/1070-1310. Loa, in/mm: 8.5-13.8/215-350. Brl, in/mm: 3.0-8.5/76-216. Rf: 6 R?. Sft: 'transfer bar' hammer block; inertia-type firing pin.

Modelo 357 Police

Small personal defence revolver. Dating from 1980, this is a minor variant of the standard 357 (qv). The improvements—a strengthened hammer, smaller 'no snag' front sight and a reversion to a plain groove back sight—assist instinctive shooting, though no-one would consider the 357 Police as a suitable target gun . . . and it possesses a vicious muzzle blast attributable to a combination of short barrel and powerful ammunition.
Cal: 0.357in Magnum. Mag: cylinder. Mag cap, rds: 6. Trg: DA, external hammer. Wt, oz/gm: 36.7/1040. Loa, in/mm: 8.4/212. Brl, in/mm: 3.0/77. Rf: 6 R?. Sft: 'transfer bar' hammer block; inertia-type firing pin.

Left: the 357 Police and 680 Inox revolvers. (Courtesy Astra.)

Modelo 680 and 680 Inox

Small personal defence revolver. The Modelo 680 is a very slight modification of and replacement for the 250 (qv), with a few small differences visible in the forging of the frame (particularly ahead of the trigger) and the shape of the recoil shield. There is also a marked difference in the hammer profile, evident from the photographs. The 680 and its stainless steel variant, the 680 Inox, date from 1981.
Cal: 0.22in LR rf, 0.22in Magnum rf, 0.32in S&W Long or 0.38in Special. All data approximately as Mo. 250, except:-
Loa, in/mm: 6.6/167.

Modelo 800 Condor

General purpose pistol. A total of 11,432 of these guns, based on the old Astra blowback system, itself derived from the Campo-Giro, were made between 1958 and 1966.

Modelo 960

General purpose revolver. The Modelo 960 is a modified Cadix (qv), with several improvements suiting it to importation into the USA under the 1968 Gun Control Act. Dating from 1973, its greatest internal change is the inclusion of a 'transfer bar' hammer-blocking safety system, which prevents the firing pin being struck until the trigger is consciously pulled. Externally, the 960 has a larger ramp on the 'no-snag' front sight, a smoother and less distinctive trigger guard, a more rounded recoil shield on the frame, grips fitting flush with the backstrap and a more massive-looking hammer. It is heavier and thus more easily controlled than its predecessor. The gun may be obtained in the same finishes as the Cadix.
Cal: 0.38in Special. Mag: cylinder. Mag cap, rds: 6. Trg: DA, external hammer. Wt, oz/gm: 38.5-43.6/1090-1235. Loa, in/mm: 8.5-11.4/215-290. Brl, in/mm: 3.0, 4.0 and 6.0/76, 102 and 152. Rf: 6 R?. Sft: 'transfer bar' hammer block; inertia-type firing pin.

Modelo 7000

Small personal defence pistol. Dating from 1973, this is a revision of the Cub (qv) chambering rimfire ammunition only and offering a few minor constructional changes. The back sight, for example, is dovetailed into the slide instead of being an integral forging, and thus is capable of limited adjustment. Similarly, the contours of the trigger guard have been refined. The power of the 0.22in LR rf cartridge is insufficient for man-stopping purposes, though it cannot be denied that the Modelo 7000 (and other guns like it) are very readily concealed. Once again, several de luxe versions are available.
Cal: 0.22in LR rf. Mag: detachable box in butt, catch on left side of butt. Mag cap, rds: 8. Trg: SA, external hammer. Wt, oz/gm: 14.6/415. Loa, in/mm: 5.0/125. Brl, in/mm: 2.4/59. Rf: 6 R?. Sft: radial lever on left side of frame behind trigger, moving down to 'fire'; hammer lock prevents accidental firing.

Auto Mag Corporation

This was founded to make the extraordinary Auto Mag high-power pistol, a recoil-operated design locked by a rotating bolt. From 1970 until c.1977, the pistol was made by or for several contractors in many guises—Models 160, 180, 260, 280, Jurras Special, etc—but then disappeared, leaving an influence disproportionate to its numbers.

Fritz Barthelmes KG

Fritz Barthelmes KG, Sportwaffenfabrik, D-7920 Heidenheim-Oggenhausen, Watzmannstrasse 17, West Germany

British agency: (trade only) John Rothery Ltd, 22 Stamshaw Road, Portsmouth, Hampshire. US agency: Pyro-Spectaculars, Rialto, California, USA. Standard warranty: 12 months.

This company was founded in 1948 by Fritz Barthelmes (d.1973), co-designer of the Walther P 38, and began to manufacture starting and signal pistols in 1954. Air pistols—covered in the companion work, *The Airgun Book*—are also made, and the company has a justifiable reputation for producing cheap, good-quality products by virtue of advanced manufacturing techniques. This also enables its very small workforce to attain an awesome annual output.

FB Record Flobert-Pistol

Practice/indoor pistol. It is very difficult to categorise this gun, which is an odd amalgam of a low-grade target pistol and a standard starting pistol! The Record Flobert-Pistol has an unconventional side-hinged breechblock and a lengthened barrel. It also has a distinctive ring-type external hammer, but the ultra-short grip prevents all but the most abbreviated 3-finger grasp. There is an auto-ejector and a rifled barrel liner within a diecast frame.
Cal: 6mm Flobert, 0.22in LR. Mag: none. Mag cap, rds: 0. Trg: SA, external hammer. Wt, oz/gm: 13.1/370. Loa, in/mm: 6.3/160. Brl, in/mm: 4.4/112. Rf: none?
Sft: none, though the hammer nose acts as a breechblock lock.

FB Record Gas-Pistol Model A

Starting and signal pistol. This gun, a single shot, handles Flobert blanks or small-diameter signal rockets. Made largely of die-castings, it features auto ejection, an external ring hammer and a safety interlock. The hammer protrudes much less than on some other Record designs, with appreciably reduced chance of snagging and premature ignition.
Cal: 6mm Flobert blanks and 10mm diameter signal rockets. Mag: none. Mag cap, rds: 0. Trg: SA, external hammer. Wt, oz/gm: 6.2/175. Loa, in/mm: 3.9/100. Brl, in/mm: NA. Rf: none. Sft: none.

FB Record Gas-Pistol Model B1S

Starting and signal pistol. This, patented by Fritz Barthelmes in 1954 (DRP 1009973), is another of the small, largely die-cast Barthelmes designs—an example of the 'front discharge' pattern of starting pistol distinguished by its external ring-pattern hammer. Like many of its contemporaries, the B1S can project signal rockets from the integral muzzle extension.

The manufacturer's literature notes the ammunition possibilities as: 6mm blanks, 15mm blast cartridges, 15mm ricochet sound cartridges, 15mm tracer blank cartridges, 10mm rockets, 15mm rockets and 6mm gas bullets. The gun is supplied in a brown finish, with chequered plastic grips.
Cal: 6mm Flobert blanks (see also text). Mag: type uncertain. Mag cap, rds: 2. Trg: SA, external hammer. Wt, oz/gm: 8.8/250 Loa, in/mm: 5.1/130. Brl, in/mm: NA. Rf: none. Sft: none.

FB Record Gas- und Signal-Pistol GP1

Starting and signal pistol. This is a variation of a tried and, perhaps, well-trodden path—deriving at least some of its inspiration from the Walther UP1 and UP2 of the 1950s and 1960s. The GP1 exhibits a unique bar type magazine block (patented by Martin Barthelmes in 1978) which slides longitudinally in the receiver. There is a radial safety/loading lever above the left grip. The foremost position, marked 'F' for *Feuer*, disengages the safety; the medial mark 'E', enables the gun to be loaded; and the rearmost position, 'S' for *Sicher*, engages the safety. The GP1 is a well made little gun, available in brown or chromed finish. An optional, interchangeable barrel may be used for signal flares and rocket ammunition.
Cal: 6mm Flobert, or 7, 10 or 15mm diameter flares. Mag: bar pattern in receiver, catch on left side of frame. Mag cap, rds: 6. Trg: DA. Wt, oz/gm: 11.6/330. Loa, in/mm: 4.3/110. Brl, in/mm: NA. Rf: none. Sft: radial lever above left grip; striker safety prevents discharge unless trigger is pulled.

FB Record Weinberg- und Signal-Pistol

Starting and signal pistol. Another of the distinctive external-hammer Barthelmes designs, this gun—in common with most of its stablemates—offers surprisingly good manufacturing quality at competitive price, achieved by attention to detail and the use of extremely advanced fabricating techniques.

Above: the Bauer 25 Auto. (Courtesy Bauer.)
Left: four FB Record pistols. From left to right, top to bottom—the Flobert-Pistole, the Model A, the Model B1S and the Model GP1. (Courtesy Barthelmes.)

The single-shot action features automatic ejection of a spent blank, while the threaded extension of the signal rocket discharger may be attached either as prolongation of the 'bore' (giving a conventional appearance) or on top of the receiver above the barrel. Both version are available only with browned finish.
Cal: 6mm Flobert blanks or 15mm diameter signal rockets. Mag: none. Mag cap, rds: 0. Trg: SA, external hammer. Wt, oz/gm: 6.5/185. Loa, in/mm: 4.9/125. Brl, in/mm: NA. Rf: none. Sft: none.

Bauer Firearms Corporation

34750 Klein Avenue, Fraser, Michigan 48026, USA.

British agency: none. Standard warranty: 90 days.

Bauer is another of the small independent US manufacturers, formed in the mid 1970s to market its small, stainless-steel personal defence pistol.

25 Auto and 25 SS

Small personal defence pistol. This is amongst the best of the guns currently available in its class, the majority of its parts being corrosion resistant stainless steel. It bears more than a passing resemblance to the FN Baby Browning (which dates from 1936), but this comparability is common among guns of this size. The Bauer may be obtained in standard or 'neutral

Below: the locking system and action of the Benelli 76.

satin stainless' finish (Model 25 SS) and with simulated pearl or chequered American black walnut grips; it offers both the principal advantages of guns of its class—easy concealability and light weight—together with the major *disadvantages*, minimal stopping power and uncomfortably abbreviated grip.
Cal: 0.25in ACP (6.35mm). Mag: detachable box in butt, catch on butt heel. Mag cap, rds: 6. Trg: SA, striker fired. Wt, oz/gm: 10.0/285. Loa, in/mm: 4.0/102. Brl, in/mm: 2.3/58. Rf: 6 R. Sft: radial lever on left side of frame behind trigger, up to safe.

Benelli Armi SpA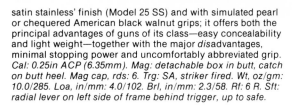

Urbino, Italy.

British agency: Yaffle (Importers & Exporters) Ltd, Sterling Works, Dagenham, Essex RM10 8ST, England. US agency: apparently none. Standard warranty: 12 months.

Benelli—claiming origins, like so many Italian gunmakers, in the mid nineteenth century—is now better known as a maker of autoloading shotguns of impeccable quality. The 1976-vintage Modello 76 pistol thus far remains Benelli's only venture into the pistol scene.

Modello 76

Military and police pistol. Benelli is better known as a maker of high quality shotguns rather than of this interesting pistol—well designed, if a little complicated, and exhibiting an unusual hesitation blowback operation in which the breechblock is displaced downward against a shoulder in the frame. The slide can easily be retracted manually, but the extreme pressure generated on firing causes a separate toggle-shaped cam-piece atop the breechblock to 'lock' the breech until the chamber pressure has dropped sufficiently to allow the breechblock to run back safely. The Benelli is largely made of traditional forgings and machined parts, is very accurate as a result of its fixed barrel and handles well because of its good balance and ideally raked grips. Early guns had a reputation for poor feed characteristics with soft point ammunition—almost always a problem when magazines are raked as far as the Benelli type (cf. Parabellum). The Modello 76 is usually blued with wood grips; they have yet to sell in large quantities. There are several guns in the series: the Modelo 76 chambers the 9mm Parabellum, while the Modello 80 chambers the appreciably weaker 7.65mm ACP. The sights may be fixed or adjustable. The two 'S' models, intended for sporting and target use, feature muzzle counterweights, extended grips and better sights.
Cal: 7.65in or 9mm Parabellum. Mag: detachable single column box, catch on left side frame behind trigger. Mag cap, rds: 8. Trg: SA, exposed hammer. Wt, oz/gm: 34.2/970. Loa, in/mm: 8.1/205. Brl, in/mm: 4.30/108. Rf: 6 R. Sft: inertia firing pin; manual safety catch on rear left side of frame above grip, moves up to safe; half-cock on hammer.

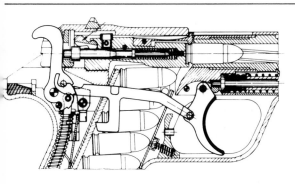

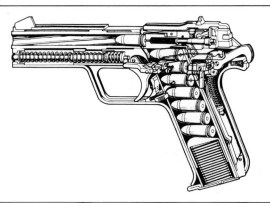

Pietro Beretta SpA

I-25063 Gardone Val Trompia (Brescia), Italy.

British agency: Gunmark Ltd, The Armoury, Fort Wallington, Fareham, Hampshire PO16 8TT, England. US agency: The Beretta Arms Company, Inc., PO Box 2000, Ridgefield, Connecticut 06877, USA. Standard warranty: 12 months

Beretta is one of the few modern gunmakers whose lineage can be traced back to the seventeenth century; in fact, based on recent researches in local archives, Beretta is now claiming a plausible connection with the master barrelsmith, Bartolomeo Beretta (c.1490-1567). The early history of the company may be learned in greater detail from the bilingual *Beretta, la dinastia industriale più antica del monde* (Beretta, the world's oldest industrial dynasty) by Morin & Held, published by Aquafresca Editrice of Chiasso in 1980 to mark the tercentenary of the *official* foundation date. As far as *The Pistol Book* is concerned, however, Beretta history begins with the introduction of a blowback general purpose pistol in 1915 and its subsequent adoption by the Italian authorities, the first of many similar pistols to be acquired. The best known of the series is the Modello 1934, an external-hammer design used in great quantities in the Second World War, during which Beretta also made vast numbers of rifles, submachine-guns and machine-guns. Operations were rebuilt after 1945, many prewar guns being put back into production while new designs were prepared. These included the Modello 951 or Brigadier, derived from the German Walther P 38, which gave the company a suitable foothold in the international military/police pistol market, selling to the armies of Italy, Egypt and Israel. Beretta has kept abreast of the times, and a policy of constant improvement has led to the comprehensive range of elegant, well-made guns described here.

Modello 20

Personal defence pistol. This gun is a modernised version of the 950 series (qv), from which it differs primarily in having a double-action trigger system and improved safety features. The principal external distinctions are the enlarged spring-steel strip forming the trigger guard, and the rather spindly trigger lever placed well forward in the guard. The gun is blued—though some minor components are anodised alloy—and the grips are black chequered plastic bearing the Beretta trademark.
Cal: 0.25in ACP (6.35mm Auto). Mag: detachable box, catch on lower left side of butt. Mag cap, rds: 8. Trg: SA, exposed hammer. Wt with empty mag, oz/gm: 10.9/310. Loa, in/mm: 4.9/125. Brl, in/mm: 2.4/60. Rf: 6 R. Sft: radial lever on rear left frame; inertia firing pin.

Modello 70

General purpose pistol. The Modello 70 is a modernised version of a series of Beretta blowbacks dating back to 1915—or, perhaps more specifically, to the Modello 1934. The most obvious external changes are the angled grip, the new thumb safety and the elegant rib running forward from the trigger guard to the muzzle. Internal changes include a lengthened barrel/receiver joint (claimed to improve accuracy), an improved trigger mechanism with a better trigger pull, a modified magazine catch and an improved dismantling system. Steel or alloy frames may be obtained, blued or black-anodised respectively; chequered plastic grips bearing the company trademark are standard, with walnut as an option. The sights consist of a fixed blade and an open notch.
Cal: 0.32in ACP (7.65mm Auto). Mag: detachable box, catch

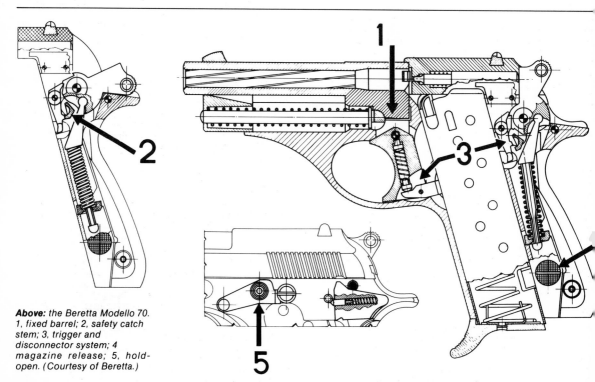

Above: *the Beretta Modello 70. 1, fixed barrel; 2, safety catch stem; 3, trigger and disconnector system; 4 magazine release; 5, hold-open. (Courtesy of Beretta.)*

Above: *the Modello 75 sporting/target pistol. (Courtesy of Beretta.)*

on lower left side of butt. Mag cap, rds: 8. Trg: SA, exposed hammer. Wt, oz/gm, steel–alloy: 23.3–18.4/660–520. Loa, in/mm: 6.5/165. Brl, in/mm: 3.5/90. Rf: 6 R. Sft: radial lever on left rear of frame (up-safe); inertia firing pin.

Modello 70S

General purpose pistol. This is a variation of the Modello 70 (qv), differing in minor respects—the most obvious of which is the grips, chequered plastic thumbrest patterns with the Beretta name surrounding the magazine release button. The 'S' guns also have an additional safety which prevents firing until the magazine has been firmly replaced. The centrefire version has fixed sights: the rimfire, the adjustable back sight of the Modello 76 (qv). The centrefire gun is usually listed as *per mercati esteri,* for export only, and its status in Italy remains uncertain.
Cal: 0.380in ACP (9mm Short) or 0.22in LR rf. Otherwise as Modello 70, except:. Wt, oz/gm (0.22in, 9mm): 22.4, 23.8/635, 675. Loa, in/mm: 6.7/170. Brl, in/mm: 3.5/90. Sft: radial lever on rear left side of frame; inertia firing pin; magazine safety.

Modello 71

General purpose pistol. This is another derivative of the Modello 70 (qv) chambering rimfire ammunition, sharing identical dimensions but appreciably lighter because of anodised alloy construction. The 71—which lacks the magazine safety of the 70S—was originally only available with the standard short (9cm) barrel, but Beretta's recent literature notes that barrels of up to 6in (15cm) can be supplied with this gun, presumably as a result of the disappearance of the Models 72, 73 and 74.
Cal: 0.22in LR. Otherwise as Modello 70, except Wt, oz/gm: 16.9/480.

Modello 72

Sporting/target pistol. The now-discontinued Modello 72 is a simple variation of the Modello 71, supplied with exchangeable 9cm and 15cm barrels. The distinction has now been removed by making long-barrelled Modello 71 guns instead. The back sight is the fixed pattern.
Cal: 0.22in LR rf. Otherwise as Modello 71, except Wt, oz/gm: 18.9/535. Loa, in/mm: 8.9/225. Brl, in/mm: 6.0/150.

Modello 73

Sporting/target pistol. The Modello 73, another of the 'Serie 70', featured the long barrel of the 72, but had an elongated grip containing a large capacity magazine. The non-reciprocating back sight was mounted above the breech rather than on the slide: a better idea in theory, perhaps, than in practice. Now discontinued.
Cal: 0.22in LR rf. Otherwise as Mo.72, except Mag cap, rds: 10. Wt, oz/gm: 19.4/550. Loa, in/mm: 9.3/235.

Modello 74

Sporting/target pistol. The Modello 74—no longer in production—is a minor variant of the 73 with an adjustable non-reciprocating back sight in which elevation is controlled by a large screw passing vertically through the leaf into the sight body, and lateral adjustments ('windage' in the USA) by small screws regulating movement of the back sight blade.
Cal: 0.22in LR rf. Otherwise as Mo.72, except Mag cap, rds: 10. Wt, oz/gm: 20.1/570. Loa, in/mm: 9.3/235.

Modello 75

A designation applied to the Modello 72 when supplied only with the 6in (15cm) barrel. No longer used, as the distinction between the models 71 and 72 has ceased.

Modello 76

Target pistol. This—together with the somewhat similar Bernardelli Modello 69 (qv)—is among the best value in its class. The blowback action is practically identical with others in the Serie 70, but the principal recognition feature is the long non-reciprocating slide extension which supports the long barrel and doubles as a muzzle weight. The fixed front and fully adjustable back sights are carried on this matted-top-rib extension, which permits the constant sight alignment not always obtainable in guns with one sight on the barrel and the other on the slide or frame. The Modello 76 has a fixed-pull factory-adjusted trigger conforming to UIT rules, and the slide stays open after the last round has been chambered, fired and ejected. The gun is blued steel apart from the muzzle extension and some minor parts, which are anodised alloy. Grips may be chequered black plastic bearing the Beretta mark or, more commonly, non-adjustable but excellent quality thumbrest walnut.

Cal: 0.22in LR rf. Otherwise as Modello 71, except Mag cap, rds: 10. Wt, oz/gm: 32.8/930. Loa, in/mm: 9.2/233. Brl, in/mm: 5.9/150.

Modello 81 and 81 Lusso

General purpose pistol. This is the first truly modern double-action Beretta—and a very good design indeed, well made and offering some very good features. It is an elegant, well streamlined gun with the partially cutaway slide so characteristic of its maker. It has an efficient double-action trigger system derived from German practice (and none the worse for it), simplified dismantling, a large capacity magazine, an extractor doubling as a loaded chamber indicator, a manual safety on *both* sides of the gun and a reversible magazine release crossbolt suited to use in either hand. The blued gunmetal slide and anodised alloy frame are complemented by plain walnut grips, though chequered black plastic may be supplied as an option. Some guns may be encountered with grooves on the front strap to improve grasp in wet or adverse conditions. The limited-availability de luxe gun *(tipo lusso)* features hand engraving, gold-plated hammer and trigger, and selected walnut grips with an inlaid gold escutcheon, and may be obtained in blue or gold finish. It is supplied in a leather case together with a spare magazine and cleaning equipment. The Beretta Modello 81 is a first-rate design, good enough to be made (with a few insignificant changes) by FN in Herstal—see FN Mle 40 DA. But then Fabrique Nationale owns a 36 per cent stake in Beretta.

Cal: 0.32in ACP (7.65mm Auto). Mag: detachable staggered-column box, catch on frame-side behind trigger. Mag cap, rds: 12. Trg: DA, exposed hammer. Wt, oz/gm: 23.5/665. Loa,

in/mm: 6.8/172. Brl, in/mm: 3.8/97. Rf: 6 R. Sft: radial lever on rear of frame, up to safe; inertia firing pin; half-cock notch on hammer; optional magazine safety.

Modello 82B

General purpose pistol. This is a derivative of the Modello 81 (qv) differing solely in its magazine arrangements and weight. *Cal: 0.32in ACP (7.65mm Auto). Mag: detachable single column box. Mag cap, rds: 9. Wt, oz/gm: 21.5/610. Otherwise as Modello 81.*

Modello 84 and 84 Lusso

General purpose pistol. A variation of the Modello 81 chambering a different cartridge, generally agreed to be a better man stopper.

Cal: 0.38oin ACP (9mm Short). Otherwise as 81 except Mag cap: 13 rounds. Wt, oz/gm: 22.6/640.

Modello 85B

General purpose pistol

This is another variation of the Modello 84, to which it bears much the same relationship as the Modello 82 does to the 81—with a single column magazine.

Cal: 0.380in ACP (9mm Short). Otherwise as Modello 81, except Mag cap, rds: 8. Wt, oz/gm: 21.2/600.

Modello 90

General purpose pistol. This is an interesting gun, but the joker in the Beretta pack. While all the other pistols are made in the Gardone factory, this one is made in Rome—strengthening a supposition that Beretta has taken over a smaller Italian manufacturer and continued production. The Modello 90 barrel is totally enclosed in the slide, with an ejection port on the right side, and the double-action trigger system incorporates a safety block raised only when the

Below: the Beretta Modello 76.   **Above right:** the Modello 84 with its large-capacity magazine. (Courtesy of Beretta

trigger is deliberately pulled (cf. Walther PPK). Beretta has clearly made some minor changes to the basic design as latest publicity photographs (not the one reproduced here) show a typical Beretta dismantling catch on the left side of the frame above the magazine release crossbolt. The slide is blued steel, the frame anodised alloy; and the grips are chequered black plastic.
Cal: 0.32in ACP (7.65mm Auto). Mag: detachable single-column box, crossbolt release behind trigger. Mag cap, rds: 8. Trg: DA, exposed hammer. Wt, oz/gm: 19.4/550. Loa, in/mm: 6.7/170. Brl, in/mm: 3.6/92. Rf: 6 R. Sft: hammer safety system; radial lever on rear left side of frame (up-safe); inertia firing pin; rebounding hammer.

Modello 92

Military and police pistol. Developed from the Modello 951 Brigadier (qv) and sharing the same recoil-activated breechblock, the Modello 92 is the first of Beretta's modernised combat pistols. Externally it has the typical-Beretta cutaway slide, exposing the top of the barrel. However, it has a more modern appearance than its predecessor and is easily distinguished by the slender trigger lever set well forward in the guard, allowing the long double-action pull. There are several catches and levers along the under-edge of the slide: from muzzle to grip these are the dismantling catch, a slide-release lever to override the hold-open feature and the manual safety catch. The Modello 92 has fixed sights and performed well in the recent US trials. However, the 92S and 92SB (qv) are more efficient progressions. The gunmetal parts are blued, the alloy parts anodised and the chequered black plastic grips display the company's trademark. Wood grips are optional and a lanyard ring lies on the butt heel.
Cal: 9mm Parabellum. Mag: detachable staggered-column box, crossbolt catch on left side of butt above lanyard ring. Mag cap, rds: 15. Trg: d/a, exposed hammer. Wt, empty mag, oz/gm: 33.5/950. Loa, in/mm: 8.5/217. Brl, in/mm: 4.9/125. Rf: 6 R. Sft: radial lever on left side of frame above grip (up-safe); inertia firing pin; rebounding hammer with half-cock.

Modello 92S

Military and police pistol. This is a derivative of the otherwise praiseworthy Modello 92, with greatly improved safety features. The old safety—which simply locked the slide and frame together—has been replaced by a Walther-type 'barrel' or rotary unit high on the left side of the slide behind the retraction grooves. This permits the hammer to be dropped on a loaded chamber in perfect safety, as rotating the lever to its 'safe' (upper) position blocks the path of the hammer to the firing pin, and breaks the contact between the sear and the trigger. This feature apart, the 92S is identical with the 92 (qv). Sight holes are cut into the back of the magazine to show how many rounds remain.
Cal: 9mm Parabellum. Otherwise generally as Modello 92, except Wt, with empty mag, oz/gm: 34.4/975. Sft: inertia firing pin; half-cock on hammer; hammer block system operated by rotary catch on left side of slide (see text).

Modello 92SB

Military and police pistol. Dating from 1981, this is the perfected double-action military Beretta and, as its predecessor is said to have been the victor of the recent US pistol trials, the 92SB must be a very good design indeed. Recoil operated, locked by an 'oscillating block' adapted from the P 38 and taken directly from the Modello 951 Brigadier, the 92SB differs from the 92S in purely minor details. The grip straps are grooved to assist grip, the plastic grips are chequered overall, and the magazine release catch has been moved up behind the trigger from its former position on the lower left side of the butt. In addition, the catch can be reversed to suit right- or left-handed firers. The changes have ensured that all the 'operating functions' (apart from slide retraction and inserting a new magazine) can be accomplished by the firing hand. It is a shame—but carping criticism!—that the slide-release lever has not been duplicated as well. The 92SB is an excellent product, well made and accurate. An appreciable amount of metal has been cut away from the left side of the frame at the top of the magazine well, but this is obviously insufficient to compromise its overall strength.
Cal: 9mm Parabellum. Otherwise as Modello 92S.

Modello 92SB Compact

Military and police pistol. This is a smaller version of the 92SB, intended for 'special purposes' and smaller than its

cousin. The slide, frame and barrel have all been shortened. The smaller grip means that the magazine capacity has also been reduced. However, the 92SB Compact is otherwise identical with the standard gun.

Cal: 9mm Parabellum. Otherwise as Modello 92SB, except Mag cap, rds: 11(?). Wt, oz/gm: 31.7/900. Loa, in/mm: 7.9/200. Brl, in/mm: 4.3/108.

Modello 93R

Military and police pistol. The 93R, adapted from the 92 (qv), is intended to double as a light machine-pistol capable of firing three-shot bursts, which is thought to be the maximum permissible in a handgun which, by definition, has low weight and a high cyclic rate—and can easily run out of control. The R suffix represents *Raffica*, or 'bursts'. This is a style of operation with which Beretta had previously flirted (see 951R), but the history of these guns goes back to the First World War. Though derived from the earlier Modello 92, the 93R looks very different. It has a more angular, modernistic appearance, and the barrel, with its three-slot muzzle brake/compensator, protrudes well past the slide. There is a large trigger guard, a folding forward handguard, an extended 20-round magazine and an optional collapsible shoulder stock. The proliferation of frame mounted catches has now reached four—from the

muzzle backward: the dismantling catch, the slide release lever, the fire selector (● for single shot, ●● for bursts) and co-axial sear-blocking safety lever. All in all, the 93R is an interesting design, perhaps a little too heavy and unwieldy to serve as a standard pistol but undoubtedly sufficiently handy and conventional to be a better long-term solution than more extreme concepts such as the US 'Arm Gun' and similar submachine-gun/pistol hybrids. Its future progress should be watched closely.

Cal: 9mm Parabellum. Mag: detachable staggered-column box, crossbolt catch behind trigger. Mag cap, rds: 20. Trg: SA, exposed hammer. Wt with empty mag, oz/gm: 41.3/1170. Loa without stock, in/mm: 9.5/240. Brl, in/mm: 6.1/156. Rf: 6 R. Sft: radial lever on rear left of frame, co-axial wityh selector, down safe; inertia firing pin. Cyclic rate: about 1100rpm, depending on ammunition.

Modello 101

General purpose pistol. This designation appeared during a 1960s 'rationalisation' for the American market, Galef then being Beretta's distributor. The Modello 101 is identical with the Modello 71 (qv), but the new model number was short-lived.

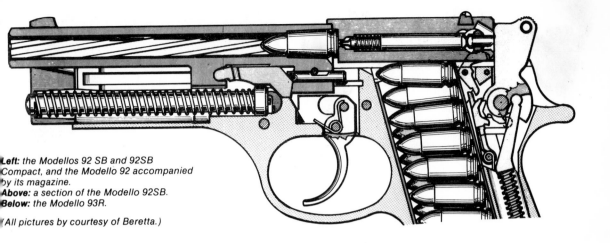

Left: the Modellos 92 SB and 92SB Compact, and the Modello 92 accompanied by its magazine.
Above: a section of the Modello 92SB.
Below: the Modello 93R.

(All pictures by courtesy of Beretta.)

Modello 102 'New Sable'

The 1960s US-market designation of the Modello 76 (qv).

Modello 104

A designation analogous to the Modello 102, but applied to the Modello 951 Brigadier (qv).

Modello 950B and 950BDI

Personal defence pistols. These are among the smallest of the Beretta blowbacks, dating back to the early 1950s. There are several unusual features including a single-shot loading capability resulting from a tip-up barrel reminiscent of the old Le Français, controlled by a spring-steel trigger guard, and the absence of an extractor (spent rounds are 'auto expelled' by residual gas pressure). The guns, once gunmetal, are now made largely of anodised alloy and have chequered black plastic grips—though the BDI, the de luxe gun, is gold-plated with walnut grips, hand engraved and supplied in a special case. Unfortunately, the ineffectual bullets fired by these guns—notwithstanding their ready concealability—make them poor man-stoppers and useful only at ultra-close quarters. Their safety arrangements are inadequate by modern standards.

Cal: 0.25 ACP (6.35mm Auto). Mag: detachable box, crossbolt catch on lower left side of butt. Mag cap, rds: 8. Trg: SA, exposed hammer. Wt, oz/gm: 9.9/280. Loa, in/mm: 4.7/120. Brl, in/mm: 2.4/60. Rf: 6 R. Sft: inertia firing pin; half-cock on hammer.

Modello 950BS (Minx)

Personal defence pistol. The 950BS is an improved version of the 950B (qv) differing only in the addition of a manual safety catch on the rear left side of the frame above the grip. This feature apart, remarks made about the earlier gun apply equally here.
Cal: 0.25in ACP (6.35mm). Otherwise as Modello 950B, except Sft: inertia firing pin; half-cock notch on hammer; radial lever on left rear frame (up-safe).

Modello 950 cc

Personal defence pistol. A smaller-calibre version of the 950B, this chambers that least powerful of handgun cartridges—the 0.22in Short rimfire—and is thus an even poorer man stopper than the 6.35mm Auto/0.25in ACP version. Though the Beretta is a well made little gun, this whole genre has little to commend it.

Modello 950 cc Special

Personal defence pistol. A longer barrelled version of the standard Modello 950 cc (qv) but otherwise identical. Perhaps worth its purchase price for plinking, but otherwise of little practical use.
Cal: 0.22in Short rf. Otherwise as Modello 950B except Mag cap, rds: 6. Wt, oz/gm: 11.3/320. Loa, in/mm: 6.1/155. Brl, in/mm: 3.7/95.

Modello 951 Brigadier

Military and police pistol

Inspired by the success of the blowbacks, Beretta embarked on the development of a stronger, locked breech design. The result was the Modello 951, or 'Brigadier', which appeared in small numbers in 1951-2 and—once perfected—from 1955 onwards in volume. The action is short recoil operated, locked by a separate block under the breech which is cammed ('propped-up') into engagement with recesses in the slide as the action closes. The principle behind this is much the same as exhibited by the prewar Walther P38, from which inference can be drawn that Beretta's technicians were well aware of the German design. There are several good features: a mechanical hold-open system, the typical open-top slide, an exposed hammer and the quality to be expected of Beretta. Much was made of a light alloy 'Ergal' frame, but this gave development trouble despite its considerable weight saving. The alloy frame was finally substituted by a stronger and less ambitious gunmetal pattern. The Brigadier, known in the late 1960s as the Modello 104 during a short-lived renumbering ploy, has sold in great quantity in the Italian armed forces, Carabinieri and police, as well as to Israel and Egypt. Egyptian guns generally have a slightly longer than standard barrel and the magazine release on the butt heel. It has also inspired a series of improved derivatives (Modello 92—qv). Currently not for sale on the Italian commercial market.
Cal: 9mm Parabellum. Mag: detachable single-column box, crossbolt catch on lower left side of butt. Mag cap, rds: 8. Trg: SA, exposed hammer. Wt, steel frame, empty mag, oz/gm: 32.1/910. Wt, alloy frame, empty mag, oz/gm: 25.3/720. Loa, in/mm: 8.0/204. Brl, in/mm: 4.5/115. Rf: 6 R. Sft: inertia firing pin; half-cock notch on hammer; manual crossbolt on rear left of frame through grip, pushes to right for fire.

Modello 951R

Military and police pistol. Several differing prototype and pre-production variants of this gun—Beretta's first combination pistol/submachine-gun—were made in the 1960s and early 1970s, but really succeeded only in paving the way for the 93R (qv). The 951R was *fully* automatic in its 'repeat' mode, and suffered the two usual drawbacks: virtual uncontrollability and almost instantaneous depletion of the small magazine! Its external features include a slightly lengthened barrel and a hollowed, folding front handgrip which pivots backwards to partly shroud the trigger guard. The selector lies on the right side of the frame behind the trigger and is marked AUT above SEM.
Cal: 9mm Parabellum. Otherwise as M951, except Mag cap, rds: 10. Wt, with empty mag, oz/gm: 47.6/1350. Loa, in/mm: 8.5/217. Brl, in/mm: 4.9/125. Cyclic rate: about 750rpm depending on ammunition.

Modello 951 Target

This only seems to have been made for the Egyptian army. It chambers the 9mm Parabellum but is otherwise practically identical with the Mo.952 Special (qv). However, the slide mounted backsight is appreciably higher and the magazine release catch lies on the butt heel.
Cal: 9mm Parabellum. Otherwise generally as Modello 952S.

Modello 952

Military and police pistol. This designation covers a variant of the Brigadier chambering the bottlenecked 7.65mm Parabellum, which shares the casehead dimensions of the 9mm pattern and thus permits a relatively straightforward transformation.

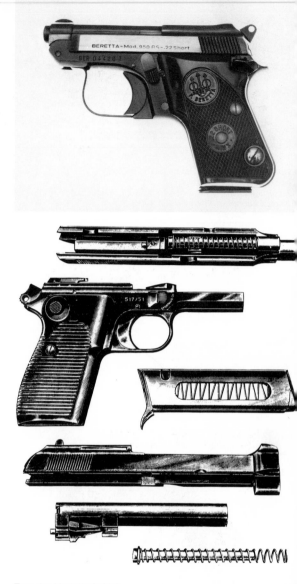

Top: the Modello 950BS.
Above, below: the Modello 951 Brigadier and its major components. (Courtesy Beretta.)

Modello 952 Special

Target pistol. This handsome gun is a specialised adaptation of the standard Modello 952 with a longer barrel, revised sights and high quality thumbrest walnut grips. The front sight is mounted on a removable sleeve around the muzzle (which facilitates dismantling) while the fully adjustable backsight lies on top of the slide. The 952 Special is capable of much better accuracy than the standard guns, though it is lighter than some guns in its class and the method in which the front sight is mounted could be theoretically objectionable should wear between the muzzle and the sight collar occur.
Cal: 7.65mm Parabellum
Otherwise as Modello 951, except Wt, oz/gm: 33.8/960. Loa, in/mm: 9.8/248. Brl, in/mm: 5.9/150.

Modello Signal 1in S ·

Signal and flare pistol. This is a relatively cheap and comparatively unsophisticated signal, flare and line-throwing gun. It is loaded simply by pulling down the lever that forms the rudimentary trigger guard, and removing the barrel. The 1in S signal cartridge, or a smaller diameter flare in a special 'reducer' insert, is then placed in the barrel, the latter replaced on the frame and the guard lever closed. There are sundry safety features, and the 1in S can also be used—with a rather curious accessory in the shape of a fishing reel—for throwing a weighted line up to 50m.
Cal: 1in (25.4mm), 0.32in ACP (7.65 Auto) blanks in reducer. Mag: none. Trg: SA, exposed hammer. Wt, oz/gm: 20.8/590. Loa, in/mm: 8.4/213. Brl, in/mm: 5.9/150. Rf: none. Sft: barrel/closing lever interlock prevents premature hammer release; inertia firing pin; rebounding hammer.

Below: the Bernardelli AMR pistol. Positioning of the front sight on the muzzle extension is far from ideal. (Courtesy of Bernardelli.)

Vincenzo Bernardelli SpA

Vincenzo Bernardelli SpA, Fabbrica d'Armi, I-25063 Gardone Val Trompia (Brescia), Via Matteotti 125, Italy.

British agency: Surrey Guns Ltd, 9 Manor Road, Wallington, Surrey SM6 0BZ, England. US agency: (formerly) Interarms, 10 Prince Street, Alexandria, Virginia 22313, USA; (from 1983) EBM Group, Inc., Room 414, Empire State Building, 350 Fifth Avenue, New York, NY 10018, USA. Standard warranty: 12 months

Vincenzo Bernardelli founded his barrel-making workshop in 1865, and soon progressed to making complete guns—with the initial assistance of Belgian-made actions. By 1900, what had become Fratelli Bernardelli had grown considerably and the period immediately after the end of the First World War saw further expansion. The first shotguns were made in 1928, alongside the Italian Modello 89 service revolver, and many ordnance supplies were manufactured during the Second World War. A series of automatic pistols was introduced in the immediate post-1945 era and the factory was entirely reconstructed in 1968-75. A range of well made, solid, dependable but rather unremarkable pistols and revolvers is now marketed.

Pistola Automatica (PA, Vest Pocket or VP)

Small personal defence pistol. According to its manufacturer, this gun was introduced in 1946. Mechanically, however, it is very similar indeed to the prewar Walther Modell 9—for example, it shares the same 'dumb bell' unit controlling the dismantling system. The Bernardelli PA was supplemented in 1968 by the Modello 68 (qv) and production was discontinued two years later. The PA is a small, rather angular design, distinguished by the old-style company trademark moulded into the black bakelite grips. An optional butt extension, which housed an extra-long magazine, could also be obtained, and the standard finish was a rich burnished black. These guns exhibit the perennial strengths and weaknesses of their class: ready concealability, but poor man-stopping qualities. Larger versions of the PA chambering 0.22in LR, 7.65mm and 9mm Short (0.32 and 0.380 ACP), were also made from 1948 until discontinued between 1960 and 1965.
Cal: 0.25in ACP, 6.35mm. *Mag:* detachable box in butt, catch on butt heel. *Mag cap, rds:* 5 (8 with extension magazine). *Trg:* SA, striker fired. *Wt, oz/gm:* 9.2/262. *Loa, in/mm:* 4.1/105. *Brl, in/mm:* NA. *Rf:* 6 L. *Sft:* radial lever on left side of frame behind trigger; magazine safety.

Pistola Automatica AMR

Sporting and target pistol. This derivative of the Modello 60—*Automatica con Mire Regolabili,* or 'automatic pistol with adjustable sights'—features a lengthened barrel and a modified slide carrying a fully adjustable backsight. The barrel carries a separate front sight located by a flat under the rearward-running matted rib, and retained by a threaded muzzle collar. The AMR is mechanically identical with the Modello 60, however. Competitively priced, it offers sufficient quality to make a useful plinking and practice pistol.
Data generally as Modello 60 (qv), apart from Wt, oz/gm: 25.6/725. *Loa, in/mm:* 8.9/227. *Brl, in/mm:* 6.0/152.

Pistola Automatica 'Baby'

Small personal defence pistol. This gun, apparently dating from the late 1940s and discontinued in 1970, is a small version of the PA (qv) chambering rimfire rather than centrefire ammunition. This makes it an even poorer performer in self-defence, but a better bet for practice because of the cheapness of the cartridges. It was supplanted in 1968 by the smallest in the Modello 68 series. The original Baby is externally similar to the PA, but its cutaway slide exposes the top of the barrel. Interestingly, Bernardelli advertised it as the 'smallest 22 caliber automatic ever made, chambered for the powerful (sic) 22 Short or Long cartridge'—a contentious claim, at best.
Cal: 0.22in Long or 0.22in Short. *Mag:* detachable box in butt, catch on butt heel. *Mag cap, rds:* 5. *Trg:* SA, striker fired. *Wt, oz/gm:* 9.3/262. *Loa, in/mm:* 4.1/105. *Brl, in/mm:* NA. *Rf:* 6 L. *Sft:* radial lever on left side of frame behind trigger; magazine safety.

Pistola Automatica USA

General purpose pistol. This is essentially an adaptation of the Modello 60 (qv) to satisfy the US Internal Revenue Service and the Gun Control Act of 1968. The principal difference between the USA and its predecessor concerns the safety system: the USA features a slide-mounted Walther-type radial or 'barrel' type firing-pin lock *in addition* to the standard radial lever on the frame and the magazine disconnector. The multiplicity of safeties is, to say the least, unnecessary—but was forced on the manufacturer by the American legislation. The extractor, on the right side of the slide, doubles as a loaded chamber indicator. The USA has the improved ramp-mounted front and fully-adjustable back sights introduced by the AMR and is usually encountered with the supposedly optional chequered walnut grips rather than the standard wraparound plastic type.

Right: *a collection of Bernardelli pistols and revolvers. From top to bottom–the Modello USA, the VB Revolver Tascabile, the VB Revolver and the Modello 68 pocket pistol (courtesy of Bernardelli).*

Cal: 0.22in LR rf, 0.32in ACP (7.65mm short) or 0.380in ACP (9mm short). Mag: detachable box in butt, catch on butt heel. Mag cap, rds: 7 (9mm), 8 (7.65mm) or 10 (0.22in). Trg: SA, external hammer. Wt, oz/gm, with empty mag: 24.3-25.0/690-710. Loa, in/mm: 6.5/164. Brl, in/mm: 3.5/90. Rf: 6 L. Sft: radial lever on left side of frame behind trigger; magazine safety; radial lever firing-pin lock on left side of slide below back sight; inertia-type firing pin.

Revolver VB ('Bernardelli-Revolver)

General purpose revolver. The VB is a competitively priced and quite well made gun based—quite closely—on contemporary Smith & Wesson practice, as a glance at comparative sectional drawings will testify. Like most modern S&W revolvers, the VB cylinder is mounted on a yoke and swings laterally from the left side of the frame after the catch beneath the hammer has been pressed. The gun offers an inertia-type firing pin and a safety system preventing the hammer slipping off full-cock unless the trigger is pressed. Blued finish and chequered walnut grips are standard fittings, and engraved or chromed versions can be obtained on special request. The VB was originally introduced in the 1950s and sold as the 'Martial', often with a barrel measuring about 4.9in (125mm).
Cal: 0.22in LR rf, 0.22in Magnum rf or 0.32in S&W Long. Mag: cylinder. Mag cap, rds: 6. Trg: DA, exposed hammer. Wt, oz/gm: 18.3-19.9/520-565. Loa, in/mm: 7.6-10.4/194-264. Brl, in/mm: 3.1-5.9/80-150. Rf: 6 L. Sft: inertia-type firing pin; full-cock safety unit.

Revolver VB MR

Target revolver. This modification of the standard long-barrel VB (qv) has micro-adjustable sights—in Italian, *Mire Regolabili*. It may be identified by its prominent front sight, pinned to the muzzle atop a chequered rib. An equally notable back sight lies above the frame immediately ahead of the hammer. The 'MR' version of the Bernardelli may be obtained with chequered wooden or simulated mother-of-pearl grips, chrome finish and several grades of engraving. It was originally marketed in the 1950s as the 'VB Special'.

Data: generally as 7.9in (150mm) barrelled VB, but only available in 0.22in LR rf.

Revolver VB Tascabile

Personal defence revolver. The VB 'T' is a standard Bernardelli with its barrel reduced and an abbreviated chequered walnut butt, the contours, heel and toe of which are rounded to reduce snagging. It may be obtained in the standard rimfire chambering, which is admirably suited to practice but has little value as a man stopper; the 0.32in S&W Long is a better choice, though still by no means perfection. The VB Tascabile was introduced in the early 1950s, when it had a parallel-side 2in (51mm) barrel and an under-muzzle lug supporting the head of the ejector rod. It was superseded in 1958 by the present model (known as the 'New Pocket Model' while the two co-existed), lacking the ejector-head support and featuring a longer tapered barrel.
Data as standard VB revolver, except Wt, oz/gm: 19.0/540. Loa, in/mm: 6.9/175. Brl, in/mm: 2.5/64.

Pistola Parabellum P 018 and P 018/9

Military and police pistol. This, dating from 1982, is Bernardelli's first entry into the big-bore combat pistol market. The two variants—differing only in calibre—are handsome, well balanced, double-action short-recoil operated pistols featuring *another* adaptation of the Browning tipping-barrel locking system (or, more precisely, of the cam-finger sub-type developed by FN and latterly modified by SIG/Sauer). The Bernardellis are made by traditional gunsmithing methods with very little evidence of advanced fabricating techniques and the synthetic parts beloved by such companies as Heckler & Koch. They feature the usual firing-pin lock, automatically disengaged as the trigger is squeezed, and the now virtually obligatory staggered-column large capacity magazine. The slide top is squared, with a sturdy durable sights (adjustable sights are supplied to order) and minimal protrusions avoid snagging. The well-placed safety lever can easily be operated by the thumb of the firing hand—though the present P 018 pistols, unlike some 'ambidexterous' rivals, suit right-handed users only. They may be supplied in blue or non-reflective

Below: *the Modello 69 Tiro Standard–a popular and efficient basic target pistol. (Courtesy of Bernardelli.)*

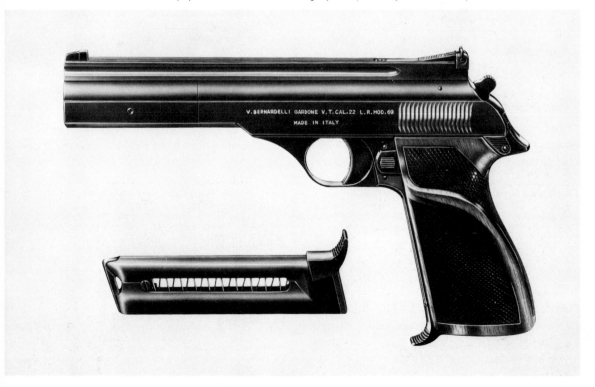

matt finish, with chequered walnut or plastic grips.
*Cal: 7.65 or 9mm Parabellum. Mag: detachable box in butt,
catch on butt heel. Mag cap, rds: 14. Trg: DA, external
hammer. Wt, oz/gm: 35.2 or 35.6/998 or 1010. Loa, in/mm:
8.4/213. Brl, in/mm: 4.8/122. Rf: 6 R. Sft: manual lever on
frame above left grip; automatic firing-pin lock; inertia firing pin.*

Pistola Automatica Modello 60

Small personal defence pistol. Dating from 1960-61, this is a
modernised version of the original large blowback Bernardelli
pistol of the late 1940s—though the alterations are largely
cosmetic. However, an appreciable change to the frame
forging is undeniably an improvement, giving a much more
comfortable raked grip. There is a standard radial-lever safety,
the point of distinction between this gun and the USA (qv)
and a magazine disconnector which restricts movement of the
trigger until the magazine is in place. Unlike many pistols in
its class and price group, the Modello 60 features dual buffer
springs to minimise impact wear on the slide. In all variants
apart from the rimfire 90mm barrel type, the magazine
platform acts as a hold-open after the last round has been
fired and ejected. The gun is usually supplied in black finish,
with chequered bakelite grips, but chromed or engraved
versions may be obtained on request. A lightweight version
with an alloy slide can be obtained in the two large calibres. In
addition, a long-barrelled (7.9in, 200mm) version of the Mod.
60 can be obtained with a replacement slide unit and a fully
adjustable back sight. This variant resembles a lengthened
AMR.
*Cal: 0.22in LR, 0.32in ACP (7.65mm Short) or 0.380in ACP
(9mm Short). Mag: detachable box in butt, catch on butt heel.
Mag cap, rds: 7 (9mm), 8 (7.65mm) or 10 (0.22in). Trg: SA,
external hammer. Wt, oz/gm: (gunmetal slide) 23.8-24.7/675-
700; (alloy slide) 18.3-18.7. Loa, in/mm: 6.5/165. Brl, in/mm:
3.5/90. Rf: 6 L. Sft: radial lever on left side of frame behind
trigger; magazine safety; inertia-type firing pin.*

Pistola Automatica Modello 68

Small personal defence pistol. Introduced, as its designation
suggests in 1968, this gun was a replacement for the PA (qv)—
though the revisions were largely cosmetic, and most of the
internal parts remained practically identical. Most of the
external changes were confined to the shape of the slide—a
more modern, rounded appearance—and the design of the
partially chequered bakelite grips. An indicator pin protrudes
from the rear of the slide when the striker is cocked. Black
finish is standard, but chromed, gilded and engraved guns
may be obtained on request—as may an extension grip
containing a large-capacity magazine.
*Cal: 0.25in ACP, 6.35mm. Mag: detachable box in butt, catch
on butt heel. Mag cap, rds: 5 (8 in extension type). Trg: SA,
striker fired. Wt, oz/gm: 9.5/270. Loa, in/mm: 4.3/108. Brl,
in/mm: NA. Rf: 6 L. Sft: radial lever on left side of frame
behind trigger; magazine safety.*

Pistola Pistola Automatica 'Baby' Modello 68

Personal defence pistol. This modified version of the original
'Baby' dates from 1968 and incorporates the cosmetic
improvements mentioned under the standard Modello 68 (qv).
The principal differences, apart from calibre, lie in the
cutaway overbarrel slide of the Baby and its lower overall
weight. Chromed, engraved and damascened versions are
available to special order, as, apparently, are simulated
mother-of-pearl grips.
*Cal: 0.22in Short or 0.22in Long rf. Mag: detachable box in
butt, catch on butt heel. Mag cap, rds: 5
Trg: SA, striker fired. Wt, oz/gm: 8.8/250. Loa, in/mm: 4.3/108.
Brl, in/mm: NA. Rf: 6 L. Sft: radial lever on left side of frame
behind trigger; magazine safety.*

Pistola Automatica Modello 69 Tiro Standard

Target pistol. The Modello 69 TS is an adaptation of the Mod.
60 (qv) for ISU standard and smallbore pistol shooting. It
features an extended barrel and extension slide-cum-
barrelweight which, integral with the backsight rib, is attached
to the muzzle by an Allen screw. As the gun is a blowback,

using the normal half-length slide, the sights and slide
extension remain stationary during firing. The magazine
follower doubles as a hold-open after the last round has been
fired and rejected. The 69 TS has a replaceable blade front
sight at the tip of the wide matted sight rib, and a fully
adjustable backsight which can handle any of several
interchangeable blades. Black finish and simple non-
adjustable burr walnut target grips complete the package,
which usually comes in a lined case complete with an extra
magazine, screwdriver, oiler and cleaning brush. The result is
a popular and surprisingly efficient gun that has found
considerable acceptance in Europe.
*Cal: 0.22in LR rf. Mag: detachable box in butt, catch on butt
heel. Mag cap, rds: 10. Trg: SA, external hammer. Wt, oz/gm,
with empty magazine: 38.0/1070. Loa, in/mm: 9.0/228. Brl,
in/mm: 5.9/150. Rf: 6 R. Sft: radial lever on left of frame behind
trigger; magazine safety; inertia-type firing pin.*

Pistola Automatica Modello 80

General purpose pistol. The current (1983) name for what was
the Modello USA (qv), usually associated with Interarms—
Bernardelli's US distributor.

Fabricas de Armas Bersa SA

Ramos Mejia, Argentina

*British agency: none. US agency: Interarms, 10 Prince
Street, Alexandria, Virginia 22313, USA. Standard
warranty: unknown*

Little is known about the background history of this
metalworking company, one of the few Argentine
manufacturers whose products are seen on the export
markets.

Modelo 97   *Modelo 622*

Modelo 97

General purpose pistol. A straightforward derivative of the 644
(qv), but chambering a larger and more powerful cartridge
and thus a better choice for self-defence.
*Cal: 0.38in ACP (9mm Short). Otherwise as Mo. 644, except
Rf: 6 R?*

Modelo 622

General purpose and target pistol. A derivative of the 644 (qv)
with a lengthened barrel on which the front sight is mounted.
Intended to provide a rudimentary target pistol, the design at
least has the merits of cheapness even though it offers no real
sophistication.
*Cal: 0.22in LR rf. Otherwise as Mo. 644, except Wt, oz/gm:
32.0, 36.0/905, 1020. Loa, in/mm: 7.0, 9.0/178, 229. Brl, in/mm:
4.0, 6.0/102, 152.*

Modelo 644

General purpose pistol. The 644 is a simple blowback semi-
automatic bearing some external affinity with the Italian
Bernadellis, reasonably well made but not in the class of many
European products. The material is usually good, but

toolmarks are evident and the blueing is not always exemplary. There are several Bersa guns, all apparently sharing common mechanical characteristics. The most distinctive external features are the position of the safety catch, the ring hammer and the slender prolongation of the frame behind the grips.
Cal: 0.22in LR rf. Mag: detachable box, catch set in lower left grip. Mag cap, rds: 7. Trg: SA, exposed hammer. Wt, oz/gm: 28.0/795. Loa, in/mm: 6.5/165. Brl, in/mm: 3.5/89. Rf: 4 R? Sft: radial lever on extreme rear left side, down to safe.

Fabbrica Armi P. Bondini

I-47020 S. Carlo di Cesena, Via Sorrento 345, Italy

British agency: Peregrine Arms Co. (see Uberti). US agency: Navy Arms (qv). Standard warranty: unknown.

Bondini makes a series of excellent single-shot flintlock and percussion pistols, the best of which come exquisitely fitted in plush-lined cases. For the sake of convenience—and as a result of the late acquisition of material, they are considered here together.

Bondini pistols

Single shot sporting and target pistols. All fire 0.45in ball ammunition with the exception of the 0.50in or 0.54in calibre Hawken, weigh between 32 and 41oz and measure 14.5-16.5in overall.

J. & S. Hawken Percussion Pistol. This reproduction of an American duelling pistol features a heavy blued barrel, a swivel rammer and a threequarter-length stock with a rather short butt. The furniture is German silver and there is a single set-trigger.

Le Page Percussion Pistol. The Le Page features the French style of the mid nineteenth century, with a fluted grip and a scroll-engraved lockplate. The pistol sports a double set-trigger and a spurred trigger guard.

Le Page Percussion Pistol This elegant gun features a rifled octagonal barrel matched with a stock à la Boutet. The furniture is German silver, with scrollwork engraving on the lockplate. A single-set trigger and adjustable sights are standard, but the gun can also be cased singly or as a matched pair.

John Manton Match Pistol. This is English-style percussion pistol has a walnut full-stock, brass furniture and an elegant spurred trigger guard.

Moore & Patrick Flintlock. This features a European walnut half-stock and an engraved lock with a roller on the frizzen. The octagonal barrel is rifled, the mounts are German silver and the trigger guard is a brass casting.

W. Parker Percussion Pistol. This is a reproduction of an English pistol made, perhaps, in the 1840s. It features double set-triggers and an elegant schnabel-tipped forestock. The butt is squared at the toe and heel, and the furniture is German silver.

F. Rochatte Pistol. This copy of a European original features a finial-tipped butt in French style and matches a highly polished simulated back-action lock with a bright polished round barrel. There is a single set-trigger.

Right: three Bondinis—the Hawken, the Le Page (II) and the Parker. (Courtesy of Navy Arms.)

Browning Arms Company

Route 1, Morgan, Utah 84050, USA, and Montreal, Province of Quebec, Canada. Browning markets the FN-made GP Mle 35 under the designation Hi-Power and the Mle 140 as the BDA 380. There is also an American-made pistol called the Challenger II (6.8in barrel) or Challenger III (5.5in) derived from the original FN Challenger pistol, but with a new wedge-locking system and generally squared contours.

Britarms

This company was formed in the mid 1970s to market the well-known Britarms target pistols, but has struggled against better established (if often inferior) products.

Model 2000

Target pistol. This appeared in 1976, an exceptionally sophisticated design owing something in its magazine construction and overall external appearance to the FAS Modelo 601 (qv). Intended as a 'Match Pistol', the 2000 offers the FAS-type top loading magazine and a combination hammer/striker firing mechanism. The breechblock is retracted by two knurled extensions running forward ahead of the trigger and the trigger lever is fully adjustable for rake, as well as longitudinally within the trigger guard; its pull can be adjusted from below 1000gm to more than 1360gm. A 'Mark 2' appeared in 1979, differing in trigger and grip arrangements. Like its predecessor, it has a low barrel line and as long a sight radius as practicable, the back sight lying at the extreme rear of the receiver. An additional 80gm weight can be attached beneath the muzzle with two Allen-head bolts. The slide is blued, the frame a satin-finish alloy and the grip stipple-roughened walnut, altogether an attractive and efficient product which has seen considerable success.
Cal: 0.22in LR rf. Mag: detachable box, catch on left side of frame behind trigger. Mag cap, rds: 5. Trg: SA, concealed hammer. Wt, oz/gm: 42.0/1215. Loa, in/mm: 11.0/280. Brl, in/mm: 5.9/150. Sft: inertia firing pin only.

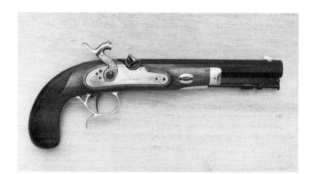

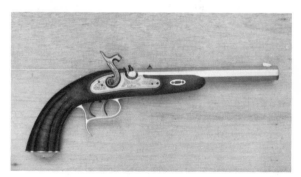

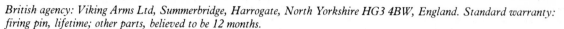

Charter Arms Corporation

430 Sniffens Lane, Stratford, Connecticut 06497, USA

British agency: Viking Arms Ltd, Summerbridge, Harrogate, North Yorkshire HG3 4BW, England. Standard warranty: firing pin, lifetime; other parts, believed to be 12 months.

Charter Arms was founded in 1964 to exploit the ideas of Douglas McClenahan, who saw a market for the small, powerful, readily concealable revolver that was to become the Undercover. The company has since been very successful—by 1978, half a million revolvers had been made—and vies for a place among the best of the American revolver manufacturers. A wide range of rimfire and centrefire designs is currently on offer.

Bulldog

Personal defence revolver. This is the first of the Charter Arms guns to be described, and deserves lengthy coverage. Great effort was made from the outset to ensure that the Bulldog was sufficiently good to gain a foothold in a very crowded marketplace. This goal was attained by virtue of several unusual features; for example, Charter Arms claims that its revolvers contain the fewest critical moving parts (the Undercover contains 54 parts in total) and are the first production double-action guns to discard the detachable sideplate. There has always been a short hammer fall of about 55°, and the unbreakable copper/beryllium firing pin carries a lifetime guarantee. The Bulldog is an elegant gun, much of which effect derives from the careful shaping of the trigger guard and the slender cylinder. The swing-out cylinder is carried on a yoke, locked by a sliding catch on the left side of the frame beneath the hammer.
Cal: 0.357in Magnum, 0.44in Special. Mag: cylinder. Mag cap, rds: 5. Trg: DA, exposed hammer. Wt, oz/gm: 19.0-21.9/540-620. Loa, in/mm: 7.3, 7.8/184, 197. Brl, in/mm: 2.5, 3.0/64, 76. Rf: 8 R. Sft: transfer bar, inertia firing pin.

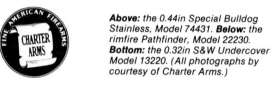

Model	Cal	Brl	Finish	Grips
34431	0.44in Spl	3.0in	blue	wood
34433P	0.44in Spl	3.0in	blue	neoprene
33521B	0.357in Mag	2.5in	blue	wood
74431	0.44in Spl	3.0in	stainless	wood
74433P	0.44in Spl	3.0in	stainless	neoprene

Above: *the 0.44in Special Bulldog Stainless, Model 74431.* **Below:** *the rimfire Pathfinder, Model 22230.* **Bottom:** *the 0.32in S&W Undercover Model 13220. (All photographs by courtesy of Charter Arms.)*

P-suffix guns feature the 'pocket' hammer, without a protruding spur, and oversize wraparound neoprene grips.

Bulldog Tracker

General purpose revolver. This variant of the Bulldog (qv) offers more substantial grips and longer barrels, suited more to sporting use than personal defence. Adjustable rather than fixed sights are fitted.
Cal: 0.357in Magnum. Otherwise as Bulldog, except Wt, oz/gm: 21.0, 24.0, 28.0/590, 680, 800. Loa, in/mm: 7.5, 9.0, 11.0/191, 229, 279. Brl, in/mm: 2.5, 4.0, 6.0/64, 102, 152

Model	Cal	Brl	Finish	Grips
63522B	0.357in Mag	2.5in	blue	wood, square
63542B	0.357in Mag	4.0in	blue	wood, square
63562B	0.357in Mag	6.0in	blue	wood, square

Explorer 2

General purpose pistol. This extraordinary-looking angular design on first glance resembles a piece of plumbing rather than the efficient firearms for which Charter Arms is renowned. However, first impressions can deceive; this is no exception. The Explorer derives from the Armalite AR7 survival rifle, its barrels being exchanged simply by unscrewing the lock-nut. The action is a reliable, simple and easily maintained blowback, fed from a box magazine ahead of the trigger. Finish may be black (Model 9228) or non-corrosive Silvertone (9228S), the grips being the quaintly named 'Shure-Hold Simulated Walnut'. The Explorer may look ungainly, but it performs remarkably well.
Cal: 0.22in LR rf. Mag: detachable box, catch in trigger guard. Mag cap, rds: 10. Trg: SA, internal hammer. Wt, oz/gm: 26.5-29.5/750-835. Loa, in/mm: 13.5, 15.5, 17.5/343, 394, 445. Brl, in/mm: 6.0, 8.0, 10.0/152, 203, 254. Rf: 8 R. Sft: radial lever on rear right side of receiver, back to safe; inertia firing pin.

Pathfinder

General purpose revolver. This popular gun shares the basic mechanical construction of the Bulldog, but chambers rimfire ammunition—permitting a return to the standard revolver cylinder capacity, of six rounds. Pathfinders may be encountered with small or large grips, the latter being standard on the longest barrel option. The various combinations of size and finish are listed on the Table. Adjustable sights are standard and the most obvious recognition feature is the short cylinder; as the standard frame is retained, a notable gap lies between the front of the cylinder and the frame.
Cal: 0.22in LR or Magnum rf. Otherwise as Bulldog, except Wt, oz/gm: 19.0-22.5/540-640. Loa, in/mm: 6.3-10.9/159-276. Brl, in/mm: 2.0, 3.0, 6.0/51, 76, 152.

Model	Ctg	Brl	Finish	Grips
22220	LR	2.0in	blue	standard
22230	LR	3.0in	blue	standard
22320	Mag	2.0in	blue	standard
22330	Mag	3.0in	blue	standard
22262	LR	6.0in	blue	target
22362	LR	6.0in	blue	target
72230	LR	3.0in	stainless	standard
72330	Mag	3.0in	stainless	standard

Police Bulldog

General purpose and personal defence revolver. This is simply a reduced-scale version of the Bulldog, chambering standard rather than magnum ammunition. P suffix guns have the pocket or spurless hammer, a B suffix indicates a heavyweight 'bull' barrel, while an S prefix signifies optional bright or silk-finish stainless steel construction. The Police Bulldog is among the best guns in its class, though its cylinder holds one less cartridge than some rivals . . . the price to pay for its compactness.
Cal: 0.38in Special. Otherwise as standard Bulldog, except Wt, oz/gm: 19.0-22.0/540-620. Loa, in/mm: 7.1, 9.0/181, 229. Brl, in/mm: 2.0, 4.0/51, 102.

Model	Brl	Finish	Grips
83820	2.0in	blue	walnut, round butt
S83820	2.0in	stainless	walnut, round butt
83820P	2.0in	blue	walnut, round butt
S83820P	2.0in	stainless	walnut, round butt
S83823P	2.0in	blue	neoprene
83842	4.0in	blue	walnut, square butt
83842P	4.0in	blue	walnut, square butt
S83842	4.0in	stainless	walnut, square butt
S83842B	4.0in	stainless	walnut, square butt

Target Bulldog

Target and general purpose revolver. This is an adaptation of the standard Bulldog with a heavier barrel, a heavy ejector shroud, adjustable sights and square-butt walnut grips. The Target Bulldog, chambering two of the most popular and powerful cartridges available, represents good value even though it is very light by target shooting standards and would undoubtedly benefit from more weight. There are two variants; the Model 43542 chambers the 0.357in cartridge, while the Model 44442 handles the 0.44in Special.
Cal: see text. Otherwise as Bulldog, except Wt, oz/gm: 29.0/570. Loa, in/mm: 9.0/229. Brl, in/mm: 4.0/102.

Undercover

Personal defence revolver. Advertised as the smallest and lightest gunmetal revolver made in the United States of America, this is basically a diminution of the Police Bulldog (qv), sharing identical mechanical characteristics. P-suffix guns have the pocket hammer, with its vestigial spur, while the finish may be blue or stainless. Undercovers were originally made in 0.22in LR and Magnum rimfire as well as the two centrefire calibres, but these were replaced by the Pathfinder (qv).
Cal: 0.32in S & W Long, 0.38in Special. Generally as Bulldog, except Mag cap, rds: 5 (0.38in) or 6 (0.32). Wt, oz/gm: 16.0, 17.0/450, 500. Loa, in/mm: 6.3, 7.5/159, 191. Brl, in/mm: 1.8, 3.0/47, 76.

Model	Cal	Brl	Finish	Grips
13220	0.32in S & W	2.0in	blue	walnut
13820	0.38in Spl	2.0in	blue	walnut
13820P	0.38in Spl	2.0in	blue	walnut
13823P	0.38in Spl	2.0in	blue	neoprene
13830	0.38in Spl	3.0in	blue	walnut
73820	0.38in Spl	2.0in	stainless	walnut
73820P	0.38in Spl	2.0in	stainless	walnut
73823P	0.38in Spl	2.0in	stainless	neoprene

Undercoverette

Personal defence revolver. This name appears to have been applied to an Undercover with a narrower butt than normal, specifically intended for women. It apparently replaced the original 1.8in barrelled Undercover, though the latter had reappeared by 1982 and the Undercoverette name had itself been discontinued.

Below: *the Target Bulldog. This particular gun is the Model 44442, chambering the 0.44in Magnum, but is also available in 0.357in Magnum. (Courtesy of Charter Arms.)*

Classic Arms Company

A division of Navy Arms Co, 689 Bergen Boulevard, Ridgefield, New Jersey, USA.

British agency: none. Standard warranty: unknown.

This company began life in the early 1970s in Palmer, Massachusetts, making replicas of some of the best known guns from early American history. It was purchased in 1977 by Navy Arms (qv) and moved to Union City, New Jersey, early the following year.

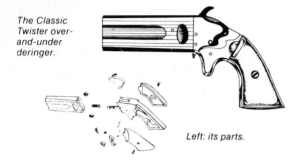

The Classic Twister over-and-under deringer.

Left: its parts.

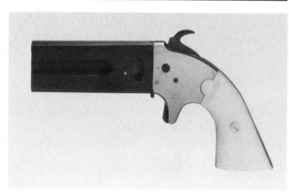

Classic Twister

Personal defence pistol. This is a copy of a gun originally made by the American Arms Company to Wheeler's Patents of 1865-6. The barrels form a single gunmetal block which rotates around a central axial pivot on the brass frame, each being fired by thumb-cocking the hammer. Loading is effected by turning the barrel cluster to its intermediate (90°) position. The Twister is extremely simple, consisting of a mere seventeen parts, and has no sights. It is obtainable in assembled or 'build it yourself' kit form.
Cal: 0.36in. Mag: none, twin barrels. Trg: SA, exposed hammer. Wt, oz/gm: 16.0/455. Loa, in/mm: 6.0/152. Rf: ? Sft: half-cock notch on hammer.

Duckfoot

Personal defence pistol. This 'early mutiny and riot arm', as its maker calls it, derives from flintlock/early percussion prototypes: times when, with ignition suspect and reloading sometimes fatally time-consuming, multi-barrelled volley guns were understandably popular. The Classic Duckfoot has three barrels (originals had as many as seven) and percussion ignition. The flanking barrels are splayed to minimise aiming errors—or hit three targets at once! Again a simple design, with only sixteen parts, it is also available in kit form.
Cal: 0.36in. Mag: none, three barrels. Trg: SA, external hammer. Wt, oz/gm: 32.0/910. Loa, in/mm: 10.5/267. Rf: none. Sft: half-cock notch on hammer.

Elgin Cutlass Pistol

Personal defence pistol. This extraordinary combination weapon was originally made for the US Navy in 1837 by C.B. Allen, under the Elgin patents. Its principal distinguishing feature—not surprisingly—is the heavy blade running forward under the barrel to give the user a second option should the gun misfire or the shot miss its target. The Elgin pistol was issued as a boarding weapon, where the blade would have been an asset. Several sizes of Elgin are known, though the military pattern was large and heavy—0.54in calibre, 16.5in/420mm overall and weighing about 37oz/1050gm. The Classic version is appreciably smaller and based on the components of the New Orleans Ace (qv). Like most of this maker's products, the Elgin is available pre-assembled or in kit form.
Cal: 0.44in. Mag: none. Trg: SA, external hammer. Wt, oz/gm: 24.0/680. Loa, in/mm: 12.0/305. Rf: none. Sft: half-cock notch on hammer.

Ethan Allen Pepperbox

Personal defence pistol. This is a replica of one of the USA's most famous early indigenous firearms—the multi-barrel pepperbox (or barrelless revolver) made by various combinations of Allen, Thurber and Wheelock in Connecticut and Massachusetts under patents granted in 1837 and 1845. The gun features a double-action self-indexing mechanism in a solid brass frame. It is also available in kit form.
Cal: 0.36in. Mag: none, four barrels in a cluster. Trg: DA, external bar hammer. Wt, oz/gm: 36.0/1020. Loa, in/mm: 9.0/230. Rf: none? Sft: none.

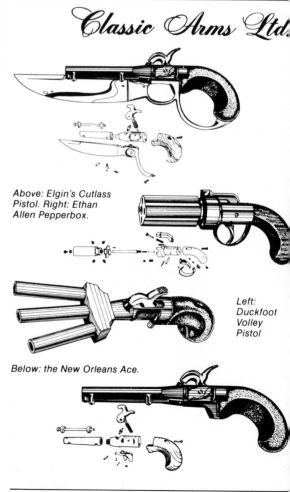

Classic Arms Ltd.

Above: Elgin's Cutlass Pistol. Right: Ethan Allen Pepperbox.

Left: Duckfoot Volley Pistol

Below: the New Orleans Ace.

New Orleans Ace

Personal defence pistol. A simple single-shot percussion-ignition pistol, the Ace has a sheath trigger and a small ramrod mounted on the left side of the barrel. It has a bird's head grip of American walnut and a solid brass frame; it can also be obtained in kit form.
Cal: 0.44in. Mag: none. Trg: SA, external hammer. Wt, oz/gm: 16.0/450. Loa, in/mm: 9.0/230. Rf: none. Sft: half-cock notch on hammer.

Snake Eyes

Personal defence pistol. The 'Deadly Deuce', a twin-barrelled muzzle-loading pocket percussion-ignition pistol favoured by Southern gentry in the early nineteenth century, has a brass frame and twin hammers. The single trigger will release one or both of the hammers if they have been cocked. Pearlite or walnut grips are standard, though a limited number of de luxe specimens (featuring hand engraving on the breech) have also been offered. The gun is popular in its kit form.
Cal: 0.36in. Mag: none, two barrels. Trg: SA, external hammers. Wt, oz/gm: 20.0/570. Loa, in/mm: 6.8/170. Rf: none. Sft: half-cock notch on hammers.

Southerner Derringer

Personal defence pistol. Introduced in 1982, this little gun is been based on the 'Southerner' made for a few years from 1867 by the Merrimack Arms & Mfg Co., and its later successor, the Brown Mfg Co. of Newburyport, Massachusetts. It is a single-shot, its barrel rotating laterally around a vertical pivot at the front of the frame—brass in the Classic version, but gunmetal in the original. The sheath trigger and white pearlite grips are also noteworthy.
Cal: 0.44in. Mag: none. Trg: SA, external hammer. Wt, oz/gm: 12.0/340. Loa, in/mm: 5.0/127. Brl, in/mm: 2.5/63. Rf: none. Sft: half-cock notch on hammer.

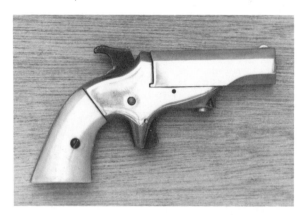

Above: the double-barrel Snake Eyes deringer. Below: the Southerner. (All drawings and photographs by courtesy of Classic Arms.)

Colt's, Inc.

Firearms Division of Colt Industries, 150 Huyshope Avenue, Hartford, Connecticut 06102, USA.

British agency: no sole agents. Standard warranty: 12 months

Colt has a long and interesting history, too tortuous to relate here; the reader seeking more detailed information is, therefore, directed to books such as Serven's or Bady's. Samuel Colt was initially associated with the Patent Arms Manufacturing Company of Paterson, New Jersey, until this venture was liquidated in 1842. Thus the success of the Colt-Walker revolvers, a little over a thousand of which were acquired by the US Army in 1847, was assured largely by the co-operation of Eli Whitney—in whose Whitneyville, Connecticut, factory they were assembled. With one government contract fulfilled, Colt sought another; his arrangement with Whitney had lapsed, so a small factory was built in Hartford and production recommenced in 1849. The rest of the story is popular history. The introduction of the Model 1851 Navy and 1860 Army percussion-ignition revolvers, acquired in great numbers during the US Civil War of 1861-5, and then of the 'Peacemaker', that most famous of Western handguns, took the company's fortunes from strength to strength—even though Smith & Wesson had stolen a march on the Colonel during the late 1850s with their Rollin White patents for bored-through cylinders. Together with early metallic cartridge ammunition, the White patents prevented Colt from competing effectively with Smith & Wesson until they expired in 1871. On into the present century, with a stranglehold on US Army sales and an ever-growing law enforcement (and underworld!) market to satisfy, Colt prospered. This prosperity was greatly helped by the lucrative association with the great arms inventor John M. Browning (1855-1926) and the then-unparalleled success of the Browning automatic pistol, in addition to the Browning Automatic Rifle and the Colt-Browning machine-guns. Thompson sub-machineguns were also made by Colt in appreciable quantities: the list is virtually endless and must be pursued elswhere, but mere mention of it indicates the extent to which the company had grown and the prominence it had attained. Colt manufactured vast amounts of ordnance *matériel* during the Second World War and re-established itself on the postwar commercial market with a series of improved variations on prewar themes. Like many American companies, Colt's firearms business has been subjected to several takeovers and reorganisations. Control passed from the Colt family to the Penn-Texas Corporation, and then to the Fairbanks-Whitney Corporation. In 1964, however, the name of the controlling group was changed to Colt Industries in honour of a century or more of tradition. In addition to various military commitments, notably for the AR-15 (M16) rifle, Colt now markets a series of variations on well-tried designs—including the renowned M1911A1 Colt-Browning pistol. In addition, a range of superb recreations of the original percussion-ignition revolvers of the mid nineteenth century has also appeared during the 1980s.

the authentic Colt BLACKPOWDER series

Sam Colt

Walker Colt

Military revolver. This is a modern recreation of the first perfected Colt percussion revolvers, named the 'Walker' in recognition of the participation of Captain Samuel H. Walker (1817-47) in its development—though also known as the 'Whitneyville-Walker' because the 1100 or so originals were made by Eli Whitney in Whitneyville, Connecticut. The revolver is really in the 'collectable' category. Although interesting to fire, it is also a test of strength as it is long, unwieldy and stupefyingly heavy. The modern version follows the original faithfully, even to the leaf-spring locked ramrod lever, which service use soon showed to be unreliable. The Walker is blued, with a colour-casehardened frame, hammer and rammer unit. The trigger guard is brass, as is the backstrap—a deviation from the Colonel's original, which was iron. The design is quintessentially Colt: a distinctive open-top frame, with the barrel attached to the large-diameter cylinder axis pin by means of a transverse wedge through the rammer housing.
Cal: 0.44in. Mag: cylinder. Mag cap, rds: 6. Trg: SA, exposed hammer. Wt, oz/gm: 73.0/2070. Loa, in/mm: 15.5/395. Brl, in/mm: 9.0/230. Rf: 7 R. Sft: half-cock notch on hammer.

First Model Dragoon Pistol

Military revolver. These guns were among the first to be made in the then-new Hartford factory (1849-50), their name acknowledging use by the US light cavalry. About 6,750 were made. The gun is substantially the same as the Walker Colt, shorter and lighter though still something of a handful. Its features include a 2.2in (55mm) cylinder, a V-mainspring, oval cylinder stops and a straight-back trigger guard. The trigger guard and grip straps are brass, most of the other parts are casehardened, and a copy of the famous engraving by W.L. Ormsby is rolled into the cylinder periphery.
Cal: 0.44in. Otherwise as Walker Colt, except Wt, oz/gm: 66.0/1875. Loa, in/mm: 14.0/356. Brl, in/mm: 7.5/191. Rf: 7L.

Second Model Dragoon Pistol

Military revolver. This is a minor variant of the First Model, with the rectangular rather than ovoid cylinder stops patented in September 1850. Only about 2,250 of the Second Model were made between 1850 and 1851.
Cal: 0.44in. Otherwise as First Model.

Third Model Dragoon Pistol

Military revolver. Another variation of the basic Dragoon Pistol, otherwise identical with the first, this displays a round-backed trigger guard, rectangular cylinder stops and a leaf pattern mainspring with an additional roller bearing to improve the hammer action. Dragoons have a blade front sight in place of the pin used on later guns. Slightly more than ten thousand of the Third Model were made between 1851 and c.1860, but few were used by the US armed forces.
Cal: 0.44in. Otherwise as First Model.

Pocket Dragoon Pistol

Personal defence revolver. This variation of the Dragoon

Pistols is built on a much smaller frame, similar to that later used on the 1851 Naval Belt Pistol (qv). It also chambers a much smaller projectile and its weight is very much reduced, befitting its purpose. Construction parallels that of the First Model Dragoon (qv) apart from omission of the ramrod. The cylinder stops are ovoid. A 'Rangers and Indians' scene is rolled into the cylinder periphery and the grips straps are silver-plated.
Cal: 0.31in. Mag: cylinder. Mag cap, rds: 5. Trg: SA, exposed hammer. Wt, Loa: NA. Brl, in/mm: 4.0/102. Rf: 7 L. Sft: half-cock notch on hammer.

Naval Belt Pistol, or Colt Navy Model 1851

Military revolver. Together with the Army gun (Model 1860—qv), this was undoubtedly the best known and most successful of the company's percussion revolvers. Production began in the early 1850s and continued until 1872-3, by which time hundreds of thousands had been made. The first substantial naval order occurred in 1855. The Navy Belt Pistol is a much smaller version of the Dragoons, with similarly squared frame and a pivoted rammer unit, but infinitely handier and better balanced. It also fires a smaller-calibre projectile and the barrel is octagonal not round. The 1851 Navy also inspired countless European and Confederate copies. Production resumed in 1971, after demand for replica had reached enormous proportions. The new guns duplicate the first of the 'Navies', with straight-backed trigger guards, now silver-plated together with the backstrap. The frame, hammer and rammer unit are attractively colour-casehardened and the result is an effective re-creation of a milestone in handgun history. Many other Navy replicas will be encountered, but few exhibit the quality of the modern Colts.
Cal: 0.36in. Mag: cylinder. Mag cap, rds: 6. Trg: SA, exposed hammer. Wt, oz/gm: 40.5/1150. Loa, in/mm: 13.1/333. Brl, in/mm: 7.5/191. Rf: 7 L. Sft: half-cock notch on hammer.

Army Holster Pistol, or Colt Army Revolver Model 1860

Military revolver. The success of the naval 'belt pistol' lead to number of derivatives, and finally to an army holster pistol in time to see extensive use in the US Civil War. The army revolver appears a very different design from its predecessor though it shares the same open-frame construction and a barrel held to the cylinder axis pin by a transverse wedge through the rammer housing. It is nearly half the weight of the Walker despite comparable overall dimensions, a result of judicious weight reductions, and has an elegance unmatched by other percussion revolvers—if not the strength or reliability (cf. Remington Army Revolver). The modern version is blued and has a colour-casehardened frame, hammer and rammer unit, the latter being an improved rack-and-pinion in place of the old pivoted pattern.
Cal: 0.44in. Mag: cylinder. Mag cap, rds: 6. Trg: SA, exposed hammer. Wt, oz/gm: 42.0/1190. Loa, in/mm: 13.8/351. Brl, in/mm: 8.0/203. Rf: 7 L. Sft: half-cock notch on hammer.

Naval Belt Pistol, or Colt Navy Model 1861

Military revolver. This represents an amalgam of the small calibre and grip shape of the 1851 navy revolver with the elegant lines, rounded barrel and improved rammer of the 1860 army type.
Cal: 0.36in. Otherwise as Naval Belt Pistol Model 1851, except Wt, oz/gm: 42.0/1190. Loa, in/mm: 13.2/335. Brl, in/mm: 7.5/191.

Navy Pocket Revolver 'Model 1862'

General purpose revolver. This gun was originally made in the 1850s, a smaller and lighter version of the standard contemporary navy revolver with the same octagonal barrel, pivoted rammer and plain rebated cylinder. Hence the modern 'Model 1862' designation is, to say the least, suspect. However, the original features are faithfully reproduced in the modern version, which has a colour-casehardened frame, hammer and rammer unit, and silvered backstrap and trigger guard assemblies. The front sight is a small silvered brass pin

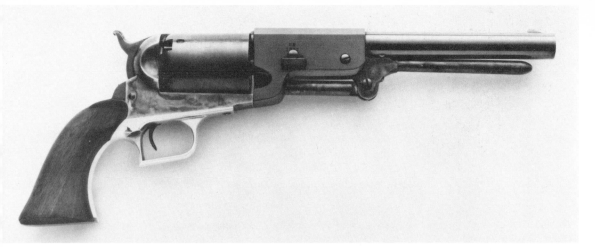

Top: the Walker Colt, one of the largest and most unwieldy of all the percussion revolvers–but a gun to which much of Colt's subsequent success can be attributed. *Above left:* the Second Pattern Dragoon, a refined version of the Walker Colt. *Above right:* that most famous of percussion revolvers, the 1851 Navy pattern.

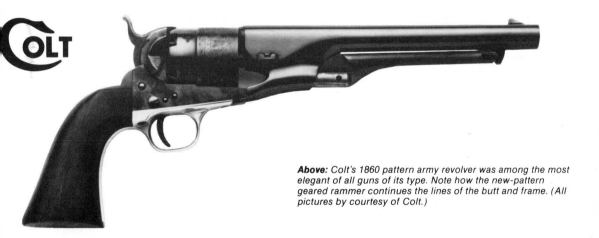

Above: Colt's 1860 pattern army revolver was among the most elegant of all guns of its type. Note how the new-pattern geared rammer continues the lines of the butt and frame. (All pictures by courtesy of Colt.)

and the back sight is represented by a groove cut in the hammer nose.
Cal: 0.36in. Otherwise as Model 1851, except Mag cap, rds: 5. Wt, oz/gm: 27.0/765. Loa, in/mm: 10.4/265. Brl, in/mm: 5.5/140.

Pocket Police Revolver Model 1862

General purpose revolver. This is a hybrid designation: the gun is really a modern version of the Colt Police Pistol of 1862. It has a rounded frame, the rack-and-pinion rammer and a partially fluted cylinder (the essentially similar 1862 pocket pistol had a plain rebated cylinder with a rolled-in stagecoach

motif). The modern version parallels this construction, allied with the same finish as the so-called Model 1862 Pocket Navy revolver (qv).
Cal: 0.36in. Otherwise as Model 1860, except Mag cap, rds: 5. Wt, oz/gm: 25.0/710. Loa, in/mm: 10.4/265. Brl, in/mm: 5.5/140.

Army Holster Pistol, or Colt Army Model 1862

Military revolver. This dubious designation covers a variant of the 1860 Army (qv) with a fluted rather than plain rebated cylinder.
Cal: 0.44in. Otherwise as Model 1860.

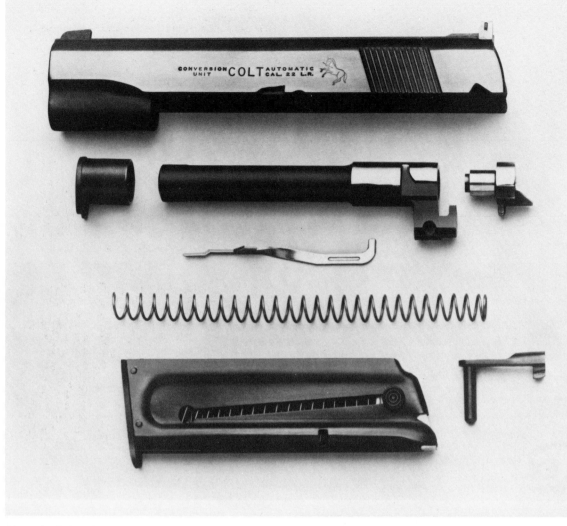

Above: the Colt rimfire conversion unit. *Below:* the Diamondback revolver. *(Courtesy Colt.)*

ce

...rget/training pistol. This is a rimfire version of the standard
...overnment Model, offering much the same weight and
...lance, but the chance of low-cost practice. The most
...teresting feature, however, is the use of a 'floating chamber'
... magnify the recoil of the small and low-powered rimfire
...und until it approximates to the 0.45in ACP! The Ace is a
...odern version of the Colt Service Model Ace introduced in
...37-8 and discontinued a little under a decade later. The
...odern gun is blued and offers chequered wooden grips; the
...ont sight is fixed, the back sight adjustable. It offers a
...rprising performance—an amazing duplication of the full
...re guns—and very good quality at a reasonable price.
*...al: .22 LR rf. Mag: detachable single-column box, catch on
...ft side of frame behind trigger. Mag cap, rds: 10. Trg: SA,
...posed hammer. Wt, with empty mag, oz/gm: 42.0/1190. Loa,
.../mm: 8.4/213. Rf: NA. Sft: as Government Model (qv).*

ombat Commander

...ilitary and police pistol. The Commander is a smaller version
...the Government Model (qv), 'an outstanding on and off-
...ty semi-automatic pistol' according to the Colt catalogues.
...is mechanically identical with the larger gun and is usually
...ued, though the 0.45in ACP version can be obtained in satin
...ckel. The Commanders have arched backstraps in M1911A1
...shion, but ring instead of spur hammers.
*...al: 0.45in ACP, 0.38in Super, 9mm Parabellum. Otherwise as
...overnment Model, except Wt, oz/gm: 36.0 or 36.5/1020 or
...'35. Loa, in/mm: 7.9/224.*

onversion unit (.22 LR)

...aining pistol. This is not a pistol in the true sense, but
...nsists of components to convert the Gold Cup and
...overnment Models to fire inexpensive rimfire ammunition—a
...w slide, muzzle bush, barrel, floating chamber, recoil
...ring, ejector, slide stop and 10-round magazine.

etective Special

...rsonal defence revolver. This is Colt's current offering in the
...mpact personal defence-gun stakes. Well streamlined, with
...urdy fixed sights and a fully shrouded ejector, it offers good
...uality at a somewhat higher price than some rivals. The
...andard finishes are blue or nickel, the grips invariably
...equered walnut. Like all Colt revolvers, apart from the
...rcussion guns and variations on the Peacemaker theme, the
...linder (which rotates clockwise) is carried on a sturdy yoke.
...e original Detective Special was introduced as long ago as
...26.
*...al: 0.38in Special. Mag: cylinder. Mag cap, rds: 6. Trg: DA,
...posed hammer. Wt, oz/gm: 21.5/610. Loa, in/mm: 6.9/175.
...l, in/mm: 2.0/55. Sft: 'transfer bar' hammer block; inertia
...ing pin; half-cock notch on hammer.*

iamondback

...eneral purpose revolver. Named, like so many of Colt's
...volvers, after a venomous snake, the Diamondback is a
...edium weight general purpose revolver on the lines of the
.../thon (qv) introduced in 1967. It has an adjustable back
...ght, a rib pierced by three slots—two in the short barrel
...rsion—and a wide serrated hammer spur. The 0.38in calibre
...rsion is a better choice for service use, while the rimfire gun
...a more economical trainer. The guns are all blued with
...equered walnut grips.
*...al: 0.22in LR rf, 0.38in Special. Mag: cylinder. Mag cap, rds:
...Trg: DA, exposed hammer. Wt, with 4in barrel, oz/gm: 31.8
...27.5/900 and 780. Loa, with 4in barrel, in/mm: 9.0/227. Brl,
.../mm: 4.0 or 6.0/102 or 152. Rf: yes. Sft: 'transfer bar' hammer
...ock; inertia firing pin; half-cock notch on hammer.*

old Cup National Match

...rget pistol. This is an advanced target-shooting version of
...e standard Government Model pistol (qv), with which it is
...echanically identical. The Gold Cup National Match offers
...e Colt Accurizor barrel and muzzle bush; the Colt-Elliason
...icro-adjustable backsight and an undercut frontsight,

mounted on a matted rib; and a wide-grooved adjustable
trigger. The grips are chequered walnut; the overall finish, a
rich blue. Unusually, perhaps, the backstrap housing is the
straight pattern normally associated with the original M1911.
The Gold Cup is an excellent performer as befits the careful
fitting and handwork lavished on it, though the design does
not have the inherent accuracy of some of its competitors.
*Cal: 0.45in ACP. Mag: detachable single-column box, catch
on left side of frame behind trigger. Mag cap, rds: 7. Trg: SA,
exposed hammer. Wt, oz/gm: 38.5/1090. Loa, in/mm: 8.8/223.
Sft: manual lever on left side of frame behind grip; grip safety;
inertia firing pin; half-cock notch on hammer.*

Government Model (Model 1911A1)

Military and police pistol. What can one say about this gun—
perfected in the early years of present century and still in
production after more than seventy years? The short-recoil
operated design is credited to John M. Browning, transformed
in stages from the first, inefficient 'parallel ruler' double-
depressor barrel locking system to the single-link tipping
barrel mechanism exemplified by the US Army Model of
1911—developed stage by stage into today's Government
Model. The current pistols feature the Colt Accurizor barrel
and muzzle bush, culmination of a number of attempts to
match accuracy with the outstanding ruggedness and

*Above: the US Government Model, or Model of 1911, was
made by several contractors; this example was made by
Remington in its Bridgeport factory.*

dependability proven in two world and countless lesser wars.
There are grip and thumb safeties, ramp front and fixed
square-notch back sights. The gun is available in blue, nickel
and satin nickel finishes, while chequered walnut grips are
now standard. The biggest problem with the full-power 0.45in
ACP version is its heavy recoil, which does not suit it to many
firers of small physique; for them, a less powerful chambering
is helpful and the Colt Government also comes in 0.38in
Super and the ubiquitous 9mm Parabellum.
*Cal: 0.45in ACP, 0.38in Super Auto, 9mm Parabellum. Mag:
detachable single-column box, catch on left side of frame
behind trigger. Mag cap, rds: 7 (0.45in), 9 (0.38in; 9mm). Trg:
SA, exposed hammer. Wt, oz/gm: 38.0 or 39.0/1075 or 1105.
Loa, in/mm: 8.4/213. Brl, in/mm: 4.7/120. Sft: radial lever on
left side of frame behind grip; grip-safety on back strap; half-
cock on hammer; inertia firing pin.*

Lawman Mk 3

Personal defence revolver. The Lawman is a competitively
priced personal defence revolver, firing magnum ammunition
and suitably strongly made. Features include fixed sights, a
wide spur hammer and, in the smaller gun, a fully shrouded
ejector rod. The side-swinging cylinder is mounted on a yoke,
the sights are fixed and the grips are slender, chequered
walnut. The trigger is serrated for better grip and the
mainspring is a coil pattern.
Cal: 0.357in Magnum (or 0.38in Special). Mag: cylinder. Mag

cap, rds: 6. Trg: SA, exposed hammer. Wt, oz/gm: 32.0, 35.0/910, 990. Loa, in/mm: 7.4, 9.4/188, 238. Brl, in/mm: 2.0, 4.0/51, 102. Rf: 6L. Sft: 'transfer bar' hammer block; inertia firing pin; half-cock notch on hammer.

The Colt Commande

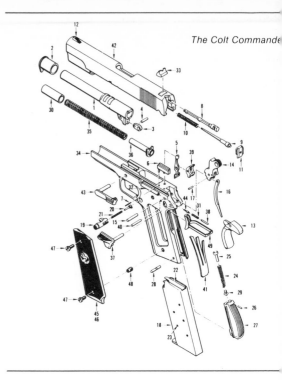

Lightweight Commander

Military & police pistol. This is simply a variant of the standard Commander (qv), with a high-strength blued alloy frame and chambering the 0.45in ACP only—which gives it a rather fearsome recoil. The gun was originally introduced in 1949 but has since been improved in several minor respects.
Cal: 0.45in ACP only. Otherwise as Government Model, except Wt, oz/gm: 27.0/765. Loa, in/mm: 7.9/200.

New Frontier

General purpose revolver/sports revolver. This is a re-introduction of a gun discontinued in the 1950s, basically a revision of the Colt Model P or 'Peacemaker' chambering rimfire ammunition, and with modern ramp-mounted front and fully adjustable backsights. The traditional hinged loading gate and offset under-barrel ejector rod remain, however, even though the grips are chequered composite rubber, displaying rampant Colt and American eagle motifs. The metal parts are blued, while the frame is attractively colour casehardened. The longest barrel version is the most accurate, the shortest the most handy—and the middle one the best compromise! Interestingly, the gun bears patent marks . . . September 1871, July 1872 and January 1875.
Cal: 0.22in LR rf. Mag: cylinder. Mag cap, rds: 6. Trg: SA, exposed hammer. Wt, oz/gm: 31.0/880. Loa, in/mm: 9.8, 11.4, 12.9/250, 290, 328. Brl, in/mm: 4.4, 6.0, 7.5/112, 152, 190. Rf: 6L. Sft: 'transfer bar' hammer block; inertia firing pin; half-cock notch on hammer.

Above: *the current version of the Combat Commander, in 0.45in ACP chambering, another of the many variants of the Colt Government Model. (Photograph by courtesy of Colt.)*

Above: *the specialised target-shooting derivative of the basic design, the Mk 4, Series 70 Gold Cup National Match— capable of very good performance indeed. (Courtesy Colt.)*

Python

General purpose revolver. Undoubtedly, the Python must be regarded as one of the world's finest revolvers; its hand-fitted and honed double-action, for example, assures smooth and dependable operation. The guns offer a full-length under-barrel ejector shroud, a ramp-mounted front and fully adjustable back sight, a ventilated rib, choice of ultra-high polish blue or nickel finishes and handsome chequered wooden grips which for 'factory' products give an excellent hold. The Python features the standard Colt trigger system, together with the transfer bar and inertia firing pin safety. Its first appearance, as factory model I-3, occurred in 1955.

Cal: 0.357in Magnum, 0.38in Special (8in barrel only). Mag: cylinder. Mag cap, rds: 6. Trg: DA, exposed hammer. Wt, with 6in barrel, oz/gm: 43.5/1235. Loa, in/mm: 7.8, 9.3, 11.3 or 13.3/198, 236, 287 or 338. Brl, in/mm: 2.5, 4.0, 6.0 or 8.0/63, 102, 152 or 203. Rf: 6L. Sft: 'transfer bar' hammer block; inertia firing pin; half-cock notch on hammer.

Trooper Mk 3

General purpose revolver. The Trooper is a heavy duty large-framed revolver intended for general and sporting purposes, and offers a range of chamberings from rimfire to magnum. Careful attention to the fit of the parts, a target hammer with a short fall (but see also Trooper Mk V), a coil mainspring and a smooth trigger action has ensured the Trooper a good reputation for ruggedness and reliability. The frontsight is a 'no snag' ramp; the backsight, an adjustable notch. The finishes are blue or nickel, the grips are chequered walnut and there are a number of barrel options.

The original Trooper Mk 1, factory model I-4, was introduced in April 1953, the 357 Magnum version following in January 1962.

Cal: 0.22in LR rf or 0.22in Magnum rf; 0.357in Magnum. Mag: cylinder. Mag cap, rds: 6. Trg: DA, exposed hammer. Wt, 6in barrel, oz/gm: 46/1305. Loa, in/mm: 9.5, 11.5 or 13.5/240, 292 or 343. Brl, in/mm: 4.0, 6.0 or 8.0/102, 162 or 203. Rf: 6L. Sft: 'transfer bar' hammer block; inertia firing pin; half-cock notch on hammer.

Trooper Mk 5

General purpose revolver. This 1982 model is the latest version of the tried, tested and popular Trooper range, with a revised and refined trigger mechanism. The hammer-fall arc has been reduced from 54° to 46° to reduce the lock-time, and changes have been made to the butt to accept a wider range of grips. A white-outline fully adjustable back sight and a red insert front sight complete the package. Finish options include blue, nickel and what is called 'Coltguard' a non-reflective and apparently self-lubricating electroless plating which provides protection externally and internally. 'Royal Coltguard' is applied over impeccable mirror polishing to give an even better finish.

Cal: 0.22in LR rf or 0.22mm Magnum rf; 0.357in Magnum. Otherwise generally as Trooper Mk 3 (qv).

Top: *a cased Colt Python, with its telescope sight and accessories.* **Above:** *blue and nickel versions of the Trooper Mk V.* *(Photographs by courtesy of Colt.)*

Cop Gun, Inc.

Torrance, California, USA. This quaintly named organisation makes the 'Cop Gun', a modernised derivative of the old Sharps four-barrel cluster deringer of the late 1850s. Made of stainless steel, the Cop Gun chambers the 0.357in Magnum cartridge—making it a handful to fire. The barrel cluster tips down to load.

Crown City Arms

Box 1126, Cortland, New York State 13045, USA. No information has yet been received concerning the activities of this company, believed to be concerned largely with the conversion of the Colt Government Model pistol (qv) to more efficient 'practical pistol' standards. Its products are as yet rarely seen in Britain.

Libero Daffini

Villaggio O. Montini, Traversa VIII, I-25100 Brescia, Italy.

British agency: none. US agency: none. Standard warranty: unknown.

Daffini, one of the smaller independent Italian gunmakers working in the Gardone/Brescia region, entered the commercial register in 1947 and worked at Vicolo Tre Archi, Brescia, prior to 1955. Hunting guns, shotguns and a series of handguns are made in small numbers.

Colt Navy

Percussion revolver. This is a straightforward copy of the gun originally made in 1851. The Daffini version is neither the best of the replicas nor the worst, and is often found in an elegant compartmented wood case containing a powder flask and a ball mould.
Cal: 0.36in. Otherwise as Colt M1851 (qv).

Colt Walker

Percussion revolver. This is a straightforward copy of the large, unwieldly Walker-Colt revolver, described in greater detail in the Colt section. The gun has hardwood grips, is browned and has a design depicting Texas Rangers pursuing Indians rolled into the cylinder surface. The Walker may be obtained in a well-fitted baize-lined case containing a scissors-type ball mould and a powder flask.
Cal: 0.44in. Otherwise as Colt version (qv).

Derringer

Personal defence pistol. This is a copy of the two-barrel Remington of the late 1860s, rather than the original percussion design attributed to Henry Deringer of Philadelphia. The two barrels are superimposed and hinge upwards at the breech for loading. The guns are blued, with black or ivory-coloured synthetic grips.
Cal: 6mm Flobert, 0.22in LR rf, 0.38in Special. Mag: none, twin barrels. Trg: SA, exposed hammer. Wt, oz/gm: 14.8/420. Loa, in/mm: about 5.1/130. Brl, in/mm: about 3.0/75. Rf: 4 R. Sft: apparently none.

Frontier

General purpose revolver. This is, quite simply, an Italian rimfire derivative of the Colt Peacemaker—otherwise quite conventional and unremarkable, with fixed sights and a single-action trigger. The guns usually have a burnished finish, though decorated versions are obtainable to special order. Grips are chequered wood.
Cal: 0.22in LR rf. Mag: cylinder. Mag cap, rds: 6. Trg: SA, exposed hammer. Wt, oz/gm: 28.2/800. Loa, in/mm: various. Brl, in/mm: 3.9, 4.7 or 5.5/100, 120 or 140. Rf: yes. Sft: none, apart from half-cock notch on hammer.

Kentucky Pistol

Flintlock pistol. The 'Kentucky' replicas are popular among the Italian gunmaking industry—easy to make and a popular sales line, especially in the United States of America. This gun has a full-length polished and sometimes carved hardwood butt/fore-end, displaying two brass ramrod pipes and a brass nosecap. The trigger guard and side plate are also brass, as are the simple fixed sights. Daffini's pistol—unlike some others—is a flintlock.
Cal: 0.44in. Mag: none, single shot. Trg: SA, exposed hammer. Wt, oz/gm: 42.3/1200. Loa, in/mm: 12.5/317. Brl, in/mm: 8.0/203. Rf: yes. Sft: half-cock notch on hammer.

Remington Army

Percussion revolver. This black-powder replica duplicates the Remington Army revolver of 1858, a strong and efficient design which rivalled the Colt for popularity in the mid nineteenth century. The Remington differs from the Colt in several respects, the most important of which are the distinctive under-barrel rib and solid-frame construction. The finish is browned; the grips, plain hardwood.
Cal: 0.36in, 0.44in. Otherwise generally as the similar gun made by Giuseppe Pietta (qv).

Sharps

Personal defence pistol. This is a modern version of the Sharps deringer of the mid nineteenth century, its four barrels contained in a tipping cluster. The gun has a blued barrel block, brass frame (from which a blued sheath trigger protrudes) and synthetic grips.
Cal: 0.22in Short, 6mm Flobert. Mag: none, multi-barrel. Trg: SA, exposed hammer. Wt, oz/gm: 9.9/280. Loa, in/mm: NA. Brl, in/mm: 4.0/101. Rf: 4 R? Sft: none.

Below: a typical reproduction percussion revolver—in this case, the 1858 army-model Remington.

Detonics Associates

2500 Seattle Tower, Seattle, Washington 98101, USA

UK distributor: no sole agency. Standard warranty: unknown.

Little is known about the background of this company, apparently founded in the early 1970s to make the well known Colt pistol derivative, as no material was received during the production of the directory.

Detonics 45

General purpose and personal defence pistol. This is basically a diminutive Colt Government Model, much shorter and lighter than the standard gun. It is built on a new investment-cast frame, rather than a modified machined gunmetal original. The Colt-type barrel bushing has been replaced by an enlarged muzzle, seating directly in the front of the slide, and the new mainspring assembly apparently solves the problems associated with 'springing' a small but unusually powerful automatic. The grip safety has been discarded (owing to the shortness of the butt) and the top rear of the slide has been cut away, but the operating system remains pure Colt. The Detonics 45 has a stronger recoil than normal—it is much lighter than the standard Government Model—and its muzzle blast verges on unpleasant. However, it represents a very powerful little package and is very widely liked.
Cal: 0.45in ACP. Otherwise as Colt, except Mag cap, 6 rounds. Wt, oz/gm: 29.0/820. Loa, in/mm: 6.8/172. Brl, in/mm: 4.5/114.

Dixie Gun Works

Gunpowder Lane, Union City, Tennessee 38621, USA.
DGW is best known as a retailer of blackpowder firearms, importing a vast range of reproductions from Italy and Spain. No company-owned gun manufacturing facilities appear to be operated in America.

Dílo Svratouch

Litomyšl, Czechoslovakia.

British agency: Edgar Brothers Ltd, Catherine Street, Macclesfield, Cheshire SK11 6SG, England. US agency: none. Export agency: Omnipol, Foreign Trade Corporation, Prahá-1, Washingtonova 11, Czechoslovakia. Standard warranty: unknown.

Dílo, a small part of the nationalised Czech firearms industry, makes a limited range of simple and reliable target pistols, quite well made for what they offer and undeniably competitively priced.

Drulóv vz.70 standard

Target pistol. This single-shot design was developed from the original 1963 pattern. The Drulóv is a bolt-loader, the breech opening being controlled by a rotary knob protruding behind the frame. This is turned clockwise, the bolt retracted, a cartridge dropped into the boltway and the action closed, cocking the striker en route. The height of the front sight can be adjusted, while the back sight can be moved laterally across the frame. The Drulóv has a long barrel—and a sight radius in excess of some current competition rules—and a one-piece walnut grip with an integral thumbrest. It shoots amazingly well for a gun in its class, but would benefit from more weight ahead of the trigger and (perhaps) a shorter barrel. The principal recognition feature is the conventional trigger lever within the angular guard.
Cal: 0.22in LR rf. Mag: none, single-shot. Trg: SA, concealed striker. Wt, oz/gm: 44.1/1250. Loa, in/mm: 14.4/365. Brl, in/mm: 9.8/250. Rf: 6 R? Sft: crossbolt catch above trigger (through to right for safe).

Drulóv vz.70 Special

Target pistol. This is a variant of the standard Drulóv (qv) fitted with a hair-trigger and a more comfortable semi-anatomical walnut grip. The basic design is instantly recognisable: the trigger-guard is enlarged, in strip form and extends below the line of the frame. Within this guard lies the 'trigger', in the form of a small button, and the setting lever projecting horizontally beneath. Pushing down the lever sets the trigger system and permits sear release with only a few grams pressure. The mechanism is by no means as sophisticated as the best, but an adequate surrogate in what is, after all, a very competitively priced product. The sights and operating systems parallel the standard gun.
Cal: 0.22in LR rf. Otherwise as Drulóv vz.70 Standard.

Drulóv vz.75

Target pistol. The 'model 75' is a minor derivative of the vz.70 with a modified set trigger, different sights and a better (though still non-adjustable) target grip. The hair-trigger is set by a lever on the left side of the trigger-button, which is pushed down to set the mechanism and returns automatically to its intial position (unlike the vz.70 type, which springs upwards only when the trigger button is pushed). The new backsight is adjustable laterally and vertically, the blade front sight being raised to suit. The result is very competitively priced and, with a certain amount of customising, provides a first-class entry into Free Pistol shooting without huge capital outlay.
Cal: 0.22in LR rf. Otherwise generally as vz.70 Special (qv)

Pav

Target pistol. The Pav, designed by Pavlíček in the early 1960s, is among the least sophisticated of all modern target pistols—but is also one of the cheapest, and undoubtedly a good basic trainer. It is an odd design, with a long slim barrel above a short cylindrical trigger housing; there is virtually no rearward prolongation behind the back of the walnut thumbrest style grip. The front sight is dovetailed into the muzzle, which permits a measure of crude lateral adjustment, and the back sight is a groove formed in the top surface of the breechblock. The Pav is loaded by pressing a thumb-catch on the left side of the breechblock and tipping the barrel downwards, after which it can be cocked by pulling the striker grip backwards. The metal parts are chemically blacked.
Cal: 0.22in LR rf. Mag: none, single shot. Trg: SA, concealed striker. Wt, oz/gm: 22.9, 26.4 or 30.3/650, 750 or 800. Loa, in/mm: 10.2, 12.2 or 14.2/260, 310 or 360. Brl, in/mm: 7.9, 9.8 or 11.8/200, 250 or 300. Rf: yes–type unknown. Sft: none.

ECHASA

Echasa-Echave y Arizmendi y Compañía SA, Eibar, Guipúzcoa, Spain.

This company was founded in 1911, but appears to have ceased trading in the late 1970s. It is included because the 'Fast' models were very widely distributed in the United States under the name 'Dickson Special Agent' and may still be encountered.

The Fast Model and the Lur Panzer are described overleaf.

Below: *the Drulóv vz.75. (Courtesy of Edgar Brothers.)*

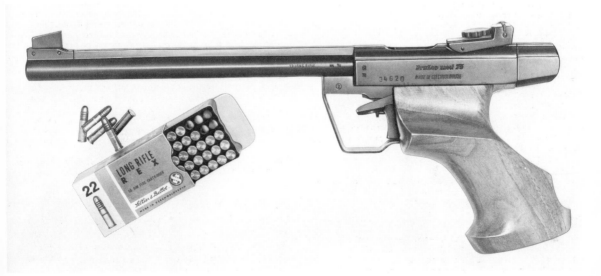

Fast Models

General purpose pistols. These existed in several subvarieties:

Fast Model 221 0.22in LR rf
Fast Model 631 6.35mm (0.25in ACP)
Fast Model 761 7.65mm (0.32in ACP)
Fast Model 907 9mm Short (0.380in ACP)

They were often made with differing degrees of ornamentation. The Fast Model 222, therefore, was simply a variant of the Model 221 with walnut grips, while the 223 was chromed with pearlite grips. All of them are simple blowbacks externally resembling the Walther PP, rather thinly blued and invariably displaying chequered plastic grips.

Lur-Panzer

General purpose pistol. This was a copy of the Erma-Luger EP22, details of which will be found in the relavant section. The quality of the Lur Panzer is not especially noteworthy, toolmarks being particularly evident internally. The most obvious identification feature is the EYA monogram inlet in the plain hardwood grips.

Em-Ge

Em-Ge Sportgeräte GmbH & Co. KG, Gerstenberger & Eberwein. D 7921 Gerstetten-Gussenstadt, Postfach 26, West Germany.

British agency: no sole distributor. US agency: no sole distributor. Standard warranty: 12 months

This is a modern re-creation of the prewar Em-Ge Moritz & Gerstenberger company, which made airguns and low-cost firearms in Zella-Mehlis prior to the end of the Second World War. It is asssumed that at least a part of the management of Moritz & Gerstenberger transferred to West Germany immediately before the postwar partition, and that this subsequently enabled the company to be rebuilt in the early 1950s. Em-Ge now makes a wide range of starting, signal and cartridge pistols alongside two air pistols. Its products have a reputation for good value at highly competitive prices.

Models 6 and 6d

Starting pistol. These conventional low priced starter pistols, dating from 1955 and 1960 respectively, have a bar-type magazine block sliding longitudinally through the receiver as the slide is operated. The exhaust port lies on top of the receiver in the Model 6, though the 6d has a conventional barrel to which a Zusatzlauf can be fitted. A spring-loaded magazine-trap cover may be found at the rear of the frame, the 6d having an additional cartridge-retaining spring on the side of its magazine. Finish may be black or chrome; the grips, chequered plastic.
Cal: 6mm Flobert blanks. Mag: bar pattern. Mag cap, rds: 6. Trg: DA, hammer fired. Wt, Loa: NA. Brl, none Sft: radial lever on left side above grips, back to safe.

Model 22GT (or 22G)

Starting and signal revolver. This 1956-vintage variant of the 22ST has a conventionally bored exhaust system and a muzzle threaded to accept an adapter (Zusatzlauf) for gas and signal ammunition.
Cal: 6mm Flobert blanks; 15mm signal or gas cartridge. Otherwise as 22ST.

Model 22ST (or 22S)

Starting revolver. This is a small, simple revolver of no great sophistication, solid framed with a double-action trigger system and no ejection other than punching out each spent case with a 'tool' such as a pencil or similar rod. The guns are usually burnished alloy with chequered synthetic grips.
Cal: 6mm Flobert blanks. Mag: cylinder. Mag cap, rds: 6. Trg: DA, exposed hammer.

Model A32

Starting and signal revolver. This gun, dating from 1969, features a side-swinging cylinder locked by an ejector rod sleeve. The double action lock-work features a hammer blocking safety bar raised only during the final stages of a deliberate trigger pull. The cylinder is steel, and with the Zusatzlauf, the auxiliary barrel attachment, virtually all types of 7mm and 9mm diameter signal/as ammunition can be fired.
Cal: 7mm blanks. Mag: cylinder. Mag cap, rds: 6. Trg: DA, exposed hammer. Wt, Loa, Brl: NA. Rf: none. Sft: automatic hammer-block bar; inertia firing pin.

Model 32ST

Starting revolver. This 1956-vintage design offers a solid frame with a manually-operated rod ejector along the right side of the barrel. This facilitates spent case expulsion . The exhaust port lies on top of the barrel, behind the front sight. The Model 32 is a dated design, but quite strongly made, with blackened alloy finish and chequered plastic grips.
Cal: 7mm Flobert (0.320in) blanks. Otherwise as A32, except Sft: none other than a rudimentary inertia firing pin.

Left: the Model 60. **Below:** the Model 324, in 0.32in S&W Long with a barrel measuring 4in (10cm) (courtesy Em-Ge).

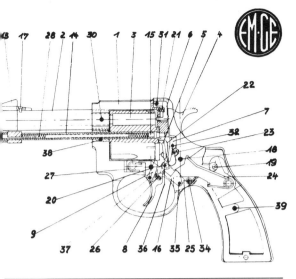

Above: a drawing of the Model 32 ST. (Courtesy Em-Ge.)

Model 38A or A-38

Starting and signal revolver. This is an enlargement of the A-32 (qv), differing principally in calibre and cylinder capacity. Signal and gas cartridges to be fired as well.
Cal: 9mm (0.380in) blanks. Otherwise as A-32 (qv), except Mag cap, rds: 5.

Model 38ST

Starting revolver. This is a Model 32ST (qv) chambering a larger cartridge and offering a commensurately reduced cylinder capacity.
Cal: 9mm (0.380in) blanks. Otherwise as Model 32ST, except Mag cap, rds: 5.

Model 60

Starting pistol. This is a variant of the Model 6, introduced in 1960, with a larger frame and conventional muzzle-exhaust; it shares the cartridge-retaining spring with the Model 6d.
Cal: 6mm Flobert blanks. Otherwise as Model 6 (qv).

Model 62

Starting and signal pistol. Dating from 1970-80, this is a minor variation of the Model 60 (qv) with a large-diameter muzzle for signal flares and gas cartridges.
Cal: 6mm Flobert blanks, 15mm diameter signal or gas cartridges. Otherwise as Model 60 (qv).

Model 63

Starting and signal pistol. This modernised Model 6d (or perhaps the 62) has a squared rather than rounded slide. The large diameter muzzle will also accept 15mm signal and gas ammunition.
Cal: 6mm Flobert blanks. Otherwise as Model 6d (qv).

Model 70

Starting and signal revolver. This solid-framed revolver is a modified Model 22 (qv) with a large diameter muzzle accepting 15mm diameter signal and gas cartridges. A rod ejector lies on the right side of the barrel.
Cal: 6mm Flobert blanks. Otherwise as Model 22.

Model 200

Target revolver. This is built on the basic frame of the A-32

starting revolver, not especially sophisticated but nonetheless offering good value. It has a longer, heavier barrel with a raised front sight atop a ventilated rib, while a micro-adjustable back sight lies at the extreme rear of the frame, its notch lying above the hammer—which has a broad, extended cocking spur. There are also thumbrest style synthetic grips.
Cal: 0.22in LR rf. Mag: cylinder. Mag cap, rds: 6. Trg: DA, exposed hammer. Wt, Loa, Brl: NA. Rf: yes. Sft: automatic hammer-blocking bar; inertia firing pin

Model 220K (formerly 22K)

This is a derivative of the 22ST with a larger frame. There is no separate ejection system, loading and unloading being effected through a laterally-swinging gate on the right side of the frame behind the cylinder. The 220K and 22ST share the same double-action trigger system and similar finish.
Cal: 0.22in LR rf. Otherwise generally as 22ST.

Model 220KS (formerly 22KS)

General purpose revolver. Introduced in 1965, this is a stronger, cartridge-firing variant of the Model 22GT (qv). The rod ejector on the right side of the barrel and the laterally-swinging loading gate on the right side of the frame behind the cylinder are most distinctive. The front sight is a fixed blade mounted on the muzzle crown; the back sight, a longitudinal groove in the top of the frame.
Cal: 0.22in LR rf. Otherwise generally as Model 22GT.

Model 223

General purpose revolver. This is an A-32 (qv), firing rimfire cartridges rather than blanks, but sharing the same construction and automatic safety. The 223 is generally black anodised alloy or chrome-plated. The grips are chequered plastic.
Cal: 0.22in LR rf. Mag: cylinder. Mag cap, rds: 6. Trg: DA, exposed hammer. Wt, Loa: NA. Brl, in/mm: 3.0/75. Rf: yes. Sft: automatic hammer-bar safety; inertia firing pin.

Model 224

General purpose revolver. This is a 223 (qv) with a longer barrel, introduced in 1969. *Cal: 0.22in LR rf*

Model 226

General purpose revolver. This is the largest of the series begun by the 223 (qv). Its long barrel makes it the easiest to shoot accurately, but the least handy.
Cal: 0.22in LR rf. Otherwise as 223 (qv), except Wt, Loa: NA. Brl, in/mm: 6.0/152.

Model 300

Target revolver. This is a larger version of the Model 200—an acceptable target revolver offering quite good sights and reasonable accuracy, but still very competitively priced.
Cal: 0.32in Smith & Wesson Long. Otherwise generally as Model 200 (qv).

Model 323

General purpose revolver. This is a sporting version of the Model 300, comparable to the 223 (qv) in a larger calibre.
Cal: 0.32in Smith & Wesson Long. Otherwise generally as Model 200 (qv).

Model 324

General purpose revolver. Dating from 1968, this is nothing more than a 323 with a longer barrel.
Cal: 0.32in Smith & Wesson Long. Otherwise as Model 323.

Model 326

General purpose revolver. The largest member of the 320 series, with a 6in (15cm) barrel, this gun offers the usual Em-Ge automatic hammer-bar safety and swing-out cylinder construction. It is reasonably sturdy and competitively priced.
Cal: 0.32in Smith & Wesson Long
Otherwise as 323, except Brl, in/mm: 6.0/152

Comparachart: personal defence guns

Revolvers

These present few problems as far as categorisation is concerned, though analysing the relative merits of small revolvers and small automatics is a subject of continual debate. The revolvers often chamber more powerful cartridges and deliver a harder punch, but the automatics are shorter, flatter and more readily concealable. The reliability of modern automatics has been improved in the last thirty years to a point where it rivals that of the revolver, though there are still champions of mechanical actuation—which minimises the effects of a misfire, difficult to clear in an automatic unless both hands are free (if the automatic has a double-action trigger system, however, the defective round may fire on the second strike). Double-action trigger systems are obviously favoured at the expense of single action, while sights should be fixed rather than adjustable (minimising the chances of accidental misalignment) and of the rounded 'no snag' type. All guns firing cartridges as ineffectual as the 0.22in LR rf have been excluded on the grounds that they are inadequate man stoppers.

GUN	CAL	VFM	CONSTR	TECH	DISMNTL	PERF	MKT	PG
Astra 250	c H M	••••	•••	•••	•••	••••	G E U	30
Astra 357 Police	L	••••	••••	••••	••••	••••	G E U	31
Astra 680 series	c d H M	••••	••••	••••	••••	••••	G E U	31
Bernardelli VB Tascabile	c d H	•••	••••	•••	••••	•••	G E U	43
Charter Arms Bulldog	L R	•••••	•••••	••••	••••	••••	G E U	46
Charter Arms Police Bulldog	M	••••	•••••	••••	••••	••••	G E U	47
Charter Arms Undercover	H M	••••	•••••	•••	••••	••••	G E U	47
Colt Detective Special	M	•••••	•••••	••••	••••	••••	G E U	53
Colt Lawman Mk III	L M	•••••	•••••	••••	••••	•••••	G E U	55
Erma ER432	H	••••	••••	•••	••••	•••	G E U	64
Erma ER438, 440	M	••••	••••	•••	••••	••••	G E U	64
FN Barracuda	J1 L M	••••	•••••	••••	••••	•••••	G E	68
H&R 632	H	•••	••••	•••	•••••	•••	U	84
H&R 732, 733	H	•••	••••	•••	•••••	•••	U	85
H&R 832, 833	H	••••	••••	•••	••••	•••	U	86
Korth Combat-Revolver	L M	•••	•••••	••••	•••	••••	E	98
Llama Piccolo	M	••••	•••	••••	••••	••••	E U	100
Llama Scorpio	M	••••	•••	••••	••••	••••	E U	100
Rossi Ranger Mo.20	H	•••	•••	••••	••••	•••	U	123
Rossi Pioneer Mo.27	M	••••	•••	••••	••••	••••	U	123
Rossi Ranger Mo.28	H	•••	•••	••••	••••	•••	U	123
Rossi Pioneer Mo.33	M	••••	•••	••••	••••	••••	U	123
Rossi Pioneer Mo.87	M	••••	••••	••••	••••	••••	U	125
Sauer TR6	M	••••	•••••	••••	•••	••••	E	127
S&W Model 12	M	••••	•••••	••••	••••	••••	G E U	132
S&W Model 15	M	••••	•••••	••••	••••	••••	G E U	132
S&W Model 19	L M	•••••	•••••	••••	••••	•••••	G E U	133
S&W Model 36	M	••••	•••••	••••	••••	••••	G E U	134
S&W Model 37	M	••••	•••••	••••	••••	••••	G E U	134
S&W Model 38, 49	M	••••	•••••	••••	••••	••••	G E U	134
S&W Model 64	M	••••	•••••	••••	••••	••••	G E U	136
S&W Model 66	L M	•••••	•••••	••••	••••	••••	G E U	136
Stm Rgr Police Service 6	K L M	•••••	•••••	•••••	••••	•••••	G E U	148
Stm Rgr Security 6	L	•••••	•••••	•••••	•••••	•••••	G E U	148
Stm Rgr Speed 6	K L M	•••••	•••••	•••••	•••••	•••••	G E U	149
Taurus Modelo 85	M	••••	•••	•••	••••	••••	E U	150
Uberti Inspector	H M	••••	••••	••••	••••	••••	G E	153
Weihrauch HW3	c d H	•••	••••	••••	••••	•••	G E	164
Weihrauch HW357	L M	••••	••••	••••	••••	•••••	G E	166
Weihrauch HW38	M	••••	••••	••••	••••	••••	G E	167
Weihrauch HW68	c d H	•••	••••	••••	••••	•••	G E	167

In addition to the guns listed above, most of which offer barrels of under 3in (76mm), any of the following can be considered if a longer barrel is acceptable: Astra Cadix, or preferably the NC-6; Astra 357; any of the smaller Charter Arms or Colt revolvers; the better Harrington & Richardson and Rossi revolvers; virtually all medium-size Smith & Wesson revolvers; Taurus revolvers Modelo 65, 66 and 85; and smallest Dan Wesson revolvers.

Pistols

GUN	CAL	VFM	CONSTR	TECH	DISMNTL	PERF	MKT	PG
AMT Back-Up	F	••••	•••••	••••	•••••	•••	G E U	25
Astra Cub	c F	•••	••••	•••	•••••	•••	G E U	27
Bauer 25	F	••••	••••	•••	•••••	•••	U	33
Beretta Mo. 950 BS	F	•••	••••	•••	•••••	•••	G E U	39
Bernardelli PA Mo. 68	F	•••	••••	•••	•••••	•••	E	44
Erma EP555	F	••••	••••	••••	••••	•••	G E U	65
Erma EP655	F	••••	••••	••••	••••	•••	G E U	65
FN Baby	F	•••	•••••	•••	•••••	•••	G E U	68
FÉG Model R,	I	••••	•••	••••	••••	••••	G E	72
Korriphila TP70	F	••••	•••••	•••••	••••	•••	G E U	98
Rigarmi Mo. 1953	F	•••	•••	•••	•••••	•••	E	118
Rigarmi Mo. 1955	F	•••	•••	•••	•••••	•••	E	118
Star Modelo DKL	O	••••	•••	••••	••••	•••••	G E U	138
Sterling M300, M300S	F	••••	••••	••••	•••••	•••	U	142
Walther TPH	c F	••••	•••••	•••••	••••	•••	G E U	163

In addition to the guns listed above, any of the following can also be considered, though they are usually a little larger and offer more powerful loadings: the Astra Constable; the excellent Beretta 81 series and its near-relation, the FN Mle 140 DA; the powerful Detonics 45 in 0.45in ACP; the Gamba RGP81, a modification of the Mauser HSc; the Přesné CZ vz.70; the Star BKM, BKS and PD (the last chambering the 0.45in ACP); the Sterling 400 series; the excellent SIG-Sauer P230; the Walther PP, PPK and the Interarms Walther American.

The Comparacharts: key to abbreviations. *GUN* is self-explanatory. *CAL* refers to the cartridge or cartridges for which the guns are chambered, keyed to Appendix 1 on pages 171-2; cartridges defined in lower case (h instead of H) are unsuitable for the purposes under review. J1 and J2 are 9mm and 7.65mm Parabellum respectively, and bracketed references indicate the existence of a suitable conversion unit. *VFM* is 'value for money'; *CONSTR* the quality of manufacture; *TECH*, the suitability of the design for its purposes and the efficiency with which it has been executed; *DISMNTL*, the ease with which the gun can be serviced; and *PERF*, an indication of the man-stopping qualities, accuracy, safety systems and general handiness of the gun. *MKT* refers to the markets in which the guns are distributed outside their country of origin—G represents Britain, E Europe and U, the United States of America. *DIS* signifies the disciplines in which target pistols are used, while *PG* is the page on which further details may be found.

The quality is indicated by the code: • poor, •• mediocre, ••• good, •••• praiseworthy and ••••• outstanding. Only the best of the guns in the book are featured on the charts. The non-appearance of a gun can mean either that it has been assessed lower than those that *are* included—or that its manufacturer supplied insufficient information to allow an adequate assessment to be made.

Left: the Smith & Wesson Model 686 revolver with a 4in (10cm) barrel—a little too large to be easily concealed, but certainly not lacking in power. (Courtesy of Smith & Wesson.)

Erma-Werke GmbH

D-8060 München-Dachau, Postfach 1269, West Germany.

British agency: John L. Longstaff (R.E.C.) Ltd, 35-37 Chapel Town, Pudsey, West Yorkshire LS28 7RZ.
US agency: apparently none at the time of writing. Standard warranty: 12 months.

This Bavaria-based company, founded in 1949, has no relationship other than in name to the prewar Erma-Werke-Berthold Geipel, producer of the Erma submachine-guns and other military equipment prior to the end of the Second World War. The original Erma ceased trading in 1945, but it must be assumed that some employees settled in western Germany and that this explains why the present company—initially a maker of metalware and slide bearings (*Gleitlager*)—so quickly and enthusiastically turned to production of well made starting and signal-pistols. A variety of cartridge-firing derivatives (some aping the lines of the Parabellum, others the Walther PP) has also appeared in the last twenty years.

Erma-Kniegelenk-Pistole EP22 (or LA-22)

General purpose pistol. Introduced in 1964, this was the first of Erma's surrogate Parabellums, displaying a blowback-operated toggle-lock rather than the short-recoil actuated original. There are many other detail differences, of course; the Erma mainspring is inclined in the back of the frame immediately behind the magazine well, where the full-bore gun's bell-crank lever would normally lie. The EP22 also has a more conventional trigger/sear system than the original, and the absence of the distinctive Parabellum cover-plate on the left side of the receiver is notable. The action is adapted from the conversion unit developed by Erma for the Pistole 08, and patented by Richard Kulisch in 1927. The EP22 was obtainable in a long-barrelled 'Navy' model and as a carbine, with a wood fore-end and a detachable shoulder stock, but was discontinued in the early 1970s. It can be identified by the pronounced rear overhang, very high front sight and a toggle raised well above the bore axis.
Cal: 0.22in LR rf. Mag: detachable box, crossbolt catch through frame behind trigger. Mag cap, rds: 8. Trg: SA, concealed striker. *Wt, oz/gm: 35.6/1010. Loa, in/mm: 7.2/183. Brl, in/mm: 3.3/83. Rf: 6 R. Sft: radial lever on left-side of frame behind grip (up-safe).*

Selbstlade-Gaspistole EGP55

Starting and signal pistol. Externally, this is all but indistinguishable from the Walther PPK, on which it has clearly been deliberately based. It has a 'barrel' or rotary safety lever on the slide and a ring hammer. It is available chromed or blued, invariably has chequered wooden grips, and the fixed sights stay true to the appearance of its prototype—but are of no practical use on a blank firer. The EGP55 can be fitted with an extension to handle signal rockets.
Cal: 8mm blanks and gas cartridges. Mag: detachable box, catch on butt heel. Mag cap, rds: 5. Trg: DA, exposed hammer. Wt, oz/gm: 15.5/440. Loa, in/mm: 5.4/137. Brl, in/mm: 2.9/73. Rf: none. Sft: rotary firing pin lock on left side of slide (up to fire); inertia firing pin; half-cock notch on hammer.

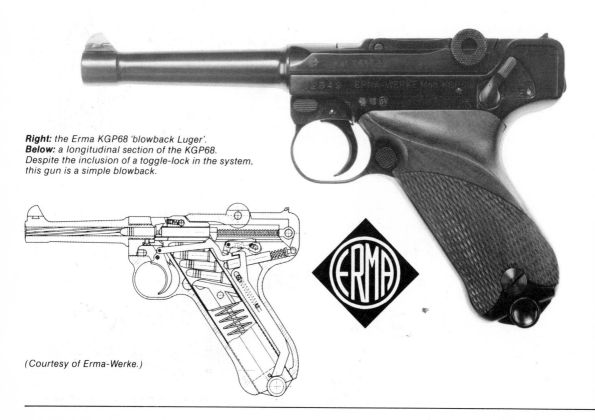

Right: *the Erma KGP68 'blowback Luger'.*
Below: *a longitudinal section of the KGP68. Despite the inclusion of a toggle-lock in the system, this gun is a simple blowback.*

(Courtesy of Erma-Werke.)

Selbstlade-Gaspistole EGP65

Starting and signal pistol. The EGP65 is a modernised derivative of the EGP55 (qv), with less obvious Walther antecedents. There are marked differences in the construction of the slide and frame, even though the components of the hammer-train remain practically unaltered. The trigger system, however, is single rather than double action and the trigger lever lies farther back in its guard than in the EGP55; the grips are usually synthetic rather than wooden, and the whole design has a much more angular appearance than its predecessors. The muzzle extension for signal flares remains optional.

Cal: 8mm blanks. Mag: detachable box, catch on butt heel. Mag cap, rds: 5. Trg: DA, exposed hammer. Wt, oz/gm: 13.8/390. Loa, in/mm: 5.3/135. Brl, in/mm: NA. Rf: none. Sft: inertia firing pin; half-cock notch on hammer.

Gasrevolver EGR66

Starting and signal revolver. This is a typical Smith & Wesson-type blank-firing revolver, with a yoke-mounted side-swinging cylinder controlled by a thumb latch on the left side. But for the Erma trademark on the grips it could easily be mistaken for an S&W. The spent cases are expelled by pushing the extractor rod, doubling as the cylinder axis pin. The guns are well made, blued with partially chequered wood grips and can be fitted with a muzzle extension to fire signal rockets.

Cal: 0.380in/9mm blank and gas cartridges. Mag: cylinder. Mag cap, rds: 5. Trg: DA, exposed hammer. Wt, oz/gm: 20.1/570. Loa, in/mm: 6.3/160. Brl, in/mm: 1.9/48. Rf: none. Sft: half-cock notch on hammer.

Erma-Kniegelenk-Pistole KGP68

General purpose pistol. This, dating from 1968, was a modified form of the EP22, refined and lightened, yet a closer approximation to the original Parabellum. It remains a blowback but chambers more powerful cartridges. The barrel (particularly), the reduced rear overhang and the lowered toggle axis are most notable, though the EP22 and the KGP68 are very similar internally. The guns feature blued alloy construction and chequered wooden grips with longitudinally grooved borders. The crossbolt dismantling catch lies ahead of the trigger guard—a departure from the radial Parabellum pattern. Like the EP22, the KGP68 shares some of the elegance, superb balance and 'pointability' of the guns on which it is based.

Cal: 0.32in ACP (7.65mm Auto), 0.380in ACP (9mm Short). Otherwise as EP22, except Mag cap, rds: 6 (0.32in) or 5 (0.380in). Wt, oz/gm: 22.6/640. Loa, in/mm: 7.4/187. Brl, in/mm: 4.0/100. Rf: 4 R.

Erma-Kniegelenk-Pistole KGP 68A

General purpose pistol. This gun is a minor variant of the KGP68 (qv), modified by the addition of a magazine and trigger safety system to satisfy the US Gun Control Act of 1968 and thus permit importation. The gun cannot be fired (even if loaded) until the magazine is pushed fully home—the subject of US Patent 3220310. The KGP 68A is externally much the same as the KGP68 but usually displays partially chequered thumbrest-style grips. The gun is sometimes called the EKP in the USA, as its correct title is the Erma-Kniegelenk-Pistole (Erma toggle-joint-pistol).

Cal: 0.32in ACP (7.65mm Auto), 0.380in ACP (9mm Short). Otherwise as KGP68, except Sft: combination trigger-block/magazine safety system; radial lever on left side of frame behind grip.

Erma-Kniegelenk-Pistole KGP69

General purpose pistol. The KGP69 is a derivative of the EP22 and KGP 68A (qv), combining the rimfire chambering of the former with the modified action and trigger/magazine safety system of the latter. It is probably the best balanced of the series, and its less powerful cartridge and greater weight (though less than the original EP22) makes it more pleasant to

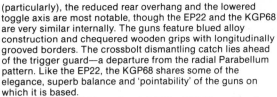

fire. Apart from the barrel shape and an appreciably higher front sight, it is virtually identical with the KGP 68A.
Cal: 0.22in LR rf. Otherwise generally as KGP 68A, except Mag cap, rds: 8. Wt, oz/gm: 29.6/840. Rf: 6 R.

Selbstlade-Gaspistole EGP75S

Starting- and signal pistol. This is a larger version of the EGP55, as comparison of dimensions will show. The two guns function practically identically, though the 75S is somewhat better made and—particularly where the extractor and dismantling systems are concerned—a little more sophisticated. The EGP75S bears an even closer resemblance to the Walther PP/PPK series than the 55, on which the rear of the slide is an almost perfect diagonal rather than the contoured version of the Walthers and the 75S. The 75S has 22 vertically milled slide-retraction grooves and a safety that moves from 0° to 60°; the 55, on the other hand, has only eight *diagonal* grooves and a safety operating in a 45-90° arc. The EGP75S can be acquired with the standard muzzle extensions, the Zusatzläufe Kal. 15mm für Signale.
Cal: 8mm blank and gas cartridges. Otherwise as EGP55, except Mag cap, rds: 7. Wt, oz/gm: 20.8/590. Loa, in/mm: 6.1/155. Brl, in/mm: 3.3/84.

Erma-Gas-Revolver EGR77

Starting- and signal revolver. This is another of Erma's 'gas alarm revolvers'; like most of its stablemates, it bears a close

type grips are often associated with the short-barrelled version
Cal: 0.22in LR rf. Mag: cylinder. Mag cap, rds: 6. Trg: DA, external hammer. Wt, oz/gm: 19.4, 21.2/550, 600. Loa, in/mm: 6.3, 7.3/160, 186. Brl, in/mm: 2.0, 3.0/50, 76. Rf: 6 R. Sft: 'transfer bar' hammer block; inertia firing pin; half-cock notch on hammer.

Erma-Revolver ER423

Personal defence revolver. This is simply a version of the ER422 (qv) chambering the more powerful Winchester Magnum rimfire round—a better man stopper than the 0.22in LR rf, though still only marginally useful for this purpose.
Cal: 0.22in Magnum rf. Otherwise as ER422.

Erma-Revolver ER432

Personal defence revolver. This short-barrelled 'snub nose' gun is comparable to the ER422 (qv), but chambers a larger and more powerful cartridge. It has also reverted to the separate striker pinned into the hammer nose, though the hammer safety arm remains an integral part of the mechanism. The cylinder yoke is operated by a thumb latch, the sights comprise a ramp-mounted blade and frame-top groove, and the chequered wooden grips display a traditional 'detective special' rounded butt.
Cal: 0.32in S&W Long. Otherwise as ER422, except Wt, oz/gm. 19.4, 21.2/550, 600. Sft: hammer-blocking arm; half-cock notch on hammer.

resemblance to the Smith & Wessons—which is probably more than merely coincidental! The cylinder is mounted on a side-swinging yoke controlled by a thumb latch on the left side of the frame, beneath the hammer. The chunky hammer has a separate replaceable firing pin, and the action includes an arm preventing the primer being struck until the trigger lever is deliberately pulled. The ejector rod is fully shrouded and, amazingly, this *blank-firer* has sturdy combat-worthy sights. Its finish is usually blue-black and the grips are generally chequered wood.
Cal: 0.38in (9mm) blanks. Mag: cylinder. Mag cap, rds: 6. Trg: DA, external hammer. Wt, oz/gm: 31.7/900. Loa, in/mm: 7.5/190. Brl, in/mm: 2.4/62. Rf: none. Sft: hammer-blocking arm; half-cock notch on hammer.

Erma-Revolver ER422

Personal defence revolver. This is, yet again, a Smith & Wesson lookalike—but chambering ball cartridges rather than mere blanks and signal rockets. It shares many parts with the Erma gas revolvers, but offers a transfer bar safety unit and the traditional S&W yoke-mounted thumb latch-controlled cylinder. There is a choice of barrel lengths, but the unsophisticated back sight is simply a longitudinal groove cut in the top of the frame above the cylinder and the EGR422 is intended for instinctive rather than deliberate shooting. The barrel is retained by two prominent pins driven laterally through the frame ahead of the cylinder, the finish is usually blue and the grips are generally chequered wood. The heel and toe of the butt may be squared, but rounded pocket-pistol

Erma-Revolver ER438

Personal defence revolver. A version of the ER432 (qv) chambering a still larger round, the reduced cylinder capacity of the 438 necessitates changes in the trigger and cylinder pawl system though the ER432 and ER438 are otherwise the same. Indeed, Erma sales literature often makes use of the same exploded-view photograph for *both* of them, though the 5-round capacity cylinder is a little too obviously the 438! Owing to its chambering, the 438 is the best Erma personal defence revolver.
Cal: 0.38in Special. Otherwise as ER422, except Mag cap, rds: 5. Wt, oz/gm: 20.1/570. Loa, in/mm: 6.3, 7.3/160, 185. Brl, in/mm: 1.8, 3.0/48, 76. Sft: hammer-blocking arm; half-cock notch on hammer.

Erma-Revolver ER440

Personal defence revolver. This is simply a corrosion-resisting stainless steel version of the ER438 (qv), which it otherwise duplicates. *Cal: 0.38in Special. Otherwise as ER438.*

Erma-Pistole EP552

Personal defence pistol. This is a bullet-firing derivative of the EGP55 (qv), imitating the lines of the Walther PPK but exhibiting constructional differences. It shares the eight diagonal retraction grooves and 45°-90° safety catch movement of the 55 (cf. EGP75S), while the sights comprise a fixed blade and a non-adjustable standing open notch integral

with the slide rib. The grips are chequered wood or plastic and the alloy parts have a blue-black anodised finish. A handy and quite well-made little gun, the EP552 unfortunately lacks enough power to be regarded as an effective man stopper.
Cal: 0.22in LR rf. Mag: detachable box, catch on butt heel. Mag cap, rds: 7. Trg: DA, external hammer. Wt, oz/gm: 14.5/410. Loa, in/mm: 5.4/137. Brl, in/mm: 2.9/73. Rf: 6 R. Sft: rotary lever on left side of slide (down safe); inertia firing pin; half-cock notch on hammer.

Erma-Pistole EP555

Personal defence pistol. This is identical with the EP552 (qv), but chambers the almost equally ineffective 0.25in ACP cartridge—very popular in Europe as the 6.35mm Auto, despite its deficiencies.
Cal: 0.25in ACP (6.35mm Auto). Otherwise as EP552.

Erma-Pistole EP652

Personal defence pistol. This is the conventional version of the EGP65 (qv), firing ball ammunition rather than blanks though construction is virtually identical. The slide has a squared, modernistic shape, with an oblique-cut tip and seventeen diagonal retraction grooves. The rotary safety lever is capable of moving from about 40° to 85°. The finish is blue-black; the grips, chequered brown plastic.
Cal: 0.22in LR rf. Mag: detachable box, catch on butt heel. Mag cap, rds: 7. Trg: DA, exposed hammer. Wt, oz/gm:

13.8/390. Loa, in/mm: 5.3/135. Brl, in/mm: NA. Rf: 6 R. Sft: rotary lever on left side of slide above grip (down safe); inertia firing pin; half-cock notch on hammer.*

Erma-Pistole EP655

Personal defence pistol. This minor variant of the EP652 chambers the 0.25in ACP (6.35mm Auto) cartridge but, apart from rifling, calibre and magazine, is identical with its companion.
Cal: 0.25in ACP (6.35mm Auto). Otherwise as EP652.

Selbstlade-Kniegelenk-Gaspistole KGP690

Starting and signal pistol. This comparatively recent introduction is a blank-firing version of the KGP69 (qv). The guns are virtually identical, though the KGP690 lacks the combination trigger block/magazine safety. In addition, the blank-firer has plain-bordered wooden grips without the thumbrest.
Cal: 8mm blank and gas cartridges. Mag: detachable box, crossbolt catch on left side of frame behind trigger. Mag cap, rds: 6. Trg: SA, concealed striker. Wt, oz/gm: 29.6/840. Loa, in/mm: 7.4/188. Brl, in/mm: 3.6/92. Rf: none. Sft: radial lever on left rear side of frame (down safe).

Note: In addition to the guns listed here, Erma recently introduced the Model 452, resembling the Colt Government Model, and the Walther-lookalike Model 752.

FAS

Fabbrica Armi Sportive SrL, I-20091 Settimo Milanese (Milano), Via E. Fermi 8, Italy.

British agency: Oliver J. Gower Ltd, Unit K1, Cherrycourt Way, Stanbridge Road, Leighton Buzzard, Bedfordshire LU7 8UH, England. US agency: no sole agency at the time of writing. Standard warranty: 12 months.

One of many small independent Italian gunmakers, FAS makes a small range of extremely high-quality target pistols (including an airgun), formerly known as the Domino, IGI or IGI-Domino. Little else is known about the previous history of FAS, which has only recently emerged from the IGI/Ravizza shadow.

PGP 75 (Pardini)

Target pistol. The Pardini, designed in the early 1970s, is among the strangest looking of the Free Pistol class. A single-shot bolt-action gun, its bore lies extremely low in relation to the grips above which tower the sights. The hair-trigger mechanism—adjustable from 5 to 300gm—is cocked by a lever protruding ahead of the walnut fore-end, the grips are either fully adjustable or fixed (seven variations of the latter are available), and various stabilisers can be obtained. The

Pardini has even been offered with oscillating and spirit-level sights. Barrel weights of 100 or 150gm can be attached as required.
Cal: 0.22in LR rf. Mag: none, single-shot. Trg: SA, internal striker. Wt, without auxiliary barrel weights: oz/gm: 35.3/1000. Loa, in/mm: 16.9/430. Brl, in/mm: 9.1/230. Rf: yes. Sft: apparently none.

Modello OP 601

Target pistol. Introduced in 1973, this is a specialised rapid-fire gun, formerly known as the IGI or IGI Domino 601. It is typical of its class, but very well made and offering some very good features—including a very low sight line (a mere 15mm above the bore), a barrel placed low in relation to the handgrip so that the bore acts virtually as an extension of the shooter's forearm, and a fully adjustable sear and trigger. The sights are also fully adjustable, while 2mm diameter gas-ports are bored into the barrel to minimise the effects of muzzle climb; there are six ports in the standard barrel, four in the 'High Speed' and only two in the 'Pentathlon' version. The optional barrel weights are 280, 400 and 450gm. The unusual 600-series magazine is inserted downwards through the open breech, permitting a much greater variety of grip shapes than most FAS rivals (but not the Britarms 2000, qv). The grips themselves are stippled walnut, adjustable, or a cheaper fixed wraparound pattern obtainable in five different sizes (3 for right-handers, 2 for left). The 601 dismantles easily, functions flawlessly and is undoubtedly among the top in its class—the winner of the gold medal at the 1980 Olympics.

Cal: 0.22in short rf. Mag: detachable box, catch on left side of frame behind trigger. Mag cap, rds: 5. Trg: SA, concealed hammer. Wt, without barrel weights, oz/gm: 27.2/770. Loa, in/mm: 11.3/288. Brl, in/mm: 6.0/152. Rf: 6 R?. Sft: inertia firing pin.

Modello SP 602

Target pistol. This is a 'sport pistol' derivative of the rapid-fire 601 (qv), with which it shares similar dimensions and construction. There are differences in the construction of the removable two-stage trigger, adjustable from 1050gm down to about 100gm, and the barrel ports have been omitted. The 601 and 602 otherwise look much the same though the latter has a more prominent front sight. Like its cousin, the 602 is cocked by means of knurled thumbpieces—larger on the 602 than the 601—running forward from the breechblock ahead of the trigger guard. Five different patterns of grip and three barrel weights (80, 240, 360gm) may be obtained.
Cal: 0.22in LR rf. Otherwise as 601, except Wt, without barrel weights, oz/gm: 28.6/810. Loa, in/mm: 11.2/285. Brl, in/mm: 5.6/142.

Modello CF 603

Target pistol. The CF 603 is the centrefire derivative of the FAS series, chambering S&W Wadcutter ammunition. Apart from calibre and weight, it duplicates of the 602 (qv). A trigger pull of 1360gm and adjustable walnut grips are standard fittings.
Cal: 0.32in S&W Wadcutter. Otherwise as 602, except Wt, oz/gm: 42.3/1200. Loa: 11.2/285. Brl: 5.3/135.

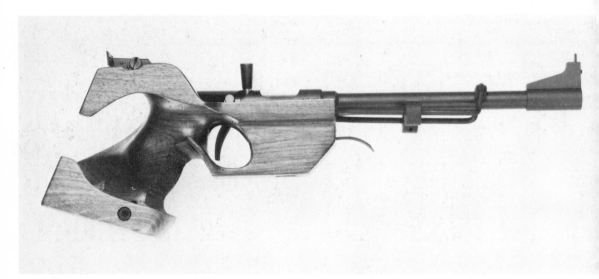

Above: *the Pardini.* **Below:** *the FAS 602. (Courtesy of Oliver J. Gower Ltd.)*

Top left: *the FN factory in Herstal, near Liège.* **Top right:** *a richly engraved FN-Browning blowback, the Mle 1900, on which the company's successful pistol business was based.* **Above:** *the Salon de Gravure (engraving hall) in Herstal. (Courtesy of FN.)*

Fabrique Nationale SA

B-4400 Herstal-lèz-Liège, Belgium

British agency: none. US agency: Browning Corporation, Route 1, Morgan, Utah 84050, USA. Standard warranty: 12 months?

Fabrique Nationale d'Armes de Guerre, as the company was originally known, was founded in 1889 by a group of Belgian gunsmiths intent on negotiating a lucrative contract to make the Mle 1889 (Mauser) magazine rifles. The success this enterprise attracted was such that FN built more Mauser rifles for export, but this was to lead to a suit filed on behalf of Ludwig Loewe & Co. of Berlin alleging that FN manufacture of the 'Spanish Model' Mauser rifle infringed patents that had not been included in the Loewe/Mauser licence to make the Mle 89. FN unsuccessfully contested the case, whereupon Loewe acquired virtually half the company shares from disgruntled shareholders and the FN board was rearranged to include German representation. This benefitted the company in the short term, however, as FN was included in a cartel organised by DWM, OEWG and Mauser to make the Mauser-system rifles. Thus established, FN went from strength to strength, rapidly graduating to blowback pistol, bicycle and automobile production. The German occupation of Belgium was a time of great conflict for FN, whose Belgian directors courageously refused to operate the plant for German benefit; their courage was rewarded in 1918 when, after confiscation of the German shareholding, FN once again became wholly Belgian owned. Success in the postwar period was ensured by sales of Browning-designed blowback pistols alongside Mauser rifles and Browning machine-guns, and the perfection of the GP pistol after Browning's death in 1926 finally ended the depression of the 1930s. But no sooner had FN begun production of the GP than war broke out again and Belgium was again occupied by the Germans. Some of the key technicians escaped to Britain, where prototypes of the Saive-designed SLEM rifle (later to become the ABL) were made during the early 1940s and inspired the postwar re-establishment of the company. The success of the improved FN FAL, the MAG medium machine-gun and a host of other guns has since raised FN Herstal to its position amongst the world's leading smallarms manufacturers. This has in no way been damaged by clever selection of foreign designs such as the Uzi and Beretta sub-machine guns, built under licence, and FN now makes items as diverse as aero engines, rocket engine components . . . and tennis rackets. It also holds a 36 per cent shareholding in Beretta, a minor modification of whose excellent double-action personal defence pistol is also being made under the FN banner.

BROWNING®

Two examples of the diversity of FN's wares: the Challenger target pistol (above) and the 'Baby' personal defence pistol (left). (Courtesy of FN.)

Baby

Personal defence pistol. The 'Baby', dating from 1936, was put back into production after the end of the Second World War. It is small, almost minuscule: 104mm long, 72mm high and a fraction under 20mm wide. It is a plain and rather austere design, blued with black chequered polyamide grips, but offers excellent quality and features such as a magazine safety. The sights are rudimentary, but the gun is intended purely for short range instinctive fire where sights are virtually superfluous. The chambering is the notoriously ineffectual 6.35mm Auto, but even this should not be underrated as the metal-jacketed bullets will penetrate up to 60mm of pine at a range of 15 metres—or even 30mm at six times that distance. *Cal: 0.25in ACP (6.35mm Auto). Mag: detachable box, catch on butt heel. Mag cap, rds: 6. Trg: SA, internal striker. Wt, oz/gm: 7.4/210. Loa, in/mm: 4.1/104. Brl, in/mm: 2.1/54. Rf: 6 R. Sft: radial lever on left side of frame ahead of grip, up to safe; magazine safety.*

Barracuda

Personal defence revolver. This is a substantial, well-made but technically rather unremarkable design based on Smith & Wesson practices. The cylinder, for example, is mounted on a laterally swinging yoke locked by a thumb latch on the left side of the frame beneath the hammer. The gun has a full-length ejector shroud, an adjustable-pressure mainspring, contoured wooden grips . . . and interchangeable cylinders to accept the rimmed revolver or rimless automatic rounds. With the rimless 9mm Parabellum cartridges, a special rosette-shaped clip must be used in the manner of the half-moon clips used by some Colt and Smith & Wesson revolvers during the First World War—not a new idea therefore, but unusual in contemporary designs. The blued, forged-steel Barracuda has sturdy fixed sights; in photographs it seems quite small, but it is in fact a surprisingly massive gun. However, Its balance is very good, however, and it will be interesting to see how

successfully it can be marketed by this major manufacturer who has hitherto relied entirely on a line of automatic pistols. *Cal: 0.357in Magnum and 0.38in Special, or 9mm Parabellum. Mag: cylinder. Mag cap, rds: 6. Trg: DA, exposed hammer. Wt, oz/gm: 36.1/1025. Loa, in/mm: NA. Brl, in/mm: 3.0/76. Rf: 6 R. Sft: 'transfer bar' hammer block; inertia firing pin; half-cock notch on hammer.*

Challenger

Target pistol. This is the first of FN's sporting pistols to be encountered, a reasonably uncomplicated (yet undeniably well made) blowback, similar in some respects to the Colt Woodsman series. It has a slender barrel carrying a prominent sight blade, a fully adjustable back sight mounted on the half-length slide and a well-raked, chequered grip in selected walnut, offering superb pointability. The trigger pull is adjustable; the trigger lever, grooved and generally gold plated. The standard finish is blue, but chrome plating and various classes of engraving are available up to the Renaissance Grade. The Challenger was discontinued in the late 1970s. *Cal: 0.22in LR rf. Mag: detachable box, catch above left grip. Mag cap, rds: 10. Trg: SA, concealed hammer. Wt, oz/gm: 35.0/995. Loa, in/mm: 8.9, 11.2/225, 285. Brl, in/mm: 4.5, 6.6/114, 173. Rf: 6 R. Sft: radial lever on left rear of frame; inertia firing pin.*

Competition, GP (or HP) Competition

Target pistol. This is a minor adaptation of the GP Mle 35, with a lengthened barrel, a fully adjustable back sight and a muzzle counterweight attached by an Allen-head bolt ahead of the slide/weight joint. The guns are specially selected and their actions hand-finished to give ultra-smooth operation, but mechanically they are identical with the standard GP. *Cal: 9mm Parabellum. Otherwise generally as GP Mle 35 (qv), except Wt, oz/gm: 34.6/980. Loa, in/mm: 9.1/230. Brl, in/mm: 5.9/150.*

'Fast Action'

Military and police pistol. This is a variant of the GP Mle 35 (qv) with a new concept in triggers—a 'semi-double-action' which permits the firer to thumb-cock the hammer and then push the hammer forwards again to its 'down' position. The gun can be fired simply by pulling the trigger; as the hammer spring is *already* in its cocked position, this permits what is effectively a double-action pull without the added force necessary to rotate the hammer against the hammer spring . . . overcoming one of the principal objections to double-action systems—a tendency for the added finger/hand pressure to pull the first shot high and to the right if the firer is right handed. The GP FA has not yet been mass produced, as Fabrique National awaits a large-scale order before taking what otherwise may be a big risk. The gun is a little longer and more streamlined than the GP Mle 35, has an enlarged ambidexterous safety lever and allegedly looks not unlike the CZ vz.75 (qv). Its sights are fixed and the current finish is grey parkerising.

Cal: 9mm Parabellum. Otherwise generally as GP Mle 35, except Trg: SDA, exposed hammer.

Grande Puissance Modèle 1935 (GP or HP 35)

Military and police pistol. Like the Colt-Browning and the Parabellum, little remains to be said about this gun, currently (1983) serving with police and military forces in more than 65 countries. Once records have been released by the manufacturer (FN remains understandably coy), the GP Mle 35 will be regarded as the most influential handgun ever made. It is a refined version of the Colt-Browning M1911, developed by John Browning and the FN Bureau d'Études during the early 1920s and allegedly inspired by publication in the early 1920s of a French declaration to re-equip. Ironically, the French have been one of the few nations never to have used the GP. US Patent 1618510 was sought at the end of June 1923 but not granted until February 1927. The gun retains the Colt-Browning breech-lock—two partly circumferential lugs on the barrel engaging recesses cut in the undersurface of the slide—but the action is controlled by a

Above: an early version of the FN GP Mle 35, dating from 1924. **Below:** the 'Competition' derivative of the GP. *(Photographs by courtesy of FN.)*

cam finger, depressed by a transverse bar, rather than a pivoted link. The patent illustrations differ greatly from the production model, perfected by FN soon after Browning's death in 1926 though mass production was delayed until 1934-5. The finalised GP (sold to Belgium, Latvia and Estonia prior to 1939) holds the dubious distinction of being the only gun to be made and used by *both* sides during the Second World War: in addition to the hundreds of thousands made for the Wehrmacht in the German-occupied FN factory, Inglis of Toronto made many more for the Chinese, Canadian, British and other armies towards the end of the war. The action is operated by short recoil, there is a single-action trigger system with an exposed hammer, and fixed or tangent leaf back sights. The standard chambering is the 9mm Parabellum rather than the larger and more powerful American 0.45in ACP, rarely favoured in Europe. One important by-product

was an increased magazine capacity which inspired the modern obsession with large, staggered or double column magazines. The GP has attained a justifiable reputation for rugged dependability and though many 'improved' military handguns have since appeared, none has even so much as loosened FN's hold on the world markets. Some guns have simply disappeared, but more than a few of the others have either been based on the GP or, in cases such as the new Hungarian FÉG (qv), simply blatant copies! Even the Cambodian insurgents of the 1950s, the Cao Dai, paid FN the compliment of copying the GP. Its several modern derivatives are discussed separately. The standard guns now feature blued finish, tangent-leaf back sights, chequered polyamide grips and an optional lanyard ring on the base of the butt. They are also often marketed under the brandname 'Captain'.

Cal: 9mm Parabellum (7.65mm Parabellum has been discontinued). Mag: detachable box, crossbolt catch on frame behind trigger. Mag cap, rds: 13. Trg: SA, exposed hammer. Wt, oz/gm: 31.7/900. Loa, in/mm: 7.9/200. Brl, in/mm: 4.7/119. Rf: 6 R. Sft: radial lever on left side of frame behind grip, up to safe; magazine safety system; inertia firing pin; half-cock notch on hammer.

Variants of the GP Mle 35

Numerical designations applied to the GP series have included:

1001 9mm Parabellum chambering, parkerised and sealed, with fixed sights and a lanyard ring on the butt. Also known as the Vigilant (qv).
1101 As above, but chambering the 7.65mm Parabellum (discontinued).
1002 A version of 1001 without the lanyard ring. 9mm Parabellum.
1102 A version of 1101 without the lanyard ring. 7.65mm calibre, but now discontinued.
1003 9mm Parabellum, black (ie, blued) finish, with lanyard ring. Another variant of the Vigilant.
1103 A 7.65mm calibre version of the 1003.
1004 A version of the 9mm Vigilant with black finish but lacking the lanyard ring on the butt.
1104 Model 1004 in the smaller 7.65mm calibre, no longer available.

2001 9mm calibre, parkerised and sealed, with a tangent-leaf back sight and the back strap slotted to receive the shoulder stock. This is currently the standard GP, often known as the Captain.
2101 A 7.65mm Parabellum derivative of the Captain (above), now discontinued.
2002 A version of the 9mm Captain without the lanyard ring.
2102 Model 2002 in 7.65mm calibre. No longer available.
2003 A version of the 9mm Captain with black (ie: blued) finish and a lanyard ring.
2103 Model 2003 in 7.65mm calibre, no longer available.
2004 The 9mm Captain with black finish, but no lanyard ring.
2104 Model 2004 chambering the 7.65mm Parabellum cartridge; no longer available.

3001 The Sport Model (qv) with modified sights and chequered walnut grips. 9mm Parabellum calibre.
3101 A 7.65mm version of Model 3001.
3002 The de luxe version of the Sport pistol with Renaissance Grade engraving, specially selected chequered grips but no lanyard ring.
3102 Identical with the 3002 model, but in the smaller 7.65mm calibre and since discontinued.
3003 A de luxe version of the standard Sport pistol, Model 3001, with selected grips and high-polish finish.
3103 The selected de luxe Sport pistol chambering the smaller 7.65mm Parabellum cartridge. No longer available.

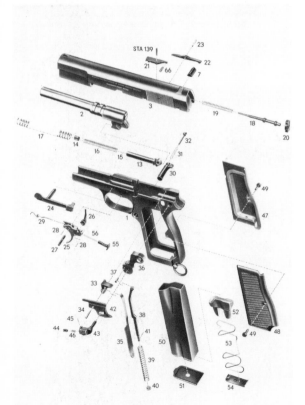

Above: *the standard GP Mle 35.* **Left:** *its components.* **Below:** *the Sport derivative. (All courtesy of FN.)*

Above: the FN International II, the company's finest target pistol. **Right:** the Medallist, International Medallist and Nomad pistols. (Courtesy of Fabrique Nationale.)

International II

Target pistol. This is the current top-of-the-range FN blowback target pistol, offering outstanding quality and performance. The features include a fully adjustable back sight, a trigger adjustable for travel and weight down to the UIT permissible minimum of 1000gm, distinct muzzle heaviness assisted by an auxiliary barrel weight, a comfortable stippled-walnut palm-rest target grip and a non-reflecting matt black finish. The trigger lever, however, is rather ostentatiously gold-plated.
Cal: 0.22in LR rf. Mag: detachable box, catch above left grip. Mag cap, rds: 10. Trg: SA, concealed hammer. Wt, oz/gm: 46.7/1325. Loa, in/mm: 11.7/298. Brl, in/mm: 5.9/150. Rf: 6 R. Sft: radial lever on left rear of frame; inertia firing pin.

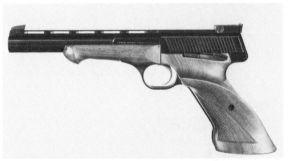

International Medallist ('Medalist' in USA)

Target pistol. This was the predecessor of the International (qv), bearing some resemblance to the Medallist but without the wooden fore-end and displaying less lavishly finished thumbrest-style grips. A ventilated rib still lies above the large-diameter barrel, however, and sights remain fully adjustable. The International Medallist has a shorter sight radius than the Medallist, conforming with ISU rules (8.6in against 9.5in). The trigger is fully adjustable; the finish, generally blue.
Cal: 0.22in LR rf. Otherwise generally as Challenger (qv), except Wt, oz/gm: 42.0/1190. Loa, in/mm: 10.9/277. Brl, in/mm: 5.9/150.

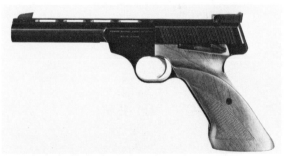

Medallist ('Medalist' in USA) or Match

Target pistol. This, once the most distinguished of FN's target pistols, has now been discontinued in favour of the International (qv). Its distinctive design incorporates a dry-firing device to allow practice without unduly harming the hammer mechanism or trigger assembly, which can be adjusted for pull and backlash. The back sight is micro-adjustable, while the other sight lies at the front of a ventilated rib on the large diameter 'bull' barrel. The wraparound thumb-rest style grip and fore-end—which camouflages the supplementary weights—are made from walnut specifically selected for the beauty of its grain. Blue has always been the

standard finish, but varying degrees of engraving, inlaying and damascening have been offered up to the Renaissance Grade. *Cal: 0.22in LR rf. Otherwise generally as Challenger (qv), except Wt, without auxiliary weights, oz/gm: 46.0/1305. Loa, in/mm: 11.3/287. Brl, in/mm: 6.7/170.*

Nomad

Target pistol. The American name for what is usually known as the 'Standard' (qv) or 'Target' model.

Sport Model (Modèle 3001)

General purpose pistol. This commercial derivative of the GP Mle 35 (qv) has a raised-blade front sight, a micro-adjustable back sight atop the slide ahead of the hammer, high quality blue finish and chequered walnut grips. A 'Sport de luxe' has been offered from time to time, differing primarily in the quality of finish and the style of the grips. *Cal: 9mm Parabellum. Otherwise generally as GP Mle 35.*

Sport Renaissance

General purpose pistol. This is a variation of the Sport (qv) distinguished by the acanthus-leaf 'Renaissance' engraving greatly favoured by FN, old silver or gold plate finish, a gold-plated trigger and specially selected walnut grips. As the engraving is invariably applied by hand, differences in detail will be encountered from gun to gun even though the basic pattern remains the same. *Cal: 9mm Parabellum. Otherwise generally as GP Mle 35.*

Standard

Target pistol. Known as the Nomad in the United States or as the 'Scheibe' or Target model in Europe, this is a more basic version of the Challenger (qv), mechanically identical and with comparable sights. The standard pistol, however, has Novadur plastic grips and may often be encountered with an alloy frame. *Cal: 0.22in LR rf. Otherwise generally as Challenger, except Wt, short barrel version, oz/gm: 34.0/965. Loa, in/mm: 8.9, 11.2/225, 283. Brl, in/mm: 4.5, 6.8/114, 172.*

Target

Target pistol. An alternative designation for the Standard (qv) FN blowback target pistol. It may also be encountered under the designation *Scheibe*, which means 'target' in German.

Vigilant, Vigilante

Military and police pistol. The Vigilant is a lightened version of the standard GP Mle 35 (qv) with an alloy frame, fixed open sights and parkerised finish. As a result of its weight, it exhibits greater apparent recoil than the gunmetal-framed GP. It may also be encountered with the standard Renaissance Grade de luxe finish. *Cal: 9mm Parabellum. Otherwise generally as GP Mle 35, but rather lighter.*

Modèle 125 (380 Auto in USA)

General purpose pistol. This is the last remaining survivor of the Browning blowbacks dating back, in this form at least, to the Modèle 10 developed in 1909. A larger version known as the Mle 10/22, with a lengthened slide and larger grip, appeared for military use in the early 1920s and has been developed in recent times into the Mle 125. The principal external features are the one-piece squared slide (the 10/22 had a two piece rounded slide), the prominent raised front and possibly superfluous micro-adjustable back sights, and the grip safety—once very common in pistols of this class, but now seen only rarely. The 125 is usually blued, with chequered black polyamide grips displaying the FN monogram, but various finishes can be obtained up to and including the Renaissance Grade. The 125 is a popular but rather dated design and doubtless will be replaced in due course by the Modèle 140 DA (qv). *Cal: 0.380in ACP (9mm Short). Mag: detachable box, catch on butt heel. Mag cap, rds: 9. Trg: SA, concealed striker. Wt, oz/gm: 25.4/720. Loa, in/mm: 7.0/178. Brl, in/mm: 3.8/96. Rf: 6*

R. Sft: radial safety on left rear of frame; magazine safety; grip safety on back strap.

Modèle 140 DA

General purpose pistol. This is, quite simply, a Belgian version of the Beretta Modello 81 (qv) with cosmetic alterations such as a closed FN-type slide and FN monogrammed polyamide grips (wood grips are optional). The 140 shares all the advantages of the Beretta, including very good quality, a multiplicity of safeties, an ambidexterous safety and (with a little alteration) magazine catches and large magazine capacity. As FN held 36 per cent of Beretta shares at the end of 1982, such collaboration is not altogether unsurprising, though FN, with a praiseworthy disregard of xenophobia, has always negotiated licences to make the best of designs such as the Israeli Uzi. *Cal: 0.32in ACP (7.65mm Auto), 0.380in ACP (9mm Short). Mag: detachable staggered column box, crossbolt catch on frame behind trigger. Mag cap, rds: 12 (0.32in), 13 (0.380in). Trg: DA, exposed hammer. Wt, oz/gm: 22.9/650. Loa, in/mm: 6.7/170. Brl, in/mm: 3.8/96. Rf: 6 R. Sft: rotary lever on slide, down to safe; magazine safety; inertia firing pin; half-cock notch on hammer.*

FÉG

Budapest, Hungary

UK distributor: Viking Arms Ltd, Summerbridge, Harrogate, North Yorkshire HG3 4BW, England. US distributor: none. Standard warranty: unknown (12 months?).

This state-owned firearms factory was formerly known as Fémaru es Szerszamgépgyär NV. Several types of pistol have been made, including the Tokagypt—a slightly modified Tokarev—and the Walam 48M, a minor modification of the Walther Polizei-Pistole. A closer copy of the PP, made for Hege-Waffen (see Hebsacker) of West Germany, was sold as the 'AP66'. Hege also disposed of large quantities of surplus Tokagypts under the brandname 'Firebird', the Egyptians understandably preferring the Beretta Brigadier.

Model FP

Military and police pistol. This is a copy of the GP Mle 35: so close a replica, in fact, that some parts are said to be interchangeable. The most obvious differences—apart from the markings—are the ventilated rib atop the slide and the revised contours of the back of the slide. The FÉG, well made of good material, usually exhibits good blueing and chequered hardwood grips. *Cal: 9mm Parabellum. Otherwise generally as FN GP Mle 35.*

Model R

Personal defence pistol. The external appearance of this small gun calls the Walther PPK to mind. However, the slide is more angular, the back of the grip is straighter and the shape of the web running back over the thumb is notably different. The slide is gunmetal; the frame, alloy. The bore is chromed, a method of prolonging its useful life that is very popular in the Eastern bloc, while the double-action trigger system incorporates a de-cocking lever and a safety system that disconnects the trigger if applied to an uncocked action. The unique dismantling system is controlled by a combination of a spring-loaded stud and radial lever on the left side of the frame ahead of the trigger guard. *Cal: 7.65mm Auto (0.32in ACP). Mag: detachable box, crossbolt catch on the left side of the frame behing the trigger. Mag cap, 6 rounds. Trg: DA, exposed hammer. Wt, oz/gm: 15.5/450. Loa, in/mm: 5.5/140. Brl, in/mm: 2.9/72. Rf: yes. Sft: Rotary 'barrel' catch on the left side of the slide above the grip; inertia firing pin.*

Above: the FN Barracuda revolver, the company's first entry into a market previously dominated by American companies such as Smith & Wesson, Colt and Ruger. (Courtesy of FN.)

Right: the FN Mle 40 DA pistol, derived from the Beretta Modelo 81. (Courtesy of FN.)

Below: a drawing of the FÉG pistol, a near-relation of the FN GP Mle 35. (Courtesy of Viking Arms Ltd.)

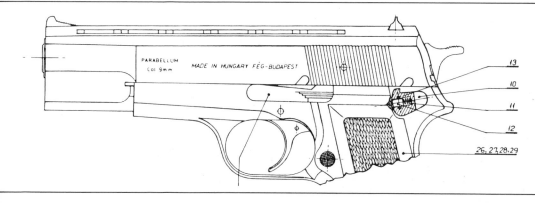

Freedom Arms

1 Freedom Lane, Freedom, Wyoming 83120, USA.

British agency: none. Standard warranty: lifetime.

This company now makes the 'mini-revolver' designed by Dick Casull, formerly made by two other independent US manufacturers—North American Arms and Rocky Mountain Arms. However, Freedom Arms existed *before* production of the Casull began in 1978 and the company appears to have been making black-powder long arms since the early 1970s.

FA-BG

Personal defence revolver. The Freedom Arms 'Boot Gun' is based on the FA-S (qv), from which it differs principally in barrel length, weight and the shape of the butt. The grips of the boot guns are generally black Velox, and are the squared Western rather than rounded bird's head style. The FA-BG was introduced in 1981.
Cal: 0.22in LR rf. Otherwise as FA-S, except Wt, oz/gm: 4.8/135. Loa, in/mm: 6.3/160. Brl, in/mm: 3.0/76.

FA-BG Magnum

Personal defence revolver. A more powerful version of the standard FA-BG, handling magnum rimfire ammunition. It is mechanically identical with the smaller gun, but has a substantially longer cylinder and frame.
Cal: 0.22in Magnum rf. Otherwise as FA-S, except Mag cap, rds: 4. Wt, oz/gm: 5.4/150. Loa, in/mm: 6.6/167. Brl, in/mm: 3.0/75.

FA-L

Personal defence revolver. A variant of the FA-S (qv) differing solely in barrel length.
Cal: 0.22in LR rf. Otherwise as FA-S, except Wt, oz/gm: 4.3/120. Loa, in/mm: 4.8/121. Brl, in/mm: 1.8/45.

FA-L Magnum

Personal defence revolver. Another variant of the Casull-designed mini-revolver, this is simply a lengthened version of the FA-L (qv) chambering magnum cartridges and thus appreciably more powerful.
Cal: 0.22in Magnum rf. Otherwise as FA-S, except Mag cap, rds: 4. Wt, oz/gm: 4.9/140. Loa, in/mm: 5.1/129. Brl, in/mm: 1.8/45.

FA-S

Personal defence revolver. This is the perfected 1977-8 version of the Casull mini-revolver previously made by Rocky Mountain Arms and North American Arms (qv). Its features include an inertia firing pin in the frame, a 'sure lock' cylinder axis pin, greatly improved lockwork and a longer butt affording a better handhold. The FA-S is very unusual by today's standards; though well made of ultra-modern materials, it is in the tradition of the deringers and sheath-trigger pocket revolvers of the nineteenth century. This, of course, is the secret of its charm. The finish is semi-polish stainless steel and the grips are Velox—a crackproof and chemical resistant synthetic ebony.
Cal: 0.22in LR rf. Mag: cylinder. Mag cap, rds: 5. Trg: SA, exposed hammer. Wt, oz/gm: 4.0/113. Loa, in/mm: 4.0/102. Brl, in/mm: 1.0/25. Rf: 6 R?. Sft: inertia firing pin; half-cock notch on hammer.

FA-S Magnum

Personal defence revolver. The FA-S Magnum is the standard gun, chambering a longer cartridge and consequently possessing a longer cylinder and frame. The guns are otherwise identical. The magnum cartridge gives surprising power for such a small and light revolver, though the muzzle blast is far from pleasant.
Cal: 0.22in Magnum rf. Otherwise as FA-S, except Mag cap, rds: 4. Wt, oz/gm: 4.8/135. Loa, in/mm: 4.3/109. Brl, in/mm: 1.0/25.

Below: left to right, top to bottom. The FA-M, FA-BG, FA-S and the FA-S in its 'belt buckle'. (Courtesy of Freedom Arms.)

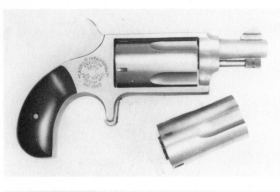

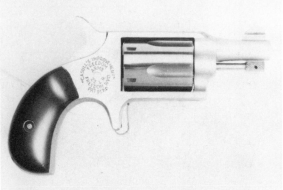

Comparachart: military pistols

The abbreviations are explained on pages 60-61.

This review of the most popular of the current big-bore military and police pistols is graded according to criteria as diverse as magazine capacity and the provision of ambidexterous safety catches. The final conclusions, however, must be personal and very subjective—even though there are points on which everyone will probably agree. There has been much debate about calibre, for example. One school of thought believes in the biggest possible bullet, with maximal stopping power but excessive recoil; the other, in a smaller cartridge with poorer 'knock down' capabilities but a better chance of accurately placed shots. Equally, experts divide over magazine capacity: should the gun carry as many cartridges as possible to minimise reloading time—the Steyr GB magazine contains 18—or remain with the more manageable, time-proven eight rounds still embodied in the Walther P5 or Heckler & Koch PSP? Large magazines do tend to give a bulkier grip, and weight distribution will change perceptibly as the cartridges are expended . . . but are thirteen, fifteen or eighteen rounds worth adjusting to the gradual change in balance? Of course, hostility also exists against guns that are made largely of synthetics or cheap-looking stampings; in the connexion, it is interesting to observe that the winner of the last series of US Army trials (another is apparently being undertaken at the moment) was the Beretta Modelo 92—very well made in traditional forged and machined style—rather than the avant garde H&K VP70Z.

The Comparachart cannot hope to be anything but a rough guide, opposing opinions being admissible. Interested readers are directed to the excellent *Combat Handguns*, by the late George C. Nonté, for assessments that occasionally differ. Major Nonté had unrivalled experience of his subject and championed the 0.45in ACP to the detriment of the 9mm Parabellum. But he was also a big, strong man; shooters of smaller physique or lower physical strength will find light, powerful guns such as the Detonics 45 and the Star PD (both chambering the 0.45in ACP) too much of a handful to be used effectively without considerable practice.

GUN	CAL	VFM	CONSTR	TECH	DISMNTL	PERF	MKT	PG
Astra A80	J1 J2 N T	••••	•••	••••	••••	••••	G E U	30
Benelli Modello 76	J1 J2	••••	••••	••••	••	•••	G E U	33
Beretta Modello 92	J1	••••	•••••	••••	••••	••••	G E U	37
Beretta Modello 92SB	J1	•••••	•••••	••••••	••••••	•••	G E U	37
Beretta Modello 51 Brigadier	J1	••••	•••••	••••	••••	••••	G E U	40
Bernardelli P 018	J1 J2	••••	•••••	••••	••••	•••	E	43
Colt Government Model	J1 N T	••••	•••••	•••	••••••	•••	G E U	53
Colt Combat Commander	J1 N T	••••	•••••	•••	••••••	•••	G E U	53
Colt Lightwt Commander	T	••••	•••••	•••	•••••	•••	G E U	54
FN GP Modèle 35	J1 J2	••••	•••••	••••	••••	••••	G E U	69
FÉG Model FP	J1	•••••	•••	••••	••••	•••••	G E	72
Heckler & Koch PSP (P7)	J1	••••	•••••	•••••	••••	•••••	G E U	88
Heckler & Koch P9S	J1 T	••••	•••••	••••••	••	•••	G E U	89
Heckler & Koch VP70Z	J1	••••	•••••	••••••	••••	••••	G E U	91
Llama Modelo VIII	N	•••	•••	•••	•••••	•••	G E U	99
Llama Modelo IX-A	T	•••	•••	•••	•••••	•••	G E U	99
Llama Modelo XI	J1	•••	•••	•••	•••••	•••	G E U	99
Llama Omni	J1 T	••••	•••	•••••	••••	••••	G E U	100
Navy Arms Mamba	J1 J2	••••	••••	••••	••••	••••	G E U	110
Přesné CZ vz.75	J1	•••••	•••	••••	••••	•••••	G E U	114
SIG P210	J1 J2	••	•••••	••••	•••	•••••	G E U	128
SIG-Sauer P220	J1 J2 N T	••••	••••	••••••	••••	••••	G E U	128
SIG-Sauer P225	J1	••••	••••	••••••	••••	•••••	G E U	128
SIG-Sauer P226	J1	•••••	••••	•••••	••••	•••••	G E U	129
S&W Model 39	J1	•••	•••••	••••	••••	•••	G E U	135
S&W Model 59	J1	••••	•••••	•••••	••••	••••	G E U	135
S&W Model 439	J1	••••	•••••	•••••	••••	••••	G E U	136
S&W Model 459	J1	••••	•••••	•••••	••••	•••••	G E U	137
S&W Model 539	J1	•••••	•••••	•••••	••••	••••	G E U	137
S&W Model 559	J1	•••••	•••••	•••••	••••	•••••	G E U	137
Star Modelo AS	N	•••	•••	•••	•••••	•••	E U	138
Star Modelo BS	J1	•••	•••	•••	•••••	•••	E U	138
Star Modelo 28 DA	J1	••••	•••	••••	••••	••••	G E U	141
Star Modelo 28 PDA	J1	••••	•••	••••	••••	••••	G E U	141
Star Modelo 28 PKDA	J1	••••	•••	••••	••••	••••	G E U	141
Steyr Model GB or Pi-18	J1	••••	••••	••••	••••	••••	G E U	144
Taurus PT-92	J1	•••••	••••	••••	••••	••••	U	150
Taurus PT-99	J1	•••••	••••	••••	••••	••••	U	150
Walther P1 (P38)	(C J1) J2	•••	•••••	••••	•••	•••	G E U	162
Walther P4	J1	••••	•••••	••••	•••	•••	G E U	162
Walther P5	J1	••••	•••••	•••••	•••	•••••	G E U	162

Industria Armi Galesi F.lli

Via Trento 10/A, Collobeato, Brescia, Italy.

British agency: none. US agency: formerly EIG Corporation. Standard warranty: unknown.

Very little is known about this manufacturer of shotguns and pistols, and the current status is uncertain. The guns are rarely seen outside Italy, though they were once relatively common in the United States prior to the demise of the distributor.

Pistola Automatica Modelo 9

Personal defence and general purpose pistols. The Galesi Fig have little in common with Rigarmi (Rino Galesi—qv), apart from a similar name and, one assumes, common ancestry. Their gun are all apparently variations on one theme; a simple rather elegant rounded-slide blowback available in a variety of shapes sizes and chamberings. Sights consist of a simple groove along the slide-top, quite adequate for their purpose

Cal: various, see table. Mag: detachable box, catch on butt hee. Mag cap, rds: between 6 and 8. Trg: SA, concealed striker. W Loa, Brl: see Table. Rf: yes, various types. Sft: radial lever on rea left side of frame, up to safe.

Nomenclature c.1965

Model	Cal.	Loa. (mm)	Wt. (gm)	Finish	Grips
503A	0.22in Short 0.22in LR 0.25in ACP	114	340	brown	black
503B	as above, except:			brown	white
504	as above, except:			chrome	white
505B	as above, except:			chrome, engraved	white
505EL	as above, except:			chrome, engraved, de luxe polish	mother-of-pearl
506A	0.22in LR	132	440	brown	black
506B	as above, except:			brown	white
507	as above, except:			chrome	white
508B	as above, except:			chrome, engraved	white
508EL	as above, except:			chrome, engraved and mirror polished	mother-of-pearl
512A	0.32in ACP	155	570	brown	black
512B	as above, except:			brown	white
513	as above, except:			chrome	white
514B	as above, except:			chrome, engraved	white
514EL	as above, except:			chrome, engraved and mirror polished	mother-of-pearl
515A	0.32in ACP	180	625	brown	black
515B	as above, except:			brown	white
516	as above, except:			chrome	white
517B	as above, except:			chrome, engraved	white
517EL	as above, except:			chrome, engraved and mirror polished	mother-of-pearl

Variations of the Galesi pistol, Modelo 9

Right: *The Hämmerli-Martini Modell 106 Free Pistol and its travelling case.*

Armi Renato Gamba SpA

Cassetta Postale 84, I-25063 Gardone Val Trompia (Brescia), Italy

British pistol agency: none. US agency: Interarms, 10 Prince Street, Alexandria, Virginia 22313, USA. Standard warranty: unknown.

Better known as a manufacturer of shotguns, Gamba forged links with Mauser-Jagdwaffen as a result of the production during the late 1970s of a special Gamba-Modell Parabellum.

RGP81

General purpose pistol. This is a modified Mauser HSc (qv), featuring refinements such as a 'combat' trigger guard, the front surface being recurved, and a large capacity staggered-row magazine. The sight channel in the top of the frame is matted and the long walnut grips are stippled rather than chequered. The guns are invariably blued.
Cal: 0.32in ACP (7.65mm Auto), 0.380in ACP (9mm Short), 9mm Police (9mm x 18mm). Otherwise generally as HSc, except Wt, oz/gm: 26.4/750. Loa, in/mm: 6.3/160. Brl, in/mm: 3.3in/84mm.

Below: *the Hämmerli-Martini Modell 106. (Courtesy Hämmerli)*

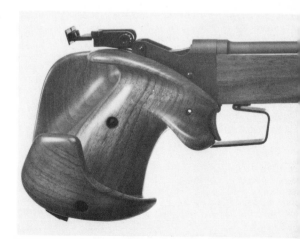

Hämmerli AG

Hämmerli AG, Jagd- und Sportwaffenfabrik, CH 5600 Lenzburg, Switzerland.

British agency: Springfield Firearms. US agency: no sole agency. Standard warranty: various.

This gunmaking business, best known for its high-grade target guns, was founded as a gunbarrel manufactory by Johann Ulrich Hämmerli in 1863. It was reorganised as Hämmerli & Hausch in 1876, the Hausch family interest continuing until Rudolf Hämmerli & Co. was formed in December 1928. Rudolf Hämmerli, grandson of the founder, continued the business until his death in 1946 whereafter control passed to a triumvirate of Thommen, Wackernagel and Bertschinger. The name changed first to Hämmerli AG and then to its present style. SIG (qv) purchased a controlling interest in 1971 and the business is now sometimes listed as SIG-Hämmerli; however, only the P 240 is rightly so-called. Hämmerli initially established a reputation for target rifles and Martini-system match pistols, the first of which was produced in 1933; in 1951, however, a licence to make the excellent Olympia-Pistole was negotiated with Fritz Walther, and Hämmerli has since produced several highly successful derivatives. These form the backbone of the Hämmerli product range, together with new Hämmerli-designed rapid-fire pistols and ultra-modern Martini dropping-block free pistols.

Hämmerli-Martini

Free pistols–a chronology

MP33	1933–49	0.22in LR rf or 0.22in Extra Long (Nr 7) rf. Octagonal barrel, 4R rifling, 3-lever set trigger. Trigger: 10–15gm. Walnut grips and schnabel-tip fore-end.
Modell 100	1950–56	As above, but 4R then 6R rifling; 5-lever set trigger and adjustable trigger let-off screw protruding from trigger lever. Trigger approx. 5gm. Butt and fore-end as MP33. First number 1001.
Modelle 101, 102, 103	1956–60	A variation of the Modell 100, with a heavy round barrel and improved trigger. The 101 has a matt browned finish; the 102, mirror polished. 0.22in LR rf only. The 103 was a de luxe version with an octagonal barrel and (often) de luxe grips.
Modelle 104, 105	1962–5	0.22in LR rf only. The gun has a tapered round barrel, a fore-end without the schnabel tip, a modified grip and a revised squared trigger guard. The 105 was identical mechanically, with an octagonal barrel and often featuring carved and decorated grips.

Modell 106

Target pistol. Introduced in 1965, this (together with its near relation, the Modell 107) was the last in a line of similar Martini dropping-block action Free Pistols dating back to the MP 33 of Rudolf Hämmerli & Co. All are operated by a lever whose tail protrudes beneath the grip, and cocked by a thumb-lever on the left side of the breech. The Modell 106 has a long, tapered round barrel with an interchangeable front sight retained by a catch spring. The fully adjustable back sight—with reversible, exchangeable notch-plate—lies on top of the breech above the heel of the adjustable sculpted grips. The gun is fitted with a five-lever set trigger of stupefying complexity . . . but undeniable efficiency, adjustable between 5 and 100 grams. A revised trigger was fitted from about 1967, distinguishable by the omission of the button projecting from the trigger lever. The grips and fore-end are high quality walnut. The Modell 106 was discontinued in 1971 in favour of the Modell 150, which exhibited a similar if modernised action. *Cal: 0.22in LR rf. Mag: none, single shot. Trg: SA, set-pattern, internal hammer. Wt, oz/gm: 45.8/1300. Loa, in/mm: NA. Brl, in/mm: 11.3/287. Rf: 6 R. Sft: inertia firing pin.*

Modell 107

Target pistol. Made between 1965 and 1971, this was simply a 106 with an octagonal barrel, or *Achtkantlauf*. These guns are often found in highly decorated form with elegant, chiselled and carved grips. The series was discontinued at number 33788. *Cal: 0.22in LR rf. Otherwise as 106 (qv).*

Modell 120 Sport pistol

Target pistol. This is a simplified single-shot Free Pistol, developed in 1969. Its bolt action is operated by a laterally moving lever on the left side of the breech. The SP120 has a simplified set-trigger which actuates a striker unit in the breechblock. The trigger lever is upside-down, the lever pivot (allowing lateral movement) lying at the *bottom* of the trigger guard. The lock-time is about 1.8 milliseconds, the trigger pull being a double pressure of 150-200 grams or a single pull of 40 to 100 grams. The new SP120 is guaranteed to place 10 shots within a 2.5cm circle at 50m. The back sight is fully adjustable with an exchangeable notch plate, and a broad blade-pattern front sight is mounted on a high ramp. The back sight can be moved longitudinally along the rear of the receiver. A short barrel SP120 has also been made in small numbers. *Cal: 0.22in LR rf. Mag: none, single shot. Trg: SA, concealed striker. Wt, oz/gm: 43.4/1230 (45.8/1300 with adjustable palm rest grips). Loa, in/mm: 15.7/400. Brl, in/mm: 10.0/254. Rf: 6 R. Sft: none.*

Modell 150

Target pistol. This extraordinary looking gun is a Free Pistol, a class characterised by extreme accuracy—and, it must be said, extreme oddity. The Modell 150 was developed to replace the excellent, but obsolescent Modelle 106 and 107 (qv); the action remains the popular Martini dropping block, opened by lifting the large lever at the left side of the breech, whereupon a cartridge can be inserted and the breech lever closed. The fully adjustable set-trigger mechanism is set by depressing the small cocking catch beneath the breech lever. Once cocked, the gun should not be treated violently if the trigger (which may be set from 5 to 100 grams) is set at its minimum pressure. The Modell 150 has a long slender unsupported barrel, below which lies the wood-encased auxiliary weight. The back sight is carried on an extension of the receiver, inset in the top of the grip to ensure the lowest possible sight time. The gun has a beautifully made semi-enveloping walnut grip and a large stamped-strip trigger guard. Two different trigger units may be fitted: the improved post-1979 version has a broad trigger lever running back to the rear of the guard, the older version being much more slender. The guaranteed accuracy is 10 shots within a 2cm diameter circle at 50m.
Cal: 0.22in LR rf. Mag: none, single shot. Trg: SA, concealed striker. Wt, oz/gm: 45.8/1300. Loa, in/mm: 16.9/430. Brl, in/mm: NA. Rf: 6 R. Sft: none.

Modell 152 Electronic

Target pistol. This is the 'high technology' Modell 150, in which the mechanical components of the trigger system have been replaced by an electromagnetic system powered by a 9V dry battery with a life of up to 5000 shots. This offers an extremely short lock time and an exceptionally light trigger pull—1.7±0.3 milliseconds or less, and 2-100 grams (±0.5 up to 20grams) respectively! Externally, the Modell 152 resembles the Modell 150 and shares its Martini action, the most obvious distinctive features being the on/off switch and two LEDs on top of the compensating weight housing immediately ahead of the breech. The red light is activated during the charging cycle of the trigger release condenser, while the green one glows only when the trigger is pulled. (**Note:** owing to the extremely sensitive 152 trigger system, *power should be switched off during loading*). The Modell 152 Electronic may be obtained with adjustable palm-rest or wraparound Martini-style grips, all in impeccably finished walnut.
Cal: 0.22in LR rf. Mag: none, single shot. Trg: electronic; striker fired. Wt, oz/gm: 46.9/1330. Loa, in/mm: 16.9/430. Brl, in/mm: NA. Rf: 6 R. Sft: none, apart from on/off switch.

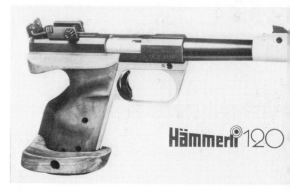

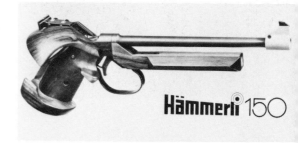

Above: *two versions of the Hämmerli Modell 120.* **Below:** *the Modell 150.*

The Hämmerli Modell 152 combines a much modified Martini-inspired dropping block action with a highly sophisticated electronic trigger, capable of such a light pull that it can virtually be blown to release the striker. (All pictures on this page by courtesy of Hämmerli GmbH.)

Modell 206 International

Target pistol. The 206 was the first of the true Hämmerli derivatives of what had previously been straightforward Walther Olympia-Pistolen—though the alterations were largely cosmetic and internal components remained practically unaltered. External appearance was quite different, however, as the contours of the frame, slide and barrel had been simplified and 'squared'. Each pistol had a well-fitted barrel weight which, especially in the later guns, often looked as though it were an integral part of the barrel (which it was not) The most important change concerned the back sight, which was placed atop a solidly built frame housing through which the slide reciprocated, removing the sights from the effects of slide wear; this also caused the slide retraction grooves—27 diagonal—to be moved ahead of the trigger guard. The 206 has an auxiliary weight beneath the muzzle, attached by two Allen-head bolts, and an extended muzzle (ahead of the front sight) displaying three diagonally-cut combination muzzle-brake and compensator slots. The Modell 206 trigger is adjustable between 350 and 1750 grams, though a special 'soft' or roll-over trigger could be obtained on request. Two versions of the Modell 206 were made between 1962 and 1968. One, chambering the 0.22in LR rf round, was destined for standard pistol competitions; the other, in 0.22in Short, being for rapid fire.
Cal: 0.22in short rf; 0.22in LR rf. Mag: detachable box, crossbolt catch on left frame behind trigger. Mag cap, rds: 6 (0.22in Short) or 8 (0.22in LR). Trg: SA, concealed hammer. Wt, oz/gm: 33.1 or 38.7/940 or 1100. Loa, in/mm: 12.5/318. Brl, in/mm: 7.1/180. Rf: 6 R. Sft: radial lever on left side of frame ahead of grip (down safe); inertia firing pin.

Modell 207 International

Target pistol. The Modell 207 is identical with its contemporary, the 206 (1962–8), apart from the substitution of adjustable French walnut palm-rest grips suitable for Free Pistol competitions. This made it longer, wider and slightly heavier, though identical in all other respects.
Cal: 0.22in Short rf or 0.22in LR rf. Otherwise as Modell 206, except Wt, oz/gm: 38.8 or 40.9/1000 or 1160. Loa, in/mm: 12.9/327.

Hämmerli-Walther

Olympia-Pistolen chronology

Modell 200	1952–62/3	0.22in Short or 0.22in LR rf. Virtually a copy of the prewar Walther, but with 20 slide retraction grooves and Hämmerli marks. Thumbrest grips and 3-part compensating weight. A three-slot muzzle-brake /compensator appeared in 1954, when the grip design changed. An adjustable trigger was fitted from 1956. In 1957, the two-slot brake appeared and the barrel weights were reduced to two.
Modell 201	1955–57	Identical with the Modell 200 with a three-slot brake, but a 24cm barrel and an adjustable trigger. The chambering could be changed from 0.22in LR (steel slide) to 0.22in Short (alloy slide) at will.
Modell 202	1955–7	A derivative of the Modell 201 (above) with adjustable palm-rest style grips, intended for free pistol competitions.
Modell 203	1956–8	This appeared after UIT rules had been revised following the 1956 Olympics. The guns usually have post-1957 two slot muzzle-brakes, revised compensating weights and slimmer than normal grips. A special version was made for the US market, differing principally in the sights.
Modell 204 'Amerikamodell'	1956–63	This was a revision of the basic Olympia-Pistole, with an omni-directional backsight and the trigger revised to conform with NRA rather than UIT rules. The hold-open was released by inserting the *next* magazine. Chambered only for the 0.22in LR rf, it had non-adjustable palm-rest grips.
Modell 205 'Amerikamodell'	1956–63	Intended for rapid fire, this was only available in 0.22in Short. Apart from the chambering and an adjustable palm-rest grip, it was identical with the 204.

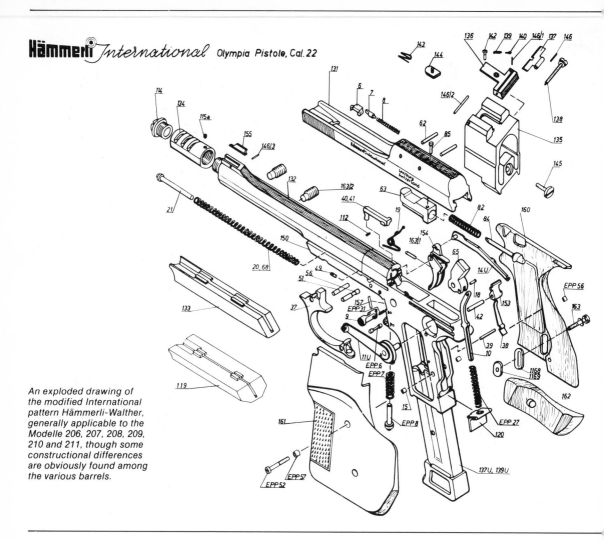

Hämmerli *International* Olympia Pistole, Cal. 22

An exploded drawing of the modified International pattern Hämmerli-Walther, generally applicable to the Modelle 206, 207, 208, 209, 210 and 211, though some constructional differences are obviously found among the various barrels.

Left: the Modelle 208, 209 and 211. *(Courtesy Hämmerli.)*

Modell 208 International

Target pistol. Dating from 1966, this modified 206/207 is destined for national rather than international 'standard pistol' competitions and therefore has no muzzle brake. Two different triggers—1000 or 1360 grams—are supplied to order; while a trigger-stop and hold-open, the latter actuated by a catch protruding above the left grip, are also fitted. Guns made before 1968-9 had standard Olympia-Pistole radial safety levers and crossbolt magazine catches, but the safety was then discarded and the magazine catch removed to the base of the butt. The 208 is an extremely popular design which betrays none of its prewar Walther origins and remains among the best in its class, and one of the most attractive and efficient. The slide, sight base and counterweights are generally sandblasted, the barrel and frame being immaculately polish-ground; the satin-finish walnut grips have an adjustable palm rest.
Cal: 0.22in LR rf. Mag: detachable box, catch on butt heel (see text). Mag cap, rds: 8. Trg: SA, concealed hammer. Wt, without auxiliary weights: oz/gm: 34.7/985. Loa, in/mm: 10.0/255. Brl, in/mm: 5.9/150. Rf: 6 R. Sft: see text.

Modell 209 International

Target pistol. The 209 was a specialised rapid-fire derivative of the Modell 208, also dating from 1966. The principal external differences are the addition of an extraordinary combination counterweight and muzzle-brake taking the form of a massive square block attached by two Allen-head bolts. It has a single large oblique-cut slot, rather than the three smaller slots found on some earlier guns. Six ports are bored vertically into the barrel above the front of the slide, acting in conjunction with the compensator to reduce the effects of 'jump' on firing and minimise the time needed to get the sights back on to target. Plugs can be screwed into the three ports nearest the breech to adjust to differing cartridge loadings. Pistols made in 1968-70 had three additional longitudinal slots cut in the barrel behind the front sight, which suggests that a tendency to pull to the left had become apparent. The trigger-pull may be adjusted between 350 and 750 grams. The Modell 209 has thumbrest-style walnut grips rather than the palm-rest version of the otherwise similar 210 (qv). The Modell 209 was short-lived, discontinued in 1970 in favour of the Modell 230—not a Walther inspired design.
Cal: 0.22in Short rf. Otherwise as Modell 208, except Mag cap, rds: 5. Wt, oz/gm: 35.3/1000. Loa, in/mm: 11.0/280. Brl, in/mm: 4.7/120.

Modell 210 International

Target pistol. This gun is a minor variant of the Modell 209 (qv), made between 1966 and 1970. It differs only in the substitution of adjustable palm-rest walnut grips for the plainer thumb-rest variety.
Cal: 0.22in Short rf. Otherwise as 209, except: Wt, oz/gm: 36.0/1020. Loa, in/mm: 11.8/300.

Modell 211 International

Target pistol. The Modell 211—introduced in 1966 and still in production—is simply a Modell 208 with plain thumb-rest grips rather than the adjustable palm-rest variety.
Cal: 0.22in LR rf. Otherwise generally as 208, but a little lighter.

Modell 212

Sporting pistol. This simplified Hämmerli International is intended for sporting use and, when fitted with the optional safety catch, to satisfy the competition regulations of the German DJV (hunting association). The 212 shares the action of the Modell 208, though its open-notch back sight is mounted on the slide; the sight blade insert can be changed to effect vertical adjustment, or moved laterally across the sight block. It has two sets of slide retraction grooves, one at the front of the slide and another directly above the grips. The result bears a surprisingly close resemblance to the prewar

Left: the Hämmerli-Walther Modell 207, one of the first of the International series.

Below: the comparatively modern Modell 212, a sporting derivative of the basic design that resembles the prewar 'Jägerausführung' or hunting pistol. *(Courtesy Hämmerli.)*

sporting version of the Walther Olympia-Pistole—the compass swinging a full circle in four decades.

Cal: 0.22in LR rf. Mag: detachable box, catch on butt heel. Mag cap, rds: 8. Trg: SA, concealed hammer. Wt, oz/gm: 31.0/880. Loa, in/mm: 8.50/215. Brl, in/mm: 5.0/126. Rf: 6 R. Sft: optional radial lever on left frame behind trigger (see 206); inertia firing pin.

Modell 215

Target pistol. The 215 is a Modell 208 (qv) with a little less care taken over finishing in an attempt to keep the costs down, not that the result is particularly inferior; as 'properly finished' Hämmerli pistols are quite simply among the best, this reduction in polishing operations must be placed in proper context. Hämmerli catalogues note that 35 of 665 machining and finishing operations have been eliminated . . . though none affects the functioning of the gun, which retains the flawless behaviour expected of its maker. Apart from its markings, the 215 may be distinguished by the simplified 'hump' on which the front sight is mounted.

Cal: 0.22in LR rf. Otherwise generally as 208 (qv).

Modell 230

Target pistol. This rapid-fire pistol has replaced the Modelle 209 and 210, which despite their great successes in the early 1960s steadily lost ground to guns such as the Walther OSP as the decade ran its course. The Modell 230 differs greatly from its Hämmerli predecessors, with a breechblock reciprocating inside the receiver, but lacks the gas-bleed ports of the later Modell 232. The 230—which was perfected in 1968 and introduced in 1970—has a fully adjustable trigger (from 240 to 300 grams) and its firing mechanism consists of a hammer-struck firing pin running through the breechblock. The system is cocked by retracting the grips behind the ejector port (ejection being leftward), but ahead of the massive back-sight housing at the extreme rear of the receiver. A Parabellum-style radial dismantling lever may be found above the trigger guard on the left side of the alloy frame. Most of the metal parts offer a non-reflecting finish, while the adjustable palm-rest grips are fine quality walnut.

Cal: 0.22in Short rf. Mag: detachable box, catch on butt heel. Mag cap, rds: 5. Trg: SA, concealed hammer. Wt, oz/gm: 43.8/1240. Loa, in/mm: 11.6/295. Brl, in/mm: 6.3/160. Rf: 6 R. Sft: inertia firing pin.

Modell 232

Target pistol. The 232, which dates from 1975, is a short-barrelled Modell 230—altering the balance—and has six gas-bleed ports (2 × 3) bored into the barrel through the upper angled sides of the approximately octagonal barrel sleeve. Sear engagement, trigger-pull weight, trigger travel and the trigger stop can also be adjusted; there are three different trigger lever sizes; the front sight blades and back sight notches may be replaced; and the entire gun can be field-stripped without tools. The Modell 232 may be encountered with adjustable palm-rest grips (232-1) or three sizes of the distinctive enveloping Morini pattern (232-2), through which the fingers of the firing hand must pass. The grips are always satin-finished walnut of impeccable quality.

Cal: 0.22in Short rf. Otherwise as 230 (qv), except Wt, oz/gm: 44.1/1250. Loa, in/mm: 10.4/263. Brl, in/mm: 5.1/130.

Below: *Hämmerli pistols model 214, 230 and (bottom) 232. (All by courtesy of Hämmerli GmbH.)*

Harrington & Richardson, Inc.

Industrial Rowe, Gardner, Massachusetts 01440, USA.

British agency: Viking Arms Ltd, Summerbridge, Harrogate, North Yorkshire HG3 4BW, England. Standard warranty: various.

H&R, as the company is better (and more conveniently) known, was founded in Worcester, Massachusetts in 1874. The principals were Gilbert Harrington, a nephew of Franklin Wesson, and William Richardson and traded first from Manchester Street and then Hermon Street in Worcester. H&R was sufficiently well-established to exhibit its revolvers at the Centennial Exposition in Philadelphia in 1876, and made its first double-action revolver two years later. A licence was concluded with Anson & Deeley in 1880, whereupon shotgun manufacture commenced. The company was reorganised in 1888 and opened new premises in Park Avenue and Chandler Street in 1894 and 1901 respectively. However, both founders died unexpectedly in 1897 and further reorganisation was undertaken in 1905. Small numbers of Webley & Scott automatics were subsequently made after a licence had been negotiated in 1909, but sales were poor and production ceased on the outbreak of the First World War; no automatics have since been made. H&R has since made huge numbers of competitively priced revolvers—hinged and solid frame alike—alongside rifles and shotguns. A move from Worcester took place in the mid 1970s and the current product range offers, to say the least, a wide range of options. The H&R revolvers are not always among the most elegant of guns, but are always well made and perform well; the auto-ejecting hinged-frame guns, seemingly increasingly unpopular on the American market in recent years, are among the most impressive.

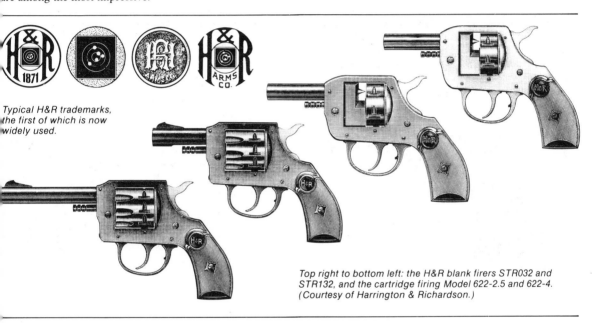

Typical H&R trademarks, the first of which is now widely used.

Top right to bottom left: the H&R blank firers STR032 and STR132, and the cartridge firing Model 622-2.5 and 622-4. (Courtesy of Harrington & Richardson.)

STR022

Starting revolver. This is a small, but quite well made starting revolver of very unusual type. It has a solid barrel without a bore, an odd cutaway ahead of the narrow cylinder, and an odd anvil-like projection in the gap thus created. This is designed—so H & R claims—to avoid the build up of fouling and over-powder which that often occurs in other designs. The cylinder is released by pulling its axis pin forward. The STR022 has satin blue finish and chequered black Cycolac grips.
Cal: 0.22in blanks. Mag: cylinder. Mag cap, rds: 9. Trg: DA, exposed hammer. Wt, oz/gm: 19.0/540. Loa, in/mm: NA. Brl, in/mm: 2.5/63. Rf: none, solid. Sft: half cock notch on hammer.

STR032

Starting revolver. The 032 is an 022 (qv) chambering a larger cartridge, which understandably reduces cylinder capacity. The finish remains satin blue (see also STR132), the grips being black Cycolac.
Cal: 0.32in S & W blank. Otherwise as STR022 (qv), except Mag cap, rds: 6.

STR122

Starting revolver. The STR122 differs from the STR022 (qv) in only one respect; the finish. This is H & R 'Hard-Guard', durable electroless matt nickel plate.
Cal: 0.22in blanks. Otherwise as STR022.

STR132

Starting revolver. A version of the STR032 (qv), featuring the electroless 'Hard-Guard' nickelled finish. Otherwise, it is the same as its companion.
Cal: 0.32in S & W blank. Otherwise as STR032 (qv).

Model 603

General purpose revolver. The Model 603 features H & R's swing-out cylinder, locked by longitudinal movement of the cylinder axis pin. This may be pulled forwards to allow the cylinder yoke to swing out to the left, whereafter the cylinder contents can be ejected by pressing the axis pin fully rearward. The H & R swing-out system is by no means as substantial as that of modern Colts or Smith & Wessons; however, it is more than adequate for the low-powered

cartridges normally chambered by H & R designs. Features include a flat-side heavyweight barrel, a fully adjustable 'Wind-Elv' back sight mounted on the frame above and ahead of the hammer, and a recessed muzzle to protect the rifling. The guns have 'Crown Lustre' blue finish and plain American walnut grips with inlaid H & R medallions. The most distinctive feature is the plain, unfluted cylinder.
Cal: 0.22in Magnum rf. Mag: cylinder. Mag cap, rds: 6. Trg: DA, exposed hammer. Wt, oz/gm: 35.0/995. Loa, in/mm: NA. Brl, in/mm: 6.0/152. Rf: yes. Sft: transfer bar hammer block; half cock notch on hammer.

Model 604

General purpose revolver. The Model 604 is a minor variation of the Model 603, except that the former has a heavyweight cylindrical 'bull' barrel. It remains a swing-out cylinder design with blue finish and American walnut grips. The gun chambers magnum rimfire ammunition and consequently displays a plain, unfluted chamber.
Cal: 0.22in Magnum rf. Otherwise as 603 (qv), except Wt, oz/gm: 38.0/1075.

Model 622

General purpose/personal defence revolver. This is the first solid-frame H & R gun, with its cylinder locked simply by a 'push-pull' or longitudinally moving axis pin. The Model 622 has fixed sights and what its maker terms a 'modified bulldog grip' . . . large enough for comfort and proper handling characteristics, but not bulky—though the abbreviated butt allows little more than three-finger grip. The finish is an attractive dual-tone Crown Lustre and satin blue (the latter on the frame only); the grips are chequered black Cycolac. The Model 622, available in two differing barrel lengths, offers good value at a very competitive price.
Cal: 0.22in LR rf. Mag: cylinder. Mag cap, rds: 6. Trg: DA, exposed hammer. Wt, oz/gm: 20.0, 26.0/565, 735. Loa, in/mm: NA. Brl, in/mm: 2.5, 4.0/63, 102. Rf: yes. Sft: transfer bar hammer block; half-cock notch on hammer.

Model 632

General purpose/personal defence revolver. This is a variant of the Model 622 (qv), differing only in calibre. Construction and finish parallel the smaller-calibre gun.
Cal: 0.32in S & W Long. Otherwise as 622 (qv).

Below: *Harrington & Richardson's Model 650 Western revolver. (Courtesy of H&R.)*

Model 642

Personal defence/general purpose revolver. The Model 642 is a modification of the Model 622, chambering Magnum rimfire ammunition and featuring a plain, unfluted cylinder. Its construction otherwise parallels the 622
Cal: 0.22in Magnum rf. Otherwise as Model 622.

Model 649 Convertible

General purpose revolver. The Model 649 is a Western-style design resembling in shape—but by no means in detail—the Colt Peacemaker. It has an angular frame with an instantly exchangeable large-capacity cylinder permitting an easy calibre change. A rod ejector lies along the right side of the barrel, expelling spent cases (or unfired rounds) through a laterally-swinging loading gate on the right side of the frame. A small open-notch back sight (adjustable laterally by driving it across its dovetail) lies above the cylinder, complemented by a large rounded blade at the muzzle. The 649 has a recessed cylinder, almost completely enclosing the case heads, and an efficient double-action trigger mechanism; coil springs are used throughout, which gives these guns—like most H & R revolvers—a reputation for reliability. Finish is dual-tone blue, offering Crown Lustre (polished) on barrel, cylinder and trigger guard, and satin on the frame. The two-piece grips are walnut-finish hardwood.
Cal: 0.22in LR or Magnum rf. Mag: cylinder. Mag cap, rds: 9. Trg: DA, exposed hammer. Wt, oz/gm: 31.0/880. Loa, in/mm: NA. Brl, in/mm: 5.5, 7.5/140, 191. Rf: yes. Sft: 'transfer bar' hammer block; half-cock notch on hammer.

Model 650 Convertible

General purpose revolver. This is a companion for the practically identical Model 649 (qv), distinguished by its 'Hard-Guard' electroless nickel finish
Cal: 0.22in LR or Magnum rf. Otherwise as 649 (qv).

Model 686

General purpose revolver. This gun is an obvious derivation of the Models 649 and 650, though several changes have been made and differing barrel lengths will be encountered. Though it remains, undeniably, a Western-styled exchangeable cylinder 'convertible' rimfire revolver with a rod ejector on the left side of the barrel and a hinged loading gate on the frame, several cosmetic changes have been made. The frame is attractively colour case-hardened, has a pronounced

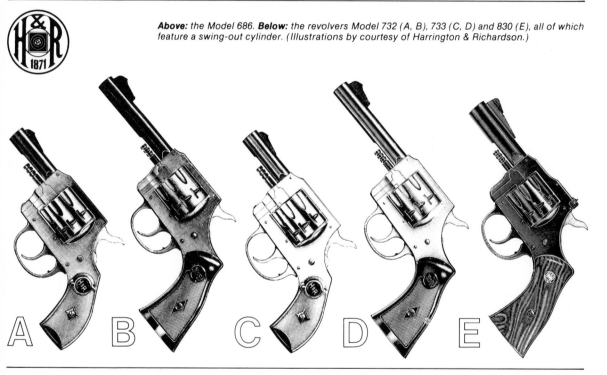

Above: the Model 686. *Below:* the revolvers Model 732 (A, B), 733 (C, D) and 830 (E), all of which feature a swing-out cylinder. (*Illustrations by courtesy of Harrington & Richardson.*)

'step' down towards the barrel and the adjustable Wind-Elv back sight above and ahead of the hammer. A revised square-contoured matted-ramp front sight graces the muzzle. The distinctive rearward extension of the trigger guard bow, similar to that of the Model 999, is another useful identification feature. Apart from the case-hardened frame and ejector rod housing, the parts are a well-polished blue; grips are walnut finished hardwood.
Cal: 0.22in LR or Magnum rf. Otherwise generally as 649 (qv), except Wt, oz/gm: 31.0, 32.0, 36.0, 39.0 and 41.0/880, 905, 1020, 1105 and 1165. Loa, in/mm: various. Brl, in/mm: 4.5, 5.5, 7.5, 10.0 and 12.0/114, 140, 191, 254 and 305.

Model 732

Personal defence/general purpose revolver. The Model 732, is available in two barrel lengths and Crown Lustre finish, is a comparatively simple and reliable H & R design in the axis-pin locked swing-out cylinder category. Its construction otherwise parallels the fixed cylinder Model 632 (qv). The longer barrelled gun has flared square-heel Western-style black cycolac grips; the shorter, abbreviated semi-rounded 'modified bulldog' grips. The latter is also available with wraparound walnut grips (Model 732WG), which undoubtedly aid handling; however, so far as holstering and pocketing are concerned, even the 732WG would benefit from a reduced, rounded hammer spur.
Cal: 0.32in S & W Long. Mag: cylinder. Mag cap, rds: 6. Trg: DA, exposed hammer. Wt, oz/gm: 23.5, 26.0/665, 735. Loa, in/mm: NA. Brl, in/mm: 2.5, 4.0/63, 102. Rf: yes. Sft: 'transfer bar' hammer block; half-cock notch on hammer.

Model 733

Personal defence/general purpose pistol. This is nothing but a variant of the Model 732 (qv) with electroless 'Hard-Guard' nickel rather than blued finish
Cal: 0.32in S & W Long. Otherwise as 732 (qv).

Model 826

Personal defence/general purpose revolver. This is an example of the H & R '800 series' chambering Magnum rimfire ammunition in a plain, unfluted cylinder. The guns share the basic all-coil spring design of the standard H & R swing-out cylinder system, described in greater detail under the Model 603 (qv). The Model 826 is only made with a large-diameter 'bull' barrel and comes with the Crown Lustre blue finish complemented by walnut grips. There are fixed ramp-

mounted front and fully adjustable 'Wind-Elv' back sights.
Cal: 0.22in Magnum rf. Mag: cylinder. Mag cap, rds: 6. Trg: DA, exposed hammer. Wt, oz/gm: 28.0/795. Loa, in/mm: NA. Brl, in/mm: 3.0/75. Rf: yes. Sft: 'transfer bar' hammer block; inertia firing pin; half-cock notch on hammer.

Model 829

Personal defence/general purpose revolver. This is a Model 826 (qv) chambering less powerful 0.22in LR rf ammunition, but with correspondingly greater cylinder capacity. The 829 is blued with walnut grips.
Cal: 0.22in LR rf. Otherwise as 826, except Mag cap, rds: 9.

Model 830

Personal defence/general purpose revolver. This is simply a Model 829 (qv) with electroless nickel Hard-Guard finish.
Cal: 0.22in LR rf. Otherwise as 829.

Model 832

Personal defence/general purpose revolver. This is another variant of the Model 826, chambering the 0.32in S & W Long and thus a better choice for self-defence—though the 0.22in LR rf version (Models 829, 830) is a better plinker. The Model 832 is blued with walnut grips.
Cal: 0.32in S & W Long. Otherwise as 826 (qv), except Mag cap, rds: 6. Wt, oz/gm: 29.0/820.

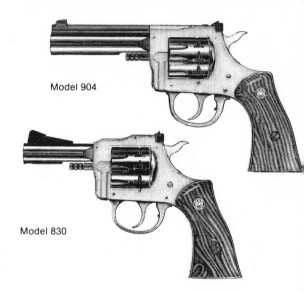

Model 904

Model 830

Model 833

Personal defence/general purpose revolver. The Model 833, in 0.32in calibre, may be distinguished from the otherwise identical Model 832 by its nickelled Hard Guard finish. The grips remain walnut with the inset H & R medallions.
Cal: 0.32in S & W Long. Otherwise as 832.

Model 903

General purpose revolver. The 903 is a variant of the Model 603 (qv) displaying the same swing-out cylinder construction and long, heavy flat-sided barrel. There is a 'Wind-Elv' back sight and the finish remains Crown Lustre blue; but there is a fluted rather than plain cylinder showing that the gun chambers the less powerful 0.22in LR rather than Magnum rimfire ammunition.
Cal: 0.22in LR rf. Otherwise as 603 (qv), except Mag cap, rds: 9.

Model 904

General purpose revolver. The 904 is a variant of the Model 903, and hence of the Model 603 (qv). Made in two barrel lengths, it may be distinguished by its heavyweight barrel— which is round rather than flat-sided. Both versions are blued with walnut grips, but the smaller is satin-finish and the larger polished Crown Lustre. The 6in (15cm) barrel gun is commonly encountered mounting the 3× H & R Model 435 Hunter/Silhouette telescope sight.
Cal: 0.22in LR rf. Otherwise as 603 (qv), except Mag cap, rds: 9. Wt, oz/gm: 32.0, 36.0/905, 1020. Brl, in/mm: 4.0, 6.0/102, 152.

Model 905

General purpose revolver. The 905 is a derivative of the Model 904, with Hard-Guard electroless nickel finish substituting for blue. The Model 905 may only be obtained with a 4in (10cm) barrel.
Cal: 0.22in LR rf. Otherwise as 4in barrel version of 904 (qv).

Model 929

Personal defence/general purpose revolver. The 929 is a derivative of the Model 732 (qv), chambering the less powerful 0.22in Long Rifle rimfire cartridge, which makes it a better choice for plinking but poorer for self-defence. The guns— made in three barrel lengths—are always blued.
Cal: 0.22in LR rf. Otherwise as 732 (qv), except Mag cap, rds: 9. Wt, oz/gm: 22.0, 26.0 or 28.0/625, 735 or 795. Brl, in/mm: 2.5, 4.0 or 6.0/63, 102 or 152.

Model 930

General purpose/personal defence revolver. This is simply a Model 929 with nickel rather than blue finish. The longest barrel option is not available.
Cal: 0.22in LR rf. Otherwise as 2.5 and 4.0in (63 and 102mm) barrel versions of the Model 929 (qv).

Model 949

General purpose revolver. The 949 is virtually identical with the Model 649 (qv) convertible Western-style rimfire revolver, but is supplied with a single cylinder chambering the 0.22in LR. An ejector rod lies under the right side of the barrel, operating in conjunction with a laterally swinging loading gate on the right side of the frame behind the cylinder. The Model 949 is blued, satin-finish on frame and polished on barrel and cylinder, while its grips are walnut stained hardwood.
Cal: 0.22in LR rf. Otherwise as 649 (qv), except Mag cap, rds: 9. Wt, oz/gm: 31.0/880. Brl, in/mm: 5.5/140.

Model 950

General purpose revolver. A derivative of the mechanically identical 949, the Model 950 offers nickelled Hard Guard rather than blued finish. *Cal: 0.22in LR rf. Otherwise as 949.*

Model 999 (Sportsman)

General purpose revolver. The Model 999 is now Harrington & Richardson's only hinged-frame revolver, a type of action much favoured in the earlier part of the century and incorporated on the single-shot H & R USRA target pistol. The mechanism, not unlike the much loved British Webley in some respects, is an auto-ejector and—consequently—much easier to load than a solid-frame design. The H & R has a sliding block system of locking the standing frame and barrel together rather than the Webley stirrup-catch, but has a similar inbuilt safety feature in that the hammer can only reach the encylindered cartridges when the breech-lock is properly closed. The popular and efficient Model 999 has adjustable sights, chequered walnut grips displaying the company medallions, Crown Lustre blue finish, weight-saving interrupted longitudinal flutes on the barrel rib, and a distinctive trigger guard with a rearward extension. The barrel of the larger gun bears the name SPORTSMAN.
Cal: 0.22in LR rf. Mag: cylinder. Mag cap, rds: 9. Trg: DA, exposed hammer. Wt, oz/gm: 30.0, 34.0/850, 965. Loa, in/mm: NA. Brl, in/mm: 4.0, 6.0/102, 152. Rf: yes. Sft: hammer-bar blocking mechanism; half-cock notch on hammer.

Below: *the Modell 999 Sportsman.*

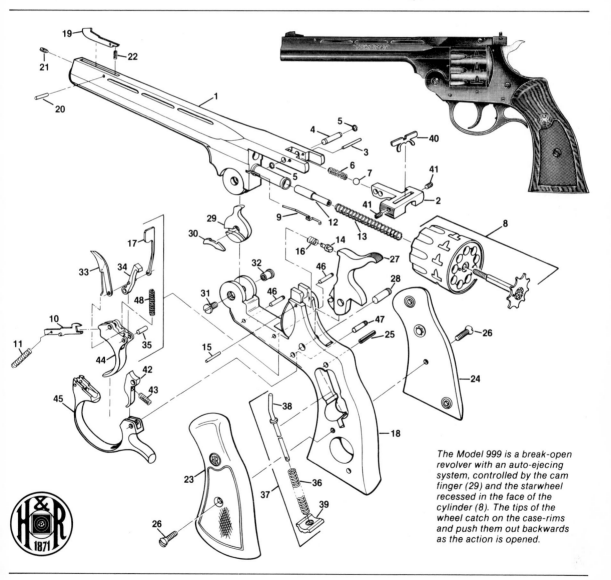

The Model 999 is a break-open revolver with an auto-ejecting system, controlled by the cam finger (29) and the starwheel recessed in the face of the cylinder (8). The tips of the wheel catch on the case-rims and push them out backwards as the action is opened.

Hebsacker GmbH

D 7170 Schwäbisch Hall, Steinbeisweg 42, West Germany.

British agency: no sole distributor, though the muzzle-loading Siber pistol may be obtained through the Mid Suffolk Gun Store, The High Street, Laxfield, Woodbridge, Suffolk. US agency: unknown.

Sometimes better known by the acronym Hege, the company trademark, Hebsacker specialises in distribution rather than manufacture. For example, large numbers of Hungarian made pistols have been sold in the last twenty years under designations such as Hege AP 66 and

Firebird (see FÉG). The best known of the current products is the Siber pistol described below.

Hege Siber

Percussion pistol. This is a re-creation of a percussion target pistol, offering extremely high quality, made by the Swiss gunsmith J.J. Siber in the mid nineteenth century. The gun is supremely elegant, with a walnut half stock featuring German silver mounts and a spurred trigger guard.

Hawes Firearms

15424 Cabrito Road, Van Nuys, California 91406, USA. No details were received from this company, an importer and distributor of Sauer and SIG-Sauer handguns in the 1970s and early 1980s, and its status remains uncertain.

Heckler & Koch GmbH

D-7238 Oberndorf/Neckar, Postfach 1329, West Germany

British agency: Parker Hale Ltd, Golden Hillock Road, Birmingham B11 2PZ, England. US agency: H&K (US), Suite 218, 933 North Kenmore Street, Arlington, Virginia 22201, USA. Standard warranty: 12 months.

Heckler & Koch is a comparatively new company, formed in 1949 after the Second World War had left the once-great Mauser empire in ruins. The principals in the new company were Edmund Heckler, Theodor Koch and Alex Seidel, all formerly Mauser employees. After building up a lucrative business making special-purpose machinery, H&K entered the smallarms field and by the 1970s numbered among Germany's largest arms manufacturers. In addition to the pistols described here, H&K makes a wide range of submachine-guns, automatic rifles, machine-guns and grenade launchers. The company has established a hard-won foothold in the vanguard of technological advance, something that is always evident in its pistols . . . which are always just that little bit innovatory.

P2A1

Signal pistol. The P2A1 is a successor to a tradition dating back way beyond the adoption by the Reichswehr of the Walther Heeresmodell signal pistol in 1926. It exhibits H&K's customary predilection for modern production techniques, however, and its synthetic grip/frame unit encloses the gunmetal operating parts. The breech is opened by depressing a catch on the rear left side of the frame, whereafter the muzzle may be swung downwards to elevate the breech and allow the auto-extractor to begin expelling the cartridge case. The barrel is simply snapped shut after reloading and the trigger system engaged by thumb-cocking the hammer. In addition to standard flare pistol ammunition, the P2A1 can project gas grenades once a discharger cup and a special sub-calibre barrel liner have been fitted.
Cal: 1.04in (26.5mm); 7.62mm NATO for insert liner. Mag: none. Trg: SA, external hammer. Wt, oz/gm: 18.2/520. Loa, in/mm: 7.9/200. Brl, in/mm: 6.1/155. Rf: none. Sft: none, though an interlock prevents firing before the breech is closed.

HK 4

General purpose pistol. The HK 4 was the first H&K pistol to gain widespread distribution. Though an uncomplicated blowback, it nevertheless offers several interesting features—not least of which is its four exchangeable barrel, mainspring and magazine units, which permit the firer to change calibres at will. The gun itself bears a resemblance to the prewar Mauser HSc, though the web at the muzzle, which houses the dismantling catch, is more austerely triangular than the Mauser's shallow curve. The double-action trigger system is allied with a Walther-type radial safety lever and a firing-pin safety lock. Replacing the barrels, the subject of German patent 1 453 916, presents little difficulty, though care must be taken to reverse the breechblock faceplate to suit the rimfire .22in round. The letter Z, for *Zentralfeuer*, or R, for *Randfeuer* appears on the front of the faceplate to suit each application respectively. The HK 4 is largely made of alloy, which conserves weight, and has a reputation for good quality.
Cal: 0.22in LR rf, 0.25in ACP (6.35mm), 0.32in ACP (7.65mm Short) and 0.380in ACP (9mm Short). Mag: detachable box in

butt, catch on butt heel. Mag cap, rds: 7 (9mm) or 8 (others). *Trg: DA, external hammer. Wt without mag, oz/gm: 16.9/480. Loa, in/mm: 6.2/157. Brl, in/mm: 3.3/85. Rf: yes. Sft: radial lever on left side of slide, turns up to 'fire'; firing-pin lock.*

PSP (Polizei-Selbstladepistole, P 7)

Military and police pistol. This gun is, perhaps, one of the most distinctive and most interesting of today's designs—and a veritable compendium of unique features. For example, it is a gas-delayed blowback in which a small part of the propellant gas is bled into a small cylinder beneath the chamber and, by acting on a piston, opposes the opening of the breech until the residual pressure has declined to a safe level. Though this idea is not new, having been tried previously in both Germany and Switzerland, H&K's is the first commercially acceptable system. The PSP trigger system also departs radically from what has previously been accepted as conventional. It must be loaded in the normal manner, by retracting the slide, but the inertia-type firing pin is only cocked when the firer squeezes the cocking lever. This replaces the front grip strap and is the subject of DBP 2 627 641. The 'squeeze' mechanism cocks the striker, whereafter pressure on the trigger fires the gun; alternatively, if pressure on the lever is released, the gun is de-cocked automatically and can be carried in perfect safety even though the chamber may be loaded. The result, so the makers claim, is a consistent trigger pull for the first *and* subsequent shots—something which cannot be achieved with conventional double-action systems. H&K has also paid considerable attention to balance and general handiness, and has even managed to fit a near-vertical magazine with the improved cartridge feed characteristics which this confers (despite the fact that the butt is angled at 110° to the bore axis). The PSP has rapidly attained a reputation for simplicity and ruggedness, and has been adopted by several West German federal authorities as the Pistole 7.
Cal: 9mm Parabellum. Mag: detachable box in butt, catch on butt heel. Mag cap, rds: 8. Trg: concealed firing pin. Wt without mag, oz/gm: 28.9/820. Wt with full mag, oz/gm: 34.6/980. Loa, in/mm: 6.5/166. Brl, in/mm: 4.1/105. Rf: polygonal, 7 R. Sft: crossbolt on rear of frame behind grip.

*Above left: the P2A1 signal pistol. **Above:** the HK4 and (**left**) its four exchangeable barrel/mainspring units. **Below:** the P9S. (All courtesy of Heckler & Koch.)*

P 9 and P 9S

Military and police pistol. This gun, the subject of DBP 1 578 392 for the locking system and DBP 1 805 399 for its frame, is a remarkable product of the designer Herbert Meidel. Roller-locking the breechblock during the infinitesimal period of ultra-high chamber pressure is not new; developed in Poland in the 1930s it has been featured by the German MG 42 and the Czech vz.52 pistol. Among the advantages claimed for it are reduction of apparent recoil, which offsets the complexity of construction, trigger and cocking systems. The roller-lock in fact falls into the 'semi-lock' or delayed

Automatic Pistol *Mod.* **P 9 S**

Cal. 9 mm / 19 Parabellum (Luger)

1 Front sight
2 Slide
3 Rear sight
4 Safety catch
5 Recoil spring
6 Barrel
7 Extractor
8 Locking rollers
9 Compression spring
10 Pressure pin
11 Compression spring for
   pressure pin
12 Locking catch
13 Pin
14 Compression spring
19 Firing pin spring
20 Firing pin
21 Spiral pin
22 Bolt head
23 Threaded pin
24 Compression spring
25 Catch bolt
26 Cylindrical pin
27 Bolt head carrier
28 Support
30 Raised head countersunk
   screw
31 Buffer housing
32 Plastic buffer
34 Barrel catch
35 Insert piece
36 Trigger spring
37 Trigger
38 Compression spring
40 Elbow spring
41 Sleeve

42 Catch lever
43 Spring for catch
44 Disconnector
45 Cylindrical pin
46 Pull bar
47 Trigger lever
48 Spring for pull bar
49 Indicator pin
50 Spiral pin
51 Hammer
52 Stop pin
53 Spring for disconnector
54 Axle for hammer
55 Threaded bush
57 Trigger guard
58 Receiver
59 Safety latch
60 Elbow spring
61 Cocking lever
62 Catch
63 Countersunk screws
64 Bearing plate, left
65 Angle lever
66 Intermediate lever
67 Bearing plate, right
68 Shank
69 Compression spring
70 Magazine catch
71 Grips
72 * Raised-head countersunk
   screw
73 Magazine housing
74 Follower
75 Follower spring
76 Support for follower spring
77 Magazine floor plate

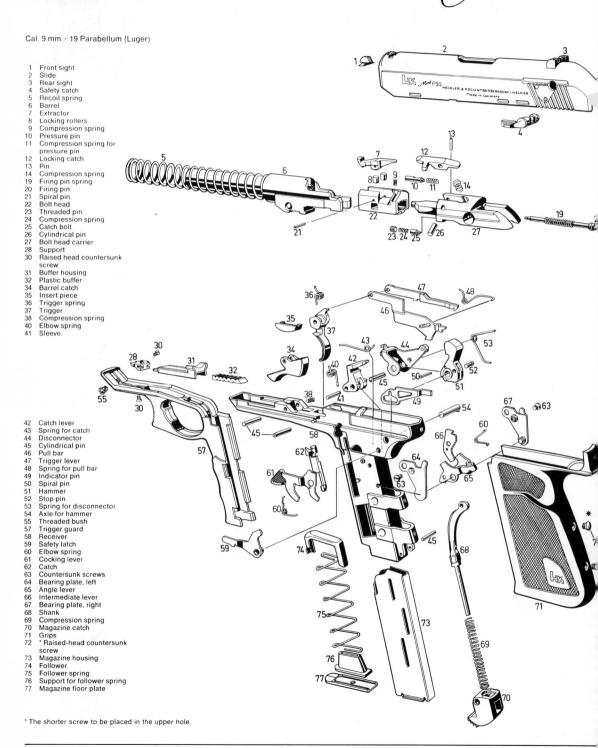

* The shorter screw to be placed in the upper hole.

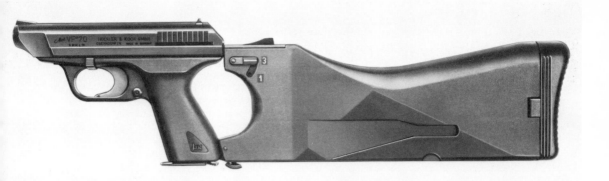

blowback category; barrel and slide recoil a short distance until the former is halted against a compressible synthetic buffer, then pressure drops far enough to permit the rollers to disengage and the slide and breechblock reciprocate alone. The P 9 series displays other unusual features: the rifling is Metford-type polygonal—once again old, but shared by no other modern weapon. It allegedly minimises gas cutting, while facilitating cleaning. A combined loaded-chamber indicator and extractor is fitted to the P 9, and a cocking indicator pin protrudes from the rear of the slide. The entire slide is enveloped in plastic, which is insensitive to extremes of temperature, and many minor parts are also synthetic. The P 9S has been quite successful but, for military and police use, the simpler P 7 is currently favoured though the P 9S remains the regulation handgun of the Saarland state police.
Cal: 9mm Parabellum. Mag: detachable box in butt, catch on butt heel. Mag cap, rds: 9. Trg: DA, concealed hammer (may be cocked with cocking lever). Wt without mag, oz/gm: 31.0/875. Wt with loaded mag, oz/gm: 37.3/1055. Loa, in/mm: 7.6/192. Brl, in/mm: 4.0/102. Rf: polygonal, 7 R. Sft: radial lever on left side of slide, moving downward to 'fire'; firing pin safety; inertia-type firing pin.

P 9 Sport (or P 9 Competition)

Convertible military and police/target pistol. This derivative of the standard P 9S features a different slide with a micro-adjustable back sight, and an extended barrel which bears a 6.7oz (190gm) muzzle weight. There is also a robust, if non-adjustable palmrest/thumbrest walnut target grip, stipple-roughened for added grip. The P 9 Sport is available in two patterns: (i) the gun, two magazines, adjustable sights, barrel weight and the anatomical grip, in a carrying case, or (ii) complete with an additional standard slide and wraparound plastic grip, which permits the sporting gun to revert to the normal 'combat' role merely by a swift change of major components. The P 9 Sport is sophisticated and performs well, but commands a price commensurate with its outstanding qualities.
All data as P 9 and P 9S, except Wt with barrel weight and full mag, oz/gm: 45.2/1280. Loa, in/mm: 9.1/230. Brl, in/mm: 5.5/140.

VP 70Z

Military and police pistol. Described by its maker as a 'robust and reliable self-defence weapon'—an apt description—the VP 70Z represents a move away from H&K's preoccupation with complex, elegant designs. A comparison between the sectional drawings of the P 9 and the VP 70Z emphasize this point: the latter, a blowback (though often misleadingly described in sales literature as recoil operated) shows the lengths to which simplification may be pursued. The gun is made largely of synthetic material, is striker fired and features a double-action-only trigger mechanism. It also has a remarkably large staggered-column magazine and the extractor, as in so many guns, doubles as the loaded-chamber indicator. Thought has been given to the dismantling procedure and the result is a simple, robust and effective design making as much use as possible of synthetic material and cost-cutting production techniques. The VP 70Z may be

accompanied by a holster-stock (protected by DBP 2 230 690) and incorporating a three-round burst firing device transforming the pistol into a rudimentary submachine-gun.
Cal: 9mm Parabellum. Mag: detachable staggered-column box in butt, catch on butt heel. Mag cap, rds: 18. Trg: DA only, concealed striker. Wt without mag, oz/gm: 29.0/820. Wt with full mag, oz/gm: 40.1/1135. Wt with full mag and stock, oz/gm: 56.1/1595. Loa, in/mm: 8.0/204. Loa with stock, in/mm: 21.5/545. Brl, in/mm: 4.6/116. Rf: polygonal, 7 R. Sft: crossbolt on frame behind trigger.

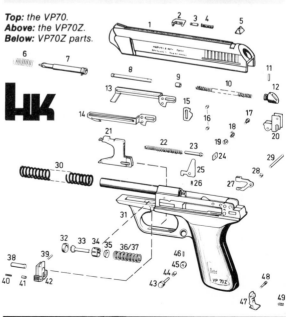

Top: the VP70.
Above: the VP70Z.
Below: VP70Z parts.

High Standard, Inc.

31 Prestige Park Circle, East Hartford, Connecticut 06108, USA

British agency: no sole distributorship, though the guns are commonly seen. Standard warranty: unknown.

Founded in 1926 to make gun barrel drills, High Standard entered the gun business—almost involuntarily—by purchasing the machinery on which the liquidated Hartford Arms & Equipment Company had been making the automatic pistols on which High Standard still relies. The pistols proved to be very successful, a silenced form being used during the Second World War by the SOE and the OSS, and the postwar commercial market equally lucrative. This was greatly helped by the steady and consistent improvement to the basic design, leading to the introduction of a number of blowback target pistols, the best of which will gain honours at the highest level. Revolvers have also been made in large numbers, though the centrefire Crusaders and Sentinels have been discontinued in favour of the rimfire.

Other High Standards

Model	General characteristics	back sight	grips
Supermatic Trophy, 1959	0.22in LR, brl 6.75, 8.0 or 10.0in	on breech	walnut
Supermatic Citation, 1959	0.22in LR, brl 6.75, 8.0 or 10.0in	on breech	laminated
Supermatic Tournament, 1959	0.22in LR, brl 4.5 or 6.75in	on slide	laminated
Supermatic Olympic, 1959	as Citation but 0.22in Short		
Olympic ISU, 1964	0.22in Short; stabiliser, wts, 6.75in brl	on slide	walnut
Olympic ISU Military, 1965	(107 series grip)		
Supermatic Trophy Military, 1965	0.22in LR, brl 5.5in bull or 7.3in fluted, military grip, adjustable trigger	on bracket	walnut
Supermatic Citation, 1965	0.22in LR, brl 5.5in bull	on slide	walnut
Supermatic Citation Military 1965	0.22in, brl 5.5in bull	on slide	walnut

Camp Gun Model 9893

Target and sporting revolver. This is High Standard's conventional yoke-mounted hinged cylinder revolver, a system described in greater detail elsewhere (see Sentinel). The Camp Gun chambers rimfire ammunition, featuring a longer barrel without the ejector-rod shroud distinguishing the larger calibre gun. The finish is blue; the grips, chequered walnut.
Cal: 0.22in LR or Magnum rf. Mag: cylinder Mag cap, rds: 9. Trg: DA, exposed hammer. Wt, oz/gm: 28.0/795 Loa, in/mm: 11.1/281 Brl, in/mm: 5.3/135 Rf: 6 R Sft: transfer bar; inertia firing pin. half-cock on hammer

Crusader

General purpose revolver. This interesting centrefire revolver, developed in 1975/6, appears to have disappeared again . . . or perhaps awaits a change in marketing policy, as its maker is currently committed to exclusively rimfire output. Notwithstanding its conventional High Standard yoke-mounted swinging cylinder design, it features refinements such as an eccentric-mounted hammer, obviating a transfer bar, and a 'geared' hammer and trigger mechanism in a quest for a smoother double-action trigger pull.
Cal: presumed to be 0.357in Magnum or 0.38in Special. Mag: cylinder. Mag cap, rds: 6. Trg: DA, exposed hammer. Wt, Loa, Brl: NA. Rf: 6 R. Sft: eccentric hammer mount (see text).

Custom Target Pistol 10-X

Target pistol. High Standard has a justifiable reputation as a manufacturer of very good rimfire target pistols—capable of competing against the best. The 10-X is currently the top of the line, descended from the Supermatic Citation and its similar relations. The 10-X has a heavyweight cylindrical 'bull' barrel and a micro-adjustable back sight mounted on a bridge at the back of the fame, through which the slide or breechblock reciprocates. The target-grade trigger features adjustments for pull weight and travel, while the hold-open works automatically once the last round has been chambered, fired and ejected. The finish is an immaculate blue; the military-style grip, chequered walnut. The grip straps are also stippled to facilitate handgrasp. Each gun is crafted individually and carries a five year guarantee.
Cal: 0.22in LR rf. Otherwise generally as Trophy.

Derringer Model

Personal defence pistol. This is an interesting modern adaptation of the Remington 'double derringer' of the mid nineteenth century. The result is a hinged double-barrel pocket pistol, one of whose major merits is flatness and ready concealability. The magnum rimfire cartridge is claimed to be as effective as the combination of an ultra-short-barrelled revolver and the 0.38in Special, as the derringer has a longer barrel. The 0.22in LR version is, however, is appreciably more economic to shoot and more favoured as a plinker. The High Standard Derringer is a popular 'desperation' weapon, or last resort. The Model 9193 is blued, chambering 0.22in LR ammunition, while the 9194 and 9306 chamber magnum cartridges; the former is blued and the latter nickelled. Models 9420 and 9421 duplicate the 9193 and 9194, but offer electroless nickel finish and chequered walnut grips.
Cal: 0.22in LR or Magnum rf. Mag: none, twin barrel. Trg: DA only, concealed hammer. Wt, oz/gm: 11.0/310. Loa, in/mm: 5.1/130. Brl, in/mm: 3.5/89 Rf: yes. Sft: None.

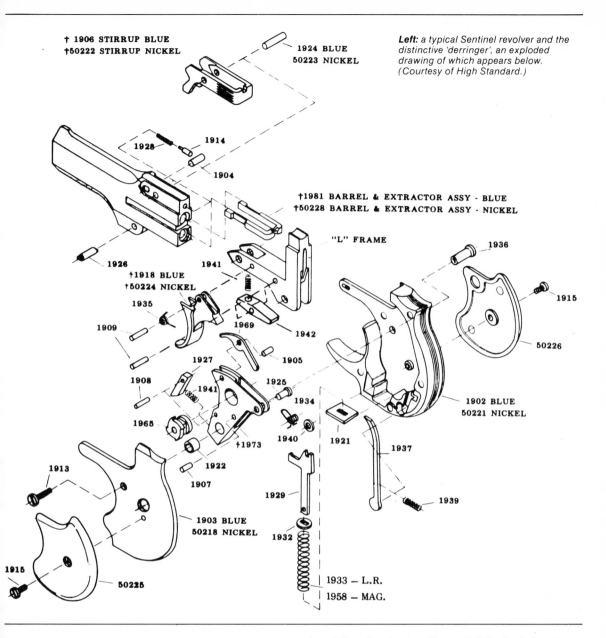

† 1906 STIRRUP BLUE
†50222 STIRRUP NICKEL

1924 BLUE
50223 NICKEL

Left: a typical Sentinel revolver and the distinctive 'derringer', an exploded drawing of which appears below. (Courtesy of High Standard.)

1928
1914
1904

†1981 BARREL & EXTRACTOR ASSY - BLUE
†50228 BARREL & EXTRACTOR ASSY - NICKEL

"L" FRAME

1936

1926
1941

†1918 BLUE
†50224 NICKEL

1915

1935
1969
1942

1909
50226

1905

1927
1908
1925

1941
1934
1902 BLUE
50221 NICKEL

1965
†1973
1940
1921

1922
1937

1913
1907

1929
1939

1903 BLUE
50218 NICKEL
1932

1915

50225

1933 — L.R.
1958 — MAG.

Duramatic M 101 (or 'Plinker')

General purpose pistol. Introduced in the early 1955, discontinued in 1963, and reintroduced a decade later—to use old stock?—this is a cheap and rather basic blowback held together by a large-head bolt upwards through the front part of the frame. The guard is a simple strip, while the plastic butt suffices as the entire grip unit. Despite its crude appearance, the M 101 performed quite adequately.
Cal: 0.22in LR rf. Mag: detachable box. Mag cap, rds: 10. Trg: SA, internal striker. Wt, Loa, Brl: NA. Rf: 6 R. Sft: Manual crossbolt at rear of frame.

Double Nine Model 9324

General purpose revolver. This pseudo-Western gun features a rather uneasy-looking amalgam of the conventional High Standard yoke-mounted swing-out cylinder and the traditional appearance of the Colt Peacemaker. The sights are adjustable, the cylinders exchangeable; the finish is blue; the

grips, plain surfaced walnut. The most distinctive feature is, perhaps, the prominent 'stepped' or reduced-width frame running forward from the vicinity of the trigger lever. The name arose from the provision of two nine-shot cylinders.
Cal: 0.22in LR or Magnum rf. Mag: cylinder. Mag cap, rds: 9. Trg: DA, exposed hammer. Wt, oz/gm: 32.0/905. Loa, in/mm: 11.0/281. Brl, in/mm: 5.3/135. Rf: 6 R. Sft: transfer bar assembly; half-cock on hammer.

High Sierra Model 9375

General purpose revolver. This is a Double Nine (qv) with a lengthened octagonal barrel. The backstrap and trigger guard are gold-plated.
Cal: 0.22in LR and Magnum rimfire. Otherwise as Double Nine, except Wt, oz/gm: 35.0/990. Loa, in/mm: 12.3/312. Brl, in/mm: 7.0/178.

Longhorn Model 9328

General purpose revolver. This Double Nine variant has a

greatly lengthened 'Buntline' type barrel—improving accuracy but greatly reducing handiness.
Cal: 0.22in LR and Magnum rf. Otherwise as Double Nine, except Wt, oz/gm: 38.0/1075. Loa, in/mm: 14.5/368. Brl, in/mm: 9.0/229

Sentinel Models 9390, 9392

Personal defence revolver. This is now available only in rimfire chanberings, reflecting a shift in company policy over the last few years from big-bore centrefire revolvers. Introduced in the late 1960s, the Sentinel once existed in four Marks:
i)   Mark 1. 0.22in LR rf, 9 shot, available with barrels of 2, 3 or 4 inches. There was a wraparound butt and fixed sights on all except the longest-barrel option.
ii) Mark 2. 0.357in Magnum, 6 shot, 2.3, 4 or 6-inch barrel. Fixed sights, squared butt.
iii) Mark 3. As Mk 2, but with adjustable back sights.
iv) Mark 4. A version of the Mk 1 chambering magnum rimfire ammunition.

It seems likely that the yoke-locking system was not as strong as that of centrefire rivals such as Colt, Charter Arms, Ruger and Smith & Wesson, and that High Standard chose to surrender this part of the market. The current Sentinels are, however, strongly made of first class material. The longer of the two variants (9392) has a full-length ejector shroud and a long, tapering front sight. The sights are fixed on the shorter model; adjustable, on the longer. The rounded chequered walnut butt affords an adequate grip and the result is an efficient gun, though lacking stopping power even in its magnum rimfire form.
Cal: 0.22in LR and Magnum rf. Mag: cylinder. Mag cap, rds: 9. Trg: DA, exposed hammer. (Data for 9892: 9890 has a 2in/51mm barrel) Wt, oz/gm: 27.0/765. Loa, in/mm: 9.1/231. Brl, in/mm: 5.3/165. Rf: 6 R. Sft: transfer bar assembly, inertia firing pin.

Sharpshooter Model 9210

Target pistol. This is the basic gun in the series culminating in the Custom Target 10-X (qv). It shares the standard blowback action and a large diameter 'bull' barrel. The principal external difference concerns the back sight, which is mounted on the slide above the rear of the grip. Other features include an 'instant barrel takedown' system controlled by a sprung latch protruding—rather surprisingly—from the front of the frame. This feature was introduced with the 104 sub-series, the squared or military grip with the 107. The result is one of America's most popular basic target pistols.
Cal: 0.22in LR rf. Mag: detachable box, catch on butt-toe. Mag cap, rds: 10. Trg: SA, concealed hammer. Wt, oz/gm:

42.0/1190. Loa, in/mm: 10.3/262. Brl, in/mm: 5.3/165. Rf: 6 R. Sft: radial lever protruding above the left side of the grip beneath the retraction grooves.

Sport King Model 9258, 9259

General purpose pistol. These, differing solely in barrel length, are the sporting derivatives of the High Standard target pistol series. Their principal distinguishing characteristics are a more rakish overall appearance, plain chequered ambidexterous walnut grips without thumbrests, and square notch back sights that can only be adjusted laterally.
Cal: 0.22in LR rf. Otherwise as Sharpshooter, except Wt, oz/gm: 39.0, 42.0/1105, 1190. Loa, in/mm: 9.3, 11.5/236, 292. Brl, in/mm: 4.5, 6.8/114, 173.

Supermatic Citation Model 9242, 9243

Target pistol. Often known simply as the 'Citation', this is an improved variant of the Sharpshooter—identical mechanically but with an improved adjustable trigger and a micro-adjustable back sight atop a frame-mounted bracket isolated from the detrimental effects of recoil, movement and wear. The Citation features exchangeable 'bull' or fluted barrels and an immaculate blue finish. Fittings such as the trigger lever and the safety catch are nickelled. A conversion unit, with a lightweight slide, transforms the pistol for rapid fire
Cal: 0.22in LR rf (a 0.22in Short rf conversion unit is available) Otherwise as Sharpshooter, except Wt, oz/gm: 45.0/1275. Loa, in/mm: 9.8, 11.6/250, 295 depending on barrel. Brl, in/mm: 5.5 (bull), 7.3 (fluted)/140, 185.

Supermatic Trophy Model 9247, 9248

Target pistol. This is practically identical with the Supermatic Citation but exhibits, in its maker's words, 'rather more flair'

Victor Model 9217

Target pistol. Dating from 1970, this represents the top of the High Standard line apart from the Custom Target, and is actually preferred by some shooters. It may be distinguished by a number of unique features; for example, its sights are mounted on a ventilated over-barrel rib rather than the fixed frame bracket. There is a full match quality trigger system, a series of auxiliary under-barrel weights and the barrel is noticeably flat-sided. The Victor has standard chequered walnut grips and a military style frame. The finish is blue, though items such as the trigger, safety and magazine release are rather ostentatiously gold plated.
Cal: 0.22in LR rf. Otherwise as Supermatic Citation, except Wt, oz/gm: 47.0/1330. Loa, in/mm: 9.6/244. Brl, in/mm: 5.5/14(

Left: the Victor competition pistol, a very popular and efficient design. *(Courtesy of Ian Hogg.)*

Hopkins & Allen

3 Ethel Avenue (PO Box 217), Hawthorne, New Jersey 07507, USA.

British agency: none. Standard warranty: 90 days.

The modern H&A has nothing do with the original company of the same name, founded in 1868 and wound up in 1917 when its factory was acquired, as part of the war effort, by the giant Marlin-Rockwell Corporation. The modern H&A was established in the early 1960s though the precise links (if any) with the Numrich Arms Corporation, under whose banner H&A percussion-ignition rifles have been sold, remains to be investigated; in addition, the Hopkins & Allen 'boot pistols' are apparently made *for* the company rather than by it.

Model 13 Boot Pistol

Percussion pistol. The much-loved H&A 'boot gun' is an extraordinary design, not only incredibly simple—the entire hammer and trigger assembly consists of two parts and two springs—but also a representative of a traditional underhammer ignition system. Production began anew in 1963. The Model 13 simply consists of an octagonal barrel hollowed at the rear to accept a solid end-cap into which the walnut grip is bolted. The mainspring doubles as the trigger guard, its forward tip slotting into the underhammer, and the back sight is a typically American 'buckhorn' pattern in which a spring-steel leaf is operated by a longitudinally sliding elevator. The ramrod is carried separately.
Cal: 0.45in. Mag: none, single shot. Trg: SA, exposed underhammer. Wt, oz/gm: 39.0/1105. Loa, in/mm: 13.0/330. Brl, in/mm: NA. Rf: 12 R?. Sft: none other than half-cock notch on hammer.

Model 13T Boot Pistol

Percussion pistol. This is an improved Model 13 (qv), with a tunnel-protected front sight and a wooden fore-end, containing the ramrod, which displays a small oval brass escutcheon on each side.
Cal: 0.45in. Otherwise as Model 13, except Wt, oz/gm: 41.5/1175.

Below: *the Model 13 Boot Pistol. (Courtesy Hopkins & Allen.)*

Interarms

10 Prince Street, Alexandria, Virginia 22313, USA.

British agency: Interarms (UK) Ltd, Interarms House, Manchester, England. Standard warranty: various.

Interarms was the brainchild of Samuel Cummings, who realised that a fortune could be made on the international arms market. Initially, the company contented itself with marketing guns made by others, but gradually acquired a number of well-known British gunmakers and set itself up as a manufacturer. The Interarms Manufacturing Division's principal factory was established at Midland, Virginia, in the 1970s, where the Virginian Dragoon revolvers and the Walther American pistol are now being made. Interarms still distributes many foreign handguns.

Virginian 22

General purpose revolver. This is a small rimfire derivative of the standard Virginian Dragoon, made in Europe by Hämmerli. The '22' features exchangeable cylinders, a fully adjustable back sight and both a transfer bar and a patented 'Swissafe' hammer block. Stainless steel and blued finishes are available.
Cal: 0.22in LR rf, 0.22in Magnum rf. Otherwise as Virginian Dragoon except Wt, oz/gm: 38.0/1075. Loa, in/mm: 10.8/274. Brl, in/mm: 5.5/140. Rf: 4 R. Sft: 'transfer bar'; 'swissafe' hammer block; half-cock notch on hammer.

Virginian Deputy

General purpose revolver. This is simply a Dragoon (qv) with traditional fixed sights and a choice of blued or stainless finish
Cal: 0.357in Magnum, 0.44in Magnum, 0.45in Long Colt Otherwise as Virginian Dragoon, except Wt, oz/gm: 49.0, 50.0/1390, 1415. Loa, in/mm: 9.0, 10.0/229, 254. Brl, in/mm: 5.0, 6.0/127, 152.

Virginian Dragoon

General purpose revolver. This an attractive version of the Colt Peacemaker single-action revolver, featuring lockwork and a transfer bar protected by US Patent 3803741 of 1974. The most obvious recognition features are the laterally adjustable back sight immediately ahead of the hammer and

the 'humpback' top frame with a prominent single longitudinal flute above the cylinder. The Dragoon can be supplied in several barrel lengths: 5, 6, 7.5, 8.4 or a mighty 12in (127, 152, 191, 213 or 305mm). The overall lengths run between 9in and 16in, the weights from about 49oz to 54oz. Some guns have fluted cylinders, others are plain. All have American walnut grips. Some are blued and some stainless, others have colour casehardened frames; engraved and cased versions may also be obtained (6in or 7.5in-barrel guns only).
Cal: 0.357in Magnum, 0.41in Magnum, 0.44in Magnum, 0.45in Colt. Mag: cylinder. Mag cap, rds: 6. Trg: SA, exposed hammer. Wt, Loa, Brl: see text. Rf: 6 R? Sft: 'transfer bar' hammer block; inertia firing pin; half-cock notch on hammer.

Virginian Dragoon Silhouette Model

Target revolver. Developed in collaboration with the International Handgun Metallic Silhouette Association (IHMSA), this gun features a greatly improved back sight, adjustable both laterally and vertically, an undercut blade front sight, corrosion-resistant stainless steel construction and a heavy parallel barrel. It also has a unusually long 12in (305mm) sight radius to achieve accuracy fit to bowl over heavy metal silhouette targets at ranges up to 200 yards. The result is a powerful but fine-handling gun.
Cal: 0.44in Magnum. Otherwise as Virginian Dragoon, except Wt, oz/gm: 53.0/1505. Loa, in/mm: 14.5/368. Brl, in/mm: 10.5/267.

Walther American

General purpose pistol. This is simply a licence-built Walther PPK/S, in whose entry further information may be sought. The Walther American (PPK/S) is a combination of the Polizei-Pistole slide with the frame of the Kriminal-Polizei-Pistole, necessary because the genuine PPK was too small to be imported into the USA after the Gun Control Act of 1968 had become law. The Interarms gun currently offers a blued finish, but a stainless-steel version will appear in the course of 1983.
Cal: 0.380in ACP (9mm Short). Otherwise generally as Walther PPK/S (qv)

Iver Johnson's Arms, Inc.

Wilton Avenue, off South Avenue, Middlesex, New Jersey 08846, USA

British agency: none. Standard warranty: unknown.

Founded when Iver Johnson bought out his one-time partner, Martin Bye, in 1883, this company originally traded as Iver Johnson Arms & Cycle Company in Fitchburg, Massachusetts. Vast quantities of revolvers have since been made, including many incorporating the 'Hammer the Hammer' safety system designed by Andrew Fyrberg and patented in 1896 after a wait of three years—the inspiration, perhaps, behind the modern preoccupation with transfer bars. The importance of Johnson has declined greatly since commercial production began again after the end of the Second World War. Many revolvers were made as late as the 1970s, in addition to Western style guns imported from Uberti, but only the Pony and a line of small 0.22in LR and 0.25in ACP personal defence pistols are currently being made.

X300 Pony

General purpose pistol. First announced in 1978 but not mass produced until 1983, this looks very much like an American version of the small Echeverria-made Starfire. Though the general lines are reminiscent of the Colt Government Model, the Pony is a simple all-steel blowback. Its back sight is adjustable laterally, the grips are usually walnut and the finish may be blue, chrome or bead-blasted matt 'military'. A long spur runs backwards above the grip to protect the web of the firer's thumb from the hammer.
Cal: 0.380in ACP (9mm Short). Mag: detachable box, crossbolt catch on left side of frame behind the trigger. Mag cap, rds: 6. Wt, oz/gm: 20.0/565. Loa, in/mm: 6.1/155. Brl, in/mm: 3.0/76. Rf: yes. Sft: radial catch on the left rear of frame; inertia firing pin.

The last revolvers

Cadet (Model 55A or 55C). A solid framed gate-loading pattern with fixed sights. *Cal: 0.22in LR or Magnum rf, 0.32in S&W Long, 0.38in S&W Long. Mag cap, rds: 8 in 0.22in, 5 in the remainder (later changed to 6). Wt, oz/gm: 24.0/680. Loa, in/mm: 7.0/177. Brl, in/mm: 2.5/63.*
Rookie. This was a more powerful version of the Sportsman with a shorter barrel and fixed sights. *Cal: 0.38in Special. Loa, in/mm: 8.8/223. Brl, in/mm: 4.0/102.*
Sidewinder and Sidewinder S (Models 50 and 50S). These were solid-frame Western-style derivatives of the Sportsman, with rod ejectors on the right side of the barrel and loading gates on the right side of the frame behind the cylinder. The finish was blue or silver satin, while the S version had adjustable sights and a range of different grips. *Cal: 0.22in LR, 22/22 Magnum. Loa, in/mm: 10.0, 11.2/253, 285. Br, in/mm: 4.7, 6.0/120, 152.*
Snub (Model 67S). A short version of the Viking, described below, made in 0.22in LR, 0.32in S&W Long, 0.32in Colt New Police, 0.38in S&W Long and 0.38in Colt New Police. Its barrel measured 2.7in (69mm), making it 7in (177mm) overall.
Sportsman and Sportsman Target (Models 55A and 57A). These were the standard guns, longer versions of the Cadet—solid framed gate loaders with the 'Hammer the Hammer' safety system and the Flash Control cylinders with a rimmed front surface. The Target version has adjustable sights and thumb-rest grips. *Cal: 0.22in LR. Loa, in/mm: 9.5, 10.7/241, 273. Brl, in/mm: 4.7, 6.0/120, 152.*
Starter. This small solid-frame blank firer, very much like the Harrington & Richardson STR 022 and STR 032, handled 0.22in or 0.32in blanks. The most obvious feature is the prominent gap ahead of the ultra-short cylinder.
Swing-Out and Swing-Out Vent Rib. These were more modern designs with a cylinder swinging out to the left for loading. The de luxe barrel had a ventilated rib, there were adjustable sights and the finish was blue. The chamberings were 0.22in LR and Magnum rf, 0.32in S&W Long and 0.38in Special. The rimfire versions were six shot; the others, five. The standard barrels measured 2, 3 and 4in (51, 76 and 102mm), though the shortest of the 'vent ribs' measured 2.5in (63mm).
Trailsman (Model 66). This was a derivative of the Viking with a six-shot cylinder, plastic thumbrest grips and adjustable sights. *Cal: 0.22in LR rf. Loa, in/mm: 11.0/279. Brl, in/mm: 6.0/152.*
Viking (Model 67). This was an eight shot break-open revolver featuring a top-latch, as well as the patented 'Hammer the Hammer' feature. The sights were adjustable; the grips, walnut finished hardwood. *Cal: 0.22in LR rf. Wt, oz/gm: 30.7, 39.5/870, 1120. Loa, in/mm: 9.5, 11.0/241, 279.*

Iver Johnson Pony Pistol.
Available in .380 ACP
caliber. Blued, Nickel or
Military.

Above: three versions of the Iver Johnson Pony. *(Courtesy Iver Johnson.)*

Izhevskii Oruzheinyi Za'vod

Izhevsk, Udmursk Autonomous Republic, RSFSR, USSR.

Export agency: V/O Raznoexport, Kalaievskaia 5, Moskva K-6, USSR. British agency: Majex (UK) Ltd, 25 High Street, Egham, Surrey, England. US agency: none. Standard warranty: unknown.

Established as an ammunition factory in 1807, this government arsenal has made vast quantities of military smallarms since the middle of the nineteenth century, including rifles, machine-guns and other stores distinguished by a bow and arrow mark. Like the Tula factory (see TOZ), Izhevsk makes guns for the civilian market in peacetime—including a range of good quality target pistols. Because of erratic deliveries to the West, however, the guns are not common.

IZh-1

Target pistol. This gun is another of the Russian Olympic Free Pistols, its Martini-type dropping-block breech operated by a lever on the left side of the grip. The fully adjustable back sight lies on the top of the elegant, adjustable palm-rest style wooden grip/fore-end unit. Opening the breech extracts the cartridge and also cocks the striker; closing the lever releases the striker safety mechanism, after which the gun may be fired. The design of the pistol is credited to Lobanov and Pletskiy, and dates from 1962.
Cal: 0.22in LR rf. Mag: none, single-shot. Wt, oz/gm: 42.0/1190. Loa, in/mm: 17.1/435. Brl, in/mm: 11.5/292. Rf: yes. Sft: mechanical firing-pin lock; inertia firing-pin.

IZh-3

Target pistol. A variant of the IZh-1 (qv) differing principally in the design of the back sight and the wraparound-style grip.
Cal: 0.22in LR rf. Otherwise as IZh-1, except Wt, oz/gm: 44.5/1260.

IZh-HR30

Target pistol. The Izhevsk-made HR30 is one of the new generation of Soviet target pistols, a modern match pistol no doubt intended to replace the Margolins. It is a distinctive design not too dissimilar from the Sako convertible (qv). Massive, perhaps a little crudely finished, but efficient and reliable, the IZh-HR30 is a striker-fired automatic pistol with a non-reciprocating fully adjustable back sight and a markedly downward slanting trigger-guard bow. The trigger too, may be fully adjusted. The slide-retraction grips lie towards the front of the gun, as the position of the sculpted, adjustable wooden grips and the back sight prevent conventional placement. The guns generally come in fitted cases with a few accessories such as pin punch, oil bottle and an extra magazine.
Cal: 0.22in LR rf. Mag: detachable box, catch on magazine base. Trg: SA, concealed hammer(?) fired. Wt, oz/gm: 41.3/1170. Loa, in/mm: 10.6/268. Brl, in/mm: 6.0/152. Rf: yes. Sft: grip safety; inertia firing pin.

IZh-HR31

Target pistol. This minor variant of the HR30 is intended specifically for rapid-fire competitions. Consequently, it chambers the low-powered 0.22in Short rf round, has a conspicuous hand-stop running rearwards at the back of the grip, and a curious two-part muzzle-brake/compensator. Its barrel is appreciably shorter than that of the HR30, while the grips may be wood or synthetic.
Cal: 0.22in Short rf. Otherwise as HR30, except Loa, in/mm: 11.6/295. Brl, in/mm: 5.3/135.

Manufacturas Jukar SA

Chancha Zelay 7, Eibar (Guipúzcoa), Spain. The Spanish commercial directories list this company as a manufacturer and exporter of 'pistols'—believed to be muzzle-loaders, though no information has yet been elicited from the company.

Korriphila

Korriphila-Präzisionsmechanik GmbH, D 7900 Ulm/Donau, West Germany

UK agency: none. US agency: see American Arms & Ammunition Co. and North American Arms Co. Standard warranty: unknown.

Little is known about this company at the time of writing, other than the fact that it has been involved in the production of the Budischowsky-system pistols, the personal defence pattern of which, the TP 70, has been widely distributed in the United States of America. In 1982, Korriphila announced a new roller-locked military and police pistol.

Budischowsky TP 70

Personal defence pistol. This is a small blowback, well made of good material but otherwise unremarkable save for its double-action trigger system. The gun has fixed sights and is made of stainless steel. The grips are usually chequered walnut.
Cal: 6.35mm Auto (0.25in ACP). Mag: detachable box, catch on butt heel. Mag cap, rds: 6. Trg: DA, exposed hammer. Wt, oz/gm: 12.3/350. Loa, in/mm: 4.6/117. Brl, in/mm: 2.6/66. Rf: yes. Sft: rotary Walther-type catch on left side of slide beneath backsight; inertia firing pin.

Budischowsky HSP 701

Military and police pistol. This is a hesitation-lock design, only the prototypes of which have thus far appeared. The locking system apparently consists of a transverse roller under the breechblock, immediately behind the magazine well. Recoil moves the actuating finger (part of the slide) back until the roller can move up into the breechblock—whereafter the mechanism can open fully. The HSP 701 has a fixed barrel, and will probably shoot quite accurately; among its other

features are a double-action trigger mechanism, an adjustable back sight and a loaded chamber indicator pin protruding above the hammer.
Cal: 7.65mm or 9mm Parabellum, 0.38in Super Auto, 0.38in WC, 0.45in ACP. Mag: detachable box, catch on left side of frame behind trigger. Mag cap, rds: 7in 0.45in, 9 in others. Trg DA, exposed hammer. Wt, unladen, oz/gm: 34.9/990. Loa, in/mm: 7.2/183. Brl: 4.0/102. Rf: 6R. Sft: rotary safety on slide (?); inertia firing pin.

W. Korth

Waffenfabrik W. Korth, Ratzeburg/Holstein, West Germany

British, US agencies: none, but once imported into the latter by Eastern Sports International. Standard warranty: unknown, but believed to be 12 months.

Korth makes a number of quite superb revolvers, with a number of unusual (but not always advisable) features. The factory's output is apparently quite small, as the guns are rarely seen outside Germany.

Korth-Revolver

General purpose revolver. This gun comes in a number of different sizes and chamberings, from 0.22in LR rf up to 0.357in Magnum. The guns offer superb quality, in addition to features such as a full-length ejector shroud, ventilated over-barrel rib, fully adjustable sights, automatic ejection once the cylinder has been swung out of the frame, adjustable firing-pin strike and an adjustable trigger; probably the worst feature, though undeniably the most distinctive, is the cylinder release catch. This lies *alongside the hammer*, where it can caught accidentally during single-action fire.
Sportrevolver—0.357in Magnum, 6-shot cylinder, 6.0in/152mm barrel, weight 38.8oz/1100gm.
Randfeuer-Sportrevolver—as above, but in 0.22in LR rf. weight 42.3oz/1200gm.
Magnum-Randfeuer-Sportrevolver—available with exchangeable cylinders for the 0.22in Magnum and the 0.22in LR rf cartridges.
Combat-Revolver—0.357in Magnum, with a barrel measuring a mere 3.0in/76mm, and the weight reduced to 33.5oz/950gm. This is heavy by American standards, but the gun shoots well as a result of the extra weight. Its sights, however, are not as good as the 'quick draw' patterns associated with Smith & Wesson and other US manufacturers.

Llama–Gabilondo y Compañía SA

Portal da Gamarra 50 (PO Box 290), Vitoria, Spain

British agency: none. US agency: Stoeger Industries, 55 Ruta Court, South Hackensack, New Jersey 07606, USA. Standard warranty: believed to be 12 months.

Gabilondo y Cía was founded in Eibar in 1904, soon progressing to manufacture of the 'Radium' automatic pistol after large quantities of cheap revolvers had been made. The 'Ruby' pistol appeared in 1914, acquired in great quantity by the French Army during the First World War. Gabilondo initially recruited other contractors to ensure supplies of the Ruby, but the contract was then thrown open on a free-for-all basis and many lesser manufacturers joined in. The quality of their guns is variable, to say the least. The first true Llama pistol was developed in 1927, the Llama trademark itself appearing on automatics after 1931—the older Ruby being relegated to revolvers. The company moved in 1966 from Elgoibar (Guipúzcoa) to a new factory in Vitoria, where good quality pistols, revolvers and the licensed Franchi automatic shotgun are being made. The Gabilondo products are always well made of good material, though—apart from the Omni pistol—rarely display evidence of original thought. Most of the revolvers follow Smith & Wesson practice, while the locked-breech automatics are pure Colt-Browning.

Modelo III-A

General purpose pistol. This is the biggest of Llama-Gabilondo's Colt lookalike blowback automatic pistols, practically indistinguishable from the models XV and X-A

apart from bore diameter, magazine and calibre marks. The gun has a blued slide topped by a ventilated rib, interrupted by the ejection port and the adjustable back sight. The grips are normally chequered plastic, but a wide selection of de luxe alternatives are available—in addition to several chromed,

damascened and engraved finishes.
Cal: 9mm Short (0.380in ACP). Mag: detachable box, catch on left side of frame behind trigger. Mag cap, rds: 7. Trg: SA, exposed hammer. Wt, oz/gm: 23.0/652. Loa, in/mm: 6.3/160. Brl, in/mm: 3.7/94. Rf: yes. Sft: radial lever on left rear side of frame; inertia firing pin; grip safety.

Modelo VIII

Military and police pistol. This is a Llama Colt-Browning copy: well-made, though not of a quality comparable to the original American product. The most distinctive feature is the interrupted ventilated rib on top of the slide. An adjustable back sight lies ahead of the exposed hammer. The slide hold-open, manual and grip safeties, magazine release and general construction are pure Colt, apart from the loaded chamber indicator inlet in the top of the slide, and the tipping barrel/link locking system is used without modification. The rear contours of the slide, thumb web and backstrap housing

differ slightly from the prototype. The finish is generally good quality blue, while the grips are plain hardwood with an inset LLAMA monogram. However, a number of de luxe finishes are also available.
Cal: 0.38in Super ACP (9mm Largo). Otherwise generally as Model III-A, except Mag cap, rds: 9. Wt, oz/gm: 00.0/1185. Loa, in/mm: 8.5/216. Brl, in/mm: 5.0/127

Modelo IX-A

Military and police pistol. This is the largest variant of the basic Llama Colt-Browning, chambering the awesome 0.45in ACP. This reduces the magazine capacity, but, owing to less weight in the barrel (the bore is bigger!), the weight has dropped to 1100gm. The guns are usually blued with plain-surfaced hardwood grips, but special finishes may be obtained on special order.
Cal: 0.45in ACP. Otherwise as Model VIII, except Mag cap, rds: 7.

Left: *drawings of the engraved large-frame automatics, generally applicable to the models VIII, IX-A and XI.*

Modelo X-A

General purpose pistol. This is a short-butt diminutive of the Colt Government model, so far as its general appearance is concerned, though internally it is a simple blowback. The standard finish is a rich blue; the grips, chequered plastic with an integral thumbrest.
Cal: 7.65mm Auto (0.32in ACP). Otherwise identical with the Modelo III-A (qv).

Modelo XI

Military and police pistol. This is simply a derivative of the Modelo VIII chambering a different cartridge. In addition, the XI is usually found with chequered wooden grips.
Cal: 9mm Parabellum. Otherwise as Modelo VIII.

Modelo XV

General purpose pistol. The smallest gun in the series including the Modelos III-A and X-A, the XV is the poorest choice as a man-stopper—firing an ineffectual rimfire bullet—but is nonetheless the best plinker.
Cal: 0.22in LR rf.. Otherwise as Modelo III-A, except Mag cap, rds: 8.

Modelo XXIII Olimpico

Target revolver. This is based on earlier Llama revolvers, and in turn on conventional Smith & Wesson practices—side-hinged yoke-mounted cylinder, frame-side thumb latch and all. There are, however, several unusual features; the most obvious is the top-quality adjustable 'orthopædic' walnut grip, designed to allow the guns to lie as low in the hand as possible, though this makes thumb-cocking the hammer more difficult than normal owing to the additional upward protrusion of the grip. There is a micro-adjustable back sight, a ventilated barrel-rib and a web joining the undersurface of the muzzle to the ejector rod housing. The result is elegant, sophisticated and among the best of the European target revolvers.
Cal: 0.38in Special. Mag: cylinder. Mag cap, rds: 6. Trg: DA, exposed hammer. Wt, oz/gm: 40.7/1155. Loa, in/mm: 12.0/305. Brl, in/mm: 5.5/140. Rf: yes. Sft: inertia firing pin; half-cock on hammer.

Modelo XXVI

General purpose revolver. This is effectively a 'plinking' or general-purpose version of the Modelo XXIX, with standard grips and a more conventional ejector rod shroud stopping well short of the muzzle. The remainder of the gun is pure Smith & Wesson, but well made of good materials and offering better value than many other S & W copies.
Cal: 0.22in LR rf. Otherwise as Modelo XXIX, except: Wt, oz/gm: 38.8, 41.4/1100, 1175. Loa, in/mm: NA. Brl, in/mm: 4.0, 6.0/102, 152

Omni

Military and police pistol. This is Llama's latest product, a remarkable gun with advanced features bordering on unique. These include a roller-bearing mounted and special double-action trigger system, though the operating system is still based on the Colt-Browning tipping barrel/link. The Omni presents an angular slab-sided appearance which is a matter for personal taste. Its most recognisable features are the upward slope to the trigger guard and the exaggerated forward slope of the trigger lever, betraying its double-action capability. It is undoubtedly an unusual design, the first reviews of which have presented conflicting views. Some of its

Right: *the engraved and damascened versions of the Llama pistols–this is a standard large-frame pattern–often present a stunning and very colourful appearance.*

Above: *an engraved form of the standard Llama small frame automatic, generally applicable to the Models III-A, X-A and XV*

Right: two versions of the Llama Comanche revolver, one of the best and most widely distributed of its type to be made in Europe. The 0.22in LR version is generally marketed in the USA as the Comanche I, the centrefire version being known as the Comanche II. (All drawings by courtesy of Stoeger/Llama.)

...aunted features may prove to be less efficient than the accompanying literature now claims, or may be reappraised once widespread service has been seen, but it cannot be denied that the Omni presents an interesting alternative to its more conventional rivals. Three models currently exist:

Omni I. A double-action design chambering the 0.45in ACP, 200mm (7.9in) long with a barrel measuring 111mm (4.4in) . The magazine holds 7 rounds and the gun weighs in at 1,110gm (39.2oz).

Omni II. This 9mm Parabellum derivative, lighter than the Omni I at 1,055gm (37.2oz), offers a nine-round magazine.

Omni III. This is a variant of the 9mm Parabellum Omni II, identical apart from the large-capacity magazine (thirteen rounds) and weighing in unladen at 1,078gm (38.0oz).

Cal: 9mm Parabellum, 0.45in ACP. Mag: detachable box, catch on left side of frame behind trigger. Mag cap, rds: see text. Trg: DA, exposed hammer. Wt, Loa, Brl: see text. Sft: rotary barrel-type safety on left side of slide beneath the back sight, down to safe; inertia firing pin.

Modelo XXIX Olimpico

Target revolver. This is a Modelo XXIII (qv) chambering rimfire ammunition—making it a better choice for practice, or for shooters in disciplines where centrefire ammunition is not permissible. Owing to the greater metal content of the cylinder and small-calibre barrel, the rimfire gun is appreciably heavier than its centrefire cousin.
Cal: 0.22in LR rf. Otherwise as Modelo XXIII, except Wt, oz/gm: 46.4/1315

Comanche

General purpose revolver. This is another adaptation of the Smith & Wesson Magnum revolvers, offering good quality and finish but otherwise quite conventional. A ventilated rib lies above the barrel and the adjustable spring-steel back sight is dovetailed longitudinally into the top of the frame above the cylinder. The finish is usually a rich blue, while the chequered walnut grips display small LLAMA medallions. De luxe finishes can be obtained on request.
Cal: 0.357in Magnum. Mag: cylinder. Mag cap, rds: 6. Trg: DA,

exposed hammer. Wt, oz/gm: 35.6, 36.7/1010, 1040. Loa, in/mm: NA. Brl, in/mm: 4.0, 6.0/102, 152. Rf: yes. Sft: transfer bar assembly; inertia firing pin.

Martial

General purpose and personal defence revolver. Essentially similar to the more powerful Comanche (qv), this gun has a third barrel option and a much more slender grip. The construction of the two is otherwise much the same, with ventilated barrel ribs and adjustable back sights. The normal finish is blue with chequered walnut grips.
Cal: 0.38in Special. Otherwise as Comanche, except Wt, oz/gm: 30.0-35.6/850-1010. Loa, in/mm: NA. Brl, in/mm: 2.0, 4.0, 6.0/51, 102, 152

Piccolo

Personal defence revolver. This is based on the standard Llamas and thus on the Smith & Wessons. The most obvious features are the double squared projections on the trigger guard and the abbreviated smooth walnut grips. Chambering the 0.38in Special, the Piccolo represents both good value and an effective man-stopper.
Cal: 0.38in Special. Mag: cylinder. Mag cap, rds: 6. Trg: DA, exposed hammer. Wt, oz/gm: 22.7/645. Loa, in/mm: NA. Brl, in/mm: 2.0/51. Rf: yes. Sft: transfer bar assembly; inertia firing pin.

Scorpio

Personal defence revolver. This is comparable to the Piccolo, but is heavier, has a conventionally rounded trigger guard and offers chequered walnut grips. The operating system is pure Smith & Wesson.
Cal: 0.38in Special. Otherwise as Piccolo, except Wt, oz/gm: 28.0/800

Super Comanche

General purpose revolver. This enlargement of the standard Comanche (qv), has a lengthened heavyweight barrel and a more robust micro-adjustable back sight in a prominent housing above the frame, directly ahead of the hammer. The gun is sufficiently powerful to chamber the most powerful of magnum cartridges.

Cal: 0.357in Magnum, 0.44in Magnum. Otherwise as Comanche, except Wt, oz/gm: 48.0, 49.6/1365, 1405. Brl, in/mm: in/mm: 6.0, 8.5/152, 216.

Lyman Products Corporation

Route 147, Middlefield, Connecticut 06455, USA. Lyman is better known as a manufacturer of reloading equipment and excellent sights than as a distributor of handguns. However, quantities of Italian-made percussion revolvers and the 'Plains Pistol' have also been handled. No handgunner who loads his own ammunition should be without a copy of the indispensable Lyman *Reloading Handbook,* now in its 46th edition.

Manufacture d'Armes de Saint-Etienne

Saint-Etienne, France. This French government-owned arsenal, designed the French Modèle 1950 service pistol in the late 1940s, basing it on the Petter (ie: Colt-Browning) principles embodied not only in the earlier Mle 1935 but also in the Swiss SIG guns.

Manufrance

Manufrance SA, Cours Fauriel 31-57, F-42033 St Etienne Cedex, France. This company was once renowned for the famous Le Français pistol, many variants of which were made until, it is believed, the early 1970s. Single-shot bolt action pistols have also been made, such as the Mle 550 Populaire and the engraved Mle 556—6mm calibre guns with an overall length of 440mm and a weight of about 900gm (17.3in and 31.7oz respectively).

MAB

Manufacture d'Armes de Bayonne, Bayonne, France.

British, US agencies: no sole distributorships. Standard warranty: unknown.

This company, founded in 1921, was unable to supply material during research and background information remains somewhat sketchy. A range of good quality automatics has been made for many years, and a modified version of the largest, the hesitation blowback Modèle R Para, has been adopted by the French armed forces and some security agencies as the PA-15.

The blowbacks

Personal defence and general purpose pistols. These may be conveniently classed under a single heading, as they share not only similar appearance but also similar operation—though variety exists among hammers and grips. One gun (the GZ) was even made by a Spanish sub-contractor.

Modèle A. This was MAB's first gun, a simple personal defence pistol based on the pocket Browning of 1906. Chambering the 6.35mm Auto cartridge (0.25in ACP), the Modèle A is 4.6in (117mm) long, has a barrel of 2.1in (53mm) and weighs about 13oz (370gm) unladen. The detachable box magazine contains 6 rounds.

Modèle C. This gun features a mainspring concentric with the barrel, adapted from Browning practice, and a grip safety unit. Initially produced in 7.65mm Auto chambering only, a 9mm Short (0.380in ACP) version was added to the production line after the end of the Second World War. The gun is 6in (15cm) long, with a barrel of 3.2in (82mm) and weighs about 22.9oz or 650gm.

Modèle D. This is simply a larger version of the Modèle C with a 4in (10cm) barrel, a lengthened grip and an extra round in the magazine. 7.65mm Auto and 9mm Short chamberings will be encountered; the gun is 7.1in, 180mm, long with a barrel measuring 3.9in (10cm) and an unladen weight of 25oz (710gm).

Modèle F. This is a rimfire version of the basic MAB blowback, with an extremely well-raked grip and adjustable sights. When fitted with a 6in (15cm) barrel, it makes a passable low-grade target pistol. It measures 10.6in (270mm) overall and weighs 29oz (825gm).

Modèle GZ. This was an exposed-hammer version of the Modèle C, made in Spain by Echave y Arizmendi (Echasa) and so marked; production, however, ceased in the 1970s. Its dismantling system also differs from the remainder of the MAB series.

Modèle R. This enlarged Modèle D features an exposed hammer and modernised slide contours. Three versions are made: the *R Court* is a blowback chambered for the 7.65mm Auto cartridge, the blowback *R Longue* chambers the unique French 7.65mm Longue round, and the hesitation-locked *R Para* is sufficiently strong to fire the ubiquitous 9mm Parabellum. The three models differ in size, the R Longue measuring 7.5in (190mm) overall and weighing 26.5oz, or about 750gm. The R Para is appreciably larger and heavier.

Modèle PA-15. This is the French service designation for an enlargement of the Modèle R Para with a 15-round staggered column magazine. Like the R Para, it is locked by rotation of the barrel in much the same way as the old Savage. The PA-15 has an unladen weight of 38.8oz (1.1kg) and measures 9.6in (244mm) overall. A specialised target-shooting variant, the PAPF-1, has also been made.

NOTE. MAB pistols have been sold in the United States of America under the Winfield banner. These have often been given names such as *Le Cavalier, Le Gendarme* and *Le Militaire*—the models C, D and R Para respectively.

Manurhin

Manufacture de Machines du Haut-Rhin, Mulhouse-Bourtzwiler, Département Alsace, France.

British agency: Viking Arms, Summerbridge, Harrogate, North Yorkshire HG3 4BW, England. US agency: none. Standard warranty: unknown.

This well-known French gunmaker derives the greater part of its revenue from its machine-tools. However, a liaison forged with Walther in the early 1950s has led to a series of 'Manurhin-Walthers'—PP, PPK and several Sport derivatives—made prior to 1964, when the production machinery was returned to the Walther factory in Ulm/Donau. Manurhin has also been involved with the assembly of the Pistolen 38, apparently in deference to treaty restrictions. Production of the interesting, efficient and popular MR73 revolver, with some unusual features and a number of differing barrel/calibre options, began in the mid 1970s.

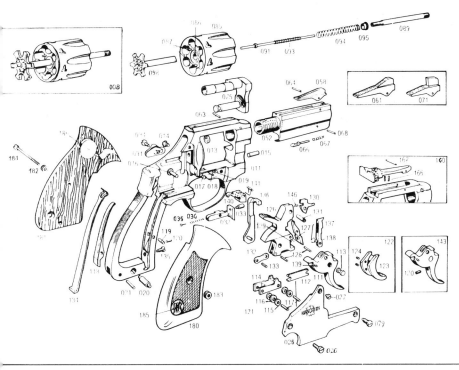

MR73

General purpose and sporting revolver. Developed in 1972, several variants of this gun (all sharing the same design) may be encountered, as tabulated below. The revolver has some unique features, not least of which is the trigger-spring bearing system—a patented combination of slider, roller bearing and leaf-spring claimed to give a smoother pull. The MR73 is obtainable with a fully adjustable back sight, dovetailed into the top of the frame, though the three shortest versions make do with a longitudinal groove and 'no-snag' front sights rather than the prominent blade of the sporting and target versions. All have side-swinging cylinders released by a Smith & Wesson type thumb-latch on the left side of the frame beneath the distinctive low-spur hammer. The guns are well blued, strongly made and have partially chequered wooden grips. Full-bore guns with an exchangeable cylinder for the 9mm Parabellum cartridge may also be obtained.

Model	Barrel in/mm	Sights front	back
MR73V	2.5/63	no snag blade	groove atop frame
MR73V	3.0/76	no snag blade	groove atop frame
MR73V	4.0/102	no snag blade	groove atop frame
MR73S	5.3/133	target blade	fully adjustable
MR73S	6.0/152	target blade	fully adjustable
MR73S	8.0/203	target blade	fully adjustable

MR73S versions are often encountered with broad, grooved auxiliary trigger shoes which can be attached by two short threaded bolts. The 'S' version also has an adjustable-travel trigger.
Cal: 0.22in LR rf, 0.22in Magnum rf, 0.32in S & W Long, 0.357in Magnum. Mag: cylinder. Mag cap, rds: 6. Trg: DA, exposed hammer. Wt, oz/gm: 33.5/950. Loa, in/mm: 9.3/235. Brl, in/mm: 4.0/102. Rf: 6 R. Sft: hammer-block safety arm.

Mayer & Söhne

D-5760 Arnsberg 1, Postfach 4340, West Germany.
Mayer makes a tipping-barrel rimfire revolver, little of which is presently known other than the fact that it may be obtained with barrels measuring 3in or 5in (7.6 or 12.7cm) and that stippled wooden or chequered plastic grips are optional. The gun is an inexpensive design, reflected in its largely alloy construction. The frame, which pivots in the manner of the British Webley, is locked by an upward moving hollow catch on the barrel extension. Mayer also makes a small range of starting pistols, similar to the older Reck models, under the tradename 'Perfecta'.

Mayer & Grammelspacher

Mayer & Grammelspacher, Diana-Werk, D-7550 Rastatt/Baden, Karlstrasse 34, West Germany

British, US agencies: none (apart from the airgun distributors). Standard warranty: 12 months.

Mayer & Grammelspacher is best known as a manufacturer of huge quantities of airguns (see *The Airgun Book*), but also makes an unusual signal pistol.

Diana SP 4

Signal pistol. This tipping-barrel design is based on some of the simplified guns procured for the Wehrmacht in the closing days of the Second World War. Made entirely of lightweight steel pressings, and generally found with a non-reflecting finish, the SP 4 has served many German police, border patrol and rescue services for more than twenty years. The breech is locked by a pivoting pressed-steel catch on the left side of the frame above the grip, a safety interlock prevents firing before the breech is closed, and there is an exposed ring hammer. The gun usually has chequered plastic grips, and a large lanyard hole through the heel of the butt.
Cal: 1.04in/26.5mm. Wt, oz/gm: 21.2/600.

Margolin

Maker and location unknown.

Export agency: V/O Raznoexport, Kalaievskaia 5, Moskva K-6, USSR. British agency: Majex (UK) Ltd, 25 High Street, Egham, Surrey, England. US agency: none. Standard warranty: unknown.

These are the work of a talented designer, Mikhail Margolin, blinded during the Second World War but responsible, nonetheless, for a remarkable series of target pistols. They are presumably made by a State organisation (one of the arsenals or a metalworking unit), but further details are not available.

MTs

Target pistol. This is the current Margolin rapid-fire target pistol derived from the models of 1949 and 1955. The original version was a plain gun, distinguished only by its reasonably sophisticated sights; the later one had a unique muzzle-brake/compensator, adjustable target-style grips and was available in 0.22in LR or 0.22in Short. The current version has a large muzzle-brake/ compensator with a single diagonally-cut slot. The MTs comes with auxiliary barrel weights, an optional palm rest and several accessories. It offers surprisingly good quality at a surprisingly low, state-subsidised price.
Cal: 0.22in LR rf. Mag: detachable box, catch on butt heel. Mag cap, rds: 6. Trg: SA, exposed hammer. Wt, without auxiliary weights, oz/gm: 37.0/1050. Loa, in/mm: 12.3/312. Brl, in/mm: 6.3/160. Rf: yes. Sft: radial lever on the left side of the frame; inertia firing pin.

MTs-2-3

Target pistol. Said to have been made in Tula and apparently designed by Mikhail Margolin in 1952, the MTs-2 and an improved derivative, the MTs-2-3, are single shot bolt-action free pistols with a sophisticated button-type set-trigger system adjustable down to 0.1oz (3gm). There is even an integral shock absorber in the trigger system. The mechanism is set by depressing the trigger-guard spur by about 10mm. The MTs-2-3 has a semi-wraparound wooden grip and a short schnabel-tip fore-end. It is a popular, efficient performer in competitions up to the highest international level. The gun is usually supplied with three front sights and three back sight bars of differing sizes.
Cal: 0.22in LR rf. Mag: none, single-shot. Trg: SA, set pattern, internal striker. Wt, oz/gm: 41.0/1165. Loa, in/mm: 17.3/440. Brl, in/mm: 11.6/295. Rf: yes. Sft: none, apart from an inertia striker.

MTs-55-1

Target pistol. This gun may have been a predecessor of the TOZ-35 (qv), or perhaps simply a modification of the MTs-2-3 'Vostok'. It has a set trigger with a lever of conventional form rather than the button pattern of the MTs-2-3, another Martini block-actioned free pistol. The trigger of the MTs-55-1 is also apparently set by moving the trigger-spur downwards. The gun has a semi-wraparound wooden grip and a short 'swamped' or reverse-tapered fore-end, from which the long, slender unsupported barrel extends forward.
Cal: 0.22in LR rf. Mag: none, single-shot. Trg: SA, set pattern, striker fired. Wt, Loa, Brl: no precise dimensions available. Rf: yes. Sft: inertia firing pin; automatic striker safety.

MTsU

Target pistol. This is a modification of the standard MTs (qv) adapted for rapid-fire competitions and thus chambering the 0.22in Short rf. It has a shorter barrel than the MTs, a detachable palm-rest and a projecting hand-stop at the top of the grip.
Cal: 0.22in Short rf. Otherwise as MTs, except Wt, without auxiliary weights, oz/gm: 35.0/990. Loa, in/mm: 11.1/282. Brl, in/mm: 5.1/130.

MTsZ-1

Target pistol. This is one of the oddest rapid-fire match pistols ever made; it caused such a sensation at the Melbourne Olympiad that the rules were rewritten to exclude it on grounds of excessive length. The gun is an upside-down version of the standard Margolin, with the barrel supported by a long sight-rib running forward from the top-feeding magazine and topsy-turvy breech. The hammer lies *under* the gun ahead of the trigger and the odd wraparound wooden grip.
Cal: 0.22in Short rf. Mag: detachable box, catch on left side of breech. Mag cap, rds: 5. Trg: SA, exposed hammer. Wt, Loa, Brl: precise dimensions unknown. Rf: yes. Sft: not known.

MB Associates

San Ramon, California, USA.

British agency: none.
Standard warranty: 90 days.

This business was founded by Robert Mainhardt and Art Biehl in 1960, to exploit any interesting new firearms projects they felt would make their fortune. The company's energies were subsequently devoted to the Gyrojet system—which enjoyed a brief heyday but then failed to overcome its inherent technical problems. The demise of the Gyrojet hastened the collapse of its backer.

MB Gyrojet Mark I Model B

Rocket pistol. This remarkable project reached fruition when a series of pistols and carbines appeared in 1965. The Gyrojet projectile is a tiny rocket, about 35mm long, containing its own propellant, a baseplate with four angled venturis (to obtain spin) and a conventional Berdan primer. The gun, therefore, is more accurately described as a hand held launcher, light and convenient, and displays exhaust ports along its barrel sides—which made the firing of the rockets a novel, spectacular and initially rather frightening experience. Ignition is accomplished by a backward-moving hammer, which slams each rocket back against a fixed firing pin and is then recocked as the projectile moves up the barrel. Poor accuracy associated with the guns may have been due, at least in part, to deformation of the projectile nose consequent on the hammer blow, but is more widely attributed to the unpredictable consumption of the propellant. The Gyrojet was an heroic failure; production ceased in the early 1970s, though launchers and rockets are still occasionally seen. The idea was not new—the Germans had tried it during the Second World War—and is sure to be resurrected as the search for caseless rounds continues. Short-barrelled and de-luxe, cased versions of the 'pistol' were also made in small numbers.
Cal: 13mm. Mag: in butt. Mag cap, 6 rockets. Trg: SA, internal hammer. Wt, oz/gm: 15.9/450. Loa, in/mm: 9.8/248. Brl, in/mm: 8.3/210. Rf: none. Sft: catch on rear of frame, up-safe.

MS Safari Arms

Little is known about the background of this American company, maker of the 'Matchmaster' (5in, 13cm barrel) and the 'Enforcer' (3.8in, 10cm barrel)—variations of the Government Model Colt-Browning automatic pistol featuring extended ambidexterous safety and slide release catches, a beavertail grip safety, adjustable sights and redesigned grips. They look a little strange, but there is no doubt that they improve on the standard Colts where practical pistol shooting is concerned. No distributor has yet been appointed in Britain, though small quantities of the Matchmaster and Enforcer are available through Coach Harness of Haughley, Stowmarket, Suffolk.

Above: *the unique Gyrojet pistol. (By courtesy of Ian Hogg.)*

Mauser-Jagdwaffen GmbH

D-7238 Oberndorf/Neckar, Postfach 1260, West Germany.

British agency: none. US agency: Interarms, 10 Prince Street, Alexandria, Virginia 22313, USA. Standard warranty: 12 months

Mauser, like so many of the German arms-making companies, finished the war in parlous state. Though the French operated the main Oberndorf factory on into May 1946, most of the facilities were then dismantled and destroyed. Gradually, Mauser rebuilt itself in the 1950s as the Bundeswehr required aircraft cannon and other heavy weapons, and, at the same time, created the sporting division—Mauser-Jagdwaffen. So far as pistols have been concerned, Mauser-Jagdwaffen has simply put two prewar designs back into production: the HSc pocket pistol, which remains among the best in its class, and the legendary Parabellum ('Luger'). New production of the latter started in the late 1960s, at the request of Samuel Cummings of Interarms, but despite preparation of many pocket, sporting and target-pistol prototypes, demand for the Parabellum was best satisfied by the production of limited numbers of commemoratives. The new HSc Super has been licensed to Renato Gamba in Italy, whose shotguns Mauser markets in Germany, while the Oberndorf plant concentrates on readying the locked-breech HSP for mass production. It seems pertinent to reflect that much of Mauser's pistol design expertise went to what is now Heckler & Koch in the late 1940s.

Modell HSc

Personal defence/general purpose pistol. This is an old but efficient design which remains in the vanguard of its class. The design history goes back to the HS, HSa and HSb of the mid 1930s, but production was interrupted in 1946 and only recommenced in the late 1960s. The HSc is a blowback with a double-action trigger and a multiplicity of safeties; externally very clean-lined, it may be distinguished by the streamlined rib running forward from the trigger-guard to the muzzle. Only the tip of the hammer spur projects from the back of the slide. A Walther-type rotary safety and de-cocking lever appears on the left side of the slide above the plain-edged walnut grip, chequered within a double-line border.
Cal: 0.32in ACP (7.65mm Auto), 0.380in ACP (9mm Short). *Mag:* detachable box, catch on butt heel. Mag cap, rds: 8 (0.32in), 7 (0.380in). *Trg:* DA, exposed hammer. *Wt, oz/gm:* 23.6, 23.3/670, 660. *Loa, in/mm:* 6.3/160. *Brl, in/mm:* 3.3/85. *Rf:* 6 R? *Sft:* rotary lever on the left side of the slide, up-safe; inertia firing pin; half-cock notch on hammer; magazine disconnector unit.

Modell HsP

Personal defence/general purpose pistol. This has been developed by Mauser, apparently to the design of the Swiss, Walter Ludwig, to give the company a competitor to the Heckler & Koch PSP (qv). The pistol is compact, but much less ambitious than the Heckler & Koch gun; recoil operated, it is locked by a pivoted arm on the barrel which is cammed out of engagement with a locking recess in the frame by cam tracks in the slide—a more complex and perhaps less sturdy solution than the modern versions of the Browning dropping link. A combination safety and de-cocking lever lies above the front of the left grip and a radial Parabellum-inspired dismantling lever above the trigger guard. The trigger is double action and the exposed tip of the hammer permits thumb-cocking. The gun is very traditionally made and blued, with chequered wood grips, and has a very distinctive rounded muzzle face. The HsP prototypes chambered the 9mm Parabellum, apart from one in 45 ACP (?) and another—a conversion unit—in 0.22in LR. Some have longer barrels and slides than that pictured here, or ovoid trigger guards.

The work necessary to convert the action to the 9mm Parabellum has apparently caused problems which have yet to be solved in their entirety, and the current status of the project is uncertain.

Cal: 9mm Parabellum. Mag: detachable box, crossbolt catch on left side of frame behind trigger. Mag cap, rds: 8? Trg: DA, exposed hammer. Wt, oz/gm: 26.5/750. Loa, in/mm: 6.5/165. Brl, in/mm: 3.3/85. Rf: 4 R? Sft: radial lever on left side of frame ahead of grip; inertia firing pin; half-cock notch on hammer.

Mauser-Parabellum 29/70

General purpose pistol. The Parabellum, 'Luger' or Borchardt-Luger pistol is too well known to require either a detailed explanation of its history—which has been recorded in several books—or of the events leading to the recommencement of Mauser production in November 1970, after many experimental prototype and pre-production guns had been made. Numbers, incidentally, began at 10.001001 (7.65mm, 1971 onwards) or 11.001001 (9mm, 1970). Several minor revisions to external parts were made during the early months, but the perfected 29/70 is a typical Parabellum of the Swiss 06/29 W + F pattern, itself derived from the 'neuer Art' of 1906. The action is powered by short recoil and is locked by the well-known rising toggle system. There is a curious laterally-acting sear, blocked by a grip safety until hand pressure releases it, and a radial dismantling catch ahead of the non-adjustable trigger. The frame is the standard Swiss pattern with a straight front-strap grip, and the front sight is dovetailed into a prominent block on the muzzle band. The safety lever head is chequered on production guns, though plain on some of the prototypes. The survival of the Parabellum is an anachronism, stemming more from sentiment rather than mechanical efficiency. The action has always been suspect with bad ammunition; the Parabellum trigger has never been capable of much refinement; and placing the back sight on the toggle link is inadvisable. In addition, the gun is extremely difficult, time-consuming and expensive to manufacture. Mauser recommenced production with high hopes, but despite initial successes the guns were understandably purchased by collectors and Lugerphiles rather than for serious combat use. The 29/70—often found with the trademarks and name of Interarms—was succeeded by the 06/73 (qv).

Cal: 7.65 or 9mm Parabellum. Mag: detachable box, crossbolt catch on left side of frame behind trigger. Mag cap, rds: 8. Trg: SA, internal striker. Wt, oz/gm: various. Loa, in/mm: 8.5, 9.3 or 10.4/215, 235 or 265. Brl, in/mm: 3.9, 4.7 or 5.9/100, 120 or 150. Rf: 4 or 6 R. Sft: radial lever on rear left side of frame, up to safe.

Mauser-Parabellum-Karabiner

Sporting pistol-carbine. This is a re-creation of the Parabellum carbines of the first decade of the twentieth century. It is a combination of the 06/73 Mauser Parabellum action with a greatly lengthened barrel, carrying an adjustable back sight above an elegant chequered walnut fore-end (which on some of the original guns contained an auxiliary recoil spring to permit more powerful ammunition to be used). The shoulder stock fits on to the T-lug on the back strap of the grip. The Parabellum–Karabiner is an anachronism, but it remains a beautiful, fascinating and desirable item.

Mauser Parabellum 06/73

General purpose pistol. The 06/73—an unofficial, but handy designation—is a modification of the 29/70 (qv), approximating more to the original Pistole 08 than to the Swiss W + F 06/29. There is a pronounced swell to the lower front grip-strap, a modified German-style safety lever and a barrel displaying an oblique-cut front sight mounted on a small saddle rather than a Swiss-style squared block. The two guns are otherwise identical, which means that the 06/73 possesses the grip safety omitted from the Pistole 08. The guns are usually blued, with chequered wooden grips, and

Mauser-Parabellum-Sport

Sporting pistol. This variation of the 06/73 Mauser Parabellum, intended for sport and target shooting, capitalises on excellent balance and handling characteristics, refined by the addition of a 'bull' barrel to give the muzzle heaviness demanded by target shooters (which does nothing for the Parabellum's good looks!). The first guns had round barrels, later ones have barrels with flattened sides. A fully adjustable back sight is attached to the back toggle link.
Cal: 7.65mm or 9mm Parabellum. Otherwise generally as 06/73, but appreciably heavier.

offer beautiful quality. Some guns have ivorine grips, others are chromed or satin-chromed; still others may be engraved or inlaid with gold. Presentation cases are often supplied for discerning clientèle. During the 1970s, Mauser became aware of the tremendous potential that lay in the Parabellum—unlike guns such as the Colt, which do not have the diversity of use or plethora of distinctive collectable models. The production of commemoratives can undoubtedly be continued for many years.
Cal: 7.65mm or 9mm Parabellum. Otherwise as 29/70.

Far left: *a short-barrelled version of the HsP.* **Left:** *a cased 29/70 Parabellum, with the 06/73 style front sight and safety lever knurling.* **Above:** *the Model 1902 Cartridge Counter commemorative.* **Below:** *the toggle and chamber marks on the Russian commemorative. (All pictures by courtesy of Rolf Gminder.)*

Commemorative Parabellums

Russian
10cm barrelled 06/73, 9mm calibre, commemorating—possibly on dubious grounds—the purchase of original DWM guns in 1906-7. There are Russian extractor and Bulgarian safety marks, and an inscription on the left side of the frame behind the cover plate. A crossed rifle mark lies over the chamber.

Bulgarian
12cm barrelled 06/73, 7.65mm calibre. Otherwise generally as the Russian model, produced in the same period, but the front sight is a block-mounted Swiss pattern and the extractor is marked in Bulgarian fashion. The toggle grips have been milled away to approximate to the 'old-pattern' 1900 model pistols ordered in 1901-2. The Bulgarian lion mark appears above the chamber.

Swiss
This appeared in 1976, a celebration of the original adoption of a Parabellum in May 1900. It is otherwise a 12cm barrelled, 7.65mm calibre 06/73, with a Swiss style block-mounted front sight. The toggle-grips are not cutaway, because the flat-face pattern associated with the 'new model' guns of 1906 has been used instead. The chamber mark is the well-known cross-on-sunburst.

Kaiserliche Marine
This distinctive gun was produced to celebrate the 75th anniversary of the adoption of the Parabellum by the Imperial Navy in December 1904. The basically 06/73 guns have 15cm barrels, the distinctive two-position rocking-L naval back sight on the rear toggle-link and a stock lug on the back strap. The guns were sold in leather cases, accompanied by a copy of the book *Luger.*

Model 1902 Cartridge Counter
This, so far as modern 06/73 construction allows, is a near replica of the US Army experimental Parabellums fitted with Powell's Cartridge Indicating Device. This consists of a transparent plastic-covered slot (originals used a sheet of mica) cut through the left grip to expose an indicator pin on the magazine follower, showing how many rounds remain. The magazine has a wooden base, in imitation of the original, while the 10cm barrel chambers 9mm cartridges. The toggle-grips are partially cut away like the original 'old models', the US displayed eagle mark lies above the chamber and a facsimile DWM monogram is to be found on the toggle link.

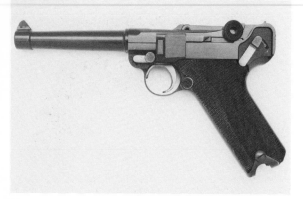

Above: the prototype 45 ACP sporting and pocket Parabellums, interesting projects which proved to be stillborn. (Courtesy of Rolf Gminder.)

The Merrill Company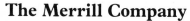

714 East Commonwealth, Fullerton, California 92631, USA

British agency: no sole distributorship. Standard warranty: unknown.

Little is known about Merrill, no details beign submitted to *the Pistol Book*. The distinctive sporting pistol appears to have been made since the mid 1970s.

Merrill Pistol

Sporting Pistol. This is another of the currently fashionable single-shot designs, presumably inspired by the success of the Thompson/Center Contender. The current Merrill—which may be chambered for a variety of cartridges—may be obtained with 9in or 10.8in (229 or 274mm) tapered half-octagonal and 14in (356mm) tapering cylindrical barrels, the shorter ones offering matted ventilated ribs. The optional sights are fully adjustable, though optical sights are usually fitted. There is a spring-loaded barrel lock, a manual safety and the trigger incorporates a roller bearing to ensure smooth action; a cocking indicator pin protrudes from the back of the frame when the mechanism is ready to fire. The grips are generally thumb-rest style walnut; the finish, blue or satin chrome. The result is one of the more popular guns of its type.
Cal: 0.22in LR Silhouette, 0.22in Magnum rf, 22 MRE, 0.22in Jet*, 0.22in Hornet, 0.256in Winchester Magnum, 7mm Merrill, 0.30in Herrett, 30/30 Winchester*, 0.357in Magnum, 0.357in Herrett, 357/44 B&D, 0.41in Remington Magnum, 0.44in Remington Magnum. (* Currently discontinued, but available on special request.) Mag: none, single shot. For other details, see text.*

Miroku Firearms Co. KK

Kochi City, Shikoku, Japan

British, US agencies: none. Warranty: unknown.

The operations of this company, now making copies of the Colt revolvers, began in 1965. Two guns are currently being made—the Miroku VI, or Model 6 (Liberty Chief), with a six-shot cylinder and 5cm (2in) barrel, and the smaller five-shot Special Police Model. Both feature side-swinging cylinders, locked by a Colt-style combination recoil shield and thumb-latch, and both chamber the 0.38in Special. Neither is common outside Japan.

MMM-Mondial

Modesto Molgora, I-20127 Milano, Via del Valtorta 38, Italy.

British agency: no sole agents. US agency: none. Standard warranty: none.

Molgora—known for its blank-firing and starting pistols—is one of Italy's leading toymakers, specialising in toy guns. None of its firearms, therefore, are especially remarkable and suffer badly by comparison with those of European gunmakers. However, Molgora's unusual background obviously plays a considerable part in this, and MMM-Mondial guns are at least very cheap.

Revolver Cobra

Starting revolver. No details yet available apart from: *Cal: 6mm Flobert blanks. Mag: cylinder. Mag cap, rds: 7. Trg: DA, exposed hammer. Wt, Loa, Brl: NA. Rf: none. Sft: half-cock notch on hammer.*

Derringer

Starting pistol. This is a copy of the nineteenth-century four-barrel Sharps deringer. It loads by tipping the barrel cluster upwards at the breech, but lacks the sophisticated lockwork of its prototype. Apart from the barrel cluster, the sheath trigger (now rarely encountered) is its most distinctive feature.
Cal: 6mm Flobert blanks. Mag: none-4 barrels. Trg: SA, exposed hammer. Wt, oz/gm: 9.5/220. Loa, in/mm: 4.9/124. Brl, in/mm: 2.5/63. Rf: none. Sft: none.

Revolver Mondial

Personal defence revolver. This represents Molgora's only true cartridge revolver—very cheap, but not on a level, technically, with the products of the world's better gunsmiths: but then Molgora is, after all, essentially a *toymaker*. The revolver is reasonably strong, but offers too little power from its tiny cartridges to be really effective. It is only available in black finish.
Cal: 0.22in short rf, 6mm Flobert. Mag: cylinder. Mag cap, rds: 6. Trg: DA, exposed hammer. Wt, oz/gm: 19.7/560. Loa, in/mm: 7.2/182. Brl, in/mm: 3.0/76. Rf: 6 R?. Sft: half-cock on hammer.

Revolver Mondial a Salve

Starting revolver. This adapation of the Mondial cartridge revolver is a more substantial product than virtually all the Molgora starting pistols with the exception of the 0.380in/9mm Smith & Wesson-based gun. It is readily distinguishable by the half-length cylinder and the conical tip to the solid barrel, protruding into the cylinder space.
Cal: 6mm Flobert blanks. Otherwise as Mondial revolver, but a little lighter.

Mondial V

Signal pistol. This is an inexpensive, but reasonably well made break-open signal or flare pistol. Pushing a knurled-head button on the frame above the trigger allows the breech to be swung upwards and partial extraction of the spent case to take place. The Mondial V has an unsophisticated die-cast frame, wood grips and a lanyard ring on the base of the butt. *Cal:* 1.0in (25.4mm). *Mag:* none. *Trg:* SA, exposed hammer. *Wt, oz/gm:* 35.3/1000. *Loa, in/mm:* 9.3/237. *Brl, in/mm:* 6.1/156. *Rf:* none. *Sft:* half-cock notch on hammer.

SM 007

Starting pistol. The SM is a modern Molgora design, drawing inspiration from the German Reck guns. It features a box magazine in the butt, a loaded chamber indicator and a safety catch. Inexplicably, it has sights (!) and handles 8mm cartridges rather than the priming-compound propelled Flobert ammunition of most other Molgora starting guns. *Cal:* 8mm blanks. *Mag:* detachable box, catch on butt heel. *Mag cap, rds:* 6. *Trg:* SA, slide-cocked before each shot. *Wt, oz/gm:* NA. *Loa, in/mm:* 4.8/121. *Brl, in/mm:* 2.3/59. *Rf:* none. *Sft:* radial lever on left side of frame behind grip.

Chief's 38

Starting revolver. No details available other than *Cal:* 6mm Flobert blanks. *Mag:* cylinder. *Mag cap, rds:* 8. *Trg:* DA, exposed hammer. *Wt, Loa, Brl:* NA. *Rf:* none. *Sft:* half-cock notch on hammer.

Chief's 320

Starting revolver. A variation of the Chief's 38, though no details are available. *Cal:* 8mm blanks. *Mag:* cylinder. *Mag cap, rds:* 7. *Trg:* DA, exposed hammer. *Wt, Loa, Brl:* NA. *Rf:* none. *Sft:* half-cock notch on hammer.

Revolver da Segnalazione Mondial 380

Starting and signal revolver. This is the best of Molgora's blank-firing guns, being a copy of Smith & Wesson practices insofar as its lockwork and yoke-mounted cylinder assembly are concerned. A safety interlock prevents firing before the yoke is properly locked in the frame, and a two-part hammer/firing pin system gives a measure of security should the gun be dropped. An adaptor may be screwed into the muzzle to project signal rockets. The standards of manufacture are adequate if unspectacular, but blank-firers do not need the strength of cartridge-firing designs. *Cal:* 0.380in/9mm blanks. *Mag:* cylinder. *Mag cap, rds:* 5. *Trg:* SA (?), exposed hammer. *Wt, Loa, Brl:* NA. *Rf:* none. *Sft:* inertia firing pin; trigger/cylinder yoke interlock; half-cock notch on hammer.

Revolver 999

Starting and signal revolver. This is identical with the Modello 1938 (qv), apart from the optional screw-on signal rocket projector which attaches to the muzzle. All details identical with Modello 1938.

*Above: the Revolver 1917. **Below left:** the Revolver 1938 (999 is virtually identical apart from its frame-marks).*

Pistola 1900

Starting and signal pistol. The 1900 is a modified 1949 (qv), adapted to fire signal rockets from the optional screw-on muzzle extension. The principal differences between the two starting pistols lie in the barrel; on the 1949 this is almost non-existent, but on the 1900 is carried practically half the length of the 'slide' to exhaust at the muzzle. This is necessary in order that the extension tube can be attached in the conventional way, but this gives the Modello 1900 a much greater depth from slide-top to butt heel. *Cal:* 6mm Flobert blanks. *Mag:* 'bar' magazine horizontally in receiver, catch on left side above grip. *Mag cap, rds:* 6. *Trg:* DA, exposed hammer. *Wt, oz/gm:* 9.3/265. *Loa, in/mm:* 4.0/102. *Brl, in/mm:* 1.8/45. *Rf:* none. *Sft:* none.

Revolver 1917

Starting and signal revolver. An odd-looking design combining the appearance of the Colt Model P 'Western' revolver with elements of a much more modern design, the 1917 has a 'spare-part' appeal. Its major advantages are an unusually large cylinder capacity and the optional screw-on muzzle extension (*Lanciarazzi*) which enables signal rockets to be fired. *Cal:* 6mm Flobert blanks. *Mag:* cylinder. *Mag cap, rds:* 12. *Trg:* DA, exposed hammer. *Wt, oz/gm:* 13.6/385. *Loa, in/mm:* 5.9/149. *Brl, in/mm:* 1.9/48. *Rf:* none. *Sft:* half-cock notch.

Revolver 1938

Starting and signal revolver. This is yet another of the inexpensive Molgora-made starting revolvers, an unsophisticated die-cast pattern based—very loosely—on Colt and Smith & Wesson practices. It is available in black, grey or nickel finish and, like so many others of its type, may be transformed by the addition of a screw-on rocket launcher. *Cal:* 6mm Flobert blanks. *Mag:* cylinder. *Mag cap, rds:* 8. *Trg:* DA, exposed hammer. *Wt, oz/gm:* 11.3/320. *Loa, in/mm:* 6.2/157. *Brl, in/mm:* 2.6/64. *Rf:* none. *Sft:* half-cock notch.

Pistola 1949

Starting pistol. The 1949 is an archetypal small starting pistol, with the general external appearance of the small Browning cartridge pistols of the early twentieth century and a possible adaptation of the Walther UP1 blank-firer of the 1950s. *Cal:* 6mm Flobert blanks. Otherwise as Pistola 1900, except *Wt, oz/gm:* 8.3/235.

Revolver 1960

Starting and signal revolver. Available in black, grey or nickel finish, this tiny revolver is virtually a toy, with fragile lockwork and decidedly inconsequential appearance. Like most of the Molgora guns, it converts for launching signal rockets by a screw-on muzzle extension. It loads by removing the cylinder axis pin and tipping the cylinder sideways out of the frame. *Cal:* 6mm Flobert blanks. *Mag:* cylinder. *Mag cap, rds:* 6. *Trg:* DA, exposed hammer. *Wt, oz/gm:* 8.8/250. *Loa, in/mm:* 5.6/142. *Brl, in/mm:* 2.2/56. *Rf:* none. *Sft:* none.

Navy Arms Company

**689 Bergen Boulevard, Ridgefield, New Jersey
07657, USA.**

British agency: no sole agents. Standard warranty: various.

This business was started by Val Forgett in 1957, as the
Service Armament Co., but rapidly transformed into
Navy Arms as soon as the first 'Reb' and 'Yank' replica
percussion-ignition revolvers were marketed. These were
made in Italy, and it can be said quite truthfully that Val
Forgett virtually single-handedly started the thriving
industry now sited in the Gardone Valley; a fact
recognised, too, by the Italian government, as Forgett was
knighted for his services to the Italian gunmaking
industry in 1978. Navy Arms Co. moved from Bogota,
New Jersey, to Ridgefield in 1960 and has since grown
considerably. Acquisitions included Replica Arms of
Marietta, Ohio, in 1974 and subsequent removal of its
plant to Union City in New Jersey; the black powder
division of the Ithaca Gun Co. followed in 1976; and then
Classic Arms (qv) of Palmer, Massachussets, in 1977.
Current offerings include an impressive range of replica
revolvers made by Pietta (qv) and single-shot percussion-
ignition pistols made by Bondini (qv) in Italy. But Navy
Arms, with an eye to diversification, is also sponsoring
the Mamba pistol, reproductions of the Remington
rolling block rifles and Colt Western-style cartridge
revolvers.

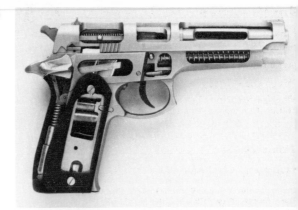

Mamba

Military and police pistol. The Mamba was originally designed
in Rhodesia (see Relay Products) but is now to be made in the
USA by Navy Arms, who was responsible for perfecting the
design. The Mamba is an interesting short-recoil pistol using
an extreme variant of the 'perfected Browning' mechanism
used by the GP35. A rib beneath the Mamba breech is moved
downwards by cam-blocks on the frame as the parts recoil—
an efficient system, but one in which downward displacement
of the breech occurs almost as soon as the recoil movement
commences (cf. SIG SP47/8). The parts are all investment
cast, including the button-rifled stainless steel barrel, and
there is a host of other features—including a 'packaged'
single-unit trigger group, an adjustable power hammer spring
and an ambidexterous safety catch. The finish is matt or blued
stainless steel, or a coating of Teflon. The Mamba slide and
grip resemble those of the Colt Government automatic, but
the front end of the frame (in particular) is radically different.
The Mamba, once perfected, will be a good performer;
however, the grip is too square to the bore axis for the gun to
point as well as the Benelli M76, though first reports suggest
that its magazine feed is more reliable. The Mamba would
benefit from a larger trigger guard . . . giving more space in
front of the trigger lever for gloved or large fingers (and,
incidentally, improving its aesthetics). Large capacity drum
magazines are allegedly being developed by Navy Arms
because the Mamba can be fitted with a selective burst
capability if required.

*Cal: 7.65 or 9mm Parabellum. Mag: detachable staggered
column box, catch on left side of frame behind trigger. Mag
cap, rds: 15. Trg: DA, exposed hammer. Wt, without magazine:
oz/gm: 37.0/1050. Loa, in/mm: 9.5/241. Brl, in/mm: 5.5/140. Rf:
12 R. Sft: manual catch on rear of frame (up-safe); inertia
firing pin; half-cock notch on hammer.*

Above: *the Navy Arms version of the Mamba, available in
blued, stainless or matt finishes.* ***Below:*** *the modernised
Remington sporting pistol, possibly made by Uberti.*

(Courtesy Navy Arms.)

Remington Rolling Block

This is a modification of the pistol apparently made for Navy
Arms by Uberti (qv), with a modernised grip, fore-end and
ventilated barrel rib. As the rolling block is a superior form of
single-shot action, it will be interesting to see what this gun
achieves. Few other details are known at the time of writing.

North American Arms Co.

Norarmco, 41471 Irwin, Mount Clemens, Michigan 48043, USA.

British agency: none. Standard warranty: unknown.

This company is believed to have been responsible for making small numbers of the Casull mini-revolver (now produced by Freedom Arms) in the early 1970s. It has also marketed the German-designed Budichowsky personal defence pistols without conspicuous success, and its current status is uncertain.

Casull Mini-revolver

Personal defence revolver. This was an improved form of the Rocky Mountain (qv) gun, with fixed blade-and-notch sights. The old external cylinder lock was discarded and changes were made in the lockwork. Production in 0.22in Short commenced in 1974, the larger 0.22in LR version appearing two years later. Production ceased in 1977 after about 8,000 had been made, but work was subsequently continued by Freedom Arms (qv).
Cal: 0.22in Short rf or 0.22in LR rf. Otherwise generally as Freedom Arms LA-S (qv).

Armi D. Pedersoli & C. SNC

Via Artigiani 53, I-25063 Gardone Val Trompia (Brescia), Italy.

British agency: none. US agency: various, but no sole distributorships. Standard warranty: unknown.

The Pedersoli company, formerly trading from Vicolo Bolognini in Gardone, is better known for its shotguns. However, at least one flintlock pistol—a 'Kentucky' copy—has also been made.

Fabbrica d'Armi F.lli Pietta di Giuseppe & C. SNC

Via Briggia 51, I-25064 Gussago (Brescia), Italy

British agency: no sole distributorship, though the guns are often seen in Britain. US agency: Navy Arms Co (qv) and others. Standard warranty: believed to be 12 months.

Little is known about Pietta, presumed to be a long-established gunmaker who comparatively recently (cf Uberti) turned to the mass production of percussion revolvers—guns in which Pietta specialises, as the entries here testify. However, percussion shotguns and even a rimfire sub-machine gun are made as well. The company was sufficiently successful to be awarded the Oscar Attivita'Economiche (business achievement award), the *Apollo d'Oro*, in 1979. The Pietta revolvers are generally regarded as the best of the Italian products other than those made by Uberti.

Colt Army Revolver M1860

Percussion revolver. This is a good quality replica of the standard army model (see Colt section), an elegant, streamlined design with a cylinder bearing a roll-engraved battle scene. Pietta's version has plain wooden grips, a colour case-hardened frame and rammer, and a brass trigger guard. The normal guns have a blued steel backstrap cut for the stock lug, but brass-strapped versions can be obtained to order. *Cal: 0.44in. Otherwise as Colt-made version.*

Colt Army Revolver M1860, Sheriff's Pattern

Percussion revolver. This is simply a standard army revolver (qv) with the barrel and rammer unit shortened by about 7cm. The result is certainly handier than the long-barrel gun, but undeniably lacks its elegance.
Cal: 0.44in. Otherwise as M1860 Army, but shorter and a little lighter.

Colt Navy Revolver M1851, Navy Yank M1851

Percussion revolver. This is Pietta's version of the authentic naval Colt of 1851, one of the landmarks in American firearms history. The blued barrel is octagonal, while the rammer assembly, frame and hammer are attractively case-hardened. The cylinder displays a plain, smooth surface into which a maritime battle scene is rolled, while the grips are well fitted walnut. Detailed coverage will be found in the Colt section. *Cal: 0.36in. Otherwise as standard Colt.*

Colt Navy Revolver M1851, 'London' Pattern

Percussion revolver. This is simply a Colt Navy with a square-backed brass trigger guard. The Pietta catalogue associates these guns with the short-lived Colt London factory, the story of which may be traced in greater detail in *Colonel Colt, London* by Joseph Rosa (Arms & Armour Press, 1976). However, most of the London guns apparently had steel guards and many early Hartford patterns had square backs. The Pietta revolver is available with brass or steel frames, and nickel- or silver-plated guard and grip straps.
Cal: 0.36in. Otherwise as M1851.

Colt Navy Revolver M1861

Percussion revolver. This is an improved 1851 Navy Colt, combining the smaller 'marine' calibre and the refined, rounded lines—and improved rammer—of the 1860 army revolver. The Pietta gun is available with a case-hardened frame and blued steel or polished-brass trigger guard and backstrap. Its cylinder displays the rolled-in naval battle scene, while its grips are polished walnut.
Cal: 0.36in. Otherwise generally as M1851 Navy Colt.

Colt Navy Revolver M1861, Sheriff's Pattern

Percussion revolver. This is a shortened, handier version of the 1861 naval revolver. It may be obtained with a polished brass or blued steel trigger guard and backstrap.
Cal: 0.36in. Otherwise as 1861 naval revolver, but 7cm shorter and a little lighter.

Colt 'Police Revolver' M1862.

Percussion revolver. This gun, somewhat misnamed (see remarks in Colt section), is a diminutive 1860 army revolver with the same elegant lines. It chambers the smaller of the two standard-calibre balls and has a rebated, fluted cylinder. The barrel and cylinder are blued; the rammer, hammer and frame, case-hardened. The trigger guard is polished brass and the grips are European walnut.
Cal: 0.36in. Otherwise, see Colt section.

Reb Nord Navy M1851

Percussion revolver. This is a variant of the standard M1851 navy revolver based on copies made in the Confederate States during the US Civil War. These featured more brass than normal, which means that these replicas have colour case-hardened steel rammers and hammers, with frames, guards and grip straps of polished brass. Some have plain cylinders; others display the rolled-in naval battle scene. The octagonal barrel is always blued, though deluxe engraved versions can be obtained to order.
Cal: 0.36in. Otherwise as M1851.

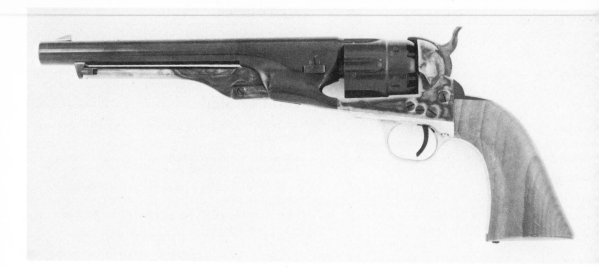

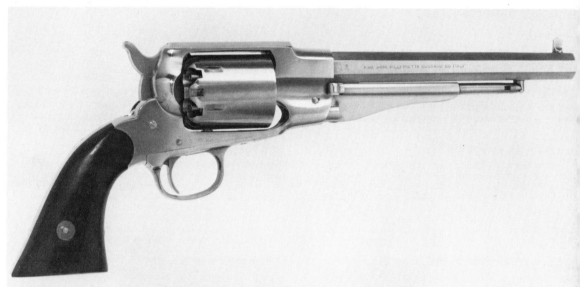

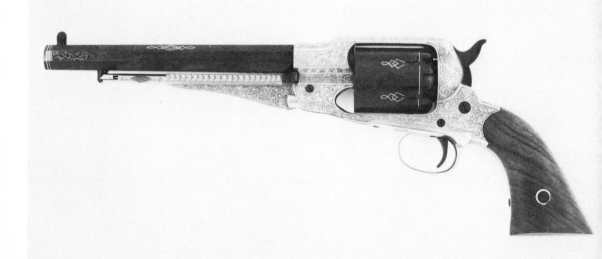

Reb Nord Confederate M1851

Percussion revolver. This gun is a version of the Colt Navy Revolver of 1851 with a brass frame, grip strap and trigger guard. Its principal distinguishing features are its round rather than octagonal barrel and plain-surface cylinder. The Reb Nord Confederate is based, somewhat loosely, on guns made by Griswold & Gunnison in Griswoldville, Georgia, during the US Civil War.
Cal: 0.36in. Otherwise as M 1851.

Reb Nord Confederate M1851, Sheriff's Pattern

Percussion revolver. This is a minor variant of the standard Reb Nord Confederate (qv), with the barrel shortened to 13cm.
Cal: 0.36in. Generally as full-length version, but shorter and a little lighter.

Reb Nord Sheriff's Model 1851

Percussion revolver. This is a Reb Nord Navy revolver (qv) with the barrel shortened by 7cm and the rammer assembly reduced to suit.
Cal: 0.36in and, apparently, 0.44in. Otherwise as Reb Nord Navy, but shorter and a little lighter.

Remington New Army Nickel

Percussion revolver. A version of the standard New Army, entirely nickel plated apart from its brass trigger guard.
Cal: 0.44in. Otherwise as New Army (qv).

Remington New Army Revolver M1858

Percussion revolver. The Remington is recognised as one of the most rugged and dependable of the mid-nineteenth century percussion revolvers, largely owing to its solid frame and sturdy parts. The Pietta version has a blued steel frame, rammer and octagonal barrel, a polished brass trigger guard and walnut grips. The most obvious recognition features are the closed cylinder aperture, a prominent web beneath the frame and rammer lever, and the plain surfaced cylinder; the interesting front sight is made from, for want of a better term, a peg with its sides milled flat. The Pietta Remington may be obtained in richly engraved 'Super deluxe' models, often with silver-plated frames and rammers.
Cal: 0.44in. Mag: cylinder. Mag cap, rds: 6. Trg: SA, exposed hammer. Wt, oz/gm: 44.0 or 46.5/1250 or 1320. Loa, in/mm: 12.5 or 13.8/317 or 350. Brl, in/mm: 6.7 or 8.0/170 or 203. Rf: 6 R. Sft: none, apart from half-cock notch on the hammer.

Remington New Army Target Revolver

Percussion revolver. This is the shorter Remington New Army (qv) with improved sights; the front sight lies on a ramp at the muzzle, while the fully adjustable back sight appears on the frame above the nipples. The gun chambers the smaller of the standard calibres in a quest for accuracy and easier control.
Cal: 0.36in. Otherwise as 17cm barrelled Remington New Army.

Remington New Army Stainless (or Inox)

Percussion revolver. Sometimes known simply as the Remington Stainless, this is a New Army differing largely in construction; apart from a polished brass trigger guard, the parts are all made from corrosion resistant stainless steel. This is a particularly useful precaution against the corrosive effect of the fulminate in percussion caps.
Cal: 0.44in. Otherwise as Remington New Army.

Sheriff's Yank M1851

Percussion revolver. This is a shortened version of the full-length gun, its barrel cut to 13cm and the rammer shortened to match. A handier gun than its prototype, particularly when carried in a belt holster, the short-barrelled Navy Colt is said to have been popular on the Frontiers . . . on both sides of the law! *Cal: 0.36in. Otherwise generally as Colt M1851.*

Texas Paterson 1836

Percussion revolver. This is one of the few re-creations of one of the earliest revolvers, the original Paterson Colt of the 1830s. The open-frame design is unique; it has a plain cylinder decorated with several circumferential grooves and a rolled-in Texas Rangers scene, and an oddly shaped frame whose flared butt is set much further forward than usual. Additionally, its forward-folding unguarded trigger is set well forward below the cylinder. The standard Pietta Paterson offers a blued frame with a similarly finished octagonal barrel, but brass-framed and specially engraved examples may also be encountered.
Cal: 0.36in. Mag: cylinder. Mag cap, rds: 5. Trg: SA, exposed hammer. Wt, oz/gm: 40.0/1135. Loa, in/mm: 13.8/350. Brl, in/mm: 9.0/229. Rf: 6 R. Sft: none, apart from half-cock notch on hammer.

Pretoria Arms Factory (PAF)
Pretoria, Republic of South Africa

This appears to have been a government smallarms factory operating on a commercial footing, the small number of 'Junior' pistols being made in the 1960s. Uncommonly encountered outside southern Africa, they are nonetheless an interesting project from a continent not noted for its handgun technology (see Relay Products).

Junior

Personal defence pistol. This is a copy of the Baby Browning (qv), without the grip safety. The first guns had raised sights; later ones, simple longitudinal grooves in the top of the slide.
Cal: 0.25in ACP (6.35mm Auto). Otherwise generally as FN-made Baby Browning.

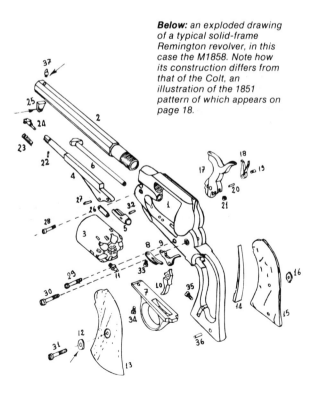

Below: an exploded drawing of a typical solid-frame Remington revolver, in this case the M1858. Note how its construction differs from that of the Colt, an illustration of the 1851 pattern of which appears on page 18.

Left: three Pietta revolvers. From top to bottom–the Colt 'Police Revolver' M1862, a stainless M1858 Remington and a richly decorated version of the standard Remington. (Photographs by courtesy of Pietta.)

PIETTA, PRETORIA ARMS FACTORY **113**

Přesné Strojírentsví

Uherský Brod, Czechoslovakia

British agency: Edgar Brothers Ltd, Catherine Street, Macclesfield, Cheshire SK11 6SG, England. US agency: apparently none. Export agency: Merkuria, 17005 Prahá 1, Argentinská 38, Czechoslovakia. Standard warranty: 12 months.

The ČZ company was originally founded in 1919 as Jihoceská Zbrojovká with a factory in Prahá (Prague) but within two years, another factory had been built in Strakoniče. After amalgamation with an engineering company, Česká Zbrojovká was formed. Large quantities of smallarms, artillery, motor cycles and machine tools have since been made—under German control during the Second World War and as part of the nationalised Czech state industry since 1948 (products then being marked 'Narodný Podnik', or 'national product'). The business was again renamed Český Zavodý Motocýklove in 1955, after which production of the pistols was transferred to Uherský Brod. A wide variety of handguns has been made since the early 1920s, the most famous being the Czech v.38 and vz.52 service pistols, the latter featuring a roller lock inspired by the German MG42 and now embodied in the Heckler & Koch P9 series.

CZ vz.70

General purpose and personal defence pistol. Obviously derived from the earlier CZ vz.50, this gun bears a considerable external resemblance to the Walther PP, and it may be presumed that the designers to whom this guns has been credited—the Kratochvil brothers—owe at least a small debt to the German design. However, there are some detail differences. The vz.70, for example, has a radial safety lever on the left side of the frame above the grip, rather than on the slide, and its trigger guard is forged intergrally with the frame (thus the dismantling system differs from that of the PP). The vz.70 is otherwise a conventional double-action blowback general purpose pistol, with angular and rather uncomfortable ribbed-heel plastic grips and an exposed ring hammer. In sum, however, it represents not only a surprisingly well made and efficient design, but also one that is competitively priced. *Cal: 7.65mm Auto (0.32in ACP). Mag: detachable box, catch on left side of frame behind trigger. Mag cap, rds: 8. Trg: DA, exposed hammer. Wt, oz/gm: 24.7/700. Loa, in/mm: 6.7/170. Brl, in/mm: 3.7/95. Rf: yes. Sft: manual lever on left side of frame above grip, up to safe (?); inertia firing pin.*

Below: *the CZ vz.75 (courtesy of Edgar Brothers).*

CZ vz.75

Military and police pistol. The action of the vz. 75 is a modified Browning link system, or perhaps more precisely the cam pattern incorporated in the Swiss SIG 47/8 (qv). The closed cam-path, cut through the material of the barrel below the chamber, elevates two partly-circumferential barrel lugs into recesses in the inside of the slide. The vz.75 also shares the SIG system of construction in which the slide-retaining grooves lie on the *inside* rather than the outside of the frame. The reasonably sturdy double-action trigger mechanism offers an exposed hammer, a reputation for smoothness and an unusually crisp double-action pull. The staggered-column magazine has the currently fashionable large capacity, obtained at the expense of considerable extra weight. The gun has distinctive lines, with narrow plastic or hardwood grips, a pronounced 'hump' to the back strap and good blueing; though it lacks the quality of some of its Western rivals, and has been unfairly criticised in some quarters, there can be no doubt that the CZ is an efficient and combat-worthy design. *Cal: 9mm Parabellum. Mag: detachable box, crossbolt catch on left side of frame behind trigger. Mag cap, rds: 15. Trg: DA, exposed hammer. Wt, oz/gm: 35.3/1000. Loa, in/mm: 8.1/206. Brl, in/mm: 4.7/120. Rf: 6 R. Sft: radial lever on left side of frame above the grip; inertia firing pin.*

Reck

Reck-Division, Umarex-Sportwaffen GmbH & Co. KG, D 5760 Arnsberg 1/Neheim-Hüsten, Donnenfeld 2 (Postfach 2720), West Germany.

British agency: none. US agency: none. Standard warranty: 12 months

Little is currently known about the history of Reck, one of Germany's leading makers of starting and signal pistols. The business was founded, apparently in the early 1950s, by Karl Arndt Reck and traded in 1966 in Lauf bei Nürnberg. A reorganisation occurred in the late 1970s and the Reck business is now owned by a large sports goods conglomerate. Reck pistols continue to offer quite good quality at competitive prices, though their hold on the market appears to have been eroded by the products of Erma (qv) and, to a lesser extent, Barthelmes.

Left: *three Reck pistols–from top to bottom, the Baby, the Cobra and the DA 38.*

(Courtesy Umarex-Sportwaffen.)

Baby

Starting pistol. This is a typical small, genuinely self-loading 'automatic' starting pistol offering reasonably conventional construction and performance, but of undeniably distinctive appearance as its alloy slide continues some distance behind the partially chequered plastic grips. The gun must be cocked and loaded by retracting the slide, but thereafter loads itself and ejects the spent blanks until the conventional box magazine is exhausted. Dismantling is begun by pressing inwards (towards the muzzle) on a locking bolt at the extreme rear of the frame, after which the slide can be removed. Unlike many guns in its class, the Reck Baby has a proper safety catch; and it rather inexplicably features quite sturdy and effective sights.
Cal: 8mm blanks. Mag: detachable box, catch on butt heel. Mag cap, rds: 5. Trg: SA, internal striker. Wt, oz/gm: 15.5/440. Loa, in/mm: 5.4/136. Brl, in/mm: 3.0/76. Rf: none. Sft: radial lever behind left grip, forward-safe.

Cobra

Starting pistol. This is a sturdy, well made and quite efficient swinging-cylinder design, with an extractor/ejector operated by a shrouded rod under the barrel. The cylinder release catch on the left side of the frame under the hammer betrays more than a hint of American lineage, and in particular the Colt (qv) of the same name. The finish is black burnished alloy; the grips, chequered plastic.
Cal: 0.380in (9mm) blanks. Mag: cylinder. Mag cap, rds: 6. Trg: DA, exposed hammer. Wt, oz/gm: 22.6/640. Loa, in/mm: 6.9/175. Brl, in/mm: 2.5/63. Rf: none. Sft: 'transfer bar' hammer block; inertia firing pin.

Commander

Starting and signal pistol. This gun bears a considerable resemblance to the Colt Commander automatic (qv) though it is, of course, a simple blowback as well as smaller and appreciably lighter than its prototype. There are rudimentary open sights and a ring hammer, anodised blue finish, and chequered synthetic or wood grips. The Reck Commander has a conventional barrel-type exhaust, the muzzle being threaded to receive the auxiliary signal flare dischargers (Zusatzläufe).
Cal: 8mm blanks. Mag: detachable box, crossbolt catch on left side of frame behind trigger guard. Mag cap, rds: 7. Trg: SA, exposed hammer. Wt, oz/gm: 21.2/600. Loa, in/mm: 6.2/158. Brl, in/mm: 3.3/84. Rf: none. Sft: radial catch on left side of frame behind grip, up to safe; inertia firing pin; half-cock notch on hammer.

DA, DA 38 or Double Action

Starting and signal pistol. This gun's appearance betrays its Smith & Wesson ancestry, particular in the design of the yoke-mounted laterally-swinging cylinder and knurled head thumb-latch beneath the hammer on the left side of the frame. Amazingly, the DA apparently features an *adjustable* back sight . . . on a starting pistol! It is an attractive, long-barrelled design, blue-finished with hardwood grips. Its muzzle is threaded to receive a Zusatzläuf. (NB: catalogue illustrations suggest that the DA was originally made with a flat topped frontsight and without the vestigial shroud or lug at the head of the ejector rod.)

Cal: 0.380in (9mm) blanks. Mag: cylinder. Mag cap, rds: 5. Trg: DA, exposed hammer. Wt, oz/gm: NA. Loa, in/mm: 10.0/254. Brl, in/mm: 6.0/152. Rf: none. Sft: 'transfer bar' hammer block; inertia firing pin.

PK800

Starting pistol. This Walther lookalike is based quite clearly on the PPK (qv), sharing the same general construction and dismantling system—even though the trigger and safety units have been greatly simplified. Black anodised, with partially chequered plastic grips, the PK800 is an elegant, efficient product. Its muzzle is threaded to receive the extension for signal flares.

Cal: 8mm blanks. Mag: detachable box, catch on butt heel. Mag cap, rds: 7. Trg: DA, exposed hammer. Wt, oz/gm: 21.2/600. Loa, in/mm: 6.1/155. Brl, in/mm: 3.3/84. Rf: none. Sft: rotary 'barrel' unit on left side of slide directly below back sight, down to safe; inertia firing pin.

PK6000 (formerly TPR?)

Starting and signal pistol. This is an interesting modern variant of the bar magazine starting pistol, adapted to project signal flares by 'bending' the exhaust tube through 90° so that the gases emerge at the muzzle. This means that what appears to be a conventional magazine base and butt-heel catch are simply dummies. The magazine is inserted after pulling down the 'hammer' (in practice serving as the magazine trap) until it is held by a ball-catch, and then operating the slide to move the magazine to its forward position. The PK6000 has an interesting double-action trigger system which incorporates, among other components, a

transporter and vertically acting hammer. The muzzle is threaded to accept the Zusatzläufe, or signal flare projectors, while the chequered plastic grips complement the black-anodised finish. Reck apparently intended to call the gun the TPR, clearly evident in the photograph reproduced here. It must be assumed that Walther—maker of the elegant TPH (qv) on which the Reck is modelled—objected sufficiently strongly for another designation to be substituted.

Cal: 6mm Flobert blanks. Mag: horizontal bar magazine in frame. Mag cap, rds: 7. Trg: DA, internal hammer. Wt, oz/gm: 12.7/360. Loa, in/mm: 5.4/138. Brl, Rf: none. Sft: radial lever on left side of slide below back sight, down to safe.

Protector or G5

Starting pistol. This is one of Reck's older designs, a predecessor of the essentially similar Baby (qv) with more dated lines—particularly at the muzzle; in the chequered synthetic grips with their long rearward extensions; and in the shape of the slide-tip and retraction grooves. The dismantling system was inherited by the Baby, but the Protector has an earlier safety in the form of a button through the left grip

Cal: 8mm blank. Otherwise generally as Baby, except Wt, oz/gm: 14.6/410. Loa, in/mm: 5.3/134. Brl, in/mm: 2.9/74. Sft: see text.

Single Action

Starting revolver. This is a 'Western'-pattern starting gun, styled after the Colt Peacemaker with a rod ejector on the right side of the barrel and a laterally swinging loading gate on the right side of the frame behind the cylinder. The SA offers sights (!), quite good construction and simulated wood-grain synthetic grips. The gun should be carried with the hammer down on an *empty* chamber.

Cal: 8mm blanks. Mag: cylinder. Mag cap, rds: 6. Trg: SA,

xposed hammer. Wt: NA. Loa, in/mm: about 10.5/267. Brl, /mm: about 5.5/140. Rf: none. Sft: half-cock notch.

Wildcat Series

ignal and starting pistols. These guns are based on the DA qv), and thus on Smith & Wesson practice, with swing-out ylinders and double-action lockwork. The guns feature ardwood grips, the Reck 'Leucht Reflexkorn' (a bright-point ont sight), the King's Road matted sight rib and an xtraordinary three-tier ventilated rib. They are apparently vailable only in blued alloy; all will take Zusatzläufe, auxiliary ignal and gas cartridge dischargers. There are several guns n the series, all chambering 0.380in (9mm) blanks. *Nomenclature:* Gepard—17in (43cm) barrel, Leopard—4in 10cm) barrel, Panther—2.5in (6.3cm) barrel, Tiger—6in 15cm) barrel.

*eft: three Reck Wildcats.
elow: a photograph and drawing of the the PK 6000. The ottom drawing shows the method of loading the magazine. Courtesy of Umarex-Sportwaffen.)*

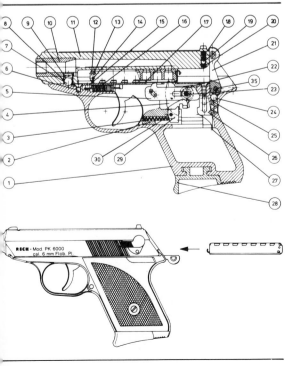

Relay Products (Pty) Ltd

Harare, Zimbabwe.

British agency: none. US agency: see remarks under Navy Arms Company.

Mamba

Military and police pistol. The Mamba is covered in the Navy Arms section, but a brief note of its unusual background is necessary here—even though many of the details are not yet clear. Design work was undertaken in Zimbabwe (Rhodesia) by combined West German/S. African/Zimbabwean interests trading through Relay Products (Pty) Ltd. of Harare. The gun was to have been offered to the South African forces and changes were made on behalf of Sandock-Austral Small Arms Company division of Gear Ratio Engineering (Pty) Ltd. So many teething troubles occurred, however, that the forces clung to the FN-Browning GP and the South African Mamba was abandoned.

Remington Arms Company

939 Barnum Avenue, Bridgeport, Connecticut 06602, USA

The Remington Arms Company was founded by Eliphalet Remington in 1816, producing a variety of handguns—including the well known percussion revolvers—but ran into financial difficulty and was reconstituted in 1886 as the 'Remington Arms Company'. It has since gone through several changes of ownership, though its trading style remains the same. The only pistol offered among Remington's current products is the odd-looking XP100, which caused a sensation in the 1960s and can be said to have inspired the current interest in single-shot pistols such as the Thompson/Center Contender and the Sterling X-Caliber. In addition, it must be remembered thhat 'Remington' revolvers, percussion and cartridge-firing alike, are being made by many companies—Pietta and Uberti among them

XP-100 Fireball

Sporting pistol. The Fireball made its debut in 1963, featuring a single-shot bolt action adapted from the Remington Model 700 rifle, which was allied with an ultra-long barrel. The pistol was intended to fire the 0.221in Remington Fireball, a bottlenecked rimless cartridge firing a light bullet at very high velocity; indeed, the Fireball is generally reckoned as a very powerful loading for a handgun. Remington's goal appears to have been to produce a handgun cartridge capable of grouping five shots in less than an inch at 100 yards, the proof of the gamble now being evident in the fact that the XP-100 is still in production after twenty years. So far as its appearance is concerned, all pretensions of beauty vanish; owing to the long barrel and the bolt unit, which has the effect of extending it, there is a very pronounced rearward overhang below which the stepped-forward bolt handle protrudes. The grip unit is an odd DuPont Zytel type with contrasting diamond motif and white-line spacer between the semi-schnabel fore-end tip. There are adjustable sights, but placing the back sight (0.221in version) on the barrel above the trigger fails to capitalise on the long sight radiius possible by placing it on the receiver bridge ahead of the bolt. For all its unconventionality, the XP-100 has proved to be an effective and noteworthy design.
Cal: 0.221in Remington, 7mm BR Remington. Mag: none. Trg: SA, striker fired. Wt, oz/gm: 60.0/1700 or 66/1870 depending on barrel. Loa, in/mm: 16.8, 21.3/427, 541. Brl, in/mm: 10.5 (0.221in), 14.8 (7mm)/267, 376. Rf: yes. Sft: thumb catch beside rear of bolt.

Rigarmi

Rigarmi di Rino Galesi, I-25100 Brescia, Via de Vitalis 1/3/15, Italy.

British agency: none. US agency: none. Standard warranty: unknown.

Rigarmi was founded in March 1951 by Rino Galesi, whose father and grandfather had been actively involved in the Italian firearms industry. Pistols, revolvers and shotguns are currently being made.

Pistola Automatica Modello 1953

Personal defence pistol. Galesi's first postwar design, though based on the prewar blowbacks, owed something to the construction of the Walther Modell 8 of 1920—an affinity evident in the dismantling system and parts of the trigger group. The Modello 1953 is an elegant but underpowered little gun, usually encountered with white simulated mother-of-pearl grips though chequered black plastic was also available. It is otherwise quite unremarkable.
Cal: 0.25in ACP (6.35mm Auto). Mag: detachable box, catch on butt heel. Mag cap, rds: 8. Trg: SA, concealed striker. Wt, oz/gm: 12.7/360. Loa, in/mm: 4.6/116. Brl, in/mm: 2.3/58. Rf: 6 R?. Sft: radial lever on rear left side of the frame, down to safe.

Pistola Automatica Modello 1954

Personal defence pistol. This is a modified version of the Modello 53 (qv), comparable in size but chambering rimfire ammunition. The slide has a larger symmetrical ejection port, cut away on the left side in addition to the right—quite unlike the earlier gun, whose smaller ejection port lies exclusively on the right side. The manual safety has been moved to the frame side behind the trigger, and a crossbolt dismantling catch has taken its place at the rear; this allows the grips to run further back on the frame.
Cal: 0.22in Short rf or 0.22in LR rf. Otherwise as Mo.1953, except Sft: radial lever on left side of frame behind trigger, up to safe.

Pistola Automatica Modello 1955

Personal defence pistol. This is a combination of the 'closed' slide construction of the Modello 53 with the revised safety and dismantling catches of the Modello 54. The 1955-vintage gun is invariably chromed and pleasantly hand engraved.
Cal: 0.25in ACP (6.35mm Auto). Otherwise as 1954 pattern.

Pistola Automatica Modello 1957

Personal defence pistol. The 1957 gun is an enlargement of the 1954 pattern, handier and better balanced but still chambering an ineffectual rimfire cartridge. It may be encountered in black, chromed or chromed-and-engraved finish, with black plastic or simulated mother-of-pearl grips.
Cal: 0.22in LR rf. Otherwise as Mo.1954, except Wt, oz/gm: 14.8/420. Loa, in/mm: 5.3/135. Brl, in/mm: 3.0/77.

Pistola Automatica Modello Italia 69

General purpose pistol. This is but a variant of the Italia Militar (qv) with a longer barrel, intended for sporting and recreational shooting. The front sight is mounted on a collar attached to the muzzle, theoretically objectionable because the alignment between the sights will be disturbed as wear sets in. The grips may be chequered plastic or plain hardwood.
Cal: 0.22in LR rf or 0.32 ACP (7.65 Auto). Otherwise as Italia Militar, except Wt, oz/gm: 24.7/700. Loa, in/mm: 8.7/220. Brl, in/mm: 6.0/152.

Revolver Navy 1851

Percussion revolver. The Navy 1851 is a close copy of the Colt pattern of the mid nineteenth century. The octagonal barrel and rammer mechanism are casehardened gunmetal, but the frame, trigger guard and grip straps—unlike the original—are brass castings and the grips are polished walnut. The Galesi Colt is adequately made, but not perhaps in the front rank of black-powder replicas.
Cal: 0.36in. Otherwise similar to the modern Colt.

Revolver Army 1860

Percussion revolver. This is a modern version of the Colt Army revolver of 1860, the matchless elegance of which is copied despite differences in construction. Unlike the original the Galesi 'replica' displays a *brass* frame and trigger guard, although the round barrel and the rammer unit are casehardened gunmetal.
Cal: 0.44in. Otherwise similar to the modern Colt.

Pistola Automatica Modello Italia Militar

General purpose pistol. This gun may be conveniently classed as an Italian Walther PP, from which, despite internal differences, it clearly derives. The rather more angular backstrap contours are a distinguishing characteristic. The trigger is double action, with an exposed ring hammer, and a typically Walther-type rotary or 'barrel' combination safety and de-cocking lever lies high on the left side of the slide above the retraction grooves. Despite the 'Militar' appellation, this is hardly a gun for military use and is more suited to the commercial market. Chromed and engraved versions (*tipo lusso*) are also obtainable.
Cal: 0.22in LR rf or 0.32 ACP (7.65mm Auto). Mag: detachable box, catch on butt heel. Mag cap, rds: 9 (0.22in) or 8 (0.32in). Trg: DA, exposed hammer. Wt, oz/gm: 24.0/680. Loa, in/mm: 6.2/157. Brl, in/mm: 3.5/90. Rf: 6 R?. Sft: inertia firing pin; rotary safety on left side of slide, down to safe.

**mod. Italia
tipo lusso**

Cromata e con finissima incisione
This is the automatic pistol in chromed and engraved type - (luxury type). Also available in bleu shining or only chromed.

Above: a typical Rigarmi pocket automatic.

Rocky Mountain Arms Corporation

Salt Lake City, Utah, USA.

British agency: none. Standard warranty: unknown.

This company produced the original Casull mini-revolver (see Freedom Arms), but was better known for its very distinctive breech-loading percussion-ignition rifle. Its current status is uncertain.

Casull Mini-revolver

Personal defence revolver. This tiny old-style revolver, made to the design of Dick Casull from 1972 until 1974, had no sights, a knurled under-barrel cylinder axis pin, a clumsy external cylinder lock running forward from the hammer, a sheath trigger and polycarbonate grips. After about 2,500 had been made, it was succeeded by the North American Arms version and finally by the Freedom Arms guns.
Cal: 0.22in Short rf. Mag: cylinder. Mag cap, rds: 5?. Trg: SA, exposed hammer. Wt, oz/gm: 4.0/113. Loa, in/mm: 3.6/92. Brl, in/mm: 1.0/25. Rf: type uncertain. Sft: half-cock on hammer.

RÖHM

Signal-Pistole RG 3

RÖHM

Selbstlade-Signal-Pistole RG 8

Above: two typical Röhm blank-firers, the RG3 and RG8.
Below: the RG9. (Courtesy Röhm.)

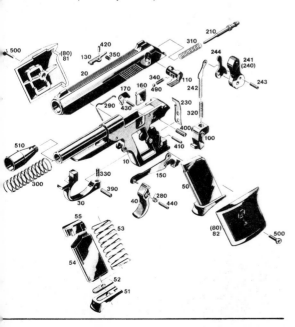

Röhm GmbH

D-7927 Sontheim an der Brenz, Postfach 60, West Germany

British, US agencies: apparently no sole distributorships, though the guns are quite widespread. Standard warranty: various—generally 12 months.

Rohm is among the best known maker of competitively-priced revolvers and starting pistols in Germany, along with Reck and Erma-Werke.

RG3

Starting and signal pistol. This is the archetypal starting pistol of the 1950s, using another variation of the horizontal bar magazine, inserted from the muzzle and moved backwards by the trigger system; once the last shot has been fired, the empty magazine block can be removed from the back of the frame. A small three-position button lies on the left side of the grip, immediately behind the trigger. F and S are the fire and safe positions respectively, while, at E (*Entleerung*), the action may be safely operated to eject a partially loaded magazine. The RG3 will accept a Zusatzlauf, or muzzle attachment, to fire signal flares. Finish may be brown or chrome, the grips being injection moulded plastic.
Cal: 6mm Flobert blanks, 9mm or 15mm signal flares. Mag: horizontal bar pattern. Mag cap, rds: 6. Trg: DA, concealed hammer. Wt, oz/gm: 10.3/290. Loa, in/mm: 4.1/105. Brl, in/mm: NA. Sft: button on frame-side-see text.

RG8

Starting and signal pistol. This modern self-loading 'automatic' starting pistol, made largely from investment castings, will fire signal flares with the assistance of Zusatzläufe. Otherwise, it is a standard small automatic with well raked synthetic grips and a detachable box magazine. The finish is dark blue-grey and sturdy-looking (but superfluous) fixed sights lie on the barrel and breech.
Cal: 8mm blanks, 9mm and 15mm signal flares. Mag: detachable box, catch on butt heel. Mag cap, rds: 6. Trg: SA, concealed striker. Wt, oz/gm: 15.2/430. Loa, in/mm: 5.1/130. Brl, in/mm: NA. Rf: none. Sft: radial lever on left side of frame behind grip, down to safe (covering red dot).

RG9, RG9L and RG9M

Starting and signal pistol. The well made, attractive little RG9 is another of the starting pistols based on the Walther TPH (qv). Typical Walther lines are evident in the Röhm gun, though the latter's grips are rather more shapeless. There are fixed sights, a double action trigger mechanism, a ring hammer, and a radial safety lever high on the left side of the slide. The guns usually display blue-grey anodised finish and chequered synthetic (RG9) or wooden de luxe grips (RG9L). However, there is also a wooden gripped nickel-plated option known as the RG9M (*M represents Matt Vernickelt*). The RG9 series will fire signal flares once the Zusatzlauf has been screwed into the muzzle.
Cal: 8mm blanks, 9mm and 15mm signal flares. Mag: detachable box, catch on butt heel. Mag cap, rds: 6. Trg: DA, exposed hammer. Wt, oz/gm: 00.0/432. Loa, in/mm: 00.0/140. Brl, in/mm: NA. Rf: none. Sft: radial lever on left rear side of slide, down to safe; inertia firing pin.

RG14

General purpose revolver. This is the first of the cartridge-firing Röhm products to be encountered, though it is little more than a conventional Smith & Wesson-inspired design with a laterally-swinging yoke-mounted cylinder, locked by a sliding ejector-rod sleeve. Its features include fixed sights, a light barrel inside an alloy 'semi-shroud' housing, a double action trigger and chequered plastic grips. The finish may be brown or nickel. The RG14 offers acceptable quality at an attractive price, but cannot be expected to compete against the best American guns.

Above: *the Röhm RG38T target revolver. (Courtesy Röhm GmbH.)*

Cal: 0.22in LR rf. Mag: cylinder. Mag cap, rds: 6. Trg: DA, exposed hammer. Wt, oz/gm: 14.8, 15.9/420, 450. Loa, in/mm: 5.7, 6.9/143, 175. Brl, in/mm: 1.8, 3.0/45, 76. Rf: 12R?. Sft: inertia firing pin.

RG23

General purpose revolver. This shares the general construction of the RG14, but has a differently shaped frame with a recurved trigger guard, an exposed coil spring on the ejector rod and an octagonal alloy barrel shroud. The sights remain fixed, though the backsight is formed as a raised notch rather than a simple longitudinal groove in the top surface of the frame. The RG23 cylinder has long, narrow cylinder locking bolt slots rather than the conventional short slots with semi-circular leads found on its predecessor. RG23 revolvers may be blue or nickel; their grips are invariably brown chequered plastic.
Cal: 0.22in LR rf. Otherwise as RG14, except:. Wt, oz/gm: 15.2/430

RG34 and RG34S Sport-Revolver

General purpose and personal defence revolver. The gunmetal construction of this gun, though it increases the weight, makes it more comfortable to fire than either the RG14 or RG23. The RG34 is the first of the Röhms thus far encountered to offer a cylinder locking catch on the left side of the frame beneath the hammer, rather than relying on the less effective sliding ejector-rod sleeve. There is a ventilated over-barrel rib, fixed sights on the standard version and a laterally adjustable back sight on the 'Sport'—which also displays a broadened hammer spur. Finish is either blue or nickel, and the chequered plastic grips bear the RG monogram.
Cal: 0.22in LR rf. Mag: cylinder. Mag cap, rds: 6. Trg: DA, exposed hammer. Wt, oz/gm: 32.4, 33.1/920, 940. Loa, in/mm: 7.2, 9.3/184, 235. Brl, in/mm: 2.0, 4.0/51, 102. Rf: 12R?. Sft: inertia firing pin.

RG34T Scheiben-Revolver

Target revolver. This is a minor variant of the standard RG34, sharing an identical action. However, the 'T' variant has a fully adjustable back sight and a raised front blade on a ramp atop the ventilated rib. The barrel is a heavy, large-diameter 'bull' pattern; both hammer and trigger have broadened finger surfaces; the trigger is honed to provide a crisp (if non-adjustable) pull; and wooden match grips will be usually encountered instead of the standard chequered plastic variety.
Cal: 0.22in LR rf. Otherwise as RG34, except:. Wt, oz/gm, with standard 6in barrel: 43.0/1220. Loa, in/mm: 8.2, 9.3, 11.2/209, 235, 285. Brl, in/mm: 3.0, 4.0, 6.0/76, 102, 152

RG35

General purpose revolver. This is a minor variant of the RG34, chambering more powerful ammunition but otherwise identical. *Cal: 0.22in Magnum rf. Otherwise as RG34.*

RG35T Scheiben-Revolver

Target revolver. Identical with the RG34T (qv), apart from the more powerful magnum chambering, this gun will also usually be found with the supposedly optional wooden target-style grips. *Cal: 0.22in Magnum rf. Otherwise as RG34T.*

RG36T Scheiben-Revolver

Target revolver. The RG36T is an RG34T (qv) chambering the more powerful 0.32in S & W round, often favoured in standard pistol shooting competitions. In common with most cartridge-firing Röhm revolvers, this gun offers acceptable performance at a reasonable price, though it is by no means top-grade. *Cal: 0.32 in S & W Long. Otherwise generally as 34T.*

RG38 and RG38S

General purpose revolver. These two guns are essentially similar, though the 'S' variant has the broadened hammer spur and adjustable sights of the standard Röhm Sport revolver. The RG38 is the most powerful of the 30-series, and the best choice for personal defence, featuring a yoke-mounted cylinder secured by a thumb-catch on the left side of the frame beneath the hammer. *Cal: 0.38in Special. Otherwise generally as RG34/RG34S (qv).*

RG38T Scheiben-Revolver

Target revolver. This is the specialised variant of the RG38, though the improvements are largely cosmetic and the gun remains firmly in the low grade category—which is not to imply severe criticism, however, as it still represents good value. *Cal: 0.38in Special. Otherwise generally as RG38.*

RG57

General purpose revolver. The RG57 is a strengthened version of the standard Röhm design, featuring a standard yoke-mounted cylinder locked by the thumb-catch on the left side of the frame beneath the broad-spurred hammer. It may be encountered with plastic or wooden sporting-pattern grips. The sights are fixed, the low-profile front sight being mounted on a ventilated barrel rib, and the basic action is sufficiently strong to chamber even magnum cartridges.
Cal: 0.357in Magnum, 0.38in Special, 0.41in Magnum, 0.44in S & W Special, 0.44in Magnum, 0.45in Colt. Mag: cylinder. Mag cap, rds: 6. Trg: DA, exposed hammer. Wt, oz/gm, with 4in barrel: 40.2/1140. Loa, in/mm: 9.4, 11.4/238, 288. Brl, in/mm: 4.0, 6.0/102, 152. Rf: yes. Sft: inertia firing pin.

RG57T Scheiben-Revolver

Target revolver. This gun is a variant of the standard RG57 (qv) with raised, adjustable sights—providing a powerful target or sporting gun for a relatively modest outlay.

RG66 and RG66M Western-Revolver

General purpose revolver. This is the first of the Röhms considered here to be based, albeit loosely, on the Colt Peacemaker. The RG66 is made largely of alloy and chambers rimfire ammunition—providing a popular plinker, but not much else. The rod ejector is mounted on the right side of the barrel, acting in conjunction with the loading gate on the right side of the frame behind the cylinder. The revolvers may be browned or nickelled, with chequered plastic semi-thumbrest grips. The M-suffix variant chambers magnum rimfire ammunition and is accompanied by a *zusätzlicher Trommel,* or auxiliary cylinder.
Cal: 0.22in LR and/or Magnum rf. Mag: cylinder. Mag cap, rds: 6. Trg: SA, exposed hammer. Wt, oz/gm, with 4.8in barrel: 31.8/900. Loa, in/mm: 10.0, 11.2, 14.2/254, 285, 361. Brl, in/mm: 4.8, 6.0, 9.0/121, 152, 229. Rf: 12R?. Sft: inertia firing pin, half-cock on hammer.

RG66T Western-Revolver

General purpose revolver. This is a target-shooting derivative of the standard RG6 (qv) with raised adjustable sights—the front of which is a modern blade rather than the old-style round type. The trigger has been improved, the pull-weight reduced and an adjustable trigger stop fitted in the back of the trigger guard. Often found with wooden, target-quality grips, this Röhm is favoured as a low-cost introduction to target shooting (though not, perhaps, in quite the same class as some of the Uberti guns). An exchangeable cylinder permits a rapid change of ammunition.
Cal: 0.22in LR and Magnum rf. Otherwise generally as RG66, except:. Wt, oz/gm, with 6in barrel: 34.2/970. Loa, in/mm: 11.1, 14.1/282, 359. Brl, in/mm: 6.0, 9.0/152, 229

RG69 and RG69M

Starting and signal revolver. These are the most impressive of this company's starting revolvers, externally resembling contemporary Charter Arms products. Their cylinders are carried on side-swinging yokes, locked by the thumb-catch on the frame-side beneath the hammer. There are gunmetal cylinders, double-action triggers and partially chequered wooden grips. Zusatzläufe, or auxiliary barrels, may be used to fire signal ammunition. The revolvers are usually blued, though 'M' suffix variants are nickelled.
Cal: 9mm blanks, 9mm and 15mm signal flares. Mag: cylinder. Mag cap, rds: 6. Trg: DA, exposed hammer. Wt, oz/gm: 25.0/709. Loa, in/mm: 7.3/185. Brl, in/mm: 2.5/64. Rf: none. Sft: inertia firing pin.

RG76

Starting and signal revolver. This is simply a lightweight blank-firer, capable of discharging signal flares (*Signalsterne*) without the barrel extension, or Zusatzlauf. There is an auto-ejector and a conventional yoke-mounted cylinder, distinguished by unconventionally angular flutes continuing into the slender cylinder locking-bolt slots. The guns are usually browned, their plastic grips displaying rounded
Cal: 6mm Flobert blanks, 9mm and 15mm signal flares. Mag: cylinder. Mag cap, rds: 6. Trg: DA, exposed hammer. Wt, oz/gm: 14.8/420. Loa, in/mm: 6.1/155. Brl, in/mm: NA. Rf: none. Sft: inertia firing pin.

RG77

Starting and signal revolver. This is simply a variant of the RG76 chambering different ammunition.
Cal: 0.22in blanks, 9mm and 15mm signal flares. Otherwise as RG76.

RG79G

Starting and signal revolver. This is an improved version of the earlier Röhm blank-firing revolvers, featuring greater strength and improved construction—the standard cylinder locking catch now lies beneath the hammer—and the chambering is even more powerful. This, however, reduces the cylinder capacity by one round.
Cal: 9mm blanks, 9mm and 15mm signal flares. Mag: cylinder. Mag cap, rds: 5. Trg: DA, exposed hammer. Wt, oz/gm: 21.5/610. Loa, in/mm: 6.9/175. Brl, in/mm: NA. Rf: none. Sft: inertia firing pin.

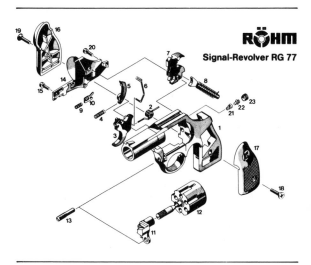

RÖHM
Signal-Revolver RG 77

RG86 and RG86M Western-Revolver

General purpose revolver. This is a strengthened, steel-frame version of the RG66 (qv), with which it is otherwise virtually identical. The sights are fixed; the guns, browned or nickelled to special request. The principal distinguishing characteristic is the pronounced vertical shoulder on the frame immediately below the hammer; in addition, the standard plastic grips lack the thumbrest often associated with the RG66. The 'M' suffix variant is supplied with an exchangeable cylinder, but is normally intended for magnum ammunition.
Cal: 0.22in LR and Magnum rf. Otherwise generally as RG66 (qv), but appreciably heavier.

RG86T and RG86TM Western-Revolver

Target revolver. These are simply variants of the RG86 (qv), chambering 0.22in LR and 0.22in LR/Magnum rimfire cartridges respectively—the latter being supplied with an exchangeable cylinder. The principal difference lies in the adjustable sights, the front of which is mounted atop a muzzle ramp.

RG88 Präzisions-Revolver

General purpose revolver. This currently represents the top of the Röhm range, an elegant double-action general purpose revolver with fixed sights and a ventilated barrel rib. Its design is quintessentially Röhm: a sideways swinging yoke-mounted

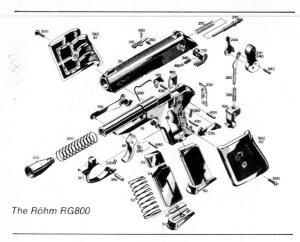

Cal: 0.357in Magnum, 0.38in Special. Mag: cylinder. Mag cap, rds: 6. Trg: DA, exposed hammer. Wt, oz/gm, with 4in barrel: 32.3/915. Loa, in/mm: 7.2, 8.2, 9.3/184, 209, 235. Brl, in/mm: 2.0, 3.0, 4.0/51, 76, 102. Rf: yes. Sft: inertia firing pin.

RG88T Präzisions-Revolver

Target revolver. This variant of the standard RG88 features adjustable target sights, broadened hammer and trigger spurs and plain-surface walnut grips. The 6-inch barrel version is standard, though shorter barrels may be obtained on request. Cal: 0.357in Magnum, 0.38in Special. Otherwise as RG88.

RG800

Starting and signal pistol. This is the most modern of the Röhm blank-firers, apart from the RG69 revolver. The RG800 is based, externally at least, on the Walther PPK, whose safety catch and dismantling system it shares. The result is both well made and reasonably efficient. The finish is normally a blue-anodised alloy, while the chequered brown plastic grips display the rG trademark. Signal flares may be fired with the aid of a Zusatzlauf, which screws into the muzzle. Cal: 8mm blanks, 9mm and 15mm signal flares. Mag: detachable box, catch on butt heel. Mag cap, rds: 7. Trg: DA, exposed hammer. Wt, oz/gm: 17.9/507. Loa, in/mm: 6.1/156. Brl, in/mm: NA. Rf: none. Sft: radial lever on left side of slide below back sight, down to safe; inertia firing pin.

The Röhm RG800

cylinder, locked by a frame-side catch immediately below the hammer. However, the trigger system incorporates a roller bearing, giving a smooth operating cycle. The RG88 is strongly made (its construction is all steel), making it durable and, therefore, good value at its price.

Amadeo Rossi SA

Amadeo Rossi SA, Metalúrgica e Munições, PO Box 28, São Leopoldo–RS, Brazil.

British agency: no sole agents. US agency: Interarms, 10 Prince Street, Alexandria, Virginia 22313, USA. Standard warranty: unknown.

The Rossi dynasty was founded by a family of Italian gunmakers which arrived in Brazil in 1881. Amadeo Rossi was officially registered in 1922, in the port of Caça, but moved to São Leopoldo in 1937, working first from rua Flores da Cunha and latterly from rua Epifânio Fogaça. Finally, in July 1968, Amadeo Rossi SA–Metalúrgica e Munições was formed. Rossi makes a wide range of pistols and revolvers (predominantly the latter) alongside rifles and shotguns, and is now the largest commercial gunmaking company in South America.

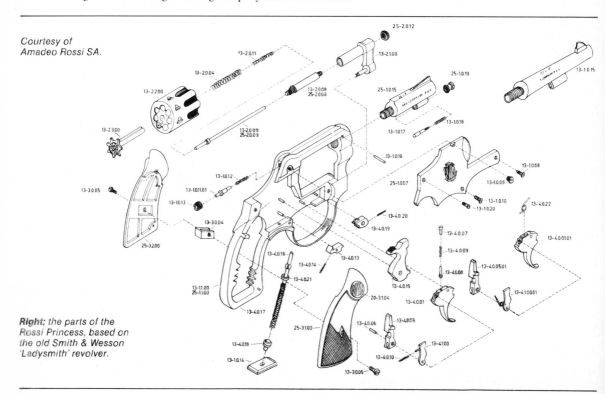

Courtesy of Amadeo Rossi SA.

Right; the parts of the Rossi Princess, based on the old Smith & Wesson 'Ladysmith' revolver.

Garrucha de dois canos, Modelo 08

Personal defence pistol. This twin-barrel side-by-side deringer, made between 1950 and 1968, was characterised by its twin triggers, twin rebounding external hammers acting on inertia-type strikers, and a self-extracting break-open action based on shotgun practice.
Cal: 0.22in LR rf or 0.320in. Mag: none–twin barrel. Trg: SA, exposed hammers. Wt, oz/gm: 9.5/270. Loa, in/mm: 6.3/160. Brl, in/mm: 2.8/72. Rf: 6 R?. Sft: inertia firing pins, rebounding hammers.

Pistola Modelo 9

General purpose pistol. This was single barrelled derivative of the Garrucha Mo.08 was introduced in 1952 and discontinued in August 1969. The grips were wood or plastic (the latter predominated) and the finish, nickel or blue. Engraved, etched and decorated specimens could also be ordered.
Cal: 0.22in LR rf. Mag: none. Trg: SA, exposed hammer. Wt, oz/gm: 10.2/289. Loa, in/mm: 9.0/229. Brl, in/mm: 4.9/125. Rf: 6 R (a few were made 6 L). Sft: inertia firing pin, rebounding hammer.

Coach Pistol Modelo 10

General purpose pistol. Dating from 1956-70, this is assumed to have been a smoothbore version of the Modelo 9 (qv), but details are lacking. It is clear, however, that a distinction was drawn between this gun ('pistolão') and the smaller predecessor ('pistola').
Cal: believed to be 36 or 40 bore. Mag: none. Trg: SA, exposed hammer. Wt, Loa, Brl: NA. Rf: none. Sft: inertia firing pin, rebounding hammer.

Princess Modelo 13

Personal defence revolver. This easily concealed gun, underpowered for its purpose and with too short a barrel to offer accuracy as a substitute for ineffectiveness, is something of an anachronism: a derivative of the old S&W 'Ladysmith' in which cylinder locking was controlled by the ejector rod, doubling as the cylinder axis pin. The lockwork, however, has some parallels with Iver Johnson practice. The Princess was Rossi's first revolver, dating from 1957, and is still in production. It has a rather delicate trigger system and the alloy frame to conserve weight. The Modelo 13 is nearly always nickelled with small wooden or synthetic mother-of-pearl grips.
Cal: 0.22in LR rf. Mag: cylinder. Mag cap, rds: 7. Trg: DA, exposed hammer. Wt, oz/gm: 11.6/330. Loa, in/mm: NA. Brl, in/mm: 3.0/76. Rf: 6 R. Sft: rebounding hammer with half-cock notch.

Ranger Modelo 20

Personal defence revolver. The 1964-vintage Ranger is a decided improvement on the Princess. A comparison between sectional drawings makes the improvements obvious; apart from the newer, stronger components in the trigger system (and the substitution of gunmetal for alloy in the frame), the Ranger has a sliding cylinder-yoke release catch below the hammer on the left side of the frame. The older Modelo 13, conversely, used the less efficient extractor-rod lock.
Cal: 0.32in S&W Long only. Mag: cylinder. Mag cap, rds: 6. Trg: DA, exposed hammer. Wt, oz/gm: 19.3/550. Loa, in/mm: NA. Brl, in/mm: 3.0/76. Rf: 6 R. Sft: rebounding hammer with half-cock notch.

Princess Modelo 25

Personal defence revolver. See remarks made under the original Modelo 13, of which this is little more than a short-barrelled derivative made from February 1965 to date. It shares its predecessor's strengths and weaknesses.
Cal: 0.22in LR rf. Otherwise as Modelo 13, except Wt, oz/gm: 11.3/320. Loa, in/mm: NA. Brl, in/mm: 1.9/47.

Pioneer Modelo 27

Personal defence revolver. Based, like all Rossi revolvers, on Smith & Wesson practice, this gun has a conventional thumb

latch beneath the hammer on the left side of the frame. This controls the cylinder yoke, which may be swung out of the left side of the frame to permit ejection. The Pioneer has a wide spur-type hammer, chequered wooden grips and optional blue/nickel finish. Derived from the Modelo 20, it was introduced in December 1966.
Cal: 0.38in Special. Mag: cylinder. Mag cap, rds: 5. Trg: DA, exposed hammer. Wt, oz/gm: 19.5/555. Loa, in/mm: NA. Brl, in/mm: 1.8/47. Rf: 6 R. Sft: rebounding hammer with half-cock notch.

Ranger Modelo 28

Personal defence revolver. A smaller version of the Modelo 27 (qv), introduced a month later in January 1967, this chambers a smaller and less powerful cartridge. This and the larger cylinder capacity apart, it is identical with the Modelo 27 and thus based on Smith & Wesson practice.
Cal: 0.32in S&W Long. Otherwise as Mo.20, except Wt, oz/gm: 18.0/520. Loa, in/mm: NA. Brl, in/mm: 1.8/47.

Pioneer Modelo 31

General purpose revolver. This long-barrelled variant of the Pioneer Mo.27 was introduced in November 1967.
Cal: 0.38in Special. Otherwise as Mo.27, except Wt, oz/gm: 21.8/622. Loa, in/mm: NA. Brl, in/mm: 4.0/101.

Pioneer Modelo 32

General purpose revolver. Another derivative of the Pioneer Modelo 27, introduced at the same time as the Mo.31 but only made in small quantities.
Cal: 0.38in Special. Otherwise as Mo.27, except Wt, oz/gm: 25.4/720. Loa, in/mm: NA. Brl, in/mm: 6.0/152.

Pioneer Modelo 33

Personal defence revolver. Identical with the Modelo 27 (qv) apart from a longer barrel, but less handy and less easily concealed, the Modelo 33 is a little better suited to deliberate shooting . . . a respect in which, however, the Modelo 31 is better still. The Pioneer 33 dates from May 1969.
Cal: 0.38in Special. Otherwise as Mo.27, except Wt, oz/gm: 20.8/595. Loa, in/mm: NA. Brl, in/mm: 3.0/76.

Modelo 38 Champion

Target or general purpose revolver. This refinement of the Pioneer series is intended for more accurate shooting. To achieve this, the barrel has been extended (see also, particularly, Modelos 40 and 41) and a more sophisticated back sight dovetailed longitudinally into the top of the frame. The sight blade can be moved laterally by a small slotted-head screw on the right side of the sight block. Vertical adjustments are controlled by a screw running down through the spring-steel sight leaf into the frame. Introduced in January 1969, the 38 is only available in blue finish with chequered wood grips. Though a good inexpensive trainer in its 6in barrelled form, it is better suited to plinking than competition use.
Cal: 0.38in Special. Mag: cylinder. Mag cap, rds: 5. Trg: DA, exposed hammer. Wt, oz/gm: 22.9/650. Loa, in/mm: NA. Brl, in/mm: 4.0/101. Rf: 6 R. Sft: rebounding hammer with half-cock notch.

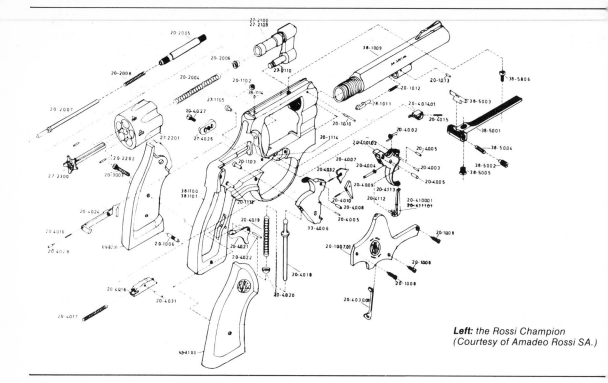

Left: the Rossi Champion
(Courtesy of Amadeo Rossi SA.)

Modelo 39 Champion

Target and general purpose revolver. Introduced in October 1969, this is a smaller calibre derivative of the Modelo 38 (qv). Otherwise identical, it offers lower power from a smaller cartridge, but offsets this disadvantage by a greater-capacity cylinder.
Cal: 0.32 S&W Long. Otherwise as Mo.38, except Mag cap: 6 rounds.

Modelo 40 Champion

Target and general purpose revolver. Dating from December 1969, this derivative of the Modelo 38—with which it is mechanically identical—features a 6in (15cm) barrel. As its overall weight has also increased, it is a better choice for accuracy than its shorter predecessor.
Cal: 0.38in special. Otherwise as Mo.38, except Wt, oz/gm: 25.4/710. Loa, in/mm: NA. Brl, in/mm: 6.0/152.

Champion Modelo 41

Target and general purpose revolver. A variation of the Modelo 39, sharing the same calibre and six-round cylinder, this also features the longer barrel of the Modelo 40. Accuracy is thus enhanced. Only small numbers of these guns are believed to have been made in the early 1970s.
Cal: 0.32 S&W Long. Otherwise as Mo.39, except Wt, oz/gm: 25.2/715. Loa, in/mm: NA. Brl, in/mm: 6.0/152.

Senator Modelo 42

Personal defence revolver. This short barrelled gun was ostensibly introduced in March 1970 but is now often confused with the Modelo 47 (qv)—the two may, in fact, be identical apart from the former's fixed sights.
Cal: 0.22in LR rf. Mag: cylinder. Mag cap, rds: 6. Trg: DA, exposed hammer. Wt, oz/gm: 20.5/580. Loa, in/mm: NA. Brl, in/mm: 1.8/47. Rf: 6 R. Sft: rebounding hammer with half-cock notch.

Senator Modelo 43

Personal defence revolver. This derivative of the Modelo 42 features a longer barrel, but is still underpowered and of no

real utility. Its designation appears to be almost interchangeable with 'Modelo 48', which apparently had adjustable rather than fixed sights.
Cal: 0.22in LR rf. Otherwise as Mo. 42, except Wt, oz/gm: 21.5/610. Loa, in/mm: NA. Brl, in/mm: 3.0/76.

Sportsman (or Champion) Modelo 47

Personal defence revolver. This is apparently a slight improvement on the Modelo 42. However, even the company textbook, *Rossi: a Marca sem Fronteiras* by Tochetto and Weingaertner, fails to distinguish clearly between the two. The ultra-short barrel of the 47 suits it more to personal defence than accuracy—and makes provision of reasonably sophisticated sights superfluous. But use of the very low-powered 0.22in LR rimfire cartridge makes the Modelo 47 an equally poor choice for personal defence. It is available only in blued finish, with chequered wooden grips.
Cal: 0.22in LR rf. Mag: cylinder. Mag cap, rds: 6. Trg: DA, exposed hammer. Wt, oz/gm: 22.4/635. Loa, in/mm: NA. Brl, in/mm: 1.8/76. Rf: 6 R. Sft: rebounding hammer with half-cock notch.

Sportsman (or Champion) Modelo 48

General purpose revolver. The Modelo 48, apparently derived from the Modelo 43 (Senator) of March 1970, is a minor variant of the Modelo 47 with a slightly longer barrel—but an insufficient improvement on the 47 to invalidate the remarks made there.
Cal: 0.22in LR rf. Otherwise as Mo.47, except Wt, oz/gm: 23.1/656. Loa, in/mm: NA. Brl, in/mm: 3.0/76.

Sportsman (or Champion) Modelo 49

General purpose revolver. Another variation of the rimfire target revolver series, The '49' is identical with the Modelo 47 apart from the barrel length and overall weight.
Cal: 0.22in LR rf. Otherwise as Modelo 47, except Wt, oz/gm: 24.5/695. Loa, in/mm: NA. Brl, in/mm: 4.0/101.

Sportsman (or Champion) Modelo 50

Target and general purpose revolver. This is a variation of the Modelo 49, and hence of the 47, with a longer barrel. Together

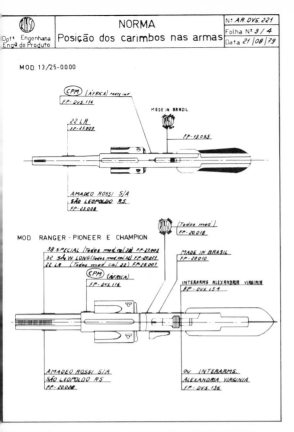

NORMA
Dptº Engenharia
Engª de Produto
Posição dos carimbos nas armas

Nº AR.DVS.221
Folha Nº 3/4
Data 21/08/79

MOD. 13/25-00.00

MOD. RANGER - PIONEER E CHAMPION

with reasonably sophisticated sights, this gives reasonable accuracy, though the low-powered rimfire cartridge is really suitable only for plinking. The Modelo 50 was introduced in May 1970, though the similar Modelo 51 is far more common. *Cal: 0.22in LR rf. Otherwise as Mo.47, except Wt, oz/gm: 25.9/735. Loa, in/mm: NA. Brl, in/mm: 5.0/127.*

Sportsman (or Champion) Modelo 51

Target and general purpose revolver. This gun, introduced in May 1970, offers the longest barrel of the Sportsman series and the greatest weight. Thus its accuracy potential is also the highest, suiting it eminently to plinking and low-grade competition shooting.
Cal: 0.22in LR rf. Otherwise as Mo.47, except Wt, oz/gm: 26.6/755. Loa, in/mm: NA. Brl, in/mm: 6.0/152.

Champion II, Modelo 68

General purpose revolver. This gun made its début in February 1973 together with the Modelos 69 and 70, and derived from the Pioneer—which it greatly resembles. The principal difference concerns the sights; on the Pioneer these had often been, as far as the back sight was concerned, a simple groove along the top of the frame. The Champion II, however, has a low-profile adjustable back sight in a slot cut laterally in the frame, and a 'no-snag' ramp-mounted front sight. The trigger and the hammer are casehardened, the finish may be blue or nickel, and the grips are chequered hardwood.
Cal: 0.38in Special. Mag: cylinder. Mag cap, rds: 5. Trg: DA, exposed hammer. Wt, oz/gm: 21.8/615. Loa, in/mm: NA. Brl, in/mm: 3.0/76. Rf: 6 R. Sft: rebounding hammer with half-cock notch.

Left: *a manufacturer's drawing of the markings applied to the Rossi revolvers for the home and export markets.*
Below: *a catalogue page showing the current range of Champion II revolvers. (Courtesy of Amadeo Rossi SA.)*

Champion II, Modelo 69

General purpose revolver. Identical with the Modelo 68, apart from the chambering. This allows another round to be carried in the cylinder, but the 0.32in bullet is appreciably less effective as a man stopper.
Cal: 0.32in S&W Long. Otherwise as Mo.68, except Mag cap, rds: 6. Wt, oz/gm: 19.4/550.

Champion II, Modelo 70

General purpose revolver. This is another derivative of the Modelo 68, but offering an even less powerful chambering in the guise of the 0.22in LR rimfire round. Thus, the best use for this gun is as a trainer for the larger-calibre versions; it has neither sufficient power to be regarded as a man stopper nor, owing to its short barrel and indifferent sights, sufficient accuracy for target use.
Cal: 0.22in LR rf. Otherwise as Mo.68, except Mag cap, rds: 6. Wt, oz/gm: 21.5/610.

Pioneer Modelo 87

Personal defence revolver. Dating from April 1981, this derivative of the original Pioneer (see Modelo 27) has a direct-strike hammer rather than relying on a separate firing pin pinned into the hammer nose. It also features corrosion-resistant stainless steel construction.
Cal: 0.38in Special. Otherwise generally as Mo.27.

Modelo 88

General purpose revolver. Rarely encountered outside Brazil at the time of writing, this is a derivative of the Modelo 87 with a longer barrel and adjustable Champion II back sight. These combine to give better accuracy and, therefore, better overall performance. The Modelo 88 made its début in April 1981 and incorporates both stainless steel construction and the 'direct hammer' action.
Cal: 0.38 Special. Otherwise as Mo.27, except Brl, in/mm: 3.0/76.

AMADEO ROSSI S.A.
METALÚRGICA E MUNIÇÕES

Oy Sako Ab

F-11100 Riihimäki, Finland.

British agency: apparently none at the time of writing. US agency: Stoeger Industries, 55 Ruta Court, South Hackensack, New Jersey 07606, USA. Standard warranty: 12 months

Sako has a long, convoluted history. It began life as the workshop of the Finnish Civil Guard, established in 1919 and later named Suojeluskuntain Ase- ja Konepaja Osakeyhtio (SAKO), 'Arms & Engineering Workshop of the Civil Guard'. The original Helsinki and later Riihimäki factories made and refurbished many thousands of rifles and other smallarms prior to the Russo-Finnish 'Winter War' (*Talvisota*) of 1939-40 but, after the peace treaty to end the Continuation War was finally signed in November 1944, Sako was rather surprisingly sold to the Finnish Red Cross and its arms-making facilities were destroyed. The rather unexpected success of the L/46 sporting rifle in the immediate postwar years permitted the company to recommence operations and it has now regained its reputation as a producer of superbly-made, dependable products. Production of the extraordinary convertible target pistols began in the 1970s. Details of Sako history will be found in the official *Sako, 1921-1971*, written in Finnish with an English précis, or 'David and Goliath: Sako and the Winter War' by John Walter, in *Shooter's Bible*, 1983.

Sako 22-32

Target pistol. The 22-32 features exchangeable barrels, suiting it to several different shooting disciplines. Though it is by no means a pioneer—the Walther GSP forestalled it by a decade or so—the Sako is an undeniably excellent design and becoming increasingly popular. It has been widely advertised as 'three pistols in one'; the package contains a single grip and three interchangeable barrel/breechblock units. These can be assembled into a match pistol in 0.22in LR rf; a centrefire pistol in 0.32in S&W Long Wadcutter; or a rapid-fire pistol in 0.22in Short rf. The units are easily exchanged. The large transverse bolt through the frame ahead of the trigger aperture is simply unfastened and the barrel section withdrawn forwards. Another unit is attached, taking care that the small intermediate spring between the frame and the barrel is in the correct position, and the retaining screw replaced. There is very little metal around the attachment point, but no user problems have been reported amd the strength must therefore be adequate. The position of the

trigger lever on the left side of the frame must be altered when changing to the rapid fire mode (0.22in Short rf) but *not* between the other two. The 22-32 is normally supplied with injection moulded ABS grips and two magazines in each calibre, but walnut grip blanks can be supplied on request. One feature of the design is the non-reciprocating sights: the Sako is a blowback, and its breech block reciprocates entirely within the gun. Cocking is accomplished by retracting the extension of the breechblock that runs forward on the right side of the barrel unit. The breechblock and extension are chromed while the remainder of the metalwork is well blued steel. The sights and trigger are fully adjustable, as is to be expected on a gun of this quality. Earliest models of the 22-32 'convertible' featured a rapid-fire breechblock/barrel unit with three ports on top of the barrel, and more cut on a diagonal alongside the front sight. There was also an optional three-slot muzzlebrake unit, but both this and the barrel ports have been omitted from latest production, as has the distinction between standard and rapid-fire grips.

Cal: 0.22in short rf, 0.22in LR rf, 0.32in S&W Wadcutter. Mag:

Sako Triace. (Courtesy Oy Sako Ab.)

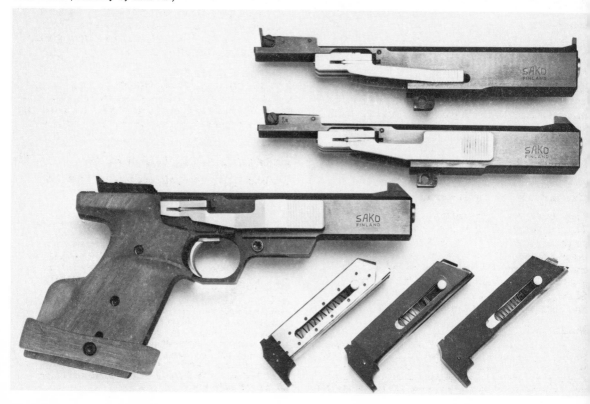

etachable box, catch on frame heel. Mag cap, rds: 5
Trg: SA, concealed striker. Wt, oz/gm, depending on mode:
44.3-48.0/1255-1360. Loa, in/mm: NA. Brl, in/mm: 5.9/150. Rf:
R?. Sft: inertia striker; no manual devices.

Sako Triace

Multi-calibre target pistol. The Triace is an adaptation of the
22-32, introduced late in 1982. There are several obvious
differences; for example, the new pistol has superb, fully
adjustable walnut anatomical grips and a new investment-cast
frame/grip unit with a support extension running forward
under the barrel units (which are the same as those of the 22-
32). In addition, the trigger guard of the Triace is horizontal,
rather than the markedly downward-slanting type of its
predecessor. Improvements have also been made to the Triace
trigger and what appears to be a hold-open catch now lies on
the right side of the frame. The opportunity has also been
taken to increase the magazine capacity of the 0.32in
centrefire version from 5 rounds to 6. The progress of Sako's
extremely interesting design will certainly be worth watching
at the highest level, as it is admirably suited to top-flight
competition.
*Details generally as 22-32, except Mag cap, rds: 5 (6 in 0.32in
S&W Wadcutter). Wt, depending on mode, oz/gm:
44.3-48.3/1255-1370.*

San Marco

**Armi San Marco di Ruffoli, Via A. Canossi 2,
I-25100 Brescia, Italy**

*British, US agencies: no sole distributorships. Standard
warranty: unknown.*

This otherwise anonymous company is known to make
shotguns and percussion revolvers, but no further details
have yet been obtained.

Armi San Paolo

San Paolo, Italy

*British agency: Helston Gunsmiths, Helston, Cornwall,
England. US agency: apparently none. Standard warranty:
unknown.*

San Paolo is now making the Sauer S&W-style revolvers
under licence, as, apparently, is the British Sterling
Armament Company! The guns are described in the
Sauer entry.

J. P. Sauer & Sohn GmbH

**D-2330 Eckernförde/Holstein, Sauerstrasse 2-6
(Postfach 1408), West Germany**

This well known gunmaking firm originated in Suhl, in
Thüringen, in 1733—though the modern organisation
perpetuates little other than the Sauer name; operations
began again in northern Germany immediately after the
end of the Second World War. Sauer made a range of
good quality revolvers until mass production of SIG-
Sauer (qv) pistols began in the late 1970s—see also Armi
San Paolo company and Sterling Armament Co.

Model SR3

Target revolver. This was the best of the Sauers based on
S&W principles, a beautifully made double-action target gun
with a special 'low resistance' trigger, adjustable wide shoe
trigger, broad hammer spur, ventilated barrel rib and fully
adjustable sights. The superbly balanced SR3 offered polished

black finish and stippled walnut grips.
*Cal: 0.22in LR, 0.38in Special. Mag: cylinder. Mag cap, 6
rounds. Trg: DA, exposed hammer. Wt, oz/gm: 37.3, 38.8/1060,
1100. Loa, in/mm: 10.5, 11.5/267, 292. Brl, in/mm: 5.0, 6.0/127,
152. Rf: yes. Sft: inertia firing pin and transfer bar assembly.*

Model TR6

Personal defence revolver. This is a Smith & Wesson-inspired
design, with a side-swinging cylinder locked by a sliding latch
on the left side of the frame beneath the hammer. The gun is
otherwise much the same as the VR4 (qv), apart from its
greatly abbreviated butt and fixed sights.
*Cal: 0.38in Special. Otherwise as SR3, except Wt, oz/gm:
19.8/560. Loa, in/mm: 7.3, 9.3/185, 236.*

Model VR4

General purpose revolver. This gun, heavier than many in its
type and thus more pleasant to shoot, shares the action of the
SR3 (qv). The front sight lies on a prominent ramp rather than
a ventilated rib, the backsight remaining fully adjustable.
*Cal: 0.22in LR, 0.38in Special. Otherwise as SR3, except Wt,
oz/gm: 35.2-38.8/1000-1100. Loa, in/mm: 8.4, 9.4, 11.4/214,
239, 290. Brl, in/mm: 3.0, 4.0, 6.0/76, 102, 152.*

Western Six Shooter

General purpose revolver. This is Sauer's amalgam of the Colt
Peacemaker and New Frontier, a well made gun whose
production was transferred to Italy in the late 1970s. The
standard gun has fixed sights, a 6in (15cm) barrel and smooth
polished grips.
*Cal: 0.22in LR or Magnum rf, 0.357in Magnum, 0.44in
Magnum, 0.45in Colt. Mag: cylinder. Mag cap, 6 rounds. Trg:
SA, exposed hammer. Wt, centrefire version, oz/gm: 42.3-
45.8/1200-1300. Loa, in/mm: 11.5/292. Brl, in/mm: 6.0/152. Rf:
yes. Sft: half cock on hammer, inertia firing pin.*

Savage Arms Corporation
Springdale Road, Westfield, Massachusetts 01085, USA.
Savage made automatic pistols at the beginning of the
twentieth century, but is now better known as a maker of
shotguns and bolt-action rifles. A single-shot Frontier-
style 'revolver', the Model 101, was made for ten years
from 1960 and may still be encountered.

Waffenfabrik Schmidt GmbH
*D-8745 Ostheim/Rhön, Nordheimer Strasse 11, West
Germany.* Schmidt makes a range of good-quality starting
pistols and rimfire/centrefire Western-style revolvers.

Semmerling Corporation

PO Box 400, Newton, Massachusetts 02160, USA

LM-4

Personal defence pistol. The rarely seen Semmerling dates
from the 1970s and deserves mention here as it is an example
of a rare class of operation: the blow-*forward*, its slide moving
away from the breech in the manner of the old Schwarzlose of
1908. The LM-4 is small, as small as the Walther TPH pocket
pistol, but chambers the powerful 0.45in ACP round and
would thus be very difficult to handle. The gun has a short
sight line, is suited only to instinctive shooting and has a
rather curious appearance; the 'retraction' grooves, for
example, lie towards the front of the slide above the trigger
guard. The striker tail of the idiosyncratic double-action
trigger mechanism protrudes through the frame/slide back
*Cal: 0.45in ACP. Mag: detachable box, 'catch' comprising
spring-latches on magazine sides. Mag cap: rds: 4. Wt, oz/gm:
25.7/730. Loa, in/mm: 5.1/130. Brl, in/mm: 3.9/100. Rf: NA.
Sft: NA, possibly none.*

SIG

Schweizerische Industrie-Gesellschaft/Société Industrielle Suisse, CH-8212 Neuhausen/Rheinfalls, Switzerland

British agency: Precision Arms Co., Paddock Wood, Kent TN12 6JE. England. US agency: Interarms, 10 Prince Street, Alexandria, Virginia 22313, USA. Standard warranty: 12 months.

SIG was founded in 1853 to make railway rolling stock but has since become one of the world's leading smallarms manufacturers, in addition to rolling stock and packaging equipment. The first guns made in the Neuhausen factory were single-shot percussion-ignition muzzleloaders, but these were soon followed by the bolt-action Vetterli and Schmidt-Rubin rifles, both of which were adopted by the Swiss armed forces, lucrative contracts being placed with SIG—as the company had been renamed in 1889. Since then many inventors have been associated with SIG, such as Adolph Fürrer, but the success of the pistol business stemmed from the patents granted to Charles Petter in the 1930s. The Petter pistol was developed into the SIG SP 47/8, now known commercially as the SP 210 and adopted by the Swiss army as the Ordonnanzpistole 49. Huge numbers of assault rifles and machine-guns have also been made, but SIG products have always had something of a justified reputation for outstanding quality at an outstandingly high price! Consequently, SIG has developed a range of low-cost pistols made by modern production techniques such as investment casting and precision stamping, and is marketing them in conjunction with the West German Sauer firm (see SIG-Sauer). SIG now also owns a controlling interest in Hämmerli (qv), but the latter still operates independently—despite the existence of the SIG-Hämmerli P 240 target pistol.

Above: SIG, Neuhausen/Rheinfalls. Below: an early SP 47/8 and accessories. Far right: the P 210-6 (courtesy SIG).

Selbstladepistole 47/8

Military and police pistol. This, one of the best automatics yet made—but undeniably the most expensive—has a history dating back to the Petters of the 1930s, which were developed by SIG to become the SP 44 and, finally, the SP 47/8. The SP 47/8 was then adopted by the Swiss armed forces as the Ordonnanzpistole 49 (OP 49) and marketed commercially as the P210. The action, operated by short-recoil, is a modified Browning dropping link with a closed cam path in the barrel block. The two semi-circumferential locking lugs lie ahead of the barrel block, mesh with recesses in the slide, and are pulled downwards as the action recoils. The barrel is then halted and the slide reciprocates alone. SIG's engineers discarded the separate barrel bushing found on some Brownings, substituting cleverly shaped slide contours instead, and developed a slide which runs *inside* the frame in place of the more conventional external slide rails.

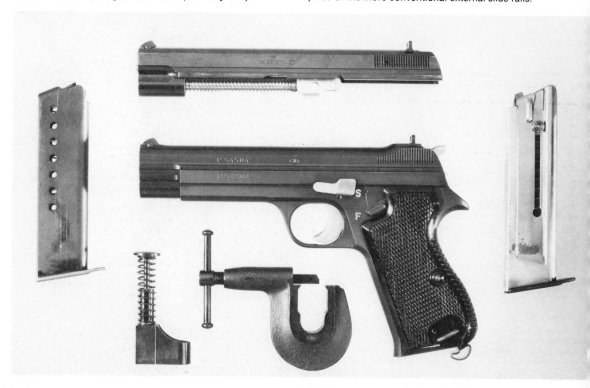

ertical barrel movement does not occur until the projectile
as left the muzzle. The result has been outstanding accuracy,
ut recently the trend has been towards the simplified SIG-
auer series.
Cal: 7.65 or 9 Parabellum. Otherwise generally as SP 210-1.

Pistole 210-2

Military and police pistol. This is a minor variant of the 210-1.
andblasted non-reflecting finish, chequered plastic grips and
 lanyard loop at the lower left side of the butt provide the
main differences.
Cal: 7.65mm and 9mm Parabellum only. Otherwise as P210-1.

Pistole 210-1

Military and police pistol. This is a slightly modernised SP
47/8, sharing identical action. It may be distinguished by its
ighly polished finish, and beech or walnut grips. The two
arger calibres use the standard locked breech, but the
convertible rimfire trainer is a simple blowback. A wide variety
of engraved and highly decorated versions of the P210-1 have
been made, a few of which are depicted here. The culmination
of this has been the Jubiläumspistole 210 (JP 210) produced
o celebrate the 125th anniversary of SIG in 1978, with

exemplary finish, gold plated hammer, trigger, dismantling
catch and safety, and deep-carved walnut grips. Only 500
guns were made (serial numbers JP001 to JP500), all
chambering the 9mm Parabellum.
*Cal: 7.65 or 9mm Parabellum (service), 0.22in LR rf (trainer).
Mag: detachable box, catch on butt heel. Mag cap, rds: 8. Trg:
SA, exposed hammer. Wt, empty w/o mag, oz/gm: 29.8-
32.0/845-910. Loa, in/mm: 8.5/215. Brl, in/mm: 4.8/120. Rf: 4 R
(7.65mm), 6 R (0.22in or 9mm). Sft: radial lever on left side of
frame behind trigger, up to safe; inertia firing pin; half-cock on
hammer; magazine safety; slide/trigger interlock.*

Pistole 210-5

Target pistol. This is a long-barrelled target-shooting
adaptation of the P210, with a carefully selected and refined
trigger giving a pull of 1750gm±250 (3.85±0.55lb) compared
to the 2250±250gm of the standard guns. The back sight,
perched atop the slide, is fully micro-adjustable while the
front sight is mounted—much more rigidly than in some
rivals—on the extended muzzle. The 210-5 is usually blued,
with chequered plastic grips, but contoured walnut examples
are also obtainable.
*Cal: 7.65 or 9mm Parabellum. Otherwise as P210-1, except Wt,
oz/gm: 35.3 or 34.3/990 or 960. Loa, in/mm: 6.0/150*

Pistole 210-6

Target pistol. The 210-6 is a minor variant of the 210-5 (qv),
with the same sights and refined trigger. It has a standard-
length barrel, however, and the front sight is mounted
conventionally on the tip of the slide.
*Cal: 7.65 or 9 Parabellum. Otherwise as P210-1, except Wt,
oz/gm: 34.0 or 33.3/950 or 940.*

SIG, Sauer and Hämmerli

See separate entries for details of distributors

The P220 series, the 230 and the 240 are the results of
varying degrees of co-operation between the SIG and
Sauer (enabling SIG-developed pistols to be marketed in
Germany) and Hämmerli, which SIG now owns.
The results have been extremely interesting.

P220

Military and police pistol. This was one of the first tangible
results of the liaison between SIG and J.P. Sauer & Sohn,
though the Swiss company had been experimenting with
simplified derivatives of the Ordonnanzpistole 49—one gun,
P57768, had been converted as early as 1958, while 36 more
were converted in 1966 and another batch in 1970. By 1974
the design had stabilised and the gun was adopted soon
afterwards as the Ordonnanzpistole 75. The object of the
experimentation was to devise a simpler locking mechanism,
less susceptible to jamming. This was achieved simply by
extending the squared breech upwards until it could be

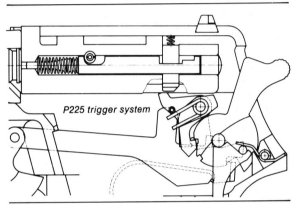

P225 trigger system

cammed into what could otherwise have been termed the
ejection port. This is very evident from the top view
reproduced here. The remainder of the elevating mechanism
was adapted from the SIG P210 (qv). There is a typically
German-style trigger mechanism with a firing-pin lock and a
de-cocking lever. The back sight block can be replaced; eight
sizes are made, ranging from +• (highest) through +, N+, N,
N—, —, —• to —••, the lowest. The P220 presents an
altogether different appearance from the P210: angular, even
ugly, made from stampings and castings wherever possible,
and generally parkerised with greyish plastic grips. However,
it works very well indeed and currently jockeys for a position
amongst the very best in its class. A blowback 0.22in LR rf
(5.56mm lfb) training conversion is also available. In addition
to the regular guns, SIG made two thousand 9mm
'Jubiläumspistolen 220', with gold-plated trigger, hammer, de-
cocking and hold-open levers, and hand-carved walnut grips.
The guns are supplied in blue plush-lined cases, numbered
JP001-JP1999 and have slides displaying the gold inlaid 125
JAHRE (SIG) 1853-1978 on the left side.
*Cal: 7.65 and 9mm Parabellum, 0.38in Super Auto, 0.45in
ACP. Mag: detachable box, catch on butt heel. Mag cap, rds: 7
(0.45in ACP), 9 (others). Trg: DA, exposed hammer. Wt,
oz/gm: 25.7-27.0/730-765. Loa, in/mm: 7.8/198. Brl, in/mm:
4.4/112. Rf: 4 R (7.65mm), 6R (others). Sft: firing-pin lock and
de-cocking system; inertia firing pin.*

P225

Military and police pistol. The P225, developed for the
German police trials, is a modification of the P220 (qv) sharing
a similar action; indeed, the guns are practically identical
internally—though the external differences prevent confusion.

There are a few minor variations in the machining of components in the double-action trigger system, but the firing-pin lock and de-cocking lever are retained. If the 220 is unattractive, the P225 is positively ugly; it is an angular, stubby design with a squared trigger guard (permitting the currently fashionable two-hand grip), a broad stamped trigger lever and a short rounded hammer. These are six different backsight blocks: +, N+, N, N—, —, —∙ from high to low. The magazine release is usually found on the frame-side, and the P225—known to the German authorities as the Pistole 6—is undoubtedly an efficient, effective handgun.

Cal: 9mm Parabellum. Mag: detachable box, catch on side of frame or on butt heel. Mag cap, rds: 8. Otherwise as P220, except Wt, oz/gm: 26.1/740. Loa, in/mm: 7.1/180. Brl, in/mm: 3.9/98.

P226

Military and police pistol. This is a minor variant of the P220 (qv), introduced in 1983 to participate in US pistol trials. The dismantling system has been simplified and there is no manual safety (though the de-cocking lever remains). The P226 is expensive, despite its undoubted efficiency.

Cal: 9mm Parabellum, otherwise generally as P220.

P230

General purpose pistol. This is SIG's entry into the personal defence/general purpose category, an elegant double-action blowback based on German practice. There are no manual safety features, but the firing-pin lock is disconnected only during the final stages of a deliberate trigger pull. This allows the loaded gun to be carried in perfect safety. The P230 was developed in the late 1960s, several experimental guns being tested by the Swiss army at the very end of the decade. There is a tiny exposed hammer, contrast sights (Von Stavenhagen patents) on a matted rib, and five heights of back sight block. The highest is marked +∙, and runs down through +, N, —, to —∙ (the lowest). There have been several revisions to the de-cocking lever head and the machining of the slide retraction grooves, which are now much more closely spaced than before.

Cal: 0.22in LR rf, 0.32in ACP (7.65mm Auto), 0.380in ACP (9mm Short), 9mm Police. Mag: detachable box, catch on butt heel. Mag cap, rds: 7, 8 (0.32in) or 10 (0.22in). Trg: DA, exposed hammer. Wt, oz/gm: 15.5-16.4/440-465 (but 27.1/690 in 9mm Police). Loa, in/mm: 6.6/168. Brl, in/mm: 3.6/92. Rf: 6 R. Sft: firing-pin lock and de-cocking system; inertia firing-pin; half-cock notch on hammer.

Above: the SIG-Sauer P220. **Left:** the locking system of the P220, showing how the breech rises into the ejection cutaway in the slide. **Below:** the P230.

arget pistol. This is a Hämmerli-made version of the SIG P 10, intended for fullbore and standard pistol competitions. ased on the standard short-recoil operated locked breech ystem, using the SIG variant of the Browning Link, the 240 is well made, accurate gun with an adjustable trigger, ompetition sights and a hand-filling walnut thumb-rest style rip. The slide runs on rails on the inside of the frame— nother feature shared with the P 210, but unusual in utomatic pistols apart from the SIGs, of course, and the zech vz/75. Unlike many guns of its type, especially the merican examples, the slide closes on an empty chamber fter the last round has been chambered, fired and ejected. lowback conversion units originally permitted changes from .38in ammunition (locked breech) to 0.22in LR or 0.32in S&W Vadcutter, but the P 240 is only currently available in 0.32in &W.

al: 0.38in Special Wadcutter, 0.32in S&W Wadcutter, 0.22in R rf. Otherwise generally as SIG P 210, except Wt, oz/gm: 3.0/1220 (0.38in), 49.0/1390 (0.22, 0.32in). Loa, in/mm: 0.5/267. Brl, in/mm: 6.0/150. Sft: radial lever on left side of ame behind the trigger, down to safe; safety notch on ammer; inertia firing pin.

elow: an exploded drawing of the P 220, from its anual. (Courtesy of SIG.)

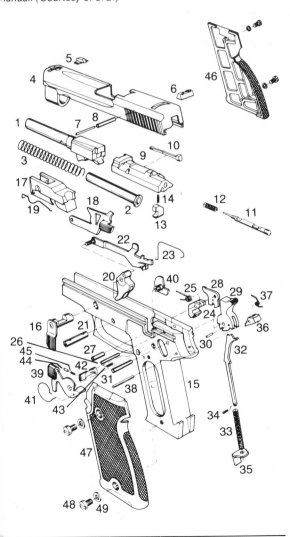

Smith & Wesson

2100 Roosevelt Avenue, Springfield, Massachusetts 01101, USA

UK agency: Springfield Firearms, 8A Eastbourne Road, St Austell, Cornwall PL25 4SZ, England. Standard warranty: 90 days.

Smith & Wesson is, with the possible exception of Colt, the world's best known pistolsmith, claiming a lineage back to 1852 when the original company—which has since gone through many changes of ownership—was formed by Horace Smith and Daniel Wesson. Their Volcanic repeating pistol received a gold medal from the Maryland Institute of the Mechanical Arts, after the Baltimore Exposition of 1854, but large-scale production proved unsuccessful financially and the business collapsed shortly afterwards. By no means discouraged by the failure of the Volcanic, Smith and Wesson joined forces again in 1856 to exploit a patent granted to Rollin White to protect a revolver cylinder in which the chambers were bored right through (unlike those of percussion guns); Smith and Wesson undoubtedly saw the potential that lay in this, when allied with their newly developed rimfire cartridges, and the first S&W rimfire *Model Number 1* revolver appeared in November 1857. The company attained great heights from such humble beginnings, though concentration on Russian contracts in the late 1860s and early 1870s—lucrative though they undoubtedly were—surrendered the home commercial market to Colt. S&W could probably have eclipsed Colt once and for all in the early 1870s, but Colt established its metallic cartridge revolvers very rapidly once White's patent had expired. The rivalry continued throughout the closing years of the nineteenth century—both companies produced revolvers with yoke-mounted cylinders that swung outwards to load, and both attempted to sell their guns not only commercially but also to the government. Colt won over the government in the end; not because its revolvers were superior (S&W guns have always been among the best), but because of the Browning automatic pistol. Smith & Wesson made a few desultory attempts to design automatics, purchasing a Belgian Clément patent in 1910, but the guns were either poor or chambered for unique cartridges. S&W currently makes excellent revolvers, of course, but also some superb automatics based on the modified Colt-Browning system. Many of these have been acquired by the US Navy and special forces, but have never succeeded in dislodging the Colt Government Model from US Army service. S&W has never entered the target pistol market with any real enthusiasm, despite the utility of the Model 41, surrendering it instead to companies such as Ruger and High Standard. Revolvers remain S&W's staple product.

No attempt has been made to catalogue minor manufacturing variations encountered in many S&W designs, particularly those that have been in production for many years. Thus, the distinctions between Model 10, 10-1, 10-5, etc., have been ignored. Further details can be sought in *History of Smith & Wesson* by Roy Jinks (Beinfeld, North Hollywood, 1977 and subsequently) or Neal & Jinks, *Smith & Wesson 1857-1945* (Barnes, New York, 1966).

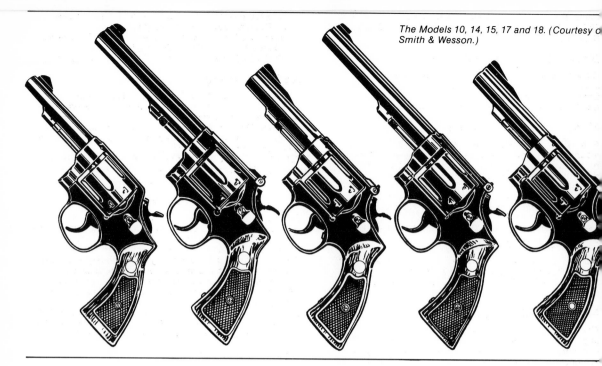

Model 10 Military & Police

General purpose revolver. This long established design
descends from the Hand Ejector Military & Police Revolver of
1899, by way of substantial changes in 1905 and 1915. Built on
the medium size K frame, the Model 10 is the archetypal Smith
& Wesson revolver: well made of impeccable material, with a
yoke-mounted cylinder that can be swung out to the left after
the thumb-latch on the left side of the frame, beneath the
hammer, has been pressed forward. There are fixed sights and
a slender walnut grip. Like all S&W guns, the Model 10 can be
obtained in blue or nickelled steel or corrosion-resisting
stainless steel. Unlike most other revolvers now made in the
United States, the Smith & Wessons do not incorporate a
transfer bar system—a testimony to the efficiency of the basic
design. Instead, the rebounding hammer, developed in 1944,
is prevented from reaching the chambered cartridge unless
the trigger is deliberately held in its rearmost position, and an
auxiliary hammer block, linked to the rebound slide, prevents
inadvertent firing unless the hammer is pulled back to its limit.
Smith & Wesson retains a seperate firing pin, pinned into the
hammer nose, rather than the frame-mounted inertia pattern
of most other comparable revolvers.
*Cal: 0.38in Special. Mag: cylinder. Mag cap, rds: 6. Trg: DA,
exposed hammer. Wt, oz/gm: 29.0-34.0/820-965. Loa, in/mm:
6.9-11.3/156-286, depending on barrel. Brl, in/mm: 2.0, 4.0 5.0
or 6.0/51, 76, 102, 127 or 152 standard weight, or 3.0, 4.0/76,
102 heavyweight. Rf: 5 R. Sft: see text.*

Model 12 Military & Police Airweight

General purpose and personal defence revolver. Introduced in
1952 and renamed 'Model 12' in 1957, this is simply the Model
10 with an alloy frame, the barrel and cylinder remaining
carbon steel. Available only in short-barrelled form, the
Airweight is appreciably lighter than the gun from which it is
derived. Like the Model 10, it uses the medium-size K frame.
*Cal: 0.38in Special. Otherwise as Model 10, except Wt, oz/gm:
18.0 or 19.5/510 or 550. Loa, in/mm: 6.9 or 9.3/156 or 235. Brl,
in/mm: 2.0 or 4.0/51 or 102.*

Model 13 Military & Police Heavy Barrel

General purpose revolver. This—developed for the New York
State Police in 1974—is essentially similar to the Model 10,
built on the K frame, but has a different barrel. In addition, it
has been strengthened to handle magnum ammunition. The
finish is blue or nickel, the stainless-steel derivative being the
Model 65.
*Cal: 0.357in Magnum or 0.38in Special. Otherwise as Model
10, except Wt, oz/gm: 33.0 or 34.0/935 or 965. Loa, in/mm: 8.3
or 9.3/217 or 235 Brl, in/mm: 3.0 or 4.0/76 or 102,
heavyweight.*

Model 14, K-38 Masterpiece

General purpose revolver. This 1947-vintage design is a target
shooting derivative of the Model 10, built on the same K-
pattern medium frame. It has a longer barrel and an adjustable
back sight comprising an elegant spring-steel rib dovetailed
longitudinally into the top of the frame. The standard back
sight insert is a square notch.
*Cal: 0.38in Special. Otherwise as Model 10, except Wt, oz/gm:
38.5 or 42.5/1090 or 1200. Loa, in/mm: 11.1 or 13.5/283 or 343.
Brl, in/mm: 6.0 or 8.4/152 or 213.*

Model 15 Combat Masterpiece

General purpose and personal defence revolver. This is
another variant of the Model 10, introduced in 1949 and
chambering the same ammunition, but with an adjustable
back sight and a Baughman Quick-Draw front sight mounted
on a plain ramp. The grips are chequered Service walnut (with
a square heel and toe).
*Cal: 0.38in Special. Otherwise as Model 10, except Wt, oz/gm:
28.0 or 34.0/790 or 960. Loa, in/mm: 7.1 or 9.1/181 or 232. Brl,
in/mm: 2.0 or 4.0/51 or 102.*

Model 16 K-32 Masterpiece

General purpose revolver. This was a variant of the Model 14
chambering 0.32in S&W Long cartridges. However, it proved
to be unpopular and was discontinued in 1973 after a
production life spanning twenty six years.

Model 17 K-22 Masterpiece

General purpose revolver. Dating from 1946, this is another
Model 10 variant, built on the medium K frame; the Model 17
is a rimfire version of the Model 14 (qv), featuring a click-
adjustable back sight, a Patridge front sight and a long barrel.
Finish is generally blue.

Cal: 0.22in LR rf. Otherwise as Model 10, except Wt, oz/gm: 38.5 or 42.5/1090 or 1200. Loa, in/mm: 11.1 or 13.5/283 or 343. Brl, in/mm: 6.0 or 8.4/152 or 213.

Model 18 Combat Masterpiece

General purpose revolver. This is a rimfire version of the Model 15. Its standard finish is blue; the grips, chequered Service pattern walnut.
Cal: 0.22in LR rf. Otherwise as 4in barrelled Model 15.

Model 19 Combat Magnum

General purpose and personal defence revolver. This is a magnum revolver built on the standard medium or K-Frame, recognisable by its bulkier Goncalo Alves Target grips (the shortest version has round-butt Service grips) and the half-length ejector shroud. The target-style grips have distinctive semi-circular 'Speedloader' cutaways. The revolvers have the standard click-adjustable back sight, but differing front sight options dependent on the length of the barrel. The two short barrels feature Baughman Quick-Draw sights on plain ramps, while the 6in barrel has a square blade sight. The finish is blue or nickel. The Model 19 was introduced in 1955.
Cal: 0.357in Magnum, 0.38in Special. Otherwise as Model 10, except Wt, oz/gm: 31.0, 35.0 or 40.0/880, 990 or 1130. Loa, in/mm: 7.5, 9.5, 11.5/190, 241 or 292. Brl, in/mm: 2.5, 4.0, 6.0/63, 102 or 152.

Model 25 1955 Target

General purpose and target revolver. This is the first of the large, or N-Frame Smith & Wesson revolvers to be encountered, the massiveness of the frame reflecting the power of the cartridges for which the guns are intended. The Model 25 is mechanically identical with the Model 10, has chequered Goncalo Alves Target grips, a plain square-blade front sight, and is invariably blued. It was originally introduced as the 45 Hand Ejector Model 1955, being renamed in 1957.
Cal: 0.45in ACP. Otherwise as Model 10, except Wt, oz/gm: 45.0/1280. Loa, in/mm: 11.4/289. Brl, in/mm: 6.0/152.

Model 25-5

General purpose and target revolver. This variant of the Model 25 1955 (qv) has a different front sight—an S&W Red Ramp,

with a coloured insert in its blade—and S&W Bright Blue finish. There are several barrel lengths.
Cal: 0.45in ACP. Otherwise as Model 10, except Wt, oz/gm: 44.0, 46.0, 52.0/1245, 1295, 1465. Loa, in/mm: 9.4, 11.4, 13.8/238, 289, 349. Brl, in/mm: 4.6, 6.0, 8.4/102, 152, 213.

Model 27 Magnum

General purpose revolver. This large, or N Frame gun is intended for magnum ammunition. Its features include three barrel options, click-adjustable back and square blade front sights and Goncalo Alves Target grips. The finish may be blue or nickel, while the top strap and barrel rib are chequered to minimise interference from reflection.
Cal: 0.357in Magnum, 0.38in Special. Otherwise as Model 25-5, except Wt, oz/gm: 41.3, 44.0, 47.0/1170, 1250, 1330. Loa, in/mm: 9.3, 11.3, 13.6/235, 286, 346.

Model 28 Highway Patrolman

General purpose revolver. This is another of the N Frame revolvers, dating from 1954, chambering magnum ammunition and featuring a half-length ejector shroud. The gun has a Baughman Quick-Draw front sight on a plain ramp and the standard click-adjustable back sight immediately ahead of the hammer. The finish is generally Satin Blue with sandblasted stippling on the barrel rib and frame edging, to minimise reflections that might disturb aim. The grips are standard chequered Service walnut.
Cal: 0.357in Magnum, 0.38in Special. Otherwise as Model 10, except Wt, oz/gm: 41.8 or 44.0/1180 or 1250. Loa, in/mm: 9.3 or 11.3/235 or 286. Brl, in/mm: 4.0 or 6.0/102 or 152.

Model 29 Magnum

General purpose revolver. This 1956-vintage is another N Frame revolver, very similar to the Model 25-5—it even has the same chequered hammer and grooved trigger—but chambering the powerful 0.44in Magnum cartridge rather than the 45 ACP. There are Goncalo Alves grips, S&W Bright Blue or nickel finish and the Red Ramp coloured-insert front sight.
Cal: 0.44in Magnum. Otherwise generally as Model 25-5, but an ounce or two lighter.

Below: *left to right, top to bottom—the M10-6, M19-6, M25-5 and M27-5 (by courtesy of Smith & Wesson).*

Model 31 Regulation Police

General purpose revolver. Production of this old design began in 1917, ceased in 1940 and began again in the late 1940s. Small and light, and thus favoured for home or 'off duty' use, the Model 31 has been popular with law enforcement agencies; in recent years, however, it has lost much ground to the magnums and is now regarded as a poor man stopper. The 0.32in S&W Long bullet is ineffectual compared with that of the 0.357in Magnum or even the 0.38in Special. The Model 31 uses the smallest of the current frame designs, the J pattern, and may be recognised by the decidedly more oval trigger guard aperture made necesasary by the smaller frame. The J Frame replaced the older I pattern in 1960. The sights consist of a fixed blade on a serrated ramp and a fixed square notch.
Cal: 0.32in S&W Long. Mag: cylinder. Mag cap, rds: 6. Trg: DA, exposed hammer. Wt, oz/gm: 20.0 or 22.0/570 or 620. Loa, in/mm: 6.5 or 7.5/165 or 190. Brl, in/mm: 2.0 or 3.0/51 or 76. Rf: 5 R. Sft: as Model 10.

Model 33 Regulation Police

General purpose revolver. Produced in much the same era as the Model 31, but ultimately discontinued in 1974, this chambered the 0.38in S&W cartridge and was issued with a 2in or 4in barrel. The shorter gun was usually known as the 38/32 Terrier, being built on the small frame usually associated with 0.32in calibre revolvers.

Model 34 1953 Kit Gun

General purpose revolver. Also known as the 22/32, this rimfire derivative of the basic J-frame design replaced the earlier Kit Gun of 1936. The guns were intended to be carried by hikers, hunters and fishermen as part of their 'kit'. They are well made, with a fixed blade front sight on a serrated ramp and the standard click-adjustable square notch back sight ahead of the hammer. Finish may be blue or nickel; the grips, chequered walnut round-butt Service pattern.
Cal: 0.22in LR rf. Otherwise as Model 10, except Wt, oz/gm: 22.5, 24.5/640, 690. Loa, in/mm: 6.0, 8.0/152, 203. Brl, in/mm: 2.0, 4.0/51, 102.

Model 35 22/32 Target

General purpose revolver. This was a variant of the Model 34 with a 6in (15cm) barrel and extended chequered walnut grips; introduced in 1953, it was discontinued twenty years later.

Model 36 Chief's Special

Personal defence revolver. This variant of the Model 31 (qv) has a round butt, which makes it fractionally shorter and lighter than its parent.

Model 37 Chief's Special Airweight

Introduced in 1952, this is a 1950-vintage Model 36 with an alloy frame, reducing its weight to a mere 14oz (395gm). Both guns chamber the 0.38in Special cartridge.

Model 38 Bodyguard

Personal defence revolver. This is a modified Model 36, dating from 1955. The most notable difference is the high-side frame, which continues upwards to shroud all but the rounded spur of the hammer. The gun is built on a modified JA alloy frame to conserve weight.
Cal: 0.38in Special. Otherwise as Model 37, but 0.5oz (15gm) heavier.

Model 39

Military and police pistol. This appeared in 1954, after tests lasting several years. It has now been superseded by the Models 439 and 539, but this general description suffices for all of them—the changes being matters of detail. The Smith & Wesson automatic is a locked-breech design operated by short-recoil, using a version of the Browning dropping link/tipping barrel system operated by actuating block integral

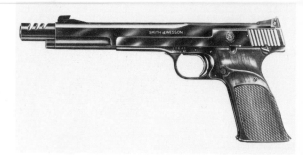

*Models 41 (**above**), 49 (**below**) and 59 (**right**).*

with the barrel. This pulls the breech downward during the recoil phase, permitting the slide to reciprocate alone. The Model 39—the development of which is normally credited to Joe Norman—has a double-action trigger system and a Walther-type safety catch high on the left side of the slide below the back sight. It has a single column magazine and a distinctive arched back strap; compact, well made, accurate and widely regarded as amongst the best of the military automatics made before the introduction of guns such as the SIG-Sauer series, the Smith & Wessons still have their champions and have been acquired in great numbers by the US armed forces.
Cal: 9mm Parabellum. Mag: detachable box, catch on left side of frame behind the trigger. Mag cap, rds: 8. Trg: DA, exposed hammer. Wt, oz/gm: 26.5/750. Loa, in/mm: 7.4/190. Brl, in/mm: 4.0/102. Rf: 5 R. Sft: see text; in addition, the firing pin is an inertia pattern.

Model 40 Centennial

Personal defence revolver. This concealed-hammer revolver, with a grip safety on the back strap, was introduced in 1952 and discontinued in 1974. Chambering the 0.38in Special, it was mechanically identical with the Model 36 (qv).

Model 41 Autoloading Pistol

Target pistol. Smith & Wesson's only rimfire target pistol, introduced in 1957, is still generally regarded as an efficient basic design. A blowback, it features a separate slide/breechblock assembly reciprocating between the frame and the fixed barrel/sight unit, ensuring that the sights are not subjected to the deleterious effects of wear and movement . . . a praiseworthy advance in which S&W can claim to have been a pioneer. The adjustable trigger offers match-grade quality and a variety of sophisticated micro-adjustable sights, barrels, barrel weights and/or compensators attached to the muzzle may be obtained. The grips are thumb-rest style chequered walnut. Several variants have been made: a shorter barrel was offered from 1958, a 0.22in Short rf version from 1961 (both now discontinued) and a Heavy Barrel option in 1965. A cheaper alternative called the Model 46, which lacked the high-quality Model 41 finish, was made for the US Air Force from 1959 until 1968.

Cal: 0.22in LR rf. Mag: detachable box, catch on left side of frame behind trigger. Mag cap, rds: 10. Trg: SA, concealed hammer. Wt, oz/gm: 42.0/1190. Loa, in/mm: 10.5/267. Brl, in/mm: 7.0/178. Rf: yes. Sft: radial lever on the rear frame behind grip; inertia firing pin.

Model 42 Centennial Airweight

Made between 1952 and 1974, this was a variant of the Model 40 with an alloy frame.

Model 43 Kit Gun Airweight

Featuring the alloy JA Frame, this was a lightened version of the Model 34 (qv). It was made between 1955 and 1974.

Model 48 K-22 Masterpiece MRF

General purpose revolver. This 1959-vintage version of the Model 17 (qv) chambers magnum ammunition. The guns are otherwise identical, which can be very confusing when the 48 is fitted with its exchangeable 0.22in LR cylinder! There are Baughman sights on the shortest barrel, squared blades on the longest, and the finish is invariably blue.
Cal: 0.22in LR and Magnum rf. Otherwise as Model 17, except Wt, oz/gm: 36.0, 39.0, 43.0/1020, 1110, 1220. Loa, in/mm: 9.1, 11.1, 13.5/232, 283, 343. Brl, in/mm: 4.0, 6.0, 8.4/102, 152, 213.

Model 49 Bodyguard

Personal defence revolver. This is simply an all-steel version of the Model 38 (qv).
Cal: 0.38in Special. Otherwise as Model 38, except Wt, oz/gm: 20.5/580.

Model 52 Master

Target pistol. This appeared in double-action guise in 1961, changing to single-action (factory model 52-1) in 1963. It is otherwise much the same as the Model 39. The M52 is longer and heavier than the M39, has a steel frame and chambers a different cartridge. Its current guise, the Master, is intended for target shooting, being offered with a special micro-adjustable back sight and a specially finished trigger. Apart from the prominent sight, the best recognition feature is the trigger stop in the back of the guard. The grips are chequered walnut, the finish a rich blue apart from sandblasting around the sighting plane to prevent undue interference from glare.
Cal: 0.38in S&W Wadcutter. Otherwise as Model 39, except Mag cap, rds: 5. Trg: SA, exposed hammer. Wt, oz/gm: 41.0/1160. Loa, in/mm: 8.6/219. Brl, in/mm: 5.0/127.

Model 53 Magnum

This chambered a unique 0.22in centrefire magnum cartridge. Built on the K Frame with three barrel options, and often supplied with an exchangeable cylinder, the Model 53 was discontinued in 1974 after a production life of thirteen years.

Model 57

General purpose revolver. This 1963-vintage revolver is practically the same as the Model 25-5, featuring the Red Ramp front sight—with its coloured insert—and chequered Goncalo Alves grips. Its most distinctive feature is its chambering, more powerful than the 0.357in Magnum without the vicious recoil and muzzle blast of the 0.44in type.
Cal: 0.41in Magnum. Otherwise as Model 25-5, but an ounce or so (30gm) heavier.

Model 58 Military & Police

General purpose revolver. This is a derivative of the Model 10, introduced in 1964, strengthened for magnum ammunition.
Cal: 0.41in Magnum. Otherwise as Model 10, except Wt, oz/gm: 41.0/1160. Loa, in/mm: 9.3/235. Brl, in/mm: 4.0/102.

Model 59

Military and police pistol. This is a modified Model 39 with a staggered-column large capacity magazine, synthetic grips and a straight backstrap. Development began in 1964, though production was delayed until 1971—and has now ceased in favour of the Models 459 and 559.
Cal: 9mm Parabellum. Otherwise as Model 39, except Mag cap, rds: 14.

Model 60 Chief's Special Stainless

Dating from 1965, this is simply a stainless Model 36 (qv).

Model 63 Stainless Kit Gun

This variant of the Model 34 (qv) is made of corrosion-resisting stainless steel and features the coloured-insert Red Ramp front sight.

Model 64 Military & Police Stainless

This 1970 design is a corrosion-resisting Model 10 (qv); variants include a 2in (51mm) barrel with a round butt, a 3in (76mm) heavy barrel with a round butt, and a 4in (10cm) barrel with a square butt.
Cal: 0.38in Special.

Model 65 Military & Police HB Stainless

This variant of the Model 13 was developed for the Oklahoma Highway Patrol in 1974 and has since been offered commercially, featuring corrosion-resisting construction.
Cal: 0.357in Magnum, 0.38in Special.

Model 66 Combat Magnum Stainless

The Model 66 of 1970 is a straightforward variant of the Model 19 (qv), with corrosion-resisting construction and the Red Ramp front sight.
Cal: 0.357in Magnum, 0.38in Special.

Model 67 Masterpiece Stainless

This is a stainless-steel Model 15 with a Red Ramp front sight.
Cal: 0.38in S&W Special.

Model 439

Military and police pistol. This is a modification of the Model 39 (qv), under which a description of its action will be found. The frame remains alloy and the grips are chequered walnut, but obvious changes have been made to the sights: the back sight now lies in prominent protectors, while the front sight is a squared blade.
Cal: 9mm Parabellum. otherwise generally as Model 39, except Wt, oz/gm: 27.0/765.

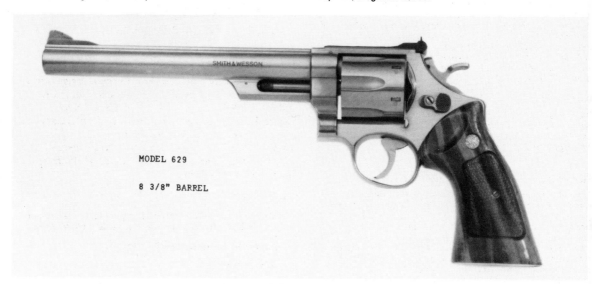

MODEL 629

8 3/8" BARREL

Above: *the long-barrelled version of the Model 629 Magnum, featuring corrosion-resisting stainless steel construction.* **Below:** *the steel-framed Model 539 automatic pistol, currently the best developed form of the original Model 39. The drawings represent the Models 586 and 686, blued and stainless steel-finish respectively, and among the best of S&W's current offerings. (Illustrations by courtesy of Smith & Wesson.)*

Model 459

Military and police pistol. This modification of the Model 59 features a staggered-column magazine, an alloy frame, a straight backstrap and synthetic grips.
Cal: 9mm Parabellum. Otherwise as Model 59, except Wt, oz/gm: 28.0/795.

Model 539

This is steel-framed Model 439 (qv).
Cal: 9mm Parabellum, Otherwise as 439, except Wt, oz/gm: 36.0/1020.

Model 547 Military & Police

General purpose revolver. This utilises the medium-size or K Frame, but is otherwise a Model 10. However, it is sufficiently strong to fire the 9mm Parabellum, has a snubbed hammer spur, and the smallest version has a grip with a noticeably sharper radius than normal—doubtless to control the recoil of such a powerful cartridge. The finish is blue, the sights fixed and the barrel a heavyweight type.
Cal: 9mm Parabellum. Otherwise as Model 10, except Wt, oz/gm: 32.0, 34.0/905, 965. Loa, in/mm: 8.3, 9.3/217, 235. Brl, in/mm: 3.0, 4.0/76, 102.

Model 559

The 559 is a variant of the Model 459 (qv) with a steel rather than alloy frame. As a result, it is appreciably heavier.
Cal: 9mm Parabellum. Otherwise as Model 459, except Wt, oz/gm: 40.0/1135.

Model 581 Distinguished Service Magnum

General purpose revolver. The Model 581 features the L frame, intermediate between the medium K and large N and permitting a sturdier cylinder. The ejector shroud runs right to the muzzle, changing the weight distribution appreciably and making the guns much more muzzle-heavy than their predecessors. They are easier to control—though the change in handling qualities remains a personal preference. The guns are mechanically identical with the Model 13.
Cal: 0.357in Magnum, 0.38in Special. Otherwise as Model 13, except Wt, oz/gm: 42.0/1190. Loa, in/mm: 9.8/244. Brl, in/mm: 4.0/102.

Model 586 Distinguished Combat Magnum

General purpose revolver. The Model 586 DCM is an adaptation of the Model 19 (qv), featuring the L Frame with its full-length ejector shroud and the Red Ramp front sight with its coloured insert. The grips remain the chequered Goncalo Alves Target type.
Cal: 0.357in Magnum, 0.38in Special. Otherwise as Model 19, except Wt, oz/gm: 42.0, 46.0/1190, 1305. Loa, in/mm: 9.6, 11.6/244, 294. Brl, in/mm: 4.0, 6.0/102, 152.

Model 629 Magnum

General purpose revolver. Built on the sturdy N frame, this is a stainless version of the Model 29 with the coloured-insert Red Ramp front sight.
Cal: 0.44in Magnum. Otherwise as Model 29.

Model 681 Distinguished Service Magnum Stainless

This is simply a corrosion-resisting version of the Model 581.
Cal: 0.357in Magnum, 0.38in Special.

Model 686 Distinguished Combat Magnum Stainless

The L-framed 686 is a corrosion-resisting version of the Model 586, with no other distinguishing features.
Cal: 0.357in Magnum, 0.38in Special.

Squires, Bingham Manufacturing Co., Inc.

Manila, Luzon, Philippine Islands.

British agency: none. US agency: none at the time of writing. Standard warranty: unknown.

Little is known about this American-backed organisation, which began production of Squibman autoloading rifles in the mid 1960s and has now entered the revolver market. Even the address is currently in dispute, some sources placing it in Makati—a southern suburb of Manila—and others in Marikina, an outlying north-easterly suburb. The guns are well made and efficient, but are rarely seen in Europe.

Model 100

General purpose revolver. This is simply a cheaper version of the Model 100D, with a plain tapered barrel and plain wooden grips.
Cal: 0.38in Special. Otherwise as 100D.

Model 100DA

General purpose revolver. This gun derives many of its operating ideals from the Colts. It has a laterally-swinging cylinder, a double-action trigger with a long hammer spur and a fully adjustable back sight above and behind the cylinder. A ventilated rib lies above the barrel, while the finish is an interesting 'velvet black'. The grips are extraordinary; made of Philippine ebony, they have a pronounced uniform circumferential flare at the juncture with the frame—quite unlike any other gun. The grips also feature skip-line chequering ('five skip four') inside a single-line border. Quality appears on a par with many European products, but the revolver is rarely seen outside the Orient.
Cal: 0.38in Special. Mag: cylinder. Mag cap, rds: 6. Trg: DA, exposed hammer. Wt, oz/gm: 29.0, 30.0, 34.7/820, 850, 985. Loa, in/mm: 8.3, 9.3, 11.2/210, 235, 285. Brl, in/mm: 3.0, 4.0, 6.0/76, 102, 152. Rf: yes. Sft: unknown, transfer bar and inertia firing pin?

Model 100DC

General purpose revolver. This is a variant of the Model 100D (see above) with a plain, ramp mounted front sight and no over-barrel ventilated rib.
Cal: 0.38in Special. Otherwise generally as 100D.

Thunderchief

General purpose revolver. This is a version of the ventilated-rib fitted Model 100D with a heavier barrel, full-length ejector shroud and fully micro-adjustable sights. It has good quality, comfortable target-style ebony grips.
Cal: 0.22in LR rf, 0.22in Magnum rf, 0.38in Special Otherwise generally as 6in barrelled version of Model 100D.

Star

Star–Bonifacio Echeverria SA, Torrekua 3, Eibar (Guipúzcoa), Spain.

British agency: Parker-Hale Ltd, Golden Hillock Road, Birmingham B11 2PZ, England. US agency: Interarms, 10 Prince Street, Alexandria, Virginia 22313, USA. Standard warranty: 12 months?

The early history of this company has been subjected to much speculation, as its records were destroyed during the Spanish Civil War (1936-9) and little real evidence is available. Operations appear to have begun in 1905 or 1906, with an automatic pistol attributed to Juan Echeverria, but which was little more than an adaptation of the Mannlicher of 1901 (or, perhaps, of the Spanish 'La Lira' copy). The Star trademark was officially registered in 1919, but was clearly being used as early as the publication in 1911 of the German ALFA sales catalogue. Most Stars made prior to 1920 were derived from the Mannlicher or the small Browning personal defence pistols of the early twentieth century; many made after that date, however, took the locked-breech Colt-Browning as their prototype. Echeverria was one of three major Spanish gunmaking businesses permitted to resume production after the Civil War had ended, and is now regarded among Spain's leading pistolsmiths. Its products are either based on the Colt-Browning or a range of blowbacks; almost without exception, the guns are solid and reliable—though, perhaps, not always with the finish associated, for example, with the best German or American makes.

Modelo AS (Super A)

Military and police pistol. The AS, or Super A as it was once more popularly known, is a modernised version of the original Model A of c 1924 incorporating the revised dismantling system discussed in greater detail elsewhere (see Model BS). The AS, which chambers the 0.38in Super Auto cartridge, is much less popular than the BS. Like the latter, however, it is a simple adaptation of the Colt-Browning link-controlled tipping barrel incorporated in the Government Models 1911 and 1911A1.
Cal: 0.38in Super Auto. Mag: detachable box, crossbolt catch on left frame behind trigger. Mag cap, rds: 8. Trg: SA, exposed hammer. Wt, Loa, Brl: generally as Colt M1911 A1. Rf: yes. Sft: radial lever on left rear side of frame, up to safe; inertia firing pin; half-cock notch on hammer.

Modelo BKM (Starlight)

General purpose pistol. The Starlight is the lightest and smallest of the locked-breech Stars chambering 9mm Parabellum ammunition, achieved by virtue of an alloy frame and a barrel/slide unit shorter than that of the Modelo BKS (qv). Current versions of the Starlight have diagonal rather than vertical retraction grooves, a plain front strap, plastic grips and a fixed backsight. Older guns generally have vertical retraction grooves. The finish is generally a well-polished blue, but de luxe versions may also be encountered.
Cal: 9mm Parabellum. Otherwise as Modelo AS except Mag cap, rds: 8. Wt, oz/gm: 25.6/725. Loa, in/mm: 7.2/182. Brl, in/mm: 3.9/99.

Modelo BKS (Starlight)

General purpose pistol. This is a lightweight Modelo BS, still chambering the full power cartridge and something of a handful—but popular because of its attractive combination of man-stopping qualities and concealability. The Modelo BKS shares the action and dismantling systems of the BS (qv), but offers an alloy rather than machined gunmetal frame. It appears to have been replaced by the Modelo BKM (qv).
Cal: 9mm Parabellum. Otherwise as Modelo BS, except Wt, oz/gm: 26.0/735. Loa, in/mm: 7.4/188. Brl, in/mm: 4.3/109.

Modelo BM

General purpose pistol. This variant of the Modelo BKM (qv) has a conventional forged and machined gunmetal frame. Very much heavier than its companion, it is more comfortable to fire if less handy to use. It is obtainable in blue or chromed finish.
Cal: 9mm Parabellum. Otherwise as BKM, except Wt, oz/gm: 34.1/965.

Modelo BS (or Super B)

Military and police pistol. This is another of Echeverria's locked breech pistols, a simple derivative of the Colt M1911/1911A1 Government Models (qv) lacking the manufacturing quality of the American guns, but honest and dependable. The BS, sometimes known as the 'Super B', is a modification of the original Modelo B of 1928, incorporating a modified dismantling system developed in the mid 1940s. This consists of a catch on the right side of the frame which enables the slide and barrel to be removed without withdrawing the slide latch/lock pin, unlike both the Colts and previous Stars. The Modelo BS, though it bears a close external affinity to the Colt M1911A1, chambers 9mm Parabellum ammunition and the rear of its slide is cut vertically on a line extended from the backstrap—quite unlike the Colt, as a comparison of photographs will testify. The Stars also have an elongated spur to protect the web of the thumb. The Modelo BS has served the Spanish armed forces as the Modelo 46. The guns are generally blued with chequered plastic (civil) or wooden (military) grips, but *Modelos de Lujo*—de luxe guns—have been made with almost every conceivable mixture of damascening, engraving, etching and inlaying of previous and semi-precious metals.
Cal: 9mm Parabellum. Otherwise as Modelo AS (qv), except Mag cap, rds: 8. Wt, oz/gm: 37.5/1065. Loa, in/mm: 8.5/216. Brl, in/mm: 5.0/127.

Modelo DKL

General purpose and personal defence pistol. The DKL is by far the smallest of the locked-breech Star-made Colt-Browning system guns, chambering the 9mm Short (called the 9mm Corto in the Iberian peninsula) and is, therefore, not particularly effective. However, the Modelo DKL is scarcely larger than many pocket guns chambering the 0.22in LR or 6.35mm Auto, any of which it totally eclipses. This Star retains all the features of its larger relations—safety, hold-open, dismantling system—and contains them in an alloy frame. The slides are blued, the frames anodised black and the synthetic grips are partly chequered.
Cal: 0.380in ACP (9mm Short). Otherwise as Modelo BS, except Mag cap, rds: 6. Wt, oz/gm: 14.8/420. Loa, in/mm: 5.7/145. Brl, in/mm: 3.2/81.

Modelo FR

General purpose pistol. This blowback is intended for sporting or 'plinking' use, adapted from the original Modelo F introduced about 1947. The older pattern featured a rather angular 'shaped' grip, the lines of which were greatly refined on the post-1965 FR series—which is also distinguished by the hold-open catch inset on the top edge of the left grip. The Modelo FR has a hefty slab-sided fixed barrel protruding well ahead of the slide, and it sights are fixed. It is usually blued with chequered synthetic grips, but highly decorated versions (*Modelos de Lujo*) have also been made.
Cal: 0.22in LR rf. Mag: detachable box, crossbolt catch on left frame behind trigger guard. Mag cap, rds: 10. Trg: SA, exposed hammer. Wt, oz/gm: 26.0/735. Loa, in/mm: 7.3/185. Brl, in/mm: 4.3/109. Rf: yes. Sft: radial lever on rear left of frame, up to safe; inertia firing pin; half-cock notch on hammer.

A cluster of Stars
top to bottom
Models 28DA, PD, BK, SS and
FR Target
(Courtesy of Parker-Hale Ltd)

Modelo FR Sport

General purpose pistol. This is a minor adaptation of the standard Modelo FR (qv) with a longer barrel and adjustable sights. The mechanism remains a simple blowback, popular and quite well made, though lacking the manufacturing quality of some of its European and American rivals.
Cal: 0.22in LR rf. Otherwise as FR, except Wt, oz/gm: 27.0/765. Loa, in/mm: 9.0/229. Brl, in/mm: 6.0/152.

Modelo FR Target

Target pistol. Available again after an absence of several years, the FRT is the most efficient of the FR series. It remains a blowback, but offers adjustable sights, a long barrel and an optional counterweight which can be attached beneath the barrel (ahead of the slide) with two Allen-head screws. The guns are generally anodised blue, while the grips are partly chequered thumbrest-pattern plastic.

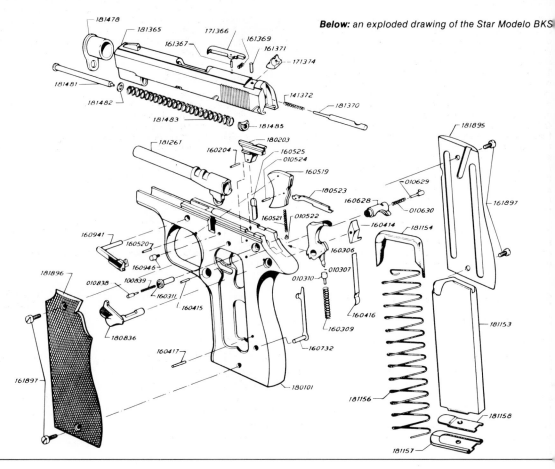

Cal: 0.22in LR rf. Otherwise as FR, except Wt, oz/gm: 29.5/835. Loa, in/mm: 10.0/254. Brl, in/mm: 7.0/177.

Modelo HK (Lancer)

Personal defence pistol. This is a pocket-size derivative of the FR series (qv) with the barrel reduced to approximately the length of the slide and the butt greatly shortened. Unfortunately, the Modelo HK chambers the ineffective 0.22in LR rf and its abbreviated butt and exaggerated thumb-web spur will not allow much more than a three-finger grip. The Modelo DKL is a better self-defence gun, which is presumably why the HK has been discontinued.
Cal: 0.22in LR rf. Otherwise as FR, except: Mag cap, rds: 7. Wt, oz/gm: 14.5/410. Loa, in/mm: 5.5/140. Brl, in/mm: 3.0/75.

Modelo PD

General purpose pistol. This is the smallest and lightest 0.45in ACP-chambered pistol currently available from series production (but see remarks under DETONICS). The Modelo PD is an interesting little gun, but suits an experienced rather than a novice firer because of its fierce muzzle blast and severe recoil. It has a gunmetal slide and an alloy frame, the front strap is grooved to assist grip and the grips are chequered hardwood. The backsight may be adjusted laterally and vertically while the front sight is a matted angular blade. The action remains an unaltered Colt-Browning, described in greater detail under the Modelo BS. Earliest guns had vertical slide retraction grooves, but grooves on newer models are diagonal (sixteen narrow).
Cal: 0.45in ACP. Otherwise as Modelo AS (qv), except Mag cap, rds: 6. Wt, oz/gm: 25.1/710. Loa, in/mm: 7.1/180. Brl, in/mm: 3.9/100.

Modelo PS

Military and police pistol. Now discontinued, this was the largest and most powerful of the Echeverria range of Colt-Browning adaptations, chambering the 0.45in ACP but by no means as popular as the 9mm Parabellum version. It replaced the original Modelo P of the mid 1930s, from which it differed principally in its dismantling system (see Modelo BS). The PS had a gunmetal frame and slide, well polished and nicely blued, and wooden or synthetic grips.
Cal: 0.45in ACP. Otherwise generally as Modelo AS, except Mag cap, rds: 7. Wt, oz/gm: 39.0/1105.

Modelo SM Super

General purpose pistol. This appears to have been an alternative designation, widespread in the United States, for what is more commonly known as the Modelo SS (qv). It is a Super M with a longer butt and one more cartridge in the magazine.

Modelo SS

General purpose pistol. This variation on the basic Echeverria 'Star' Colt-Browning theme chambers the 0.380in ACP (9mm Short, or 9mm Corto in Spain), underpowered compared to the 9mm Parabellum but resulting in a gun that is notably pleasant to fire—though undeniably larger and bulkier than many others (see Modelo DKL). However, this makes it more suitable for a novice and its greater accuracy, owing at least in part to its longer sight radius, represents a welcome bonus.
Cal: 0.380in ACP (9mm Short). Otherwise as Modelo AS, except Wt, oz/gm: 22.0/625. Loa, in/mm: 6.5/165. Brl, in/mm: 4.0/102.

Modelo 28 DA

Military and police pistol. The 28 DA, the latest of the Stars, is competing strongly for adoption as the Spanish service pistol of the 1980s. It will be interesting to compare the progress of the 28 DA and the Astra A-80, refined but conventional, against the allegedly revolutionary Llama 'Omni' (qv). The Star is a clever combination of the basic Colt-Browning operating system with easy dismantling and a carefully packaged' double-action trigger system contained in the modular back-strap assembly; the hammer, hammer spring, disconnector, sear and ejector can simply be slid out at will. Other features include a SIG-type slide, running *inside* the frame rails, and a German-style rotary or 'barrel' combination firing-pin lock and de-cocking lever. The Modelo 28 DA has squared contours, plastic grips and fluting—to aid grip—on both grip straps and the reverse-curved front section of the trigger guard. The ambidexterous safety is placed high on the slide, under the fully adjustable back sight, while the serrated angular front sight blade lies at the front of the matted slide-top. The location of the slide retraction grooves is one rather odd feature of an otherwise very good design: they are difficult to grip in the wet or with gloved fingers despite the assistance afforded by the safety catch. It is notable that the derivatives of the basic design, 28 PDA and 28 PKDA, feature grooves moved forward away from the safety.

Cal 9mm Parabellum. Mag: detachable staggered column box, crossbolt catch behind the trigger guard.. Mag cap, rds: 15. Trg: DA, exposed hammer. Wt, oz/gm: 40.2/1140. Loa, in/mm: 8.1/205. Brl, in/mm: 4.3/110. Rf: yes. Sft: rotary lever on slide-side, down to safe; inertia firing pin; firing-pin lock; half-cock notch on hammer.

Modelo 28 PDA

General purpose pistol. This is a shortened version of the standard Modelo 28 DA (qv), sharing the same locking system and double-action trigger. However, the slide retraction grips have been moved forward ahead of the safety catch and the front under-edge of the recoil spring housing has been contoured rather than simply straight-cut. The grips display more extensive chequering.
Cal: 9mm Parabellum. Otherwise as 28 DA, except Wt, oz/gm: 38.8/1100. Loa, in/mm: 7.6/193. Brl, in/mm: 3.9/98.

Modelo 28 PKDA

General purpose pistol. This is simply a variant of the 28 PDA (qv) with a light alloy frame to conserve weight. The two guns are otherwise identical.
Cal: 9mm Parabellum. Otherwise as 28 PDA, except Wt, oz/gm: 30.4/860.

Sterling Arms Corporation

211 Grand Street, Lockport, New York State 14094, USA.

British agency: no sole distributorship at the time of writing. Standard warranty: 90 days.

Sterling began life in the rather quaintly named town of Gasport, NY, in the mid 1960s, making a series of blowback target pistols which failed to find any large-scale markets. However, the contemporary personal defence pistol was considerably more successful and paved the way for the current range of personal defence and general purpose automatics-the larger of which has attained a justifiably high reputation for quality and reliability. Thus, the position of Sterling on the US arms-making scene has been consolidated and the company was sufficiently encouraged to enter the single shot hunting/sporting pistol scene with the 1982-vintage X-Caliber, an interesting design intended to compete with guns such as the Merrill and the Thompson/Center Contender—though the latter, particularly, has been available for several years and has a strong hold on the market.

Model 45DA

Military and police pistol. Dating from 1979, this represents Sterling's most impressive offering—a double-action experimental service automatic chambering the 0.45in ACP. The 45DA incorporates another variation of the Colt-Browning tipping-barrel locking system, which it allies with an adjustable muzzle bushing. There is an adjustable backsight, a ring hammer protruding above the long rearward thumb-web spur and a clearly labelled slide-mounted ambidexterous safety. The gun is angular and rather ugly, but currently exists only as a prototype and refinement would obviously be effected were it to be marketed commercially.
Cal: 0.45in ACP. Mag: detachable staggered-column box, crossbolt catch on left side of frame. Mag cap, rds: 8. Trg: DA, exposed hammer. Wt, oz/gm: 36.0/1020. Loa, in/mm: 7.5/191. Brl, in/mm: 4.3/108. Rf: yes. Sft: radial lever on left side of slide (can be repositioned on right side); inertia firing-pin.

Model 283 Target Cup

Target pistol. This, now discontinued, was a target shooting derivative of the Trapper (see Model 285), featuring a huge blade-type front sight and an equally prominent micro-adjustable square notch back sight atop the slide directly above the slide retraction grooves. The Target Cup has an adjustable trigger and optional auxiliary weights. It was mechanically identical with the 285 Trapper (qv) and had an equally rapid demise, possessing insufficient good qualities to compete with the similar but better established Rugers, Smith & Wessons, High-Standards and Colts. Finish was blue; grips, chequered black Cycolac.
Cal: 0.22in LR rf. Mag: detachable box, catch on butt heel. Mag cap, rds: 10. Trg: SA, exposed hammer. Wt, oz/gm: 36.0/1020. Loa, in/mm: 9.0/229. Brl, in/mm: 4.5/114. Rf: yes. Sft: manual sear-lock safety; inertia firing-pin.

Model 284 Target Cup

Target pistol. The 284 was a variant of the Model 283 with a tapered 6in (15cm) barrel, but otherwise identical.
Cal: 0.22in LR rf. Otherwise as 283, except Wt, oz/gm: 38.5/1090. Loa, in/mm: 10.5/267.

Model 285 Trapper

Sporting and general purpose pistol. This was one of the earliest Sterling pistols, contemporary with the Models 283 and 284 and apparently dating from 1968/9. The 285 is a blowback firmly rooted in the tradition of the Colt Woodsman, whose general appearance and half-slide construction it shares. However, the Sterling has a hammer spur to permit thumb-cocking and a differently shaped barrel. Tapered barrels were standard but a cylindrical 'bull' heavyweight could be obtained on request. The blade front sight was mounted directly on the muzzle crown (4.5in barrel) or atop a matted ramp (6in barrel), the back sight being a fixed square notch on the slide-top. The finish was generally blued; the extremely raked grips, black Cycolac. Unfortunately, the distinctly odd appearance contributed to its untimely demise.
Cal: 0.22in LR rf. Otherwise generally as 283, except Wt, oz/gm: 36.0, 38.5/1020, 1090. Loa, in/mm: 9.0, 10.5/228, 267. Brl, in/mm: 4.5, 6.0/115, 152.

Model 286 Trapper

Sporting and general purpose pistol. A version of the 285, this simply featured the 4.5in heavyweight 'bull' barrel.

Right: *several Sterling pistols–from top to bottom, the stainless Model 300S and 302S personal defence pistols, the double-action Model 400 Mk II and the 402S Mk II. (Courtesy of Sterling Arms.)*

Model 287 PPL

Personal defence pistol. This appears to have been an ultra-short Trapper, with a shortened barrel, frame and butt, but little else is known. It was especially short-lived because of the success of the Model 300 (qv).
Cal: 0.22in LR rf. Mag: detachable box, catch on butt heel. Mag cap, rds: 5. Trg: SA, exposed hammer. Wt, oz/gm: 22.5/640. Loa, in/mm: 5.4/137. Brl, in/mm: 2.0/51. Rf: yes. Sft: manual crossbolt (?); inertia firing-pin.

Model 300

Personal defence pistol. This popular little blowback is a modern American-made variation on a traditional European theme: a small, easily concealable 0.25in ACP (6.35mm Auto) calibre pocket gun. The Model 300 is well made and blued, if very conventional. Its grips are black fluted cycolac with silvered 'SA' (Sterling Arms) monograms.
Cal: 0.25in ACP (6.35mm Auto). Mag: detachable box, catch on butt heel. Mag cap, rds: 6. Trg: SA, concealed striker. Wt, oz/gm: 13.0/370. Loa, in/mm: 4.8/122. Brl, in/mm: 2.0/51. Rf: yes. Sft: radial lever on left side of frame behind trigger, down to safe; inertia firing-pin.

Model 300S

Personal defence pistol. This is a variant of the Model 300 (qv), made of corrosion-resisting stainless steel. It is mechanically identical with its near relation.
Cal: 0.25in ACP (6.35mm Auto). Otherwise as Model 300.

Model 302

Personal defence pistol. The Model 302, contemporary with the 300 (qv), is another pocket Sterling—but this time chambering rimfire ammunition and a poorer choice for personal defence than its 0.25in ACP cousins; it is, however, a more economical 'plinker' or practice weapon. The finish is blue; the grips, black Cycolac.
Cal: 0.22in LR rf. Otherwise as Model 300.

Model 302S

Personal defence pistol. This is simply an Model 302 (qv) with non-corrosive stainless steel finish.
Cal: 0.22in LR rf. Otherwise as Model 300.

Model 400 Mk II

General purpose pistol. This the first of the larger blowback Sterlings, introduced in the mid 1970s in 'Mark I' guise (a retrospective designation). The Mark II followed in 1979, with a slimmer slide and frame, modified hammer, a modified crossbolt magazine release, and a revised fully adjustable back sight let into the top surface of the slide. The Sterling 400—blued, but with a stainless steel barrel—bears some resemblance to the Walther PP, part of which is due to the rotary or 'barrel' safety unit placed on the left side of the slide below the back sight and the ring hammer. However, the Sterling is bigger, has walnut grips and the frame contours beneath the muzzle are radically different. The result is a well made, efficient and popular gun which quickly established itself on the North American market.
Cal: 0.380in ACP (9mm Short). Mag: detachable box, crossbolt catch on left side of frame behind trigger. Mag cap, rds: 7. Trg: DA, exposed hammer. Wt, oz/gm: 26.0/735. Loa, in/mm: 6.5/165. Brl, in/mm: NA. Rf: yes. Sft: rotary catch on left side of slide, up to safe; inertia firing-pin; half-cock notch on hammer.

Model 400S Mk II

General purpose pistol. This is a version of the standard 400 Mk II (see above) with stainless steel construction.
Cal: 0.380in ACP (9mm Short). Otherwise as M400.

Model 402 Mk II

General purpose pistol. The 402 series—comprising the Models 402 and 402S—is a small-calibre version of the Model 400, chambering the 0.32in ACP. Thus the larger 400 is a better man stopper and, consequently, a more popular choice for those to whom controlling its greater recoil presents no difficulty. The Model 402 is mechanically identical with its predecessor, blued with a stainless steel barrel, and has chequered walnut grips.
Cal: 0.32in ACP (7.65mm Auto). Otherwise as 400 (qv).

Model 402S Mk II

General purpose pistol. This is nothing more than a stainless steel version of the standard 402, whose design it otherwise parallels.
Cal: 0.32in ACP (7.65mm Auto). Otherwise as Model 400 (qv).

X-caliber

Target pistol. Dating from 1982, this is Sterling's competitor to the Thompson/Center Contender, the Merrill and other single-shots designed for sporting or hunting use. The X-caliber is a tipping-barrel design locked by a push-button on the left side of the receiver directly above the trigger. Its features include an octagonal barrel carrying a ramp-mounted blade front sight, the fully adjustable back sight lying in a massive faired housing on the barrel directly above the breech. The hammer

is powered by a coil-spring and plunger system inside the grip retaining cylinder (stock stud). The front of the trigger guard is concave, to permit a comfortable two-handed grip, while the fore-end and laminated butt are made of Goncalo Alves wood. The X-caliber may be obtained in two standard barrel lengths and a number of differing calibres described below. Calibre changes may be effected simply by removing the fore-end and then the barrel pivot pin. The firing pin can also be changed to suit rimfire or centrefire cartridges.

Sterling X-caliber Nomenclature

Model	Calibre	Barrel	Weight
X-22-8	0.22in rf	8in	58oz
X-22-10	0.22in rf	10in	62oz
X-22M-8	0.22in Mag rf	8in	58oz
X-222-10	0.22in Mag rf	10in	62oz
X-357-8	0.357in Mag	8in	56oz
X-357-10	0.357in Mag	10in	60oz
X-44-8	0.44in Mag	8in	54oz
X-44-10	0.44in Mag	10in	58oz

Cal: see table. Mag: none, single shot. Trg: SA, exposed hammer. Wt, oz/gm: 54-62.0/1530-1760. Loa, in/mm: 13.0, 15.0/330, 381. Brl, in/mm: 8.0, 10.0/203, 254. Rf: yes. Sft: hammer-block arm; inertia firing-pin.

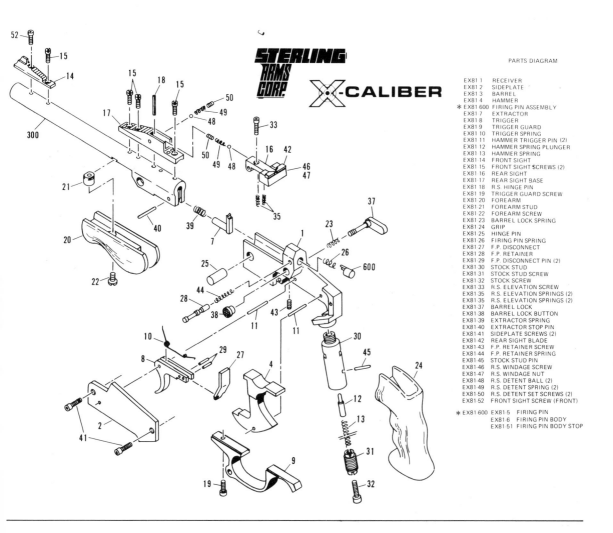

STERLING ARMS CORP.

X-CALIBER

PARTS DIAGRAM

EX81·1	RECEIVER
EX81·2	SIDEPLATE
EX81·3	BARREL
EX81·4	HAMMER
* EX81·600	FIRING PIN ASSEMBLY
EX81·7	EXTRACTOR
EX81·8	TRIGGER
EX81·9	TRIGGER GUARD
EX81·10	TRIGGER SPRING
EX81·11	HAMMER TRIGGER PIN (2)
EX81·12	HAMMER SPRING PLUNGER
EX81·13	HAMMER SPRING
EX81·14	FRONT SIGHT
EX81·15	FRONT SIGHT SCREWS (2)
EX81·16	REAR SIGHT
EX81·17	REAR SIGHT BASE
EX81·18	R.S. HINGE PIN
EX81·19	TRIGGER GUARD SCREW
EX81·20	FOREARM
EX81·21	FOREARM STUD
EX81·22	FOREARM SCREW
EX81·23	BARREL LOCK SPRING
EX81·24	GRIP
EX81·25	HINGE PIN
EX81·26	FIRING PIN SPRING
EX81·27	F.P. DISCONNECT
EX81·28	F.P. RETAINER
EX81·29	F.P. DISCONNECT PIN (2)
EX81·30	STOCK STUD
EX81·31	STOCK STUD SCREW
EX81·32	STOCK SCREW
EX81·33	R.S. ELEVATION SCREW
EX81·35	R.S. ELEVATION SPRINGS (2)
EX81·35	R.S. ELEVATION SPRINGS (2)
EX81·37	BARREL LOCK
EX81·38	BARREL LOCK BUTTON
EX81·39	EXTRACTOR SPRING
EX81·40	EXTRACTOR STOP PIN
EX81·41	SIDEPLATE SCREWS (2)
EX81·42	REAR SIGHT BLADE
EX81·43	F.P. RETAINER SCREW
EX81·44	F.P. RETAINER SPRING
EX81·45	STOCK STUD PIN
EX81·46	R.S. WINDAGE SCREW
EX81·47	R.S. WINDAGE NUT
EX81·48	R.S. DETENT BALL (2)
EX81·49	R.S. DETENT SPRING (2)
EX81·50	R.S. DETENT SET SCREWS (2)
EX81·52	FRONT SIGHT SCREW (FRONT)
* EX81·600 EX81·5	FIRING PIN
EX81·6	FIRING PIN BODY
EX81·51	FIRING PIN BODY STOP

Sterling Armament Co. Ltd

Sterling Works, Dagenham, Essex RM10 8ST, England.

US distributor: Lanchester (USA) Inc., PO Box 47332, Dallas, Texas 75247, USA.
Standard warranty: 12 months?

Sterling, better known for its own submachine-guns and licensed Armalite rifles, annnounced in 1983 that it would be making the range of S&W-pattern revolvers formerly associated with Sauer. Sterling also makes a very short submachine-gun as the 'Pistol Mk 7'; for the purposes of this work, however, this is regarded as a submachine-gun rather than a handgun!

Sterling-Sauer revolvers

These are described in greater detail in the Sauer section, as they are also being made under licence in Italy (see San Paolo). The good quality Sterlings are marketed thus:

Compact—0.38in Special, short barrel, fixed sights and an abbreviated rounded butt.
Competition—0.38in Special, 6in (15cm) barrel, with a squared target-style grip and adjustable sights.
Competitor—a variant of the Competition chambering the 0.22in LR rimfire cartridge.
Service Special—in 0.38in Special, 4in (10cm) barrel, with an adjustable back sight, a 'no snag' front sight and a slender squared butt.

Steyr-Daimler-Puch AG

A-1010 Wien 1, Kärntnerring 7, Austria

UK agency: no sole distributorship; guns available through John Slough, 35 Church Street, Hereford, and others. US agency: LES, 2301 Davis Street, North Chicago, Illinois 60064, USA.

Once better known as Österreichische Waffenfabrik Gesellschaft (OEWG), this organisation makes Mannlicher system rifles. Many handguns were made in the early twentieth century, but recent attempts—which included a personal defence gun known as the SP, discontinued in 1965—have not been as successful. The company's hopes are current pinned on the Pi 18.

Right: *the Stoeger STLR-4. The GB is pictured on page 20.*

Pistole 18 (Pi 18) or Model GB

Military and police pistol. Known in the USA as the Rogak P-18, this is an unusual delayed blowback, gas being bled into the annular space between the slide and the barrel to prevent the premature opening of the breech. The Pi 18 also has an unusually large-capacity magazine and provision, in some variants at least, for selective fire and/or a burst facility. It is well made, very comfortable to fire (gas operated pistols rarely exhibit harsh recoil) and allegedly suffers little from propellant fouling, the traditional curse of guns of its type. *Cal: 9mm Parabellum. Mag: detachable box, catch on left side of frame behind trigger. Mag cap, rds: 18. Trg: DA, exposed hammer. Wt, empty, oz/gm: 33.2/940. Loa, in/mm: 8.9/226. Brl, in/mm: 5.4/137. Rf: yes. Sft: rotary catch on left rear of slide beneath back sight; inertia firing pin.*

Stoeger Industries

55 Ruta Court, South Hackensack, New Jersey 07606, USA

Stoeger is better known as the publisher of *Shooter's Bible* but also markets blowback Lugers made elsewhere in the United States—apparently by Replica Arms

Stoeger Luger

General purpose pistol. This simple blowback 're-creation' of the world famous short-recoil operated toggle-locked Parabellum was made of alloy until 1982 (steel thereafter) and chambering 0.22in LR rimfire ammunition—which makes it a popular plinker. There have been several variants:

STLR-4—4.5in barrel, fixed sights.
STLR-5—5.5in barrel, fixed sights.
TLR-4—4.5in barrel, adjustable sights.
TLR-5—5.5in barrel, adjustable sights.

Sturm, Ruger & Co., Inc.

Lacey Place, Southport, Connecticut 06490, and Newport, New Hampshire, USA.

British agency: Viking Arms Ltd, Summerbridge, Harrogate, North Yorkshire HG3 4BW, England.
Standard warranty: none.

Sturm, Ruger was founded in January 1949 to exploit the automatic pistol patent sought by William B. Ruger in November 1946, though this was not to be granted until October 1953 . . . by which time two of the *improvements* to the basic design had been both sought and accepted. Production of the Mark 1, later renamed Mark 1 Standard, commenced in 1949 and the company's future was assured by the time a target-shooting derivative appeared on the market early in 1951. By 1957, Ruger had manufactured more than 150,000 automatic pistols as well as a number of Single Six revolvers, and the company has since become one of the best known of the US manufacturers. Shotguns, bolt- and block-action rifles are now being made alongside the Ruger Mini-14 autoloader (a reduced-scale M14, itself derived from the famous Garand) and a variety of pistols and revolvers. Ruger jealously guards its reputation for producing some of the best available designs and for keeping abreast with technology. Particularly worthy of mention among an entire series of notable products is the Old Army percussion revolver—an old idea, but built on the most modern of lines.

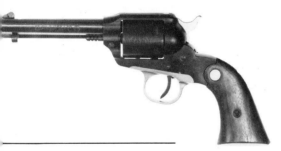

Above: the Blackhawk. Below: the Bearcat

Bearcat (old and new models)

General purpose revolver. The Bearcat was a cheaper, less sophisticated version of the Single Six (qv) with fixed sights, one rimfire chambering and only a single barrel-length option. A reduced-scale Colt Peacemaker lookalike, it had an alloy or gunmetal frame, brass trigger guard and a plain roll-engraved cylinder. The Bearcat was introduced in 1958, improved by the addition of 'new model' features in 1973 (see Blackhawk) but discontinued shortly afterwards.

Cal: 0.22in LR rf. Mag: cylinder. Mag cap, rds: 6. Trg: SA, external hammer. Wt, Loa: NA. Brl, in/mm: 4.0/102. Rf: 6 R. Sft: see Blackhawk.

Blackhawk (old and new patterns)

General purpose revolver. The original Blackhawk appeared in 1955, a derivative of the rimfire Single Six (qv) chambering more powerful centrefire ammunition. There have been many variations, including a 'Super' handling the most powerful of the Magnum rounds. Externally, the Blackhawk is a near facsimile of the Colt Peacemaker, a gate-loading single-action Western-style revolver with an ejector rod alongside the barrel. Internally, however, there is little similarity, the Ruger being a much more modern and efficient product; its springs, for example, are all of the coil pattern. The loading gate, the transfer bar system on post-1973 guns, and the hammer all interlock to prevent accidental firing. The squared front sight is mounted on a short muzzle ramp while a fully adjustable open-notch back sight lies atop the frame ahead of the hammer. The finish is normally an immaculate blue; the grips, well fitted walnut. (NB: Blackhawks made prior to 1973, and the implementation of the Gun Control Act of 1968, lacked the transfer bar safety system allowing the hammer to strike the frame-mounted inertia firing pin only during a deliberate trigger pull. These guns have three axis-screw heads on the

right side of the frame compared with only two axis-pin heads on post-1973 examples.
Cal: see table. Mag: cylinder. Mag cap, rds: 6. Trg: SA, external hammer. Wt, Loa, Brl: see table
Rf: 6 R. Sft: transfer bar; inertia firing pin; half-cock notch on hammer on post 1973 guns.

Blackhawk variants   * Exchangeable cylinders

Calibre	wt, oz	Loa, in	Brl, in	Finish
0.30in Carbine	44.0	13.1	7.5	blued
0.357in Mag	40.0	10.4	4.6	blued, stainless
0.357in Mag	42.0	12.3	6.5	blued, stainless
0.357in Mag, 9mm P*	40.0	10.4	4.6	blued
0.357in Mag, 9mm P*	42.0	12.3	6.5	blued
0.41in Mag	38.0	10.4	4.6	blued
0.41in Mag	40.0	12.3	6.5	blued
0.45in Colt	38.0	10.4	4.6	blued
0.45in Colt	40.0	13.1	7.5	blued
0.45in Colt, 0.45in ACP*	38.0	10.4	4.6	blued
0.45in Colt, 0.45in ACP*	40.0	13.1	7.5	blued

Hawkeye

Single-shot pistol. Introduced in 1963, the Hawkeye was Ruger's short-lived solution to the problems caused by chambering revolvers for excessively powerful cartridges, and the consequent jamming by case set-back in the cylinder. The Hawkeye was built on the frame of the Blackhawk, but its 'cylinder' is really a laterally-swinging breechblock and the cartridges are placed directly in the barrel. The breechblock can then be swung back and the hammer cocked and fired; the blow from the hammer is transmitted by the firing pin running through the block. The Hawkeye was very powerful and very accurate, but perhaps out of step with contemporary requirements; consequently, production ceased in 1967.
Cal: 0.256in Remington Magnum. Mag: none, single shot. Trg: SA, exposed hammer. Wt, oz/gm: 43.6/1235. Loa, in/mm: 14.1/358. Brl, in/mm: 8.5/216. Rf: 6 R. Sft: inertia firing pin; half-cock notch on hammer.

Mark 1 Bull Barrel

Target pistol. This gun is a derivative of the Mark 1 Standard (qv) with a heavy cylindrical barrel and the adjustable target sights. This ruins the handling qualities of the standard pistol, but caters rather better for the needs of most target shooters, who prefer additional weight at the muzzle.
Cal: 0.22in LR rf. Otherwise as Mark 1 Standard, except Wt, oz/gm: 42.0/1190. Loa, in/mm: 9.3/235. Brl, in/mm: 5.5/140.

Mark 1 Standard

General purpose pistol. Designed immediately after the end of the Second World War and put into production in 1949, though the US patent (2655839) was not granted until 1953, this blowback was the foundation stone on which the Ruger empire has been built. The gently tapered barrel, grip angle and general lines of the Mark 1 parallel those of the Parabellum, which is no mere coincidence—the Ruger shares the latter's superb handling qualities. The cylindrical breechblock reciprocates inside the receiver, which isolates the immobile sights from the effects of wear in the mechanism. The front sight is a blade on the muzzle crown, the back sight a block dovetailed into the receiver-top and thus capable of lateral adjustament. The Rugers are well blued with chequered Butaprene synthetic rubber grips. Coil springs are used throughout and, together with care taken during manufacture and assembly, confer on this Ruger a notable reputation for reliable, trouble-free operation. One of the company trial guns, for example, fired more than 40,000 rounds without a parts-breakage or malfunction attributable to the gun. The Mark 1 was, however, replaced at the end of 1981 by the improved Mark 2 (qv).
Cal: 0.22in LR rf. Mag: detachable box, catch on butt heel. Mag cap, rds: 9. Trg: SA, internal hammer. Wt, oz/gm: 36.0 or 38.0/1020 or 1075. Loa, in/mm: 8.8 or 10.0/224 or 254. Brl, in/mm: 4.8 or 6.0/122 or 152. Rf: 6 R. Sft: manual catch on frame behind left grip, up to safe.

Mark 1 Target

Target pistol. This was derived from the original standard pistol, introduced in 1951 after the Mark 1 had demonstrated potentially excellent shooting qualities. The principal changes are the lengthened barrel and the revised sights, an undercut blade mounted on the muzzle crown and a fully adjustable square notch back sight atop the receiver behind the ejection port. The Ruger Target is generally regarded among the best in its class, to which testimony is paid by the purchase of many thousands for the US armed forces. They have a reputation of out-performing many more expensive and supposedly more sophisticated designs.
Cal: 0.22in LR rf. Otherwise as Mark 1 Standard, except Wt, oz/gm: 42.0/1190. Loa, in/mm: 10.9/277. Brl, in/mm: 6.9/175.

Mark 2 Bull Barrel

Target pistol. This version of the heavy-barrelled Ruger automatic was introduced in 1982, a simple derivation of the original Mark 1 incorporating the improvements described under Mark 2 Standard (qv).
Cal: 0.22in LR rf. As Mk 1 Bull Barrel, except Mag cap, rds: 10.

Mark 2 Standard

General purpose pistol. Introduced on the first day of 1982 to replace the Mark 1 (qv), this features a mechanical hold-open, whose catch lies above the left grip; a redesigned magazine and magazine release catch; modified butt contours; a modified safety allowing the pistol to be unloaded or the mechanism to be operated when the catch is applied; a modified trigger system to facilitate dismantling; a new investment-cast trigger lever; and, lastly, a receiver cut away in front of the retraction grips to facilitate grasp. The Mark 2 is otherwise identical with the Mark 1—and thus certain to inherit its predecessor's enviable reputation.
Cal: 0.22in LR rf. Otherwise as Mark 1, except Mag cap, rds: 10.

Mark 2 Target

Target pistol. An improved 1982-vintage Mark 1 Target (qv), this gun incorporates the changes described in greater detail in the section devoted to the Mark 2 Standard.
Cal: 0.22in LR rf. Otherwise as Mark 1 Target, except Mag cap, rds: 10.

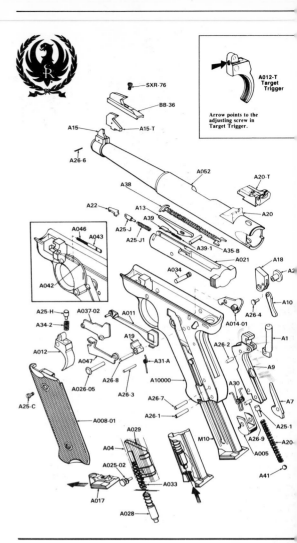

A012-T Target Trigger

Arrow points to the adjusting screw in Target Trigger.

Old Army

Percussion revolver. Introduced in 1972, this is, incontrovertibly, the finest percussion revolver yet made—incorporating, as it does, chrome-molybdenum or stainless steel construction and the highly-advanced Ruger single-action revolver lockwork. It is basically a modified Blackhawk with a plain-surfaced cylinder displaying the rolled-in circumferential legend FOR BLACK POWDER ONLY, and a multi-stage rammer assembly beneath the barrel. The result looks like an amalgam of the Remington New Army revolver of 1858 and the Colt Peacemaker! The Ruger will, of course, find little favour with the traditionalists opposed to innovation on the black powder scene; however, it is finding *every* favour with those whose quest is simply the best possible shooting performance from a black-powder burner . . . The Old Army has a fully adjustable back sight, a ramp-mounted blade-pattern front sight, blued or stainless finish and an American Walnut grip.

Cal: 0.44in. Mag: cylinder. Mag cap, rds: 6. Trg: SA, exposed hammer. Wt, oz/gm: 46.5/1320. Loa, in/mm: 13.2/335 Brl, in/mm: 7.5/191. Rf: 6 R. Sft: transfer bar; inertia firing pin; half-cock notch on hammer.

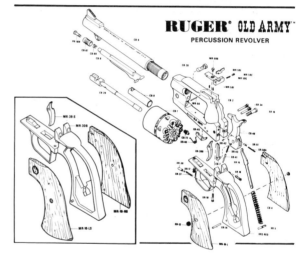

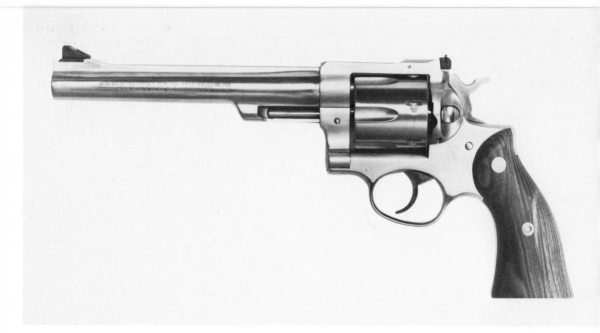

Police Service Six

General purpose and personal defence revolver. This is quite simply the standard Security Six (qv) with modified grip contours and fixed sights consisting of a longitudinal groove on the frame and a low no-snag blade. This prevents accidental misalignment of the sights, which could cost a life in situations where a fast, accurate first shot is vital.
Cal: 0.357in Magnum, 0.38in Special, 9mm Parabellum. Otherwise as Security Six (but see also Table).

Redhawk

General purpose and personal defence revolver. The Redhawk of 1979 is a greatly enlarged version of the Security Six (qv), its identical action strengthened for the powerful Magnum cartridge. The guns have plain American walnut grips and brushed satin finish on their stainless steel parts. This results in a handsome and extremely advanced design rating among the best in its class. An interesting accessory for the Redhawk is the exchangeable front sight, which includes white dot or red wedge contrast patterns and others of yellow, red, blue or white Delrin—for use against different backdrops or in varying terrain . . . and not nearly as outlandish as cursory examination of the idea may suggest.

Cal: 0.44in Magnum. Otherwise generally as Security Six, except Wt, oz/gm: 52.5/1490. Loa, in/mm: 13.0/330. Brl, in/mm: 7.5/191.

Security Six

General purpose and personal defence revolver. This gun appeared in 1971, the company's first foray into a market dominated by Colt and Smith & Wesson. The Ruger features another laterally-swinging yoke mounted cylinder system, locked by a thumb-latch inlet in the recoil shield on the left side of the frame behind the cylinder. Great care has been taken in its construction, as the Security Six can be entirely dismantled in a matter of minutes using nothing more than a small coin. Safety features include the transfer bar and inertia firing-pin assembly, and interlocks preventing either the hammer being cocked while the cylinder is open or the cylinder being opened while the hammer is cocked. Unlike the Colts, Smith & Wessons and the majority of the competing designs, the Ruger is a truly solid frame design with no separately fitted side-plate. Its trigger system is carried on a modular sub-assembly inserted into the action through the bottom of the frame. The variants of what is widely regarded as a highly successful design are tabulated below.
Cal: 0.357in Magnum. Mag: cylinder. Mag cap, rds: 6. Trg: DA,

Variants of the Security Six (SE), Police Service Six (PS) and Speed Six (SP) revolvers

* Target grip and contrast sights

Type	Model	Calibre	Sights	Finish
PS	107	0.357in Magnum	fixed	blue
PS	108	0.38in Special	fixed	blue
PS	109	9mm Police	fixed	blue
SE	117	0.357in Magnum	adjustable	blue
SE	117T*	0.357in Magnum	adjustable	blue
SP	207	0.357in Magnum	fixed	blue
SP	208	0.38in Special	fixed	blue
SP	109	9mm Police	fixed	blue
PS	707	0.357in Magnum	fixed	stainless
PS	708	0.38in Special	fixed	stainless
SE	717	0.357in Magnum	adjustable	stainless
SE	717T*	0.357in Magnum	adjustable	stainless
SP	737	0.357in Magnum	fixed	stainless
SP	738	0.38in Special	fixed	stainless
SP	739	9mm Police	fixed	stainless

RUGER
SPEED-SIX®
Revolver

The Ruger Speed-Six revolver is identical to the Police Service-Six model with round-butt frame design which is ideal for use when carrying comfort and concealability are important considerations. The 2¾" barrel model weighs 31 ounces and is 7¾" long overall. 9mm blued model is available with 2¾" and 4" barrel lengths, and with 4" barrel length in stainless steel.

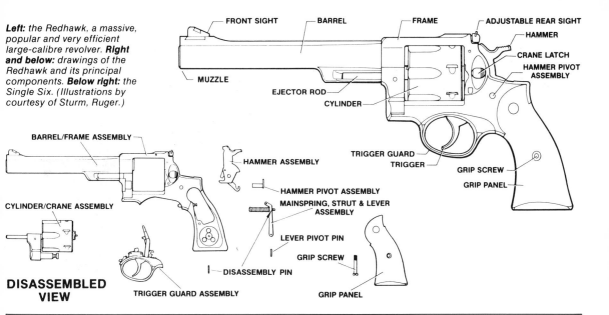

Left: the Redhawk, a massive, popular and very efficient large-calibre revolver. **Right and below:** drawings of the Redhawk and its principal components. **Below right:** the Single Six. (Illustrations by courtesy of Sturm, Ruger.)

FRONT SIGHT — BARREL — FRAME — ADJUSTABLE REAR SIGHT — HAMMER — CRANE LATCH — HAMMER PIVOT ASSEMBLY — MUZZLE — EJECTOR ROD — CYLINDER

BARREL/FRAME ASSEMBLY — HAMMER ASSEMBLY — TRIGGER GUARD — TRIGGER — GRIP SCREW — GRIP PANEL — CYLINDER/CRANE ASSEMBLY — HAMMER PIVOT ASSEMBLY — MAINSPRING, STRUT & LEVER ASSEMBLY — LEVER PIVOT PIN — GRIP SCREW — DISASSEMBLY PIN — GRIP PANEL — TRIGGER GUARD ASSEMBLY

DISASSEMBLED VIEW

exposed hammer. Wt, Loa, Brl: see Table. Rf: 6 R. Sft: transfer bar; inertia firing pin; safety interlocks between hammer and cylinder.

Speed Six

Personal defence revolver. The Speed Six is derived from the Security Six (qv), distinguished by fixed sights, short barrel and rounded butt. Some guns may be encountered without hammer spurs, suitable only for double-action fire.
Cal: 0.357in Magnum, 0.38in Special, 9mm Police. Otherwise as Security Six (qv), but see Table.

Single Six (old, new, convertible or super)

General purpose revolver. The original Single Six appeared in 1953 to satisfy demands for a rimfire Colt Peacemaker lookalike, and has since become one of the best known (and undeniably most efficient) guns of its type. It is a typical 'Western' copy, with a barrel-side rod ejector and a laterally-swinging loading gate on the right side of the frame behind the cylinder. Coil springs are used throughout the action, which on post-1973 guns incorporates the transfer bar safety pioneered by the Blackhawk (qv). Several different combinations of barrel and finish may be obtained, summarised in the Table below. The Single Six was originally made only in 0.22in LR rf chambering, but this was rapidly supplemented by a magnum version. Modern convertible guns are supplied with two exchangeable cylinders and will shoot equally well with either round; though the cylinders of the old guns can be exchanged with equal facility, differences in the pitch of the rifling lead to much poorer accuracy. The ' Super' models are made with adjustable back sights, those of the standard guns being fixed.
Cal: 0.22in LR rf or 0.22in Magnum rf. Mag: cylinder. Mag cap, rds: 6. Trg: SA, exposed hammer. Wt, Loa, Brl: see Table. Rf: 6 R. Sft: as Redhawk.

Variations of the Single Six Convertible

Wt (oz)	Loa (in)	Brl (in)	Finish
31.5	9.9	4.6	blue
33.0	10-8	5.5	blue
33.0	10.8	5.5	stainless
34.5	11.8	6.5	blue
34.5	11.8	6.5	stainless
38.0	14.9	9.5	blue

Super Blackhawk (old and new patterns)

General purpose revolver. This chambers the mighty 0.44in Remington Magnum cartridge introduced in 1957, having succeeded a short-lived 'Ruger 44 Magnum' revolver based on the Blackhawk in the late 1950s. The cartridge proved to be too hot a load for even the superbly made Ruger, and thus the Super Blackhawk made its début in 1962-3. The most obvious feature is the plain-surfaced cylinder, together with the square-backed trigger guard and the slight but perceptible downward curl to the tip of the hammer spur. The frame was strengthened, though the mechanism remained pure Blackhawk (and thus, by extension, Single Six). New Model Super Blackhawks have the post-1973 transfer safety system; earlier, old-style guns do not. The revolvers are very well made, nicely blued with polished walnut grips, and offer good value.
Cal: 0.44in Magnum. Otherwise as Blackhawk, except Wt, oz/gm: 48.0 or 51.0/1360 or 1445. Loa, in/mm: 13.4 or 16.4/340 or 417. Brl, in/mm: 7.5 or 10.5/191 or 267.

Fabbrica d'Armi Giuseppe Tanfoglio

Magno-Gardone Val Trompia (Brescia), Italy. Not much is known about this company, operations of which may have ceased. It appears to have succeeded Sabati & Tanfoglio in 1958, making a cartridge 'Derringer' (the well known Remington double-barrel type) and an odd four-shot cluster-barrel pistol with a tipping barrel block. Both chambered the 0.22in LR rf round, but are rarely seen.

Forjas Taurus SA

Estrada Fortes 511 (PO Box 44), 90.000 Porto Alegre-RS, Brazil

UK agency: none. US agency: International Distributors, Inc., 7290 West 42nd Street, Miami, Florida 33155, USA. Standard warranty: believed to be 12 months.

Little is known about the background of this company, which rose to prominence in Brazil in the mid 1960s, as no information was supplied during research. Pistols and revolvers are made in great numbers, but are currently more common in the Americas than in Europe.

Taurus pistols and revolvers

These are either yoke-mounted swinging cylinder revolvers—based on Smith & Wessons, but with very distinctive wedge-shape front sights—or Beretta Model 92 automatic pistols manufactured under licence in Brazil. The revolvers are well made of quite good material, but lack the quality of the genuine Smith & Wessons. The automatics also appear to be well made, but may be distinguished from the Beretta by their trigger-guards, the front surfaces of which are concave to suit the currently fashionable two-hand grip. This means that the two Taurus pistols, the PT 92 and PT 99, resemble the Beretta 92 (see page 38) but have guards shaped more like that of the Navy Arms Mamba (page 110).

Model	Type	Calibre	Shots	Weight (oz)	Barrel length (in)	Grip	Sights	Finish
65	revolver	0.357in Mag	6	34, 35	3.0, 4.0	Target	Fixed	Royal blue, satin
66	revolver	0.357in Mag	6	35.0, 36.0, 38.0	3.0, 4.0, 6.0	Target	adjustable	Royal blue, satin
73	revolver	0.32in Spl	6	20.2	3.0 heavyweight	Service, heavy	adjustable	Blue, satin
80	revolver	0.38in Spl	6	33.0, 34.0	3.0, 4.0	Service	fixed	blue, satin
82	revolver	0.38in Spl	6	34.0. 35.5	3.0, 4.0 heavywt	Service	fixed	blue, satin
84	revolver	0.38in Spl	6	34.0	4.0	Service	adjustable	blue, satin
85	revolver	0.38in Spl	6	21.0	3.0	Service, round	fixed	blue, satin
86	revolver	0.38in Spl	6	34.0	6.0	Service	adjustable	blue, satin
PT92	pistol	9mm Para	15	34.0	4.9	synthetic	fixed	blue
96	revolver	0.22in LR	6	35.5	6.0	Service	adjustable	blue, satin
PT99	pistol	9mm Para	15	35.2	4.9	walnut	adjustable	blue

Some guns bear names in addition to the model designations. These include *Heavy Barrel* (Model 82), *Protector* (Model 85, but now associated with the PT 99 as well), *Target Grade* (Model 84), *Target Master* (Model 86) and *Target Scout* (Model 96). However, none of the three revolvers are genuinely suitable for target shooting, as they are really the service patterns with adjustable rather than fixed sights. The two pistols are the best buys among the Taurus range.

Ernst Thälmann

VEB Fahrzeug- und Jagdwaffenfabrik Ernst Thälmann, DDR-60 Suhl, Meininger Strasse 222, German Democratic Republic

Exporter: Suhler Jagdwaffen, DDR-60 Suhl, Wilhelm-Pieck-Strasse 16. UK agency: Viking Arms Ltd, Summerbridge, Harrogate, West Yorkshire HG3 4BW. US agency: none. Standard warranty: unknown.

This state-operated conglomerate gathered together all the small gunsmithing establishments in Thüringen and elsewhere in the early 1950s, and has since made large quantities of military and sporting guns of all kinds, including shotguns, airguns and a few very competitively priced target pistols. The distribution system is such that the guns are only rarely available in the West—and then only in small numbers. However, they are usually well worth seeking out.

Zentrum (or Centrum)

Target pistol. This is an oddity, a classical falling-block design with a parentage traceable back directly to the Tell, and Luna pistols made in Suhl by Büchel and others before the outbreak of the Second World War. There is a colour case-hardened frame, whose breech is operated by the finger lever forming the trigger guard. There is an external control for the manual extractor on the left side of the breech, and the fully adjustable trigger may be set by the small lever on the left side of the frame, immediately ahead of the handsome oil-finished grip. The blued barrel is octagonal and the back sight is carried high above the grip on an extension of the frame. The sculpted palm-rest grip and the short wooden fore-end are oil-finished, the resulting gun being efficient and very competitively priced.
Cal: 0.22in LR rf. Mag: none, single shot. Trg: SA, set pattern. Wt, oz/gm: about 45.0/1275. Loa, in/mm: 13.9/353. Brl, in/mm: 10.0/254. Rf: yes. Sft: none.

Ziegenhahn Modell IV

Target pistol. This is apparently made under the auspices of the Büchsenmacher Handelsgesellschaft (BÜHAG)in Suhl, but probably not by the factory responsible for the Zentrum. It is an interesting rapid-fire pistol with an odd exposed hammer and its back sight carried on a bracket on the frame in the manner of the French Unique DES/69 (qv), a gun which the Ziegenhan resembles in other ways—though by no means sharing the same quality. Ports are bored into the barrel to adjust to the power of differing cartridges, and the well raked palm-rest style grips are adjustable. The slide/breechblock retraction grooves lie almost at the muzzle, owing to the position of the grips and the relationship between the barrel and back sight: like most rapid fire guns, the Ziegenhan is intended to lie as low in the hand as possible. It offers good (but not outstanding) quality at a very competitive price, but is seen only intermittently in the West.
Cal: 0.22in Short rf. Mag: detachable box. Mag cap, rds: 5. Trg: SA, exposed hammer. Wt, oz/gm: 47.7/1355. Loa, in/mm: 11.8/300, Brl, in/mm: 6.0/152. RF: 6R. Sft: none.

S.L. Theyma

Apartado 110, Zarauz (Guipúzcoa), Spain. According to the Spanish commercial directories, Theyma manufactures and distributes 'pistols'—though it is not explained what is covered by this definition. No information has yet been elicited from the company itself, but the guns are believed to be muzzle-loaders.

Thompson/Center Arms

Farrington Road, Rochester, New Hampshire 03867, USA

British agency: none. Standard warranty: unknown.

This began life in 1945 as the K. W. Thompson Tool Company, which grew steadily and moved to Rochester, New Hampshire in 1962. As increasing numbers of gun parts were being cast in the plant during the early 1960s, the decision was taken to move into the firearms business when Warren Center joined the firm in 1965, bringing with him the Contender pistol. By 1968, the gun business was flourishing and a purpose-built factory had been erected; the line has since been extended several times, as Thompson/Center began to make black-powder longarms, both flintlock and percussion-ignition, alongside the highly successful Contender. The products are always in the forefront, Thompson/Center paying great attention to them and constantly seeking improvements; the Contender, in particular, has inspired several competitors—few of which are as elegant or sophisticated as their prototype.

Left: the standard Contender. **Above:** the choke. **Below:** the Patriot and its lock. (Courtesy Thompson/Center.)

Contender

General purpose pistol. Developed in early 1960s—the first production gun was made in 1967—this is a very unusual gun, of a pattern with many European antecedents but now almost exclusively American. The single-shot Contender is intended specifically for hunting and sport shooting and has chambered a very wide range of cartridges (see list), in addition to being offered in many styles of barrel, grip and decoration. The action is opened by a rapid upward and rearward pull on the trigger guard spur, permitting the barrel to be pivoted downwards in shotgun style. As the action opens, the extractor moves the chambered case outwards, a hammer safety block restrains the hammer until the trigger is pulled again, the striker and trigger re-engage and the sear is positioned for the next shot. A small crossbolt safety on the hammer head can be activated to project a stop-pin from the face, thereby preventing the hammer reaching the striker. The safety catch is usually set for right-handed firers but can be reversed if required. Other features include dual rim or centrefire firing pins, an adjustable trigger and perhaps the simplest exchangeable barrel in its class. The fore-end screw is removed, and with it the fore-end, after which the hinge pin can be tapped out and the barrel replaced. NB: there are two fore-end screws in Super 14 models. The Contender is an outstanding design by any standards.
Cal: various–see table. Mag: none, single shot. Trg: SA, exposed hammer. Wt, with std 10in barrel, oz/gm: 43.0/1220. Loa, with std 10in barrel, in/mm: 13.5/343. Brl, in/mm: 10.0/255. Rf: 12 R?. Sft: see text.

Standard Contender barrel options

10in octagonal—ramp mounted front sight, fully adjustable back sight.

10in round heavyweight ('bull')—otherwise as above*
10in ventilated rib, round—with flip-up laterally adjustable backsight*
14in 'Super 14' round heavyweight—standard sights.

* Barrels thus marked can receive a removable internal choke to fire special shot cartridges. A distinctive key tool is used to remove the choke unit.

Patriot

Target pistol. Modelled on the duelling/target pistols of the first half of the nineteenth century and introduced in 1972, this is a remarkable product. Like the cartridge-firing Contender, it is among the leaders in its field. Features include a modern colour case-hardened coil-spring percussion lock, made to today's standards and giving commensurate performance; modern sights, the front mounted in a tunnel and the back fully adjustable; a well conceived set-trigger; a beautiful walnut half-stock with a saw-handle butt and cast or machined brass furniture . . . and a lifetime warranty. The octagonal barrel is rifled to improve accuracy and, together with accessories such as the adjustable powder measure and scissors-type ball moulds, the result is quite outstanding.
Cal: 0.45in. Mag: none. Trg: SA, external hammer. with set/hair trigger. Wt, oz/gm: 36.0/1020. Loa, in/mm: NA. Brl, in/mm: 9.0/230. Rf: 12 R? Sft: half-cock on hammer

NOTE

The list of the cartridges for which the Contender has been chambered—more than thirty of them, ranging in size from the 0.17in Ackley Bee to the 45/410—will be found on page 14.

TOZ

Tulskii Oruzheinyi Za'vod, Tula, RSFSR, USSR

British agency: Magex (UK) Ltd, 25 High Street, Egham, Surrey. US agency: none. Export agency: V/O Raznoexport, Kalaievskaia 5, Moskva K-6, USSR. Standard warranty: unknown.

This Russian arsenal, 110 miles south of Moscow, was established in 1595 by Tsar Boris Gudonov, though smallarms were not made in quantity until 1705-14. Tula has been an important arms-making centre since the mid nineteenth century, making large numbers of rifles, machine-guns and pistols.

TOZ-35 ('Vostok')

Target pistol. Credited to a team led by Khaydurov, the TOZ-35 free pistol appeared in the West in 1963. The gun features a Martini-pattern dropping-block action operated by a lever protruding from the base of the adjustable wooden grip. The set trigger, controlled by a screw under the fore-end ahead of the trigger guard, is set (from 0.4oz to 3oz) by a lever on the left side. The fully adjustable back sight lies high above the grip on an extension of the breech; the front sight is carried above the bore on a prominent ramp. *Cal: 0.22in LR rf. Mag: none, single-shot. Trg: SA, 'set' pattern, striker fired. Wt, oz/gm: 45.0/1275. Loa, in/mm: 17.3/440. Brl, in/mm: 11.8/300. Rf: yes. Sft: apparently none.*

Aldo Uberti & C. SaS

Via G. Carducci 41, Ponte Zanano (Brescia), Italy

British agency: Peregrine Arms Co., 105 London Lane, Bromley, Kent BR1 4HF, England. US agency: Navy Arms Co. (qv) and others. Standard warranty: 12 months.

Uberti is a comparatively youthful company, having been founded in 1959 to produce replica percussion revolvers, a field in which it has since specialised—though increasingly large numbers of cartridge guns have been made as well. Uberti replicas are regarded as among the best available, and the company takes great pride in them, recently introducing a replica of the *original* Colt Model 1873 revolver correct down to the conical firing pin. (Most other 'replicas' incorporate changes made during the Colt's long life.) The revolvers are available in standard or charcoal blue, nickel-plated or, in some cases, made from corrosion resisting stainless steel. Some guns, such as the Walker Colt, come attractively cased, while several grades of engraving—culminating in the inlaying of precious metal—are also obtainable to special order. Guns seen in Britain are often fitted with black buffalo horn or genuine ivory grips, but these are the work of Peregrine Arms, the British distributor, rather than the manufacturer.

Army Colt, M1860

Percussion revolver. This gun re-creates one of the most elegant of all percussion revolvers as faithfully as modern manufacturing techniques and materials allow. The barrel is round, slightly tapered, and flares at the breech to contain the 'creeping' rack-type rammer. The distinctive double-diameter cylinder maintains the trim lines while accommodating the largest possible calibre, and the open-top frame is colour case-hardened. The steel backstrap will receive a shoulder stock, and the trigger guard is brass. Uberti makes several variants: the standard gun; a second lacking the stock cut, but with brass 'civilian' butt straps; and a third with silvered 'Western' fittings. Fluted-cylinder variants are also made *Cal: 0.44in. Otherwise generally as Colt version (qv).*

Augusta Navy Colt

Percussion revolver. This is a modern version of the Colt-pattern revolvers made for a short time during the US Civil War by the Confederate Machine Works of Augusta, Georgia. These are practically identical with the 1851 Navy Colt, but have brass (rather than case-hardened steel) frames. Uberti also makes a variant with the barrel shortened to 5in (127mm), overall length and weight being reduced commensurately. Mechanically, however, it is identical with the full-length gun. *Cal: 0.36in. Otherwise generally as Navy Colt (qv).*

Baby Dragoon Colt, or M1848

Percussion revolver. This was originally produced to satisfy demands for a small and handy revolver which, despite its diminution, shared the undeniably good features of the full size Dragoons. The Baby Dragoon chambers a much smaller ball than its military cousins, has a smaller cylinder capacity and lacks the rammer assembly beneath its octagonal barrel. The trigger guard and backstrap are brass, but may be disguised by silver plating in the 'Western' subvariety. The frame and hammer are attractively colour case-hardened and the one-piece grip is plain walnut.

Cal: 0.31in. Mag: cylinder. Mag cap, rds: 5. Trg: SA, exposed hammer. Wt, oz/gm: 22.9/650. Loa, in/mm: 9.5/240. Brl, in/mm: 4.0/102 (barrels of 3in and 5in, 76 and 127mm, are also obtainable). Rf: 7 L? Sft: half-cock on hammer.

Buckhorn SA Buntline, Buntline Target

General purpose revolver. This is simply the standard Uberti Buckhorn magnum revolver with a fascinating (if superfluous) 18-inch barrel.

Buckhorn SA Quick Draw

General purpose revolver. The Buckhorn is a Cattleman (qv), strengthened for magnum-power cartridges. The construction remains pure gate-loading rod-ejecting Colt, the standard versions offering case-hardened frames and brass or steel grip straps. The grips are invariably plain walnut. *Cal: 0.44in Magnum. Otherwise generally as Cattleman, except Wt, oz/gm: 43.0-45.0/1220-1275. Loa, in/mm: 10.6, 11.8, 13.3/270, 300, 338. Brl, in/mm: 4.8, 6.0, 7.5/122, 152, 190.*

Buckhorn SA Quick Draw Convertible

General purpose revolver. This variant of the standard magnum Buckhorn is supplied with exchangeable cylinders chambering the 0.44in Magnum or the 44/40 Winchester. A long-barrelled fixed-stock carbine derivative is also

Buckhorn SA Target

General purpose and target revolver. This is little more than a standard Buckhorn revolver with fully adjustable sights, the other obvious external change being the square-shouldered frame. *Cal: 0.44in Magnum. Otherwise as Buckhorn (qv).*

Buckhorn SA Target Convertible

General purpose and target revolver. A variant of the Buckhorn Target featuring exchangeable cylinders for the 0.44in Magnum and the 44/40 Winchester rounds.

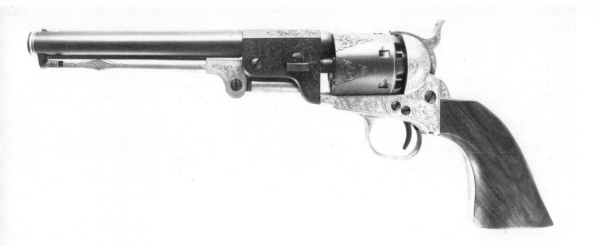

Cattleman SA Buntline, Buntline Target

General purpose revolver. This is simply an ultra-long barrelled derivative of the Cattleman (qv), named in honour of the writer 'Ned Buntline', at whose request the first such gun was made. It subsequently caused a sensation at the Philadelphia Exposition of 1875. The long barrel, though it improves accuracy, unbalances the revolver unless the skeletal shoulder stock is fitted.
Cal: 0.357in Magnum, 44/40 Winchester, 0.45in Colt. Otherwise as Cattleman, except Wt, oz/gm, without stock: 58.2/1650. Loa, in/mm: 23.5/597. Brl, in/mm: 18.0/457.

Cattleman SA Quick Draw

General purpose revolver. The Cattleman is the standard Uberti Colt Peacemaker replica, a well-made gun reproducing the majority of the original features within the limitations of modern metallurgy and production techniques . . . and the idiosyncratic Italian laws governing production of certain calibres. The Cattleman has a colour case-hardened steel frame, the backstrap and trigger guard being steel or brass; the grip is a single piece of walnut. A revolving carbine, with a permanently attached wooden stock, is also made.
Cal: 0.22in LR rf, 0.22in Magnum rf, 0.357in Magnum, 0.38in Special, 44/40 Winchester, 0.45in Colt. Mag: cylinder. Mag cap, rds: 6. Trg: SA, exposed hammer. Wt, oz/gm: 37.0-40.6/1050-1150. Loa, in/mm: 10.1, 10.8, 12.8/257, 274, 325. Brl, in/mm: 4.8, 5.5, 7.5/122, 140, 191. Rf: 7 L?. Sft: half-cock on hammer; inertia firing pin?

Cattleman SA Stainless

General purpose revolver. This is a variant of the standard Cattleman made of corrosion-resisting stainless steel.

Above: a fetchingly engraved Griswold & Gunnison Navy Colt. Below: the Inspector. (Courtesy Peregrine Arms.)

Cattleman SA Target

General purpose and target revolver. This variant of the Cattleman features improved sights—a fully adjustable open notch and a ramp mounted blade—and a square shouldered frame adjoining the barrel.

Cattleman SA Target Stainless

General purpose and target revolver. This is simply a derivative of the Cattleman Target featuring corrosion-resisting construction.

First Model Dragoon Colt

Percussion revolver. Further details of the Dragoon, lighter and handier than the Walker Colt (though still a very large gun), may be found in the Colt section. The Uberti version features a colour case-hardened steel frame, rammer assembly and hammer, the remainder of the parts being attractively blued, apart from the polished brass backstraps and trigger guard. Dragoon revolver cylinders display a rolled-in scene from the Texan-Mexican War.
Cal: 0.44in. Otherwise as Colt-made version (qv)

Griswold & Gunnison Navy Colt

Percussion revolver. This is another replica of a Confederate Colt, the original being made in Griswoldville, Georgia, during the US Civil War. It features a brass frame, a round rather than octagonal barrel, and a plain-surfaced cylinder. A shortened variant may also be obtained, as well as a full size gun chambering larger 'Army calibre' balls.
Cal: 0.36in, 0.44in. Otherwise generally as 1851 Navy Colt.

Inspector

General purpose and personal defence revolver. This is Uberti's first foray into that most competitive of markets: the modern double-action personal defence revolver. The Inspector is based on Colt practice, its side-swinging yoke-mounted cylinder being retained by a combination thumb-catch and recoil shield on the left side of the frame beneath the broad-spurred hammer. The ejector rod is fully shrouded. Finish may be blue or satin chrome, while the well-chequered grips are selected walnut. The shorter barrelled versions feature fixed sights atop solid barrel ribs, but the two longest barrel options may be obtained with fully adjustable back sights and ventilated ribs. The Uberti Inspector is efficient and competitively priced: good value, therefore, though the 0.32in version fires a somewhat ineffectual cartridge.
Cal: 0.32in S & W Long, 0.38in Special. Mag: cylinder. Mag cap, rds: 6. Trg: DA, exposed hammer. Wt, oz/gm, with 3in barrel: 24.7/700. Loa, in/mm, with 3in barrel: 8.0/203. Brl, in/mm: 2.1, 2.5, 3.0, 4.0 or 6.0/55, 64, 76, 102 or 152. Rf: yes. Sft: inertia firing pin (and transfer bar?).

Leech & Rigdon Navy Colt

Percussion revolver. This gun re-creates copies of the Navy Colt made during the US Civil War by Leech & Rigdon of Memphis, Tennessee, and Greensboro, Georgia. Several thousand revolvers were made with Colt-type steel frames, rather than the brass that typifies other Confederate wares. Uberti faithfully reproduces this frame, along with the round barrel and plain surfaced cylinder.
Cal: 0.36in. Otherwise generally as Navy Colt (qv)

Maverick (or New Maverick) Derringer

Personal defence pistol. This is another of the modern Italian versions of the Remington 2-barrel 'over/under' deringer of 1866-7, but handling more powerful than normal ammunition and—consequently—made of steel rather than alloy. The barrel unit, locked by a lever and cam system, pivots upwards and back around the top of the frame. There is a sheath trigger, a wood-gripped bird's head butt and blue finish.
Cal: 0.38in Special (0.357in Magnum and 0.45in Long Colt have been discontinued). Mag: none, twin barrels. Trg: SA, exposed hammer. Wt, oz/gm: 14.8/420. Loa, in/mm: 5.1/130. Brl, in/mm: 2.8/71. Rf: yes. Sft: none.

Navy Colt, M1851

Percussion revolver. This gun is, perhaps, the best known of all percussion revolvers and is described in greater detail in the Colt section. Uberti's version is among the best of the replicas, featuring a blued octagonal barrel, colour case-hardened frame and hammer, brass trigger guard and backstrap and a one-piece walnut grip. The standard gun has a rounded guard, but several variants are available, including a 'Western' derivative with silvered straps, a gun with a square-backed brass guard, and a 'Western' square-guard model. There is also the so-called 'London Pattern' (but see remarks in Colt section) with a square-backed steel guard, and a similar gun with its backstrap slotted to receive a shoulder stock. Uberti calls this last variant the 'Third Model Navy'.
Cal: 0.36in. Otherwise as Colt-made gun (qv).

Navy Colt, M1851, Sheriff's

Percussion revolver. This is simply an 1851-pattern Navy Colt with its barrel shortened from 7.5in to about 5in, reducing its overall length and also its weight. The guns are made in the 'normal' Uberti variants—brass frame/oval brass guard, the silvered-strap 'Western' version, and a square-backed guard with its westernised equivalent.
Cal: 0.36in. Otherwise as Navy Colt, but shorter and lighter.

New Army Remington, M1858

Percussion revolver. This is a re-creation of the most famous revolver of the percussion era other than the Colt—the robust Remington. The latter undoubtedly lacks lacks the elegance of the contemporary Colts and has a reputation of being more difficult to clean, but is unquestionably the stronger design; its solid-top frame confers a considerable advantage over the open-topped (and thus incontrovertibly weaker) construction favoured by Colt prior to 1872. The Uberti Remington has a blued steel frame, a blued octagonal barrel, a brass trigger guard and polished walnut grips.
Cal: 0.44in. Mag: cylinder. Mag cap, rds: 6. Trg: SA, exposed hammer. Wt, oz/gm: 42.7/1210. Loa, in/mm: 13.8/350. Brl, in/mm: 7.5/191. Rf: yes. Sft: half-cock notch on hammer.

New Army Remington, Stainless

Percussion revolver. This is simply a variant of the standard New Army made of corrosion-resisting stainless steel.

New Army Remington Target

Percussion revolver. This is simply a standard 1858 pattern with a fully adjustable backsight and a raised, ramp-mounted front sight. *Cal: 0.44in. Otherwise as New Army.*

New Army Remington Target, Stainless

Percussion revolver. This is a corrosion-resisting derivative of the standard New Army Revolver.

New Navy Colt, M1861

Percussion revolver. This is conveniently described as an amalgam of the Navy and Army Colts of 1851 and 1860, combining the navy-style calibre, grip, frame and cylinder with the army's toothed-rack rammer in its streamlined shroud. Construction and finish otherwise parallel the original 1851-pattern navy revolver. The Uberti replica comes in standard, civilian, Western and fluted-cylinder variants.
Cal: 0.36in. Otherwise generally as M1851 Navy Colt (qv).

New Navy Remington, M1858

Percussion revolver. This gun is derived from the Remington New Army (qv), from which it differs primarily in its smaller calibre and reduced overall dimensions. It retains the single-action trigger, however, together with blued octagonal barrel, blued frame, brass trigger guard and walnut grips.
Cal: 0.36in. Otherwise as New Army, except Wt, oz/gm: 40.6/1150. Loa, in/mm: 12.5/318. Brl, in/mm: 6.5/165.

Below: Uberti's version of the 1858-pattern Remington percussion revolver. **Above right:** the Remington Rolling Block target pistol, one of the few modern versions of a timeless design. **Right:** the Sharps cluster deringer. (All courtesy of Peregrine Arms.)

New Navy Target Remington, M1858

Percussion revolver. This is, quite simply, the New Navy (qv) with adjustable sights.
Cal: 0.36in. Otherwise as New Navy.

Outlaw (Army SA Remington M1875)

General purpose revolver. The Outlaw re-creates the revolver developed by Remington—albeit unsuccessfully—to compete with the Colt Peacemaker. The Remington had a reputation for smooth operation, being distinguished from its otherwise similar-looking rival by the elegant tapering web under the barrel and the different grip/frame prolongation, the shallower curves of which allow the Remington to lie lower in the hand than the Colt. The Uberti version has a blued barrel and cylinder, a colour case-hardened frame, a brass trigger guard and walnut grips. Nickel plating may be obtained on request.
Cal: 0.357in Magnum, 44/40 Winchester, 0.45in Colt. Mag: cylinder. Mag cap, rds: 6. Trg: SA, exposed hammer. Wt, oz/gm: 44.1/1250. Loa, in/mm: 13.8/350. Brl, in/mm: 7.5/191. Rf: yes. Sft: half-cock on hammer.

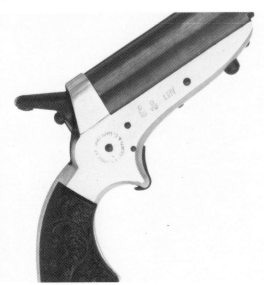

Philadelphia Derringer

Percussion pistol. This is a modern version of the tiny percussion-ignition pocket pistols originally made by Henry Deringer—his name is frequently misspelled—in mid nineteenth-century Philadelphia, and thereafter by sundry imitators. The decorative little Derringer is often encountered in cased sets. Its barrel is damascened a russet brown, while the back-action lockplate and external hammer are colour case-hardened; the mounts and front sight are German silver, while the cap-box is case-hardened steel set in a solid nickel mount. The selected walnut stock is well chequered.
Cal: 0.41in. Mag: none, single shot. Trg: SA, external hammer. Wt, oz/gm: 7.5/210. Loa, in/mm: 5.5/240. Brl, in/mm: 2.5/63. Rf: none. Sft: half-cock on hammer.

Pocket Colt, M1849

Percussion revolver. This was a logical progression from the Baby Dragoon, introduced a year previously. Indeed, the two guns are much the same—open frame percussion revolvers with five-shot cylinders—but the 1849 pattern has a pivoting rammer assembly to facilitate reloading. The backstrap and trigger guard are brass, or silver plated in the Western variant; the frame, hammer and rammer assembly are colour case-hardened, and the remaining metal parts are blued, while the grips are smooth surfaced walnut.
Cal: 0.31in. Otherwise generally as Baby Dragoon, except Wt, oz/gm: 24.7/700.

Pocket Colt, Navy Caliber, M1862

Percussion revolver. This is an adaptation of the M1862 'Police' revolver, with the old style pivoting rammer assembly, an octagonal barrel and generally squared contours. The cylinder is the double-diameter pattern. Frames are colour case-hardened, barrels and cylinders are blued, and grips are walnut. Western, or silvered-strap variants are made in each of the three barrel lengths.
Cal: 0.36in. Otherwise as M1862 'Police' revolver (qv).

Police Colt, M1862

Percussion revolver. This gun—of rather dubious parentage (see Colt)—can be considered either as a diminutive of the M1860 army revolver or a logical development of the 1849 pocket revolver. The gun is supremely elegant, the shrouded creeping-rack rammer preserving the almost unbroken sweep from the toe of the butt to the tip of the muzzle. The double-diameter cylinder permits progression from the standard

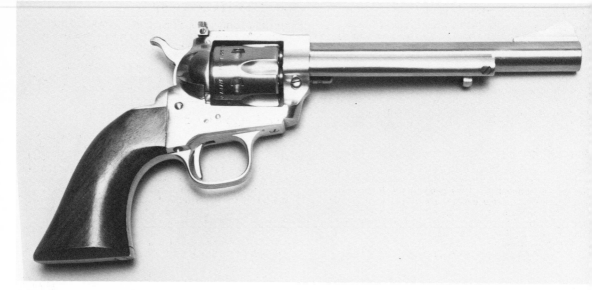

0.31in pocket pistol calibre to the 0.36in generally associated with the navy guns, though the Police Colt remains a five-shot. The frames are case-hardened, with brass or silvered brass (Western) grip straps. The remainder of the external parts are blued and the grips are invariably walnut.
Cal: 0.36in. Generally as Colt-made model (qv), except Wt, oz/gm, with 5.5in barrel: 25.4/720. Loa, in/mm, with 5.5in barrel: 10.5/267. Brl, in/mm: 4.5, 5.5, 6.5/115, 140, 165

Rolling Block Target

Single-shot pistol. This interesting gun is a replica of the Remington rolling block pistols of the late nineteenth century—strong, elegant and reliable. Uberti's version has a slender half-octagonal barrel, a brass trigger guard, a saw-handle walnut butt with a walnut fore-end, and a colour case-hardened frame. The essence of the rolling block lies in its two-part interlocking hammer/breechblock assembly, which can be opened easily once the hammer has been thumbed back, but forms a rigid, locked strut when closed. The adjustable front sight and American-style 'semi-buckhorn' open back sight make the pistol a good sporting gun. In addition, Uberti produces a modernised adaptation of the Remington for Navy Arms (qv) and a carbine based on the same action.
Cal: 0.22in LR or Magnum rf, 0.357in Magnum. Mag: none, single shot. Trg: SA, exposed hammer. Wt, oz/gm: 44.1/1250. Loa, in/mm: 14.0/356. Brl, in/mm: 9.9/250. Rf: yes. Sft: none.

Second Model Dragoon Colt

Percussion revolver. This, rarer in its original form than the First Model (which it greatly resembles), may be distinguished by squared cylinder locking bolt slots. Those of the First Model were ovoid.
Cal: 0.44in. Otherwise as First Model.

Sharps' Derringer

Personal defence pistol. This is another version of the Sharps four-barrel pistol of the nineteenth century. The Uberti version has a polished brass frame, a blued steel barrel cluster and decorative synthetic grips. The automatic firing pin fires each barrel in turn.
Cal: 0.22in Short. Mag: none, multi-barrel. Trg: SA, exposed hammer. Wt, oz/gm: 8.8/250. Loa, in/mm: 4.8/122. Brl, in/mm: 2.5/63. Rf: yes–4R? Sft: none.

Stallion Convertible Quick Draw

General purpose revolver. Once known as the 'Frontier', this is a slightly reduced-scale version of the Colt Peacemaker, whose lines and general construction it shares. The Stallion

Above: the Stallion Single Action Target revolver, popular in the United States under several names. This convertible model is supplied with exchangeable cylinders for the 0.22in LR and Magnum rimfire rounds. (Courtesy of Peregrine Arms.)

features a colour case-hardened frame, blued steel barrel, an exchangeable cylinder in which the caseheads are fully recessed, and one-piece walnut grips. The principal distinguishing characteristics are the fixed old-style sights and the gently downward-curving contours at the front frame. The ejector rod runs along the right side of the barrel, operating in conjunction with the hinged loading gate behind the cylinder on the right side of the frame.
Cal: 0.22in LR or Magnum rf. Mag: cylinder. Mag cap, rds: 6. Trg: SA, exposed hammer. Wt, oz/gm: 36.3-38.1/1030-1080. Loa, in/mm: 10.1, 10.8, 11.8/257, 275, 300. Brl, in/mm: 4.8, 5.5, 6.5/122, 140, 165. Rf: 4 R. Sft: half cock on hammer, inertia firing pin?

Stallion Quick Draw Stainless

General purpose revolver. This is a variant of the standard gun made of corrosion-resisting stainless steel.

Stallion Target Convertible

General purpose and target revolver. This derivative of the Stallion Quick Draw (qv) displays an adjustable back sight, a ramp mounted front sight and abrupt, squared contours at the front of the frame where it joins the barrel. (Note: these surfaces are slightly chamfered on newer guns.)
Cal: 0.22in. LR or Magnum rf. Otherwise as Stallion Quick Draw, except Wt, oz/gm: 37.2, 38.3/1055, 1085. Loa, in/mm: 10.8, 11.8/275, 300. Brl, in/mm: 5.5, 6.5/140, 165.

Stallion Target Stainless

General purpose and target revolver. A variant of the standard gun featuring corrosion-resisting stainless steel construction.

Texas Dragoon Colt

Percussion revolver. This gun commemorates an order placed with Tucker, Sherrard & Co., of Lancaster, Texas, during the US Civil War—though few, if any, of these Dragoon-style revolvers were ever made. Uberti's version is practically identical with the Third Model Dragoon (qv), but features a square-backed brass trigger guard and a brass backstrap. The roll-engraved cylinder features a five-point star, TEXAS ARMS and two half-armoured pikemen supporting a cartouche of thirteen stars, above two cannons in saltire. A small series of de luxe commemorative guns has also been made.
Cal: 0.44in. Otherwise as Third Model Dragoon Colt.

Third Model Dragoon Colt

Percussion revolver. The Third Model Dragoon is a derivative of the First, from which it differs in several minor respects. The most obvious is the appearance of a shoulder-stock attachment slot in the frame and a diminishing-taper rammer lever in place of the 'swamped' or swell-taper pattern on the First and Second Models. Uberti makes three variants of the Third Model: the genuine Dragoon, with steel backstrap and brass oval trigger guard, a Civilian version with brass straps but no stock-cut, and a silvered-strap 'Western' gun.
Cal: 0.44in. Otherwise as First Model (qv).

Walker Colt

Percussion revolver. This is Uberti's version of the well known revolver described in greater detail in the Colt section. The gun features a colour case-hardened hammer, frame and rammer assembly, a steel backstrap and a brass trigger guard. The remaining parts are blued, apart from the cylinder (supplied 'in the white'), and the one piece grip is usually European walnut. The cylinder surface displays a facsimile of the Ormsby 'Rangers and Indians' scene.
Cal: 0.44in. Otherwise as Colt-made version.

Very Signal Pistol Model 101

Pyrotechnic pistol. This is a copy of the well-known Very Pistol, originally introduced during the First World War. It features a tipping barrel action locked by a Webley-type stirrup catch on the right side of the frame. The metal parts are parkerised, while the grips are chequered plastic.
Cal: 1.00in, 25.4mm. Mag: none, single, shot. Trg: SA, exposed hammer. Wt, oz/gm: 32.6/925. Loa, in/mm: 9.5/241. Brl, in/mm: 5.5/140. Rf: none. Sft: none.

Wells Fargo Colt, M1849

Percussion revolver. This is a curious amalgam of the Baby Dragoon and the Pocket Colt of 1849. The rammer assembly has been omitted, the opinion of Wells, Fargo & Co. obviously being that its personnel would never have time to reload and that, therefore, the rammer was an unnecessary encumbrance. Consequently, most genuine Wells Fargo Colts were made with very short barrels. Construction and finish otherwise parallel Uberti's version of the M1849, apart from the square backed trigger guard.
Cal: 0.31in. Generally as 1849-pattern Pocket Colt, except Wt, oz/gm, with 3in barrel: 21.9/620. Loa, in/mm, with 3in barrel: 8.5/216. Brl, in/mm: 3.0, 4.0, 5.0/76, 102, 127.

Unique

Manufacture d'Armes des Pyrénées Françaises, F-64700 Hendaye, France

British agency: Arthur E.S. Matthews Ltd, Epworth House, 25-35 City Road, London EC1Y 1AR. US agency: unknown. Standard warranty: 12 months.

This company was founded in 1923, making large quantities of cheap blowback pistols under a wide variety of brandnames until the beginning of the Second World War. One example of the numbered Unique prewar series-the Modèle 17, eventually modified by the substitution of an exposed hammer for the concealed original—was made under during German supervision during the occupation of France, and production began again after the war with the first of a series of similar guns that continues today. However, Unique is best known for its efficient and competitively-priced target pistols.

The blowbacks

General purpose and personal defence pistols. These are considered under a single heading, as they all share the same unsophisticated blowback action, exposed hammer and good quality. The slides of the models B, D, K and L are cut away, exposing the barrel-top in Beretta fashion, while the Modèle R is more conventional.

Modèle Bcf or Bcf-66. This solid well made gun, chambering the 0.32in ACP (7.65mm Auto), has a nine-shot magazine, a barrel extending forward of the slide and synthetic grips with a thumb-rest. There are magazine and manual safeties (the former being a feature of dubious utility). The gun is 6.6in (168mm) long, has a barrel of 4in (102mm) and weighs 25.7oz, 730gm, unladen.

Modèle D6. This is a 0.22in LR adaptation of the Bcf intended for plinking and low-grade target shooting, displaying a 6in/15cm barrel and adjustable sights. It bears a resemblance to some of the rimfire sporting Star pistols (qv).

Modèle Kn (Mikros). This is a pocket variant of the basic design chambering the 6.35mm Auto cartridge, with a six-round magazine and the standard safeties; the Mikros is 4.4in (112mm) long and weighs only 9.2oz, 260gm.

Modèle L. There are three variants of this pattern, *Lc* in 0.22in LR rf, *Ld* in 9mm Short and *Lf* in 7.65mm Auto (0.32in ACP). The guns are 5.9in (148mm) long and weigh betwen 21.2 and 23.6oz (600-670gm) depending on calibre.

Modèle Rr. This is a derivative of the wartime Kriegsmodell, its most obvious features being the closed-top slide and the grip, which is very square to the axis of the bore. The Rr chambers the 7.65mm Auto cartridge, or 0.32in ACP, and has a nine-round magazine. It weighs about 27.5oz (780gm) and measures 5.8in, 146mm, overall.

DES/69

Target pistol. This is one of the most popular and efficient guns in its class, relatively inexpensive but capable of outstanding results. Indeed, up to 1980, shooters using the DES/69 had won the French standard pistol championship for twelve years in succession and held the French national record at 581x600. The gun is an uncomplicated blowback, but is extremely well made. Its most notable features are the position of the back sight, carried on an extension of the frame running behind and above the adjustable palm-rest walnut grips, and the gap between the exposed hammer and back sight bracket within which the breechblock reciprocates. The trigger is fully adjustable, while the fixed cylindrical barrel is usually enveloped by one of the optional supplementary barrel weights (100, 150, 260 or 350gm). An integral dry-firing device facilitates practice, while an automatic hold-open retains the slide after the last round has been chambered, fired and ejected.
Cal: 0.22in LR rf. Mag: detachable box, catch on bottom left side of the grip. Mag cap: 10 rounds. Trg: SA, exposed hammer. Wt, without auxiliary weights, oz/gm: 35.3/1000. Loa, in/mm: 10.6/270. Brl, in/mm: 5.9/150. Rf: yes. Sft: radial lever on left side of frame behind trigger, down to safe; inertia firing pin.

DES/VO

Target pistol. This variant of the DES/69 is intended for rapid-fire competitions. The VO has a squared barrel casing, displaying four ports drilled down into the bore to minimise muzzle jump during firing. The other obvious features include the grooved polygonal breechblock or half-slide, and the massive back sight housing. Internally, the VO (*Vitesse Olympique*) is identical with the DES/69, apart from the chambering.
Cal: 0.22in Short rf. Otherwise generally as DES/69, except Wt, oz/gm: 43.7/1240. Loa, in/mm: 10.0/255.

Above: the Unique DES/69 target pistol. (Courtesy of Arthur E.S. Matthews Ltd.)

Lothar Walther Feinwerkzeugbau GmbH & Co.

D-7923 Königsbronn (Württemberg), Postfach 90, West Germany. Walther does not make its own guns, despite claims occasionally made to the contrary, but is instead a specialist manufacturer of sub-calibre barrel inserts—Zusatzläufe— for a wide variety of guns, providing a means of undertaking very low cost practice with primer-propelled 4mm ammunition and low-powered rimfire rounds. Details of these units will be supplied on request.

Carl Walther Sportwaffenfabrik GmbH

D-7900 Ulm/Donau, Postfach 4325, West Germany.

British agency: Accuracy International Ltd, 43 Gladys Avenue, North End, Portsmouth, Hampshire PO2 9AZ, England. US agency: Interarms, 10 Prince Street, Alexandria, Virginia 22313, USA. Standard warranty: 12 months

Walther, founded in Zella St Blasii in 1886, is one of the best known German firearms makers. After a slow but steady start making sporting rifles, Carl Walther (1860-1915) marketed a small personal defence automatic pistol from 1910-11; this, the blowback Walther Modell 1, proved to be the first of many handguns that finally established the Walther name among the giants of firearms history. The company moved to a large factory in Zella in 1915, and managed to survive the depression following the First World War by developing new designs culminating in the Polizei Pistole of 1929: a design so good that it remains, after more than half a century, one of the best available personal defence pistols. The locked-breech military P 38 followed in the late 1930s, to be adopted by the Wehrmacht as a replacement for the ageing Parabellum. The Walther plant lay in the Soviet occupation zone at the end of the Second World War and was subsequently dismantled. Fritz Walther and his family had departed westwards, however, and the firearms business was rebuilt in the 1950s after the prewar calculators and adding machines had been put back into production to provide the necessary capital. The P 38 was re-adopted by the Bundeswehr in 1957 and the postwar commercial market proved as receptive to the PP and PPK as it had been before the war. Walther has since produced some very sophisticated target pistols alongside variations of the P 38 and PP, and built a reputation as a maker of high-class items. Airguns, sporting and target rifles are also made in large numbers, attaining success at the highest international level.

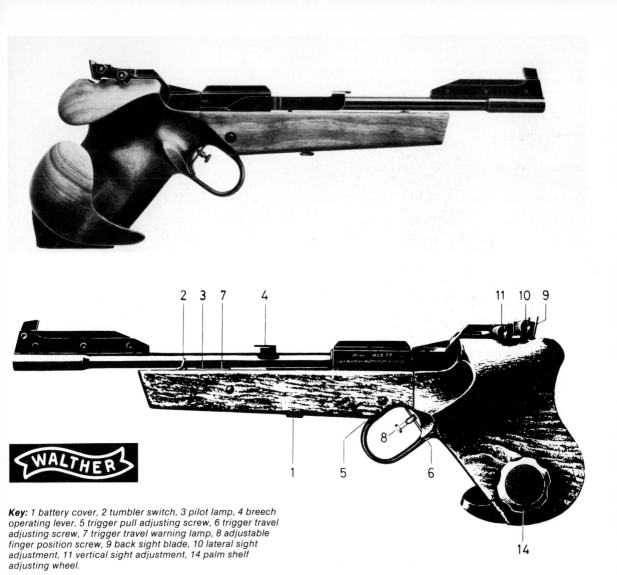

![WALTHER]

Key: 1 battery cover, 2 tumbler switch, 3 pilot lamp, 4 breech operating lever, 5 trigger pull adjusting screw, 6 trigger travel adjusting screw, 7 trigger travel warning lamp, 8 adjustable finger position screw, 9 back sight blade, 10 lateral sight adjustment, 11 vertical sight adjustment, 14 palm shelf adjusting wheel.

Above: the Walther Freie-Pistole, or FP, is among the world's most sophisticated Free Pistols-capable of the highest performance. (Courtesy Walther.)

Freie-Pistole (FP)

Target pistol. This is Walther's free pistol design, developed in the late 1970s and marketed from 1979. Like so many guns in its class, the FP features a dropping-block action, operated by a lever running forward on the right side of the barrel. Opening the breech automatically breaks the electronic ignition circuit; once the breech has been closed, the circuit is completed again—but the firer must wait until a light on the front left side of the fore-end, behind the on/off switch, indicates that the gun is ready to fire. The 9v battery is contained in the fore-end. The FP is an extraordinary-looking gun, with a fully adjustable button-style trigger and an all-enveloping handgrip, above which the backsight is carried on an extension of the receiver. The palm rest is adjusted by a large knob on the left side, while the front sight can be moved along the barrel to alter the sight radius from as little as 347mm to as much as 452.

Cal: 0.22in LR rf. Mag: none, single shot. Trg: electronic. Wt, oz/gm: 47.6/1350. Loa, in/mm: 17.3/440. Brl, in/mm: 11.8/300. Rf: NA. Sft: contact breaker activated when breech is open; on/off switch.

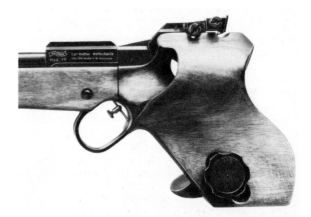

Gebrauchs- und Standard-Pistole (GSP)

Target pistol. This design, introduced in 1967, has proved extremely popular and a regular winner of international honours. The GSP is a surprisingly large but not unhandsome gun, with a sculpted walnut grip and a detachable box magazine lying ahead of the trigger guard—in which, very unusually, the trigger is pivoted at the base. Trigger units may be detached, to be replaced either with alternative triggers or dry-firing units. The locking latch for the interchangeable receiver units lies on the left side of the frame above and ahead of the trigger. The guns are blowbacks, their breechblocks reciprocating within the slide and retained by a transverse bar doubling as the cocking grips. The GSP is made in two versions, rim and centrefire; the former has a small recoil spring and small retraction grips, while the latter has a heavier breechblock, a more powerful recoil spring and larger retraction grips to permit the greater purchase needed to cock the action against the extra spring resistance. The 0.32in S & W long magazines have large basal weights or extensions, while the microadjustable non-reciprocatory backsight lies above the *front* of the grip. Early guns had the rear of the receiver cut diagonally, but newer ones are distinctly squared. (See also OSP.)

Cal: 0.22in LR rf, 0.32in S & W Wadcutter. Mag: detachable box, ahead of trigger, catch on frame behind trigger heel. Mag cap, rds: 5. Trg: SA, concealed hammer.
Wt, oz/gm: 41.6, 45.1/1180 (0.22in), 1280 (0.32in). Loa, in/mm: 11.5/292. Brl, in/mm: 4.2/107. Rf: NA. Sft: radial lever on left side of frame ahead of grip, down to safe; inertia firing pin.

Major exchangeable GSP/OSP components

(i) GSP 0.22in receiver/breechblock assembly
(ii) GSP 0.32in receiver/breechblock assembly
(iii) OSP 0.22in receiver/breechblock assembly
(iv) GSP trigger unit; adjustable 1000/1360gm pull
(v) OSP trigger unit; adjustable down to 100gm pull
(vi) GSP/OSP practice 'dry firing' trigger assemblies

Kriminal (or Kurz) Polizei Pistole, PPK

Personal defence pistol. Dating from as early as 1931, this is a shortened derivative of the PP—the latter being older by two years. The PPK is a small blowback, distinguished by its excellent quality, but is little more than a shortened, lightened Polizei-Pistole with reduced magazine capacity. Like its big brother, it has a rotary 'barrel'-type combination firing pin lock and de-cocking lever high on the left side of the slide below the fixed back sight, and the typical Walther dismantling system controlled by a hinged trigger guard. There is usually a small extension to the magazine and a lanyard loop on the base of the butt. Comments made about the PP (qv) apply equally to the PPK, whose original name (Kriminal or Kurz) has excited much controversy.

Cal: 0.22in LR rf, 0.32in ACP (7.65mm Auto), 0.380in ACP (9mm short). Otherwise as PP except Mag cap, rds: 7 (0.22in; 0.32in), 6/0.380in). Wt, oz/gm: 19.7–20.8/560–590. Loa, in/mm: 6.1/155. Brl, in/mm: 3.3/83.

PPK, Sonderfertigung (PPK/S)

Personal defence pistol. This was derived from the PPK to satisfy the US Gun Control Act 1968 which limited the maximum *height* of certain classes of gun. The PPK/S, therefore, features a shortened version of the rather more bulky PP slide and just exceeds the statutory minimum dimension!

Kurz-Pistole 38 (P38K)

Military and police pistol. Dating from the mid 1970s, this is simply a version of the Pistole 38 (qv) with the barrel cut to 7cm and the front sight—normally mounted on the muzzle crown—removed to the front of the frame. The P38K shares the squared hammer and revised retraction grooves of the P4 (qv). Though it retains full power ammunition, it is more readily concealed than its parent design . . . but increased recoil and a less than pleasant muzzle blast are among the penalties. The P38K can be considered a temporary (if quite popular) expedient, introduced while the improved P5 (qv)

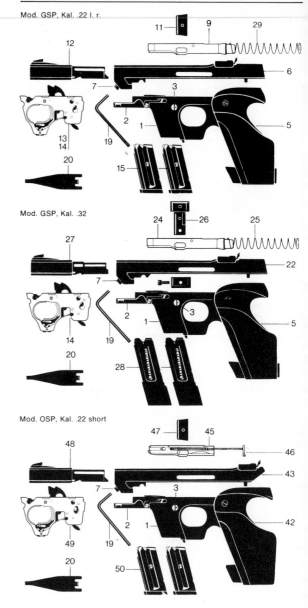

Mod. GSP, Kal. .22 l. r.

Mod. GSP, Kal. .32

Mod. OSP, Kal. .22 short

Below: *the Pistole 4 (courtesy Walther).*

was being developed. It is generally encountered with chequered plastic grips and an oxidised non-reflective finish.
Cal: 9mm Parabellum. Otherwise as P38, except Wt, oz/gm: 27.2/770. Loa, in/mm: 6.3/160. Brl, in/mm: 2.8/70.

Olympia-Schnellfeuer-Pistole (OSP)

Target pistol. The OSP was the first of Walther's modern blowback target pistols, introduced in 1962. The earliest guns had a round barrel with an auxiliary under-muzzle weight, the magazine aperture cut diagonally and rather slender grips which abutted rather than enveloped the rear of the frame. After the late 1960s, the design of the OSP was gradually merged with the then new Gebrauchs- und Standard-Pistole (qv) and the two shared virtually identical receiver/frame assemblies from 1971. However, the OSP is usually found with grips which allow the gun to lie lower in the hand, and chambers the 0.22in Short. The fully adjustable back sight lies at the extreme rear of the slide to give the maximum possible sight radius—desirable for rapid-fire competition. The OSP, like the GSP, has attained the highest of international honours.
Cal: 0.22in Short rf. Otherwise as GSP, except Wt, oz/gm: 39.5/1120. Loa, in/mm: 11.5/292. Brl, in/mm: 4.3/108.

Pistole 4 (P4)

Military and police pistol. The P4, introduced in the mid 1970s, is an 'intermediate' version of the standard Pistole 38—longer however, than the ultra-short P38K. Its alloy frame conserves weight, the hammer is squared and the retraction grips extend forward of the rotary safety/de-cocking lever on the slide. The back sight is adjustable laterally, while an arm in the trigger system lifts the firing pin (if the rotary safety catch permits) to be struck by the hammer face only during the final stages of a deliberate trigger pull; at rest, the firing-pin head enters a cutaway in the hammer and cannot be struck forward. The P4, like the P1/P38 and P38K, is a short-recoil operated design locked by a swinging block under the barrel.
Cal: 9mm Parabellum. Otherwise as P38, except Wt, oz/gm: 28.4/805. Loa, in/mm: 7.9/200. Brl, in/mm: 4.3/110.

Pistole 38 or Pistole 1 (P38, P1)

Military and police pistol. This, together with the Colt-Browning and the FN GP Model 35, is perhaps the best known of the current military pistols. Developed in the 1930s and put back into production in the 1950s, the P38 is a classic short-recoil operated design locked by a block below the barrel block cammed up, as the action closes, into recesses in the slide. Many guns have come and gone since the P38 was adopted by the German armed forces in February 1940, but derivatives of the P38 (renamed 'P1' by the West German Bundeswehr in 1963), and its near relative, the Beretta 951 Brigadier, remain in service in large numbers—a tribute to what is perhaps a timeless design. Several variants of the P38 have been made, the best being produced by Walther prior to 1942. Two other major contractors, Mauser and Spreewerke, were involved during the Second World War—but some of the guns dating from 1944-5 are poorly made and may even be potentially dangerous. Many wartime guns are still encountered, as the French, Czechs, East Germans and others used them into the 1950s. The modern alloy framed P38/P1 offers both a rising firing-pin lock, disconnected only during the final stages of triggering, and a standard Walther rotary 'barrel'-type combination safety and de-cocking lever on the side of the slide. There are strong fixed sights, chequered plastic grips with a lanyard loop on the left side of the butt, and a hold-open above the trigger on the left side of the frame (a short distance behind the Parabellum-style dismantling lever). The P38 suffers by comparison with newer designs; for example, it lacks ambidexterous safety features and has a relatively small capacity single-column magazine. Yet it is sturdy, well balanced and reliable, and remains the service pistol of the Bundeswehr. In 1968, Walther strengthened the slide of the P38/P1 as a few slides had cracked where the maker's mark had been struck too deeply. Post-1968 guns, therefore, display a small star proof on their slides. A 7.65mm Parabellum-chambered P38 was made until 1978, primarily for export to Italy, and a rimfire trainer appeared in 1976. This externally resembles the standard pistols, but beneath the surface lies a simple blowback with a rifled .22in calibre liner inserted in a standard bored-out barrel

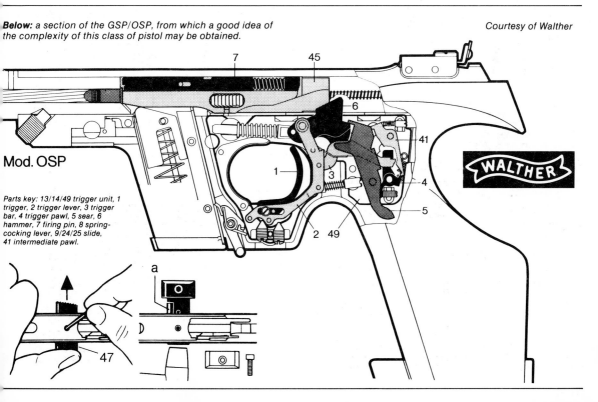

Below: *a section of the GSP/OSP, from which a good idea of the complexity of this class of pistol may be obtained.*

Courtesy of Walther

Mod. OSP

Parts key: 13/14/49 trigger unit, 1 trigger, 2 trigger lever, 3 trigger bar, 4 trigger pawl, 5 sear, 6 hammer, 7 firing pin, 8 spring-cocking lever, 9/24/25 slide, 41 intermediate pawl.

The operation of the P5

A chambering the first round by retracting the slide, keeping the finger clear of the trigger.

B double-action fire; the trigger is pulled straight through to operate the hammer.

C single-action fire; the hammer is cocked by the thumb before the trigger is pulled.

D after the last shot has been fired and ejected, the hold-open keeps the slide to the rear.

E the slide can be closed by pressing the catch above and ahead of the left grip, overriding the hold-open system and allowing the slide to run forward. The finger should be kept off the trigger.

F if the hammer has been cocked unnecessarily, or if the shot is not taken, the trigger mechanism can be actuated—by pressing the de-cocking lever—and the hammer dropped quite safely on a loaded chamber. The firing-pin head enters the safety recess on the hammer face. (All drawings courtesy Walther.)

---

forging. Blued or parkerised guns are available, as are engraved, cased, inlaid and damascened versions to order. *Cal: 9mm Parabellum (see also text). Mag: detachable box, catch on butt heel. Mag cap, rds: 8. Trg: DA, exposed hammer. Wt, oz/gm: 28.2/800. Loa, in/mm: 8.5/216. Brl, in/mm: 4.9/125. Rf: 4 R. Sft: rotary lever on left side of slide, locking firing pin, down to safe; rising firing-pin lock; inertia firing pin.*

Pistole 5 (P5)

Military and police pistol. The P5, which appeared in the mid 1970s, is essentially a Pistole 38 with a light alloy frame and a shortened barrel within an enveloping slide, but has a different trigger mechanism. The slide mounted safety/de-cocking lever has been replaced by a firing-pin elevating mechanism, which works in similar fashion to that of the P4 (qv), and a separate radial de-cocking lever ahead and above the left grip.

The adjustable back sight is also shared with the P4. The P5 retains the dismantling system of the standard P38 and, rather unusually, features 'leftward' ejection. Lack of ambidexterous controls is one of its possible weaknesses; its small capacity magazine (by modern standards) may be another. It is by no means a handsome gun, lacking the long barrelled elegance of the P38 but indisputably more handy; part of its clumsy appearance is caused by the deep slide, but as this narrows laterally ahead of the locking block, balance does not suffer. Several German police forces think sufficiently highly of the P5 to have adopted it, but the Walther still jockeys for supremacy against the P6 (SIG-Sauer P225) and P7 (Heckler & Koch PSP).
Cal: 9mm Parabellum. Otherwise as P38, except Wt, oz/gm: 28.0/795. Loa, in/mm: 7.1/180. Brl, in/mm: 3.5/90. Sft: firing-pin elevator system; de-cocking system with half-cock notch and interceptor; inertia firing pin.

Polizei-Pistole (PP)

General purpose pistol. The Polizei-Pistole is another old design. Patented in Germany as long ago as 1929, its historical significance is considerable: it featured the first commercially successful double-action trigger mechanism and has since inspired virtually every gun in this class. Many so-called 'rivals' have simply been direct copies. The survival of the PP and its smaller derivative, the PPK, is explained by one factor: the gun was so well conceived initially that little improvement could be made despite the passage of five decades. It remains a simple blowback with a sophisticated double-action trigger, distinguished by a ring hammer; it differs little from its prewar antecedents, though the safety system has been subjected to occasional revisions, and dismantling is still controlled by a downward hinged trigger guard. The guns are normally blued, with chequered plastic grips, but oakleaf or scrollwork engraving, burnishing, parkerising and chrome, silver or gold plating are all obtainable to special order.
Cal: 0.22in LR rf, 0.32in ACP (7.65mm Auto), 0.380in ACP (9mm Short). Mag: detachable box, crossbolt catch on left side of frame behind trigger. Mag cap, rds: 8 (7 in 0.380in). Trg: DA, exposed hammer. Wt, oz/gm: 22.6–23.5/640–665. Loa, in/mm: 6.7/170. Brl, in/mm: 3.9/98. Rf: yes. Sft: rotary lever on left side of slide below back sight; inertia firing pin.

Super-Polizei-Pistole (PP Super)

General purpose pistol. The PP Super, a modernised Polizei-Pistole, appeared in 1973. Its shares the same dismantling system, controlled by the trigger guard, but the original safety has been superseded by that of the Pistole 5 (qv). There is no conventional safety in the accepted Walther tradition; instead, the firing pin is only lifted into the hammer path during the final stages of deliberate trigger pull. At all other times, the head of the firing pin lies *inside* the hollowed hammer face. The lever on the left side of the slide, when depressed, acts as a de-cocking device—unlike earlier designs, however, it returns automatically to its upper position once released. The PP Super betrays its lineage quite clearly, but has a fashionable squared trigger guard (to facilitate two-hand grasp) and more combat-worthy grips.

Cal: 0.380in ACP or 9mm Police. Mag: detachable box, crossbolt catch on left frame behind trigger. Mag cap, rds: 7. Trg: DA, exposed hammer. Wt, oz/gm: 27.5/780. Loa, in/mm: 6.9/176. Brl, in/mm: 3.6/92. Rf: 6 R? Sft: inertia firing pin; firing-pin elevator system.

Taschen-Pistole (TP)

Personal defence pistol. The TP, introduced in May 1961 and discontinued in 1977 after only about 15,000 had been made, is one of the few comparative failures in the Walther production line. It was little more than a revision of the prewar Modell 9—an old blowback internal-striker design, patented in 1920/21—with much the same dismantling system controlled by a 'dumb-bell' shape locking piece in the rear of the frame. The TP features an odd radial safety on the side of the slide above the front of the grip and a sear bar inlet in an exposed channel on the left side of the frame.

Taschen-Pistole mit Hahn (TPH)

Personal defence pistol. Introduced in October 1968, this interesting little gun replaced the disappointing TP (qv). It is mechanically a diminutive of the Polizei-Pistole, with a similar double-action trigger mechanism, unusual among guns of its class, and a combination firing-pin lock and de-cocking lever. The grip is well-raked, if a little short for anything better than three-finger grasp; and the TPH is a good choice for instinctive short-range shooting, helped by square notch and blade sights with contrast markings. Unfortunately, its most powerful chambering is the ineffectual 0.25in ACP cartridge and its value as a credible man stopper may thus be questioned. The two versions are identical in all respects other than chambering and the omission from the rimfire gun of the loaded chamber indicating signal pin. The standard finish is blue, but polished black finish and oakleaf or arabesque engraving can be obtained on request.
Cal: 0.22in LR rf, 0.25in ACP (6.35mm Auto). Mag: detachable box, catch on butt heel. Mag cap, rds: 6. Trg: DA, exposed hammer. Wt, oz/gm: 11.4/325. Loa, in/mm: 5.3/135. Brl, in/mm: 2.8/71. Rf: 4 R (0.22in), 6 R (0.25in). Sft: radial lever on left side of slide above back of grip, down to safe; inertia firing pin.

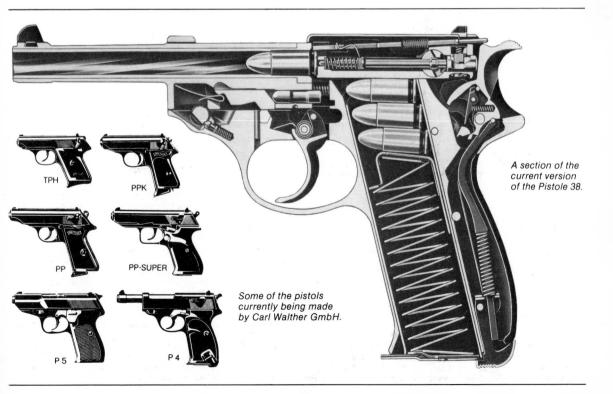

TPH

PPK

PP

PP-SUPER

P 5

P 4

A section of the current version of the Pistole 38.

Some of the pistols currently being made by Carl Walther GmbH.

Hermann Weihrauch KG

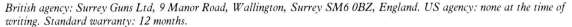

D-8744 Mellrichstadt/Bayern, West Germany

British agency: Surrey Guns Ltd, 9 Manor Road, Wallington, Surrey SM6 0BZ, England. US agency: none at the time of writing. Standard warranty: 12 months.

Founded in Zella St Blasii in 1899, this company made 'Thüringen' brand bicycles and sporting guns prior to 1945, when its factory found itself in the Russian occupation zone. However, the Weihrauch family, like the Walthers, had already fled westward and operations were successfully re-established in eastern Bavaria in 1948. The first airguns were made in 1950 and provided such a lucrative business that Weihrauch rapidly became one of the leading German manufacturers. Cartridge and blank-firing revolvers have been made since the 1960s under the brandname *Arminius*, previously associated with the Zella-Mehlis based Friedrich Pickert Waffenfabrik, whose operations ceased with the end of the Second World War. Weihrauch now also makes a range of excellent Western-styled revolvers based on the Colt Peacemaker.

Arminius HW1G

Starting and signal revolver. This is a typical Weihrauch/Arminius swing-out cylinder design of the class in which the movement of the cylinder yoke is controlled by the knurled sleeve surrounding the under-barrel ejector rod. The revolver has a short bird's head 'bulldog' butt, with chequered plastic grips, and is available in blue or chrome finish. Like most revolvers in its class—perhaps to preserve the integrity of its appearance—the HW1G actually possesses sights.
Cal: 9mm blanks or 15mm diameter signal rockets. Mag: cylinder. Mag cap, rds: 5. Trg: DA, exposed hammer. Wt, oz/gm: 22.9/650. Loa, in/mm: 7.2/182. Brl, in/mm: 3.0/75. Rf: none. Sft: 'transfer bar' hammer block; inertia firing pin.

Arminius HW1S

Starting and signal revolver. This is a minor variant of the HW1G (qv), sharing the same action but with a lateral gas vent—and, therefore, unable to fire signal rockets. The principal distinguishing characteristics, excluding the vent, are the square-tipped butt and 'notched ramp' mounted front sight. The HW1S may be obtained in blue or chrome finish, usually accompanied by chequered plastic grips.
Cal: 9mm blanks only. Otherwise as HW1G.

Arminius HW2R

Starting and signal revolver. Another of Weihrauch's 'gas revolvers', this is usually encountered with a short muzzle extension. It has a square tipped butt, yet is otherwise much the same as the HW1G. The company parts lists consider this gun, the HW1S and the HW6 to be one and the same. The finish may be blue or chrome, the chequered plastic grips dark brown or black.
Cal: 9mm blanks, 15mm diameter signal and detonating rockets. Otherwise generally as HW1G, though the muzzle extension (when fitted) adds some 0.5in (13mm) to the overall length.

Arminius HW3

Personal defence revolver. A typical snub-nose small rounded-butt and plastic-gripped pocket revolver, the HW3 offers the standard sleeve-controlled swing-out cylinder design and an interchangeable cylinder in 0.22in calibre. Unlike the HW68, the HW3 has a conventional gunmetal frame (contributing more than 200 grams of extra weight) and the usual optional blue or chrome finish. There are very prominent fixed sights, the forward of which sits on a notched plateau-type rib.
Cal: 0.22in LR and Magnum rf, or 0.32in S&W Long. Mag: cylinder. Mag cap, rds: 8 (0.22in) or 7 (0.32in). Trg: DA, exposed hammer. Wt, oz/gm: 26.4 or 24.1/750 or 685. Loa, in/mm: 7.0/178. Brl, in/mm: 2.8/70. Rf: 12 R? Sft: as HW1G.

Arminius HW4/2.5

Practice revolver. This designation covers two practically identical guns, based on the HW1 and HW2 series, but firing primer-propelled and rimfire ammunition—offering very little power indeed, but the chance of relatively safe practice in confined areas. The HW4 is another of the Arminius guns with

the sleeve-locked cylinder yoke. There are the standard finish options—blue or chrome—and a very distinctive short over-barrel rib. Being a pocket revolver, the squared butt and grips afford only a somewhat abbreviated grip.
Cal: 4mm M20 or 4mm rf. Mag: cylinder. Mag cap, rds: 8. Trg: DA, exposed hammer. Wt, oz/gm: 25.7/730. Loa, in/mm: 6.7/170. Brl, in/mm: 2.5/63. Rf: none. Sft: as HW1G.

Arminius HW4/4 and 4/6

Target revolver. This entry deals with two guns differing only in barrel length. One fires the 4mm M20 primer-propelled (Flobert) ammunition, the other the equally ineffective 4mm rimfire type. Both offer a chance to practice in confined or otherwise unsafe areas. The guns have very distinctive ventilated barrel ribs and cylinder yokes controlled by under-barrel sleeves shrouding the ejector rod. Both can be supplied in blue or chrome finish and are usually encountered with thumbrest style target grips.
Cal: 4mm M20 or 4mm rf. Otherwise as HW4/2.5, except Wt, oz/gm: 29.2 or 34.9/830 or 990. Loa, in/mm: 9.1 or 11.0/230 or 280. Brl, in/mm: 4.0 or 6.0/102 or 152.

Arminius HW5

General purpose revolver. The HW5 ia a derivative of the HW3, featuring a longer barrel and a longer flared-heel butt. All other constructional details are identical with the smaller gun (qv). The finish, as usual, is blue or chrome; but there is no barrel rib.
Cal: 0.22in LR or Magnum rf (exchangeable cylinders), 0.32in S&W Long. Mag: cylinder. Mag cap, rds: 8 (0.22in) or 7 (0.32in). Trg: DA, exposed hammer. Wt, oz/gm: 27.5 or 25.6/780 or 725. Loa, in/mm: 8.7/220. Brl, in/mm: 4.0/102. Rf: 12 R? Sft: 'transfer bar' hammer block; inertia-type firing pin; half-cock notch on hammer.

Arminius HW5T

Target revolver. This is a variant of the HW5 (qv) with a micro-adjustable rather than fixed back sight and a taller front sight atop a small rib. The HW5T, unlike the HW7T, is rarely found with the contoured thumbrest target-type grips but instead exhibits the flared-heel HW5 pattern.
Cal: 0.22in LR or Magnum rf (exchangeable cylinder), 0.32in S&W Long. Otherwise as HW5, except Wt, oz/gm: 30.0 or 28.2/850 or 800.

Arminius HW6

Starting and signal revolver. This is a minor variation of the HW2R, with which it is practically identical apart from the different calibre and the absence of a muzzle extension. The finish may be blue or chrome, while the chequered plastic grips have a squared toe and heel. The HW6 has a larger cylinder capacity than most Arminius gas revolvers.
Cal: 0.22in, 6mm gas cartridges and 15mm diameter signal rockets. Otherwise generally as HW1G.

Arminius HW7

Target revolver. The HW7 is an enlargement of the HW5, distinguished by the longer barrel and the over-barrel

Above: *some of the Weihrauch Arminius revolvers. Reading clockwise from the top, or 12 o'clock position, they are— HW357, HW9ST, HW38 with 4in barrel, HW7S, HW38 with 2.5in barrel, HW3 and HW68. (Courtesy of Weihrauch.)*

Right: *the current Weihrauch/Arminius trademarks.*

ventilated rib. The butt has a flared heel, the finish is blued or chromed, and the cylinder locking system is the well-tried annular ejector-rod sleeve (less satisfactory in many respects than the S&W frame-side latch featured on some other Weihrauch revolvers). The HW7 is quite accurate and competitively priced, but at a disadvantage to some of the better guns in the Arminius range.

Cal: 0.22in LR or Magnum rf (exchangeable cylinders), 0.32in S&W Long. Mag: cylinder. Mag cap, rds: 8 (0.22in) or 7 (0.32in). Trg: DA, exposed hammer. Wt, oz/gm: 30.9 or 28.2/875 or 800. Loa, in/mm: 10.4/265. Brl, in/mm: 6.0/152. Rf: 12 R? Sft: 'transfer bar' hammer block; inertia firing pin; half-cock notch on hammer.

Arminius HW7E

General purpose revolver. This is a derivative of the Colt Model P (see also HW 3575), modified to accept rimfire ammunition. The revolver features gate loading and the traditional offset ejector rod, and may be blued or chromed alloy. The grips are wood or chequered plastic.
Cal: 0.22in LR rf. Mag: cylinder. Mag cap, rds: 6. Trg: SA, exposed hammer. Wt, oz/gm: NA. Loa, in/mm: 11.8/300. Brl,

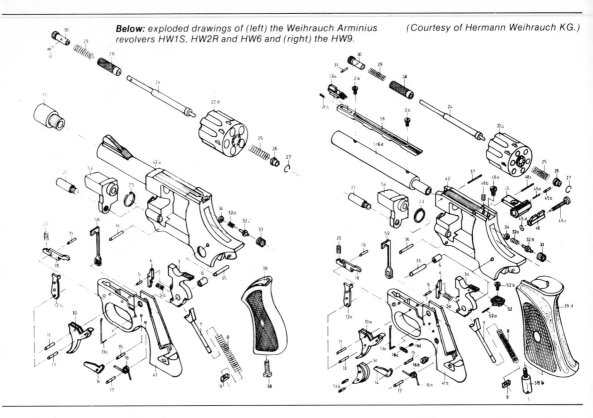

Below: *exploded drawings of (left) the Weihrauch Arminius revolvers HW1S, HW2R and HW6 and (right) the HW9.*

(Courtesy of Hermann Weihrauch KG.)

in/mm: 6.0/152. Rf: 12 R? Sft: inertia firing pin; half-cock notch on hammer.

Arminius HW7T

Target revolver. The HW7T is a variant of the basic HW7 in the same way that the HW5T is derived from the HW5—with a new ventilated barrel rib, micro-adjustable back sight, raised front sight and contoured thumbrest-style oversized target grips. As a result of the grip and the lengthened barrel, it is both longer overall and heavier than the gun from which it is derived. Blued or chromed finishes are standard.
Cal: 0.22in LR or Magnum rf (exchangeable cylinders), 0.32in S&W Long. Otherwise as HW7, except Wt, oz/gm: 32.8 or 30.3/930 or 860. Loa, in/mm: 11.0/280. Brl, in/mm: 6.0/152.

Arminius HW9

Target revolver. Developed from the HW38, this gun handles rimfire ammunition—which, together with low cost, makes it a good trainer for competition shooting. It has a ventilated-rib barrel (three slots), a ramp-mounted interchangeable blade front sight, a fully adjustable back sight, an adjustable trigger pull and a wide trigger shoe. The spur hammer has a widened thumbpiece and the grips are usually thumbrest plastic or wood, though full-scale palm-rest target grips can be supplied if required. The action is the normal Weihrauch/Arminius pattern in which the cylinder yoke is locked in place by the cylinder axis pin sleeve. The finish is always 'anodised blue', the frame being alloy rather than gunmetal.
Cal: 0.22in LR rf. Otherwise as HW38, except Wt, oz/gm: 38.8/1100. Loa, in/mm: 11.6/295. Brl, in/mm: 6.0/152.

Arminius HW7S

General purpose revolver. The 'S' derivative of the HW7 sub-series may be defined as the HW7T—target grips and ventilated over-barrel rib included—with simplified sights. The revolver only chambers rimfire ammunition and is invariably blued; it is quite adequate for its intended purpose.
Cal: 0.22in LR rf. Mag: cylinder. Mag cap, rds: 8. Trg: DA, exposed hammer. Wt, oz/gm: 32.6/925. Loa, in/mm: 11.0/280.

Brl, in/mm: 6.0/152. Rf: 12 R? Sft: 'transfer bar' hammer block; inertia safety pin; half-cock notch.

Arminius HW9ST

Target revolver. This is a minor variant of the HW9, chambering the same rimfire ammunition but with all-steel (ST—*stahl*, steel in German) construction. The HW9ST is generally found with hardwood target style grips, but has four slots under the ventilated rib rather than three and is appreciably heavier than its predecessor. Like the HW9, it has a prominent rib at the rear of the trigger guard.
Cal: 0.22in LR rf. Otherwise as HW9, except Wt, oz/gm: 42.7/1210. Loa, in/mm: 11.8/300. Brl, in/mm: 6.0/152.

Arminius HW357

Personal defence/general purpose revolver. This variant of the HW38 displays the standard Weihrauch yoke-type construction and the ventilated barrel rib carrying the ramp-mounted front sight. The back sight is fixed and the frame is tempered steel (most other Arminius frames are alloy) to withstand the greater power generated by the magnum cartridges. The guns are available in blued or chromed finish and usually feature chequered wooden grips. They are competitively priced and acceptably efficient, though the method of locking the cylinder yoke—the sliding annular ejector rod sleeve—is not as efficient as the S&W-type frame latch.
Cal: 0.357in Magnum. Otherwise as HW38, except Wt, oz/gm: 30.3, 31.7 or 35.3/860, 900 or 1000. Loa, in/mm: 7.5, 9.1 or 10.9/190, 230 or 278. Brl, in/mm: 2.5, 4.0 or 6.0/63. 102 or 152.

Arminius HW357 Match

Target revolver. This represents not only the top of the Weihrauch swing-out cylinder line, but also extremely good value—though the yoke-locking system is perhaps bettered by some rival designs. The 357 Match is practically identical with the HW9T apart from the chambering, and is invariably found with 'orthopædic' or palm-rest type target grips. The finish is invariably blue.

Cal: 0.357in Magnum or 0.38in Special. Otherwise as HW9, except Wt, oz/gm: 38.1/1080. Loa, in/mm: 11.8/300. Brl, in/mm: 6.0/152.

Arminius HW357 (T)

General purpose/target revolver. A variant of the standard HW357 (qv), this has a fully adjustable back sight, a higher ramp mounted front sight and—in the case of the longest barrelled version at least—semi-thumbrest wood grips. Finish may be blue or chrome, and most of the key parts are made of gunmetal rather than alloy. The power of the magnum cartridge makes this obligatory.
Cal: 0.357in Magnum or 0.38in Special. Otherwise as HW357, except Wt, oz/gm: 33.5, 35.3 or 37.0/950, 1000 or 1050. Loa, in/mm: 8.5, 9.1 or 11.3/215, 230 or 286. Brl, in/mm: 3.0, 4.0 or 6.0/75, 102 or 152.

Arminius HW38

Personal defence/general purpose revolver. This designation covers three essentially similar guns differing primarily in their barrel lengths—though the smallest also has a slim rounded-heel butt rather than a medium-size flare heel pattern. All three revert to the modern S&W yoke-latching system, a thumb catch on the left side of the frame beneath the hammer replacing the annular sleeve on the ejector rod. All have ventilated barrel ribs (exiguous in the case of the smallest) and may be obtained in blue or chrome finish. They are sturdy and quite well made, though not, perhaps, in the class of Colt, Smith & Wesson and other leading US products; however, the Weihrauch Arminius guns are considerably cheaper.
Cal: 0.38in Special. Mag: cylinder. Mag cap, rds: 6. Trg: DA, exposed hammer. Wt, oz/gm: 27.0, 30.9 or 33.5/765, 875 or 950. Loa, in/mm: 7.1, 8.9 or 10.8/180, 225 or 275. Brl, in/mm: 2.5, 4.0 or 6.0/63, 102 or 152. Rf: 12 R? Sft: 'transfer bar' hammer block; half-cock notch; inertia firing pin.

Arminius HW38T

General purpose/target revolver. There are three versions of the HW38T, varying only in barrel length—between 3in and 6in (75m-152mm). All three are typical Weihrauch products, with ventilated rib and fully adjustable back sights. There are also thumbrest-style chequered plastic grips and the standard 'Arminius' cylinder yoke release. Available in blue or chrome finish.
Cal: 0.38in Special. Otherwise as HW38, except Wt, oz/gm: 28.2, 33.0 or 34.7/800, 935 or 985. Loa, in/mm: 8.6, 9.3 or 11.3/219, 235 or 286. Brl, in/mm: 3.0, 4.0 or 6.0/75, 102 or 152.

Arminius HW68 Lightweight

Personal defence revolver. The HW68 is a typical Arminius design, with an ultra-short ribless barrel (cf. HW4/2.5) and a short squared butt. It features a weight-saving alloy frame, an exchangeable cylinder for two differing 0.22in rf rounds, black anodised finish and chequered plastic grips. The cylinder release is the popular under-barrel knurled sleeve around the ejector rod.
Cal: 0.22in LR or Magnum rf, 0.32in S&W Long. Mag: cylinder. Mag cap, rds: 8 (0.22in) or 7 (0.32in). Trg: DA, exposed hammer. Wt, oz/gm: 18.7 or 16.7/530 or 475. Loa, in/mm: 6.7/170. Brl, in/mm: 2.5/63. Rf: 12 R? Sft: 'transfer bar' hammer block; inertia firing pin; half-cock notch on hammer.

Arminius Western Six Shooter ARM3575

General purpose revolver. This designation covers a number of essentially similar guns based on the Colt Model P of 1873, but incorporating a transfer-bar safety system and an inertia firing pin to satisfy the US Gun Control Act of 1968. All the guns display the traditional side-hinged loading gate and offset ejector rod mounted on the right side of the barrel. Their grips may be wood or chequered plastic, displaying the ARMINIUS trademark, while the finish is usually a deep, beautifully lustrous blue. However, Weihrauch will supply chromed, gold-plated, colour casehardened or even polished *brass* frames on request.

Cal: 0.357in Magnum. Mag: cylinder. Mag cap, rds: 6. Trg: SA, exposed hammer. Wt, oz/gm: 44.1/1250. Loa, in/mm: 11.0/280. Brl, in/mm: 5.5/140. Rf: 12 R. Sft: 'transfer bar' hammer block; inertia firing pin; half-cock notch on hammer.

Variants

ARM445. 0.44in Magnum, 40.9oz/1160gm, otherwise as 3575.
ARM455. 0.45in Long Colt, otherwise as 445.
ARM3577. 0.357in Magnum, 13.0in/330mm overall, 7.5in/190mm barrel, 47.3oz/1340gm. Otherwise as 3575.
ARM447. 0.44in Magnum, 43.4oz/1230gm. Otherwise as 3577.
ARM457. 0.45in Long Colt, 41.6oz/11180gm. Otherwise as 3577.

Arminius Target Six Shooter ARM3576T

Target revolver. This is a variant of the company's excellent Western or Colt Peacemaker replica, with a high blade front sight and a fully adjustable back sight on the frame ahead of the hammer, which facilitates accurate shooting. The gun, which is almost invariably blued, is otherwise the same as the 3575 (qv).
Cal: 0.357in Magnum. Otherwise as ARM3575, except Wt, oz/gm: 48.0/1360. Loa, in/mm: 12.0/305. Brl, in/mm: 6.0/152.

Variants

ARM446T. 0.44in Magnum, 44.1oz/1250gm, otherwise as 3576T.
ARM456T. 0.45in Long Colt, 42.3oz/1200gm, otherwise as 3576T.

Dan Wesson Company

**293 Main Street, Monson,
Massachusetts 01057, USA**

*British agency: John L. Longstaff (R.E.C.) Ltd,
35-37 Chapel Town, Pudsey, West Yorkshire LS28 7RZ.*

Wesson was another of the companies unable to assist in research, but is well known for its replaceable barrel revolvers—though the guns themselves, the removable barrels apart, are relatively conventional. However, they are very well made of excellent material and have attained a good reputation.

Wesson Revolver

General purpose revolver. This is a conventional swing-out cylinder design, with unique interchangeable barrels which screw into the frame once the barrel shroud, which carries the sights, and the lock nut have been removed. Feeler gauges are supplied to ensure the correct barrel/cylinder clearance. Most of the guns display interchangeable walnut grips and are finished in satin blue.

Series 8. In 0.38in Special with barrels of 2.5, 4.0, 6.0 or 8.0in (63, 102, 152 or 203mm). The revolvers have fixed sights and weigh between 30 and 42oz (850 and 1190gm).
Series 9. A duplicate of Series 8, with adjustable sights and, consequently, a little heavier.
Series 14. The Series 8 in 0.357in Magnum.
Series 15. The Series 9 in 0.357in Magnum.
Series 15-2V. The barrels of these guns had ventilated ribs; 10, 12 and 15in barrels (254, 305, 381mm) were also available.
Series 15-2HV. These guns duplicate the Series 15-2V, but their barrels are considerably heavier.
Series 22. As Series 15, but chambering 0.22in LR rimfire ammunition rather than 0.357in Magnum.
Series 22-2V and 22-2HV. The rimfire equivalents of Series 15-2V and Series 15-2HV, excepting the three longest barrels.

Wesson also makes a 'Pistol Pac' containing one 8in-barrelled revolver, three additional barrels (2.5, 4 and 6in), an extra grip, four coloured front sight inserts and a belt buckle, in a special case.

Wildey Firearms Co., Inc.

PO Box 447, Cheshire, Connecticut 06410, USA

UK agency: Coach Harness, Haughley, Stowmarket, Suffolk IP14 3NS, England. Standard warranty: unknown.

The Wildey company was founded in the early 1970s to exploit what it claims to be the first gas-operated pistol to achieve production status, a claim that obviously hinges on the definition of 'production status' (see also Steyr Model GB). Various prototype guns were made in Cold Springs and New Windsor, New York State, before the move to Cheshire occurred in 1980.

WM 450 series

Sporting pistol. Developed by W.J. Moore, apparently inspired by a Swedish Husqvarna prototype, these pistols chamber the most powerful of the current pistol cartridges (disregarding the currently defunct Auto Mag). The annular piston surrounding the Wildey barrel is forced rearward when gas bleeds out of six radially bored barrel ports to rotate and unlock the recessed-face 3-lug bolt. The grip and frame are similar to those of the Colt Government Model, but there any resemblance ceases: the barrel and unmistakably Wildey slide-front differ greatly from the Colt. Most Wildeys are made of stainless steel and feature fully adjustable sights. It is generally agreed that gas operation gives smoother operation than recoil operation, and the powerful but very heavy Wildeys are not notably unpleasant to fire. Their barrels measure 5, 6, 7, 8 and 10in (13, 15, 18, 20 and 25cm)—all but the shortest featuring ventilated ribs. The guns are designated by barrel length; the WM 456 has a 6in (15cm) barrel, while the WM450 offers the 10in (25cm) type.
Cal: 9mm or 0.45in Winchester Magnum. Mag: detachable box. Mag cap: 8 (0.45in) or 14 (9mm). Trg: DA, exposed hammer. Wt, oz/gm: 64.0/1815 with 5in (13cm) barrel. Loa, in/mm: 11.0/281 with 7in (18cm) barrel. Brl, in/mm: see text. Rf: yes. Sft: manual lever on left rear of frame; inertia firing pin.

Right: two representative Wildey pistols: the WM 455 and the WM 458. (Courtesy Wildey Firearms.)

Zastava

Crvena Zastava, Kraguyevac, Yugoslavia. The products of this government-owned firearms factory are occasionally seen in the West, including an indigenous version of the Soviet Tokarev, known as the Model 57, and a personal defence pistol of uncertain designation. At the time of writing, distributorships exist neither in Britain nor in the United States of America.

Antonio Zoli SpA

Via Zanardelli 39, I-25063 Gardone Val Trompia (Brescia), Italy

British agency: no sole distributorship. US agency: Navy Arms Co., 689 Bergen Boulevard, Ridgefield, New Jersey 07657, USA. Standard warranty: 12 months.

Zoli is best known as a manufacturer of percussion longarms such as the 'Zouave' rifle, but has also made quantities of Kentucky-style flintlock and percussion pistols. It is believed that replicas of the US Harper's Ferry and British 'Tower' flintlocks have been made as well, but further information is still awaited.

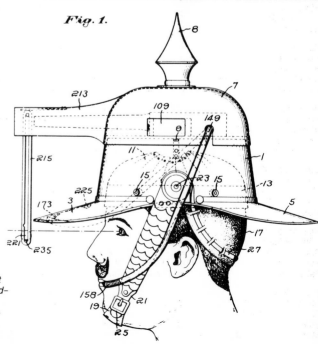

Fig. 1.

Right: from the sublime to the ridiculous. Just to show that there are still some old designs yet to be properly exploited- this 'hat gun' was patented by Albert Pratt of Lyndon, Vermont, in 1915 (other patents were sought elsewhere at different times). One dreads to think what would have happened had the gun fired a powerful cartridge.

Comparachart: target pistols

Categorisation of target pistols presents an especially difficult task, owing to the part played in selection by unadulterated personal preference. The review here is, therefore, very subjective though supported as far as possible by reviewers in many countries. Magazines such as *Target Gun, Handgunner, Guns Review,* the *Deutsches Waffen Journal, Diana-Armi* and a plethora of US publications should also be consulted before any choice is made. However, assessments of 'value for money' in particular, are certain to excite some controversy. Guns rated here as good value need not necessarily be those with which Olympic Gold will be gained; indeed, they may actually be low-grade training weapons. It is important, therefore, to remember that this particular part of the class in which the gun is intended to perform—both fiscal and from a shooting viewpoint. The high price of the recently introduced Agner, for instance, must inevitably reflect in the assessment; but it cannot be denied that the gun is superbly made . . .

No attempt has been made to indicate whether guns may conflict with competition rules; some of the trainers certainly will, and some sight radii offend ISU or national rules. It is obviously left to the shooter to determine whether a gun reviewed here satisfies the requirements of his specific discipline.

GUN	CAL	VFM	CONSTR	TECH	DISMNTL	PERF	DIS	PG
Agner M80	C	•••	•••••	•••••	••••	•••••	Std	25
Astra TS-22	C	••••	•••	•••	••••	••••	Prct	28
Beretta Modello 71	C	••••	••••	•••	••••	•••	Plnk	35
Beretta Modello 76	C	••••	•••••	••••	••••	••••	Prct	35
Beretta Mo. 952 Special	J2'	••••	•••••	••••	••••	••••	Ctrfr	41
Bernardelli Mo.69 TS	C	••••	••••	••••	••••	••••	Prct	44
Britarms Model 2000	C	••••	•••••	•••••	••••	•••••	Std	45
Colt Gold Cup Ntnl Mtch	T	••••	••••	•••	••••	••••	Ctrfr	53
Dílo Drulóv vz.70	C	•••••	••••	•••	••••	•••	Prct	57
Dílo Drulóv vz.75	c	•••••	••••	•••	••••	••••	FP	57
Dílo Pav	C	••••	••••	••	•••••	•••	Prct	57
Em-Ge Models 200, 300	C H	••••	•••	•••	••••	•••	Prct	59
FAS PGP 75 (Pardini)	C	••••	••••	••••	••••	•••••	FP	65
FAS OP 601	B	•••••	•••••	•••••	••••	•••••	Rpd	65
FAS SP 602	C	•••••	•••••	•••••	••••	•••••	Std	66
FAS CF 603	H	•••••	•••••	•••••	••••	•••••	Ctrfr	66
FN GP Mle 35 Competition	J1	••••	•••••	•••	••••	••••	Ctrfr	69
FN International II	C	••••	•••••	••••	••••	••••	Std	71
FN Practice 150	C	••••	•••••	••••	••••	•••	Std	71
Hämmerli 120	C	••••	•••••	••••	••••	••••	FP	77
Hämmerli 150	C	••••	•••••	•••••	•••	•••••	FP	78
Hämmerli 152 Electronic	C	••••	•••••	•••••	•••	•••••	FP	78
Hämmerli 208 International	C	••••	•••••	••••	••••	••••	Std	81
Hämmerli 212	C	••••	•••••	••••	••••	••••	Prct	81
Hämmerli 215	C	••••	••••	••••	••••	••••	Std	82
Hämmerli 232	B	•••••	•••••	•••••	••••	•••••	Rpd	82
Heckler & Koch P9 Sport	J1 T	••••	•••••	•••••	•••	••••	Ctrfr	89
High Standard CT 10-X	C	••••	•••••	••••	••••	••••	Std	92
High Standard Sharpshooter	C	••••	••••	••••	••••	•••	Prct	94
High Standard Supermtc Cn	C (B)	••••	••••	••••	••••	••••	Std:rpd	94
High Standard Trophy	C (B)	••••	•••••	••••	••••	••••	Std:rpd	94
High Standard Victor	C	••••	•••••	••••	••••	••••	Std	94
Izhevsk Izh-1	B	•••••	•••	••••	••••	••••	FP	97
Izhevsk Izh-30	C	•••••	•••	••••	••••	•••••	Std	97
Izhevsk Izh-31	B	•••••	•••	••••	••••	•••••	Rpd	97
Llama XXIII Olimpico	M	••••	••••	••••	••••	••••	Ctrfr	100
Llama XXIX Olimpico	C	••••	••••	••••	••••	••••	Std	101
Margolin MTs-2-3	C	••••	•••	••••	••••	•••	Std	104
Margolin MTsU	B	••••	•••	••••	••••	•••	Rpd	104
Merrill	various	••••	••••	••••	•••••	••••	Lrng	108
Remington XP-100	E	••••	••••	••••	••••	••••	Lrng	117
Röhm RG34T, 35T, 38T	C D M	••••	•••	••••	••••	•••	Prct	120
Röhm RG88T	L M	••••	••••	••••	••••	••••	Ctrfr	122
Sako 22-32	B C M	••••	•••••	•••••	•••••	•••••	Conv	126
Sako Triace	B C M	••••	•••••	•••••	•••••	•••••	Conv	126
Sauer SR3	C M	••••	•••••	••••	••••	••••	Prct	127
SIG P210-5, P210-6	J1 J2	•••	•••••	••••	••••	••••	Ctrfr	129
SIG-Hämmerli P240	C H M	••••	••••••	••••	••••	••••	Var	130
S&W Model 41	C	••••	•••••	••••	••••	•••	Std	134
Star Modelo FR Target	C	••••	•••	•••	••••	••••	Prct	139

GUN	CAL	VFM	CONSTR	TECH	DISMNTL	PERF	DIS	PG
Sterling X-Caliber	Various	••••	••••	••••	•••••	••••	Lrng	143
Sturm Ruger Mk 2 Target	C	•••••	••••	••••	••••	••••	Prct	146
Thälmann Zentrum	C	•••••	••••	•••	••••	••••	FP	150
Thälmann Ziegenhahn	B	••••	•••	•••	••••	••••	Rpd	150
Thmpsn/Center Contender	Various	•••••	••••	••••	•••••	•••••	Lrng	151
TOZ-35 (Vostok)	C	•••••	•••	••••	••••	••••	FP	152
Unique DES/69	C	•••••	•••••	••••	••••	•••••	Std	157
Unique DES/VO	B	•••••	•••••	••••	••••	•••••	Rpd	157
Walther FP	C	•••••	•••••	•••••	••••	•••••	FP	159
Walther GSP	C H	•••••	•••••	•••••	••••	•••••	Std	160
Walther OSP	B	•••••	•••••	•••••	••••	•••••	Rpd	160
Weihrauch HW7T	C D	••••	••••	•••	••••	•••	Prct	166
Weihrauch HW9ST	C	••••	••••	••••	••••	••••	Prct	166
Weihrauch HW357 Match	L M	••••	••••	••••	••••	••••	Ctrfr	166

The abbreviations are explained on pages 60-61.

Additional abbreviations, unique to the 'Target Chart': *Ctrfr* centrefire, *FP* Free Pistol, *Lrng* long range, *Plnk* plinking, *Prct* practice, *Rpd* rapid fire, and *Std* standard pistol.

Below: *the Em-Ge Model 300 revolver (courtesy Em-Ge).*

Appendices

Twenty popular cartridges

A history of the handgun cartridge—even if it were to be as condensed as far as possible—would require a book in itself and shall not be attempted here, though it must be acknowledged that many different cartridges have been tried over the years and more will undoubtedly be tried in the future. Experiments have been undertaken with many methods of ignition, but the worst of these have long since been consigned to the scrapheap of history. Even the pinfire, once extremely popular, has long since fallen into disrepute (its cartridges could be ignited too easily by a careless blow), while experiments with self-contained ammunition—the rockets exemplified by the Gyrojet, and the caseless rounds—have yet to provide an adequate substitute for the self-contained metallic-case cartridge.

Handguns have been chambered for a tremendous variety of cartridges, from the tiny 0.17in Ackley Bee up to the 45/410, which was based, as its name suggests, on a shotgun round. The diversity is clearly apparent in the list of cartridges chambered in the Thompson/Center Contender single-shot pistol (see page 14). The 0.17in cartridge was a passing craze; many other unusual 'wildcat' cartridges, produced by private experimentation, have also appeared in a short-lived blaze of glory, failed to win market approval, and rapidly returned to the melting pot or the collector's shelf. Virtually all cartridges begin life as private or corporate experiments, but the latter have a much better chance of success than the former—as witness the success of the 0.357in Magnum round, conceived by Smith & Wesson as long ago as 1934 in consultation with the late Philip B. Sharpe, against the failure of other experimental cartridges of much the same size and power that simply failed to excite sufficient interest.

The list that follows does not contain all the cartridges mentioned in this book, many of which are to be placed firmly in the 'wildcat' category even though Thompson/Center or The Merrill Company may chamber single-shot pistols for it. In addition, there are so many possible permutations of bullet and propellant charge—and so many manufacturers involved—that no attempt can be made to list them individually. This will have to await *The Ammunition Book...*!

A. 0.22in BB Cap RF★
Case type: straight rimmed
Ignition system: primer propelled
Case length: 270
Rim diameter: 278
Body diameter: 225
Neck diameter: 225
Bullet diameter: 225
Typical velocity: NA
Typical muzzle energy: NA
Remarks: the propellant of this tiny cartridge can consist either entirely of priming compound or priming compound with a small black powder charge. Usually stated to be of no use whatsoever, the BB Cap may be fired in most 0.22in rimfire revolvers and *will* provide ultra low-power practice in circumstances where even the 0.22in Short rf cannot be used.

B. 0.22in Short RF★
Case type: straight rimmed
Ignition system: rimfire
Case length: 421
Rim diameter: 278
Body diameter: 226
Neck diameter: 225
Bullet diameter: 225
Typical velocity: 1050 fps with bullet weighing 29 gr
Typical muzzle energy: 70 fp
Remarks: Introduced by Smith & Wesson in 1857, this round survives principally for rapid-fire competition use, where its ultra-low power is helpful. This minimises the disturbance to aim during firing and enables the firer to return his sights to the target in the shortest possible time.

C. 0.22in Long Rifle RF★
Case type: straight rimmed
Ignition system: rimfire
Case length: 613
Rim diameter: 278
Body diameter: 226
Neck diameter: 225
Bullet diameter: 225
Typical velocity: 1150 fps with bullet weighing 40 gr
Typical muzzle energy: 115 fp
Remarks: apparently developed for or by the Stevens Tool & Arms Company in 1887, this has become very popular in recent years—practically every manufacturer offers at least one loading, from cheap low-grade plinkers up to the finest competition ammunition.

D. 0.22in Winchester Mag. RF★
Case type: straight rimmed
Ignition system: rimfire
Case length: 1055
Rim diameter: 294
Body diameter: 242
Neck diameter: 242
Bullet diameter: 224
Typical velocity: 2000 fps with bullet weighing 40 gr
Typical muzzle energy: 355 fp
Remarks: introduced in 1959 to replace the Winchester RF of 1890, this is among the most powerful of all rimfire cartridges and a popular (if more expensive) substitute for the Long Rifle variety. Many revolvers, in particular, are supplied with exchangeable cylinders.

E. 0.221in Remington Fireball★
Case type: bottleneck rimless
Ignition system: centrefire
Case length: 1400
Rim diameter: 378
Body diameter: 377
Neck diameter: 253
Bullet diameter: 224
Typical velocity: 2600 fps with bullet weighing 50 gr
Typical muzzle energy: 750 fp
Remarks: introduced in 1963 for the XP100 bolt-action pistol, the only pistol to chamber it, this was based on the 0.222in Remington rifle cartridge. It develops more power in the long XP100 barrel than most short barrelled 0.357in Magnum revolvers.

F. 6.35mm Auto ★ (0.25in ACP)
Case type: straight rimless
Ignition system: centrefire
Case length: 612
Rim diameter: 301
Body diameter: 276
Neck diameter: 276
Bullet diameter: 251
Typical velocity: 810 fps with bullet weighing 50 gr
Typical muzzle energy: 73 fp
Remarks: this was developed in Europe and introduced in 1906 along with the Baby Browning, appearing in the USA with the Colt automatic in two years later. It develops a high velocity for so small a case, but its jacketed bullet is notoriously ineffectual; it has been remarked quite frequently that the lead-bulletted 0.22in Short rf is a better man stopper than the 6.35mm Auto.

G. 0.256in Winchester Magnum
Case type: bottleneck rimmed
Ignition system: centrefire
Case length: 1281
Rim diameter: 440
Body diameter: 380
Neck diameter: 285
Bullet diameter: 257
Typical velocity: 2200 fps with bullet weighing 60 gr
Typical muzzle energy: 650 fp
Remarks: developed in 1960, this was first used two years later. Despite attempts to develop suitable revolvers in this calibre, only the Ruger Hawkeye and new designs such as the Thompson/Center Contender (both single-shot) have been able to handle it.

H. 0.32in Smith & Wesson Long
Case type: straight rimmed
Ignition system: centrefire
Case length: 920
Rim diameter: 380
Body diameter: 337
Neck diameter: 337
Bullet diameter: 315
Typical velocity: 780 fps with bullet weighing 98 gr
Typical muzzle energy: 132 fp
Remarks: developed for the S&W First Model Hand Ejector in 1903, this was once widely favoured for police use until the advent of more powerful rounds such as the 0.38in Special and, ultimately, the 0.357in Magnum. The 0.32in S&W Long fires a modest bullet, but is very accurate and often used for centrefire competition shooting. It is also generally regarded as the smallest practicable cartridge for small game shooting.

I. 7.65mm Auto (0.32in ACP)
Case type: straight rimless
Ignition system: centrefire
Case length: 680
Rim diameter: 352
Body diameter: 336
Neck diameter: 336
Bullet diameter: 309
Typical velocity: 960 fps with bullet weighing 71 gr
Typical muzzle energy: 145 fp
Remarks: developed by John M. Browning and Fabrique Nationale, introduced in 1899, this is widely used in small automatic pistols. It is, however, a poor man stopper and of only marginal effectiveness against even the smallest of game—particularly when the jacketed bullets are used.

J. 9mm Parabellum
Case type: straight rimless
Ignition system: centrefire
Case length: 760
Rim diameter: 390
Body diameter: 390
Neck diameter: 380
Bullet diameter: 357
Typical velocity: 1140 fps with bullet weighing 115 gr
Typical muzzle energy: 332 fp
Remarks: developed by Georg Luger and DWM in 1902, this is now the world's most popular and widely distributed pistol and submachine-gun cartridge. When loaded with the right bullets, the 9mm Parabellum (also known as the 9×19mm) makes a good hunting cartridge, though its virtues as a man stopper, particularly when loaded with jacketed bullets, has been widely questioned.

K. 9mm Police★
Case type: straight rimless
Ignition system: centrefire
Case length: 709
Rim diameter: 374
Body diameter: 380
Neck diameter: 380
Bullet diameter: 355
Typical velocity: NA
Typical muzzle energy: NA
Remarks: this was developed by Hirtenberg Patronenfabrik in 1969 to explore the limits of blowback operation in automatic pistols, and has since been chambered in several European pistols (such as the Walther PP Super). It is also known as the 9×18mm, though this designation is too easily confused with the 9mm Parabellum.

L. 0.357in Magnum★
Case type: straight rimmed
Ignition system: centrefire
Case length: 1290
Rim diameter: 440
Body diameter: 379
Neck diameter: 379
Bullet diameter: 359
Typical velocity: 1430 fps with bullet weighing 158 gr
Typical muzzle energy: 717 fp
Remarks: developed in the mid 1930s by Smith & Wesson in collusion with Philip Sharpe, this is basically a lengthened derivative of the 0.38in Special—but infinitely more powerful and a better man stopper, though recoil may be excessive in lightweight guns.

M. 0.38in Special★
Case type: straight rimmed
Ignition system: centrefire
Case length: 1155
Rim diameter: 440
Body diameter: 379
Neck diameter: 379
Bullet diameter: 360
Typical velocity: 730 fps with bullet weighing 200 gr
Typical muzzle energy: 236 fp
Remarks: developed by Smith & Wesson in 1902, this is widely regarded as the most accurate of handgun cartridges—but by no means the best choice for personal defence, though incomparably superior to the 6.35mm and 7.65mm Auto pistol cartridges and the 0.32in S&W Long. Once universally used in police revolvers, it has been losing ground steadily to the 0.357in Magnum. It is still used for centrefire competition work.

N. 0.38in Super Auto Pistol★
Case type: straight semi-rim
Ignition system: centrefire
Case length: 900
Rim diameter: 406
Body diameter: 384
Neck diameter: 384
Bullet diameter: 356
Typical velocity: 1275 fps with bullet weighing 130 gr
Typical muzzle energy: 468 fp
Remarks: this round made its debut in 1929, offering an improvement over the older 0.38in Colt Auto cartridge. Known as the 9mm Long or 9mm Largo in Europe, it is very powerful; well suited to hunting and personal defence, the recoil of the pistols in which it is chambered may be quite fierce. In the opinion of some commentators, this cartridge is superior to both the 9mm Parabellum and the 0.45in ACP.

O. 0.380in ACP (9mm Short)
Case type: straight rimless
Ignition system: centrefire
Case length: 675
Rim diameter: 374
Body diameter: 374
Neck diameter: 372
Bullet diameter: 356
Typical velocity: 955 fps with bullet weighing 95 gr
Typical muzzle energy: 192 fp
Remarks: designed by Browning and Fabrique Nationale and introduced in Europe in 1912, this was at one time the service pistol cartridge in several European armies—as well as popular on the commercial market. It is about the smallest cartridge that can be taken seriously for personal defence, but may be limited by its jacketed bullets. However, anything the 7.65mm Auto round does well, the 9mm Short (9mm Corto in the Iberian Peninsula) does much better, and the guns in which it chambers are often very light and handy.

P. 0.41in Magnum
Case type: straight rimmed
Ignition system: centrefire
Case length: 1280
Rim diameter: 488
Body diameter: 433
Neck diameter: 432
Bullet diameter: 410
Typical velocity: 1305 fps with bullet weighing 210 gr
Typical muzzle energy: 793 fp
Remarks: developed by S&W in 1964, for the Model 57 revolver, this provides a gun more powerful than the 0.357in Magnum but with less of a recoil than the 0.44in pattern (though still by no means easy to fire). The 0.41in round is frequently adjudged a failure in its intended police role, but is the best all-round sporting cartridge of the three Magnums.

Q. 0.44in Magnum★
Case type: straight rimmed
Ignition system: centrefire
Case length: 1285
Rim diameter: 515
Body diameter: 457
Neck diameter: 456
Bullet diameter: 432
Typical velocity: 1470 fps with bullet weighing 240 gr
Typical muzzle energy: 1275 fp
Remarks: introduced by S&W in 1955, after consultation with Elmer Keith, this is among the most powerful of revolver cartridges. It will exhibit fearsome recoil and muzzle blast, and is certainly not to be recommended to a beginner or a shooter of small stature. However, once the recoil has been controlled, the cartridge is capable of superb accuracy and the large bullets perform superbly as a man stopper or on game.

R. 0.44in S & W Special★
Case type: straight rimmed
Ignition system: centrefire
Case length: 1160
Rim diameter: 510
Body diameter: 441
Neck diameter: 441
Bullet diameter: 440
Typical velocity: 755 fps with bullet weighing 246 gr
Typical muzzle energy: 311 fp
Remarks: developed by S&W from the 0.44in Russian round in 1907, this was never loaded to its full potential and was subsequently eclipsed by the 0.44in Magnum which derived from it. However, the 0.44in Special fires a large bullet with good knock-down capabilities, as a result of which it has found renewed popularity in revolvers too small and light to handle the 0.44in Magnum.

S. 0.45in Colt Revolver★
Case type: straight rimmed
Ignition system: centrefire
Case length: 1285
Rim diameter: 512
Body diameter: 480
Neck diameter: 480
Bullet diameter: 455
Typical velocity: 855 fps with bullet weighing 255 gr
Typical muzzle energy: 405 fp
Remarks: introduced in 1872-3, this was the cartridge that tamed the Wild West, along with the 44/40 Winchester. It is regarded as very accurate, a good man stopper, and one of the most powerful revolver cartridges obtainable prior to the advent of the 0.44in Magnum.

T. 0.45in ACP
Case type: straight rimless
Ignition system: centrefire
Case length: 900
Rim diameter: 474
Body diameter: 472
Neck diameter: 470
Bullet diameter: 450
Typical velocity: 855 fps with bullet weighing 230gr
Typical muzzle energy: 405 fp
Remarks: this, one of the best known cartridges of all time, was conceived by John Browning in 1905 and adopted by the US Army in 1911. It is extremely powerful and a very good man stopper, although the jacketed bullets are something of a hindrance. However, the 0.45in ACP exhibits severe recoil and is not suited to a novice or a shooter of small stature, who would be advised to use a gun chambering the 9mm Parabellum or even the 9mm Short.

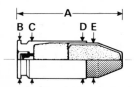

Key to measurements. Cartridge shown is 9mm Parabellum

A case length, **B** rim diameter, **C** body diameter, **D** neck diameter, **E** bullet diameter

All dimensions are given to the **nearest thousandth of an inch**, being adapted from *The Cartridge Book* by Ian Hogg (Arms & Armour Press, 1982). Cartridges marked with a star (★) are named in accordance with the recommendations of the Commission Internationale Permanente pour l'Épreuve des Armes à Feu Portatives (CIP) and accepted for classification purposes by the International Standards Organisation. Most of the performance data have been adapted from the excellent *Cartridges of the World* by Frank C. Barnes (DBI Books, various editions). The key letters (A to T) are used as abbreviations in the Comparacharts.

Accuracy and velocity

Many excellent articles and a fair number of books have been written about the performance of handguns and their ammunition, but it is clear that many of these 'tests'—especially in the magazines—lack consistent interpretation. Each writer has a different data collection system; each applies different criteria; each possesses differing equipment; few analyse data on an acceptable mathematical basis. The claims for the most powerful or most consistent shooting gun, as well as those for extreme long-range accuracy or unbelievable penetration, usually lack suitable scientific bases.

Collecting data is easy, but it takes time to do it properly. Too many velocity trials consist of ten hasty shots into the nearest chronograph, and accuracy has been assessed on the doubtful evidence of as few as three 5-shot groups. This is clearly wrong; few people seem to have realised that most combinations of gun and ammunition (and there may often be a *very* wide variety of cartridges for a given calibre) will give fluctuating performance from day to day or under differing conditions. Performance can be degraded by temperature, by substituting one kind of propellant for another, by using different types of bullet (even if nominally the same calibre) and by a host of other limiting factors. Handguns, unlike airguns—the subject to which most of this appendix was originally applied—depend largely on their ammunition to achieve their performance. Consequently, unlike the airguns, the variables apply much more to the cartridge than to the gun's mechanism, although, especially where autoloaders are concerned, lubrication and the fit of some key components undoubtedly have parts to play in the attainment of consistency. Similarly, too few experimenters appear to have been concerned that their neat one-hole or cloverleaf groups might be several inches from the other "looser" ones and, therefore, of appreciably less value. This deviation could mean missing that vital head shot, missing an animate target completely or—far worse—inflicting a non-fatal wound or one that causes a horrible, lingering death. It may also mean a zero score on a target.

After much abortive preliminary work, an analysis system was drafted on the basis of standard statistical principles. A professional mathematician eliminated errors before the system was committed to print, and it is hoped that, assuming the corrections were all made, claims made here are wholly defensible.

The first requirement is a set of *usable velocity figures*, preferably obtained from a reputable chronograph, many types of which are readily available. To be acceptable mathematically, the results of at least 25 shots fired under as near identical conditions as practicable must be obtained. Because friction and the combustion of the propellant raise the temperature in the handgun barrel during a rapid sequence of shots, this ideal state is theoretically impossible; however, the effects of bore heating are sufficiently negligible to be ignored provided that the 25 trial shots are not literally fired one after another. The results should be listed in tabular form, preferably one beneath another. The following hypothetical trial series shall serve as a demonstration. The first step is to calculate an *average velocity* (to be called V_x) from the *actual velocity* figures (V_a). This may be done simply by totalling the V_a column and dividing by the number of shots in the sequence, which we shall label **n**; in this case, in accord with the statistical principles discussed previously, **n** is 25. The average is found to be a little over 1112fs. There is a high shot, 1146fs, the 13th in the series, and a low one (number 22) at 1080fs. The greatest difference, between the two extremes (**GD**), is 66fs—is this gun/pellet pairing a consistent performer? 66fs is 5.9 per cent of 1112: an adequate index of performance? The answer, in short, is most

definitely no: it is clear that a lot of the shots—ten of 25—were recorded with ±10fs of the mean value of 1112fs, from which it may be concluded, quite reasonably, that this gun/cartridge combination deserves a higher rating. This point is brought out by comparing these 'trial sequences':

shot	Va	d	d²
1	1127	+15	225
2	1133	+21	441
3	1102	−10	100
4	1139	+27	729
5	1134	+22	484
6	1130	+18	324
7	1093	−19	361
8	1087	−25	625
9	1112	0	0
10	1082	−30	900
11	1115	+3	9
12	1119	+7	49
13	1146	+34	1156
14	1122	+10	100
15	1122	+10	100
16	1100	−12	144
17	1127	+15	225
18	1098	−14	196
19	1087	−25	625
20	1108	−4	16
21	1115	+3	9
22	1080	−32	1024
23	1113	+1	1
24	1097	−15	225
25	1123	+11	121
TOTAL	27,811		8,189
Average	1112.4*		327.6**

s = 18.09 (or $\sqrt{327.6}$)

* ie: 27811 divided by 25   ** 8189 divided by 25

Ctg A	Ctg B	Ctg A	Ctg B
1127	1080	1100	1080
1133	1146	1127	1146
1102	1080	1098	1080
1139	1090	1087	1146
1134	1146	1108	1080
1130	1146	1115	1146
1093	1080	1080	1080
1087	1146	1113	1146
1112	1089	1097	1080
1082	1146	1123	1146
1115	1080		
1119	1146	1112—Average	
1146	1146	1080—Minimum velocity	
1122	1080	1146—Maximum velocity	
1122	1146		

The combination of the gun and cartridge A is clearly shooting better than with cartridge B; yet if we were to concentrate only on the 'final' criteria—average velocity (1112fs) or maxima and minima (1146, 1180fs)—the trials would appear identical. Hence the index of performance of 3.3 per cent, which could apply equally to either series, needs to be modified to favour A at B's expense. This may be accomplished by the use of *Standard Deviation* (**s**), which will effect the desired improvements if a majority of shots groups around the average velocity. The value of **s** may be obtained by calculating the difference between each value of V_a and the average velocity, $\mathbf{V_x}$: this difference shall be called **d**, and should be calculated without regard to whether $\mathbf{V_a}$ lies above or below $\mathbf{V_x}$. The values of **d** are then squared and the $\mathbf{d^2}$ figures listed—to be totalled, divided by the number of shots (**n**), and square-rooted to provide the requisite value of **s**. Note how, from Table 1, the extreme shots have a disproportionate effect on $\mathbf{d^2}$; shots numbers 2 and 11 differ by 21fs and 3fs from the mean respectively—or, put another way, the deviation of one is seven times the other. The $\mathbf{d^2}$ values, however, increase this apparent difference to forty-ninefold. But then shot 11 is practically an average shot and ought, by rights, to have as little adverse effect as possible on the index of performance.

Applying these calculations, using Table I, should give **s** a value of 18.09 for Gun A . . . and 32.34 for Gun B. These are respectively 1.6 and 2.9 per cent of the average velocity ($\mathbf{V_x}$) and represent a better method of assessing performance. Can further progress be made? The trials and interpretation thus far undertaken have given a reasonable index for one particular combination of gun and cartridge, undertaken on one specific occasion. Can it now be developed to apply to *all* trials undertaken by this gun and any batches of the cartridges in question, assuming that no deterioration occurs? Another statistical term must be introduced—*Confidence Limits* (**C**), an expression of probability. *The Airgun Book* (Arms & Armour Press, London, 1981 and 1982) advocated the use of 2.33 as a value for **C**, representing a probability of 98 per cent, which, it was believed, allowed at least a small concession to unforeseen performance fluctuations.

This enables an equation for the average velocity of **all** shots fired by the gun/cartridge pairing to be derived:

$$V_x \pm \frac{Cs}{\sqrt{n}}$$

In other words: the average velocity, plus or minus the confidence limit, multiplied by the standard deviation and divided by the square root of the number of trial shots. Our combination becomes:

$$1112 \pm \frac{2.33 \times 18.09}{5} \text{ or } 1112 \pm 8.43\,\text{fs.}$$

8.43fs must be doubled, to 16.8, as one limit lies above the average and the other below. What it says, effectively, is that it is 98 per cent probable that the average velocity of all shots fired from the gun/cartridge system will lie somewhere between 1104 and 1020fs. The value of 16.8fs—the *Velocity Deviation Limit* or **VDL**—represents 1.5 per cent of the average velocity, a highly acceptable final index of performance. It is obviously influenced by the number of shots in the trial, owing to the inclusion of **n** in the final expression given above; strings of 100 trial shots would have been better, minimising the variables still further, but this is far too time-consuming and increases the possibility of performance deterioration over such a long sequence.

Should there be a correlation between constant muzzle velocity with the 'tightness' of a group on the target? Unfortunately, while there is a strong velocity/accuracy correlation, too many limiting factors prevent us expressing the mythical 'conversion factor' numerically. Insufficient rifling pitch, for example, may give the bullet so little gyro-stability that—after emerging from the bore—it rapidly wanders away from its supposed flight path. This need not be obvious during its travel down the bore and so, despite a near-perfect shot-to-shot velocity maintenance, the accuracy may still be unacceptably poor; similarly, a deformed or irregularly-shaped bullet may also hinder true flight only *after* emerging from the muzzle. Nevertheless, the attainment of consistent velocity is a good indication of the quality and efficiency of the ammunition. The absence of this consistency considerably reduces the chance of accurate shooting.

Assuming that at least a part of what happens when a trigger is pulled is known, then what happens to the bullet between the time it begins to move and the instant it reaches the target? A possible correlation between consistent generation of velocity and performance at the target has been already suggested; and that, therefore, a gun whose velocity fluctuates greatly will not normally shoot accurately—though

one whose velocity fluctuates by only a few feet per second will probably shoot reasonably well. This claim is still defensible, but by no means an inviolable rule. For example, bullets may pass consistently down a bore to the muzzle and be chronographed with little fluctuation, but it is equally possible for the rifling to be completely unsuited to the projectiles in question. The chronograph will often detect a bullet that has stripped in the rifling, but cannot detect that the rifling pitch is too slow to give the bullet acceptable gyro-stability in its flight. Alternatively, the bullet may rotate too quickly and wander from its intended path; in neither case is the accuracy likely to be noteworthy. Yet consistent power generation is a departure point from which an assessment of accuracy may be attempted, as most gunmakers are well-versed in styles of rifling and rarely make serious mistakes.

Manufacturers' test results are usually obtained from a rest and can seldom be duplicated consistently in the field, even though *better* results are occasionally obtained by chance: even an Olympic marksman is incapable of damping out every muscle tremor and thus keeping his gun rock steady through every shot. Thus enters an element of 'shooting at the moment the sights register perfectly on the target' (not the approved coaching method!) and, therefore, a firer may be lucky enough to pull the trigger at the precise moment his gun oscillates across the bull's eye...five or ten times in succession. In field shooting, the problems are rarely as apparent or, perhaps, as important—though the target area for a humane kill on some animate targets is very small.

Manufacturers who supply test targets with their guns invariably confine themselves to five or at best ten shots. Ten is obviously the best criterion, as the chances of getting five good shots from any sequence is high: and, therefore, little use can be made of a five-shot group as an indicator to what may happen, for example, with a hundred. Equally, one would not expect a cheap 'plinker' to give the accuracy of a top-class pistol costing perhaps ten times as much; yet it rarely shoots ten times worse. One extraordinarily good target, particularly if it has been specially selected, can be an unrealistic guide to gun quality if the remainder is poor. Thus, the problems of deciding how many shots represent a sequence return. Where pistols and revolvers are concerned, we have encountered the additional problem of magazine capacity and the attendant problem of repositioning a gun in its rest if it has been removed for reloading—though even this difficulty is not insuperable. A good five-shot group is fine, and a gun which gives five consecutive tight groups may also be desirable; but what if one, two or even all five of the groups landed in different places? There is rarely an indication from groups illustrated in magazines and gun books that the centre of one group may be displaced from another by several inches. Consider these-

Who is to say that, if all twenty five shots are combined, the shot-fall diagram would not look like this?

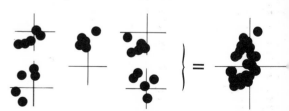

Would this gun be purchased on the basis of the large group? Perhaps, had the purchaser seen the five 5-shot groups *separately*. This then, is a major influencing factor and the *position* of test groups has a vital significance. The best sequences are probably of 25 shots; not too many to be impossible to shoot, sufficient to ensure mathematical acceptability, sufficient to highlight the worst excesses of displaced shots, and adequate to escape the worst effects of deterioration or barrel heating during the short test period.

The next steps are best illustrated by means of hypothetical test groups, fired as 5 five-shot groups, which removes the difficulty of measuring shot-fall in the large ragged 25-shot hole indicated by the 'total plot'.

Once the groups have been obtained, some numerical expression of their size and quality must be deduced. The simplest way is to measure their diameter, which provides a rough and ready guide but makes no concession to the relative distances of the shots away from the centre. The groups drawn below illustrate this point; it is noticeable that only one of the five shots in target (A) is displaced from the centre, yet all five of (B) are widely spaced. If we were aiming at a tiny target, (A) may obtain as many as four hits; (B), possibly none at all. Thus, (A) is clearly superior.

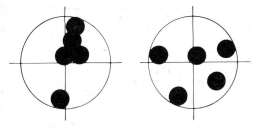

Unfortunately, the 'diameter measurement' system credits them with the same size—and is, as a result, potentially very misleading. Just as it can be contended that there exists a fairer system than normal methods of velocity assessment, so a similar argument can be used for determination of accuracy. A simple measurement is *not* a fair arbiter.

Many systems of accuracy determination have been mooted in the past and, indeed, the British Army once used a system known as 'Figure of Merit' —explained in some detail in Appendix IX of Christopher Roads' book, *The British Soldier's Firearm, 1850-1864* (Herbert Jenkins, London, 1964), and in the *Text Book of Small Arms* (1929).

Figure of Merit, like most similar methods, was based on the radial displacement of each shot from the group centre—a principle accepted both for *The Airgun Book* and for this work.

Acceptance of the radial displacement theory, however, can involve extensive measurements and a number of time-consuming calculations. But if it prevents accuracy claims of the type widely used elsewhere (an average diameter of three five-shot groups, for example), then the time and trouble will have been worthwhile. The first step, as outlined above, is to obtain the results of 25 shots, the easiest and most convenient of which, at short range at least, is to fire 5 five-shot groups; at longer ranges, where the shots are likely to be more widely distributed, it is often possible to fire all 25 on one target . . . quite acceptable assuming the fall of each can be accurately plotted.

However, it will not be obvious from the 5 separate groups where the centre of the entire sequence lies, which necessitates some calculation. This is where the aim-point mark shows its secondary use. Taking the first of the groups, the distance each shot lies *from the aim point* must be measured. In addition, these should be plotted on the horizontal (x) and vertical (y) axes. Once all the shots of each of the five groups (or the single 25-shot one) have been traced, the table of dimensions should resemble the one given here.

Thus far, we have measured the distances each shot lies from the aim-point mark, horizontally and vertically. These the table states as positive values if the shots lie to the right of the aim-point horizontally, or negative if they lie to the left; similarly, a shot that strikes above the aim-point is regarded as positive vertically, but is negative if it lies below. These 'plus or minus' elements have an important effect on calculation of the real centre of the large 25-shot group.

Column A on the Table represents the measurements of the shots in the horizontal direction. Nineteen of them struck to the right of the mark; the remaining six, to the left. Therefore, 19 have values ranging from +0.8 to +13.9, and the remainder between –0.7 and –5.5. If the values of all the 'positive' shots are added together, a total of +116.1 is obtained while the 'negatives' amount to –16.6. The sum of these two is +99.5, which indicates that the centre of the group lies to the right of the aim-point. As 25 shots were fired, the actual displacement of the centre is found by dividing the total (99.5) by the number of shots, giving a value of 3.98—or approximately 4mm as we are working to the nearest tenth.

One co-ordinate of the group centre has now been fixed, and we must repeat the process in the vertical plane to discover whether the group centre lies above or below the aim-point. Five of the 25 shots have positive values (which means that they lie above the aim-point), +0.3 to +5.6, and the remaining twenty are negatives (–0.4 to –17.7). It is clear that the centre must lie beneath the aim-point as the total of the 'negatives' is –146.7 and that of the 'positive shots' a mere +15.3. The sum of these is therefore 131.4, and as there are 25 shots contributing to the total, the actual displacement (total divided by shots) is –5.26. . . called 5.3mm for our purposes. As this has a negative value, the actual group centre lies *below* the aim-point.

So far, so good. Now that the group centre is known, the distance each shot lies from this centre can be calculated. However, there is *still* a problem. We know from columns A and B how far each shot lies from the aim-point, as they have all been measured individually. But it has also been discovered that the aim-point and the group centre are nothing like the same thing. In fact, the latter lies 4mm to the right and 5.3mm below the former. Consequently, an allowance must be made before further progress can be made and, effectively, the value of +4 must be added to all figures in column A and the value of –5.3 subtracted from the figures in column B. Subtracting a minus quantity, of course, is the same as adding 5.3 to the figures in B. This creates the two additional columns C and D. Note that correction can mean that shots previously allocated positive values horizontally can now be negative, and that some which were negative vertically are now positive. This simply indicates that though they lie to the right or below the aim-point, they are actually to the left or above the group centre (which, as we have seen, is rarely the same thing).

	A	*C*	*E*	*B*	*D*	*F*	*G*
1	+13.9	+9.9	98.01	+0.3	+5.6	31.36	11.4
2	+11.6	+7.6	57.76	-5.0	+0.3	0.09	7.6
3	+5.0	+1.0	1.00	-9.5	-4.2	17.64	4.3
4	-3.2	-7.2	51.84	-12.5	-7.2	51.84	10.2
5	-5.5	-9.5	90.25	-15.8	-10.5	110.25	14.2
6	+3.9	-0.1	0.01	+3.3	+8.6	73.96	8.6
7	-0.7	-4.7	22.09	-3.4	+1.9	3.61	4.9
8	+6.5	+2.5	6.25	-6.5	-1.2	1.44	2.8
9	+11.8	+7.8	60.84	-11.9	-6.6	43.56	10.2
10	+9.8	+5.8	33.64	-16.1	-10.8	116.64	12.3
11	+4.9	+0.9	0.81	+5.0	+10.3	106.09	10.3
12	-3.6	-7.6	57.76	-0.4	+4.9	24.01	9.0
13	+3.3	-0.7	0.49	-2.6	+2.7	7.29	2.8
14	+7.8	+3.8	14.44	-1.2	+4.1	16.81	5.6
15	+1.3	-2.7	7.29	-17.7	-12.4	153.76	12.7
16	+4.3	+0.3	0.09	+5.6	+10.9	118.81	10.9
17	+1.6	-2.4	5.76	-1.9	+3.4	11.56	4.2
18	-0.9	-4.9	24.01	-7.5	-2.2	4.84	5.4
19	+4.3	+0.3	0.09	-6.8	-1.5	2.25	1.5
20	+8.5	+4.5	20.25	-5.6	-0.3	0.09	4.5
21	-2.7	-6.7	44.89	+1.1	+6.4	40.96	9.3
22	+0.8	-3.2	10.24	-2.1	+3.2	10.24	4.5
23	+6.2	+2.2	4.84	-1.5	+3.8	14.44	4.4
24	+7.4	+3.4	11.56	-7.4	-2.1	4.41	4.0
25	+3.3	-0.7	0.49	-11.3	-5.0	25.00	5.0
	+116.1 (19)			+ 15.3			
	– 16.6 (6)			-146.7			
	+ 99.5			-131.4			180.6

The next steps are best understood from one of the actual groups.

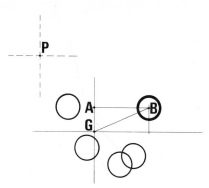

This diagram shows the aim-point, which was already established, and the relative position of the combined group centre (not the centre of this *particular* group but rather that resulting from all 25 shots in the sequence). The distance the centre of shot 1, called **B**, lies from the centre of the 'big group' **G** is obtained by simple geometry—Pythagoras's Theorem, which states that, in a right angle triangle, the square on the hypoteneuse is equal to the sum of the squares of the other two sides. The square of our displacement distance BG is, therefore, equal to the square of the length of AB added to the square of the length AG. AB is the horizontal displacement, taken from the corrected column C on our first table, while AG is the vertical displacement taken from Column D. For the first shot, the values are 9.9 for AB and 5.6 for AG, as the shot struck to the right and above the calculated group centre.

Using $BG^2 = AB^2 + AG^2$, we get $BG^2 = 9.9^2 + 5.6^2$ or 98.01 plus 31.36 (a total of 129.37). Columns E and F on Table 3 display the squared values of C and D respectively. Remembering that the value obtained, 129.37, is actually the square of the displacement distance BG, we have to use a calculator or square-root tables to obtain the actual value: $\sqrt{129.37}$ is 11.37, and thus the first shot lies about 11.4mm away from the centre of the 'big group'. The process is repeated for all 25 shots, until it is discovered (column G) that the nearest shot to the group centre is the nineteenth, only 1.5mm away, and that the farthest is number 5—14.2mm distant.

Finally, the values in the last column are added together to total, in this instance, 180.6mm—the total displacement of all 25 shots considered individually without regard to the direction in which they lie from the group centre. A case can be made for using the 'string total' as the final result, but most shooters talk in terms of 'group diameter' and it is better to fall into line with this method. The average radial displacement (total divided by shots) of the 180.6mm test string is 7.22mm. Of course, *diameter* is twice the value of radii; thus we may consider a value of twice 7.22, 14.44mm, to be a reasonable 'diameter' assessment of the trial under consideration. This is a lower value than the average diameter of the five groups, which would have been about 19.1mm, but has been obtained by different means and can be expected to minimise the effect of strays or fliers. However, had there been a consistently large quantity of wild shots, the overall figure could easily have been worse; as it may also have been had one of the supposedly good groups been displaced in relation to the remainder.

Now that the system of assessment has been explained, we need to look at it further. What else can be done with it? One additonal use enables us to derive an acceptable theoretical prediction of the performance of the same gun firing the same ammunition on virtually any occasion, which makes it easy to see whether misfortune is about to befall the cartridges, but involves the same statistical procedures outlined during the sections on velocity measurement. Use of standard deviation and confidence limits makes this process mathematically acceptable, though theory and practice will probably be reconciled only after a lot of experimentation. Our accuracy system also lends itself to setting realistic, acceptable standards. It is well known that two pistols—even of the same make—rarely perform alike, but one can still expect that all high-class target pistols, for example, to be very accurate. Sporting guns will rarely approach this on the target range, but may perform much better outdoors. These figures can be reconciled by expressing the variable range in terms of a constant measurement, such as a minute of angle. The best unit is a thousandth part of the range. Thus a gun shooting a 1-metre diameter group at 1,000 metres is said to have an accuracy of 1.0; but so would a gun that shoots a diameter of 2.5cm at 25m, or a centimetre at 10m. For instance, the gun shooting the 1cm group at 10m can be said to be performing the same as one shooting a group of 2.2in at 60yd.

The best target pistols may need to develop accuracy better than 0.3 units to be not only reasonable value for money but also capable of winning competitions if the firer is good enough; mid-grade sporting guns may need to better 1 unit; low-price plinkers, 2.5 and so on. (5 units would mean that groups at 25m would be 125mm or nearly 5 inches in diameter, which is not particularly good.)

Below: the stainless steel version of the Colt 1806 Army-pattern percussion revolver. Some of these shot quite well—but we would like to learn of the results of trials undertaken in the manner described above . . . . (Photograph by courtesy of Colt.)

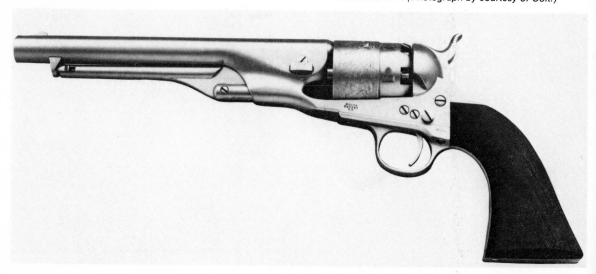